Civil Society, Democracy, and Civic Renewal

Civil Society, Democracy, and Civic Renewal

edited by
Robert K. Fullinwider

ROWMAN & LITTLEFIELD PUBLISHERS, INC.
Lanham • Boulder • New York • Oxford

ROWMAN & LITTLEFIELD PUBLISHERS, INC.

Published in the United States of America
by Rowman & Littlefield Publishers, Inc.
4720 Boston Way, Lanham, Maryland 20706

12 Hid's Copse Road
Cumnor Hill, Oxford OX2 9JJ, England

British Library Cataloguing in Publication Information Available

Library of Congress Cataloging-in-Publication Data

Civil society, democracy, and civic renewal / edited by Robert K.
  Fullinwider.
        p.   cm.
    Includes bibliographical references and index.
    ISBN 0-8476-9355-4 (cloth : alk. paper). — ISBN 0-8476-9356-2
(pbk. : alk. paper)
      1. Political participation—United States.   2. Civil society—
United States.   3. Democracy—United States.   I. Fullinwider,
Robert K., 1942–   .
JK1764.C5267   1999
301'0973—dc21   98-48272
                                                                      CIP

Printed in the United States of America

∞ ™ The paper used in this publication meets the minimum requirements of
American National Standard for Information Sciences—Permanence of Paper for
Printed Library Materials, ANSI Z39.48–1992.

Contents

Part Three: Trust and Civic Virtue

Part Four: Religion and Race

Part Five: Public Deliberation

Part Six: International Civil Society

Preface

The essays in this book were produced for the National Commission on Civic Renewal, whose report *A Nation of Spectators* was issued in June 1998. Many of the essays were written by members of the Commission's Working Group on Civil Society, which met twice in Washington, D.C., in 1997. The rest were written by members of the Institute for Philosophy and Public Policy.

The work of the National Commission was made possible by a grant from the Public Policy Program of the Pew Charitable Trusts and by the unswerving encouragement of Pew's president, Rebecca Rimel, the director of the Public Policy Program, Paul Light, and program officer Betsy Hubbard. Neither the Commission nor this book would have existed without their support, for which we are grateful. The book also benefited from the active involvement of many people at the Institute. Special mention must be made of Arthur Evenchik, the Institute's editor, who shepherded the essays through various stages. Thanks are due also to Carroll Linkins, Teresa Chandler, Henry Clifford, and Steve Aylward for their efforts in advancing the Commission's research agenda.

Introduction

Robert K. Fullinwider

Alexis de Tocqueville, on his visit to the United States in 1831, was struck by this country's rich and variegated stratum of "civil associations," a stratum that Europeans might fail to appreciate, he noted, "because we have hardly ever seen anything of the kind." Cooperative associations seemed to define the very essence of American life. "Wherever at the head of some new undertaking you see the government in France, or a man of rank in England," observed Tocqueville, "in the United States you will be sure to find an association."[1]

The American habit of associating grew in part out of our tradition of limited government, which reserved to local communities extensive powers of decision making, and in part out of our political and social egalitarianism, which allowed individuals of all stations to mingle and work together in common endeavors. Finally, the vibrancy of American civil society was in part an artifact of our tradition of church-state separation. The disestablishment of religion in our early national history put church support—and the influence that goes with support—in the hands of church members themselves. (Kathryn Kish Sklar develops these points in chapter 7.)

The proclivity to associate still characterizes American life. Our society exhibits an impressively extensive and active civil society—"a realm of associational life independent of the market and the state."[2] This realm has recently moved to the forefront of domestic political and academic discussion for several reasons.

First, many people, disillusioned with centralized governmental programs that deal with poverty, joblessness, crime, drug addiction, and community decay, now look to the institutions of civil society as the preferred agents for addressing these problems. In their view, private, com-

1

munity-rooted organizations are more flexible and effective than large-scale government programs, better able to tailor their activities to community needs and circumstances. The recent political debate on welfare reform constitutes one dimension of this "return to civil society."

Second, many people now look to civil society for regeneration of political life in America. For decades, voter turnout has steadily declined. Likewise, polls consistently show great dissatisfaction among the electorate with political institutions and political actors. In this context, the institutions of civil society strike many as particularly attractive, either as possible sources for renewing the civic spirit of individuals and prompting them to greater engagement with political life, or as alternative sites of self-government in which individuals can organize more effectively to solve community problems.

Third, and more generally, scholars and policy makers increasingly perceive the private, voluntary sector of associational life as a vital source of "social capital," those "features of social life—networks, norms, and trust—that enable participants to act together more effectively to pursue shared objectives," as Robert Putman puts it.[3] Both Putman (*Making Democracy Work: Civic Traditions in Modern Italy*, 1993) and Francis Fukuyama (*Trust: The Social Virtues and the Creation of Prosperity*, 1995) have produced impressive studies emphasizing the salutary effects of such "social capital." Putnam sums up these effects in this way:

> [N]etworks of civic engagement foster sturdy norms of generalized reciprocity and encourage the emergence of social trust. Such networks facilitate coordination and communication, amplify reputations, and thus allow dilemmas of collective action to be resolved. When economic and political negotiation is embedded in dense networks of social interaction, incentives for opportunism are reduced. At the same time, networks of civic engagement embody past success at collaboration, which can serve as a cultural template for future collaboration. Finally, dense networks of interaction probably broaden the participants' sense of self, developing the "I" in the "we," or (in the language of rational-choice theorists) enhancing the participants' "taste" for collective benefits.[4]

If "social capital" arises principally out of the activities of civil society, that puts civil associations on the front line in any project of civic renewal.

Finally, just at this time of renewed appreciation—in both the academy and the polity—of the vital contributions civil society makes to political, economic, and social life, disturbing signs indicate that the American tradition of joining is under stress or even in decline.[5] In his famous 1995 article, "Bowling Alone," Putnam notes declines over the last several decades not just in political participation but also in the memberships of churches, labor unions, fraternal organizations, mainline civic clubs, and the like.[6] His findings have sparked an intense academic and public debate.[7] Whether in fact our habit of associating has declined or remained healthy, however, another trend is indisputable. Three decades of polling data show that the *trust* Americans once placed in major institutions, and in each other, has eroded significantly.

Our domestic concern about the health of civil society converges with a second stream of contemporary debate. As the nations of Eastern Europe and the former Soviet Union labor to replace the totalitarian state with something different and democratic, they invoke "civil society" as the touchstone of regeneration. Civil society means, for these countries, filling spaces once occupied by the state with private, volunteer associations—civic, religious, political, and cultural—and it also means (in contrast to our domestic focus) creating free markets and private businesses in place of the command economy.

Both the broader international attention and the more narrow domestic concerns generate several questions about civil society: how best to conceive it, how to understand its relation to government, how to gauge its various effects, and how to define its own preconditions. The chapters in this book join the debate that has recently welled up in the halls of Congress and animated numerous academic conferences. Most were produced by a working group attached to the National Commission on Civic Renewal. The Commission, cochaired by William J. Bennett and Senator Sam Nunn, made its report public in June 1998. It surveyed the country's civic health broadly, looking at (1) increases in violent crime, divorces, and out-of-wedlock births over the last several decades; along with (2) declines in political participation, group memberships, and public and personal trust; and (3) mounting public complaints about the quality of our common culture and the adequacy of our public schools. At the heart of the Commission's deliberations and recommendations, however, lay concern about the renewal of civil society—something it found already under way at the grass roots in countless communities across the country.

The chapters in this book provide a broad-ranging consideration of civil society. To best see its democratic potential, Benjamin Barber (chapter 1) wants us to think of civil society as the "free space in which democratic attitudes are cultivated and democratic behavior is conditioned." Other contributors, too, pay special attention to the relation between civil society and democracy. Like Barber, William Sullivan (chapter 2) emphasizes the importance of a civic culture that supplies to people public goals that transcend their personal (and often conflicting) projects. Sullivan and Barber both are especially concerned with the transformation of the privately focused "I" into a publicly spirited "we," an effect Putnam attributes to participation in civil associations.

Jean Cohen (chapter 3) draws attention to the "public sphere," the communicative dimension of civil society. This dimension gets obscured, she fears, by Putnam's focus on standard associations such as the PTA, Elks clubs, and bowling leagues. Such a focus overlooks "social movements" (a point also made by Fredrick Harris in chapter 13) which, along with mainline associations, help shape public opinion, as they force new terms of argument onto the public agenda or rally to preserve older understandings of the public good. Cohen also worries that the focus on standard associations neglects the important role of the state in the creation of social trust. The legal protection of rights and the operation of official democratic forms greatly influence the formation and operation of associations within civil society, which take on the character of the larger political and legal framework.

The connection between official political structures and the character of civil society institutions is very much on Xiaorong Li's mind, too, as she attempts (in chapter 17) to parry "civil society determinism"—the view that strengthening private institutions within an authoritarian state will inevitably propel it toward democratic political reform. David Crocker, in turn, explores (in chapter 16) the contributions certain kinds of civil society institutions can make as former authoritarian states embark upon the transition to democracy and attempt to address the human rights abuses of previous regimes.

Judith Lichtenberg (chapter 14) and Robert Wachbroit (chapter 15) take up two special dimensions of the "public sphere." Lichtenberg looks at the growth of "public journalism" and its roots in a particular theory of democracy—"deliberative democracy." Public journalism seeks to create opportunities for citizens to deliberate about community problems and solutions. Wachbroit dwells on the problem of expert knowledge: how can the public make informed decisions about issues laced with technical and scientific disputes or uncertainties? He looks at different models of the expert-public relationship, as embodied in different health organizations this century.

Another major theme in the book traces the relationship between civil society and government. William Schambra (chapter 4) sees central government as the enemy of civil society when it becomes enthralled with the idea of "national community," attempting to stamp a single pattern on diverse communities. Steven Rathgeb Smith (chapter 5) examines the complex interplay between government policy and the activities of groups in the voluntary sector. Government for decades has relied on nonprofits to deliver public services. One upshot has been the proliferation of nonprofits. However, involvement with government frequently pushes nonprofits toward a professional-staff model and away from a broad volunteer base or deep community roots. Mark Sagoff (chapter 6) explores the bureaucratic paralysis that occurs when an agency such as the Forest Service must impose a single federal mandate across a range of different situations, and he describes how the Forest Service is increasingly turning to community groups to shape environmental policy to local circumstances.

Kathryn Kish Sklar (chapter 7) describes women's volunteer efforts in the nineteenth and early twentieth centuries, which were given momentum by the desire of reform groups to enlist government power in the service of broader social responsibilities and by the resistance of government organs to assuming such expanded roles. Kathleen McCarthy (chapter 12) tells a related story in describing the central place churches and religious organizations have assumed in civil society. Fredrick Harris (chapter 13) describes the condition of civil society among African Americans, showing that civic activism in the black community has often been a manifestation of oppositional politics.

A last major theme has to do with attitudes and behavior. Does a flourishing civil society make us more trusting and more civically and morally virtuous? Robert Wuthnow (chapter 8) offers survey data about public trust, exploring different factors that might underlie contemporary expressions of distrust. David Wasserman (chapter 9), Nancy Rosenblum (chapter 10), and Loren Lomasky (chapter 11) each consider a facet of civil society's putative function as a nurturer of virtue. Wasserman takes up self-help groups, which have proliferated enormously in the past thirty years, and ponders the moral and civic effects such groups might produce on their members. Rosenblum asks what it is that individuals seek when they join different groups and associations. She argues that the effects of membership are so various that we must be cautious in generalizing about the contribution civil society makes to individual virtue. Lomasky undertakes a complementary philosophical task. He offers a picture of the virtues—what they are and how they are manifested—and develops a liberal theory of virtue and vice.

NOTES

1. Alexis de Tocqueville, *Democracy in America II* (New York: Knopf, 1945), 110, 114.

2. Alan Wolfe, "Is Civil Society Obsolete?" *Brookings Review* 15 (Fall 1997): 12.

3. Robert D. Putnam, "The Strange Disappearance of Civic America," *American Prospect*, no. 24 (Winter 1996): 34.

4. Robert D. Putnam, "Bowling Alone: America's Declining Social Capital," *Journal of Democracy* 6 (1995): 67.

5. See Putnam, "The Strange Disappearance of Civic America."

6. Putnam, "Bowling Alone," 68–70.

7. For some responses to Putnam, see Robert J. Samuelson, " 'Bowling Alone'

Is Bunk," *Washington Post*, 10 April 1996, A19; Nicholas Lemann, "Kicking in Groups," *Atlantic Monthly* (April 1996): 22–26; Michael Schudson, "What If Civic Life Didn't Die?" *American Prospect* 25 (March–April 1996): 17–20; and Everett C. Ladd, "The Data Just Don't Show Erosion of America's 'Social Capital,' " *Public Perspective* 7 (June–July 1996): 1–22.

PART ONE

CIVIL SOCIETY:
IDEA AND ACTUALITY

1

Clansmen, Consumers, and Citizens

Three Takes on Civil Society

Benjamin R. Barber

Civic renewal rooted in the revitalization of citizenship is a worthy ideal, but it is also nebulous, even incoherent, in practice, because there is so much confusion about the meaning of the term that defines citizenship's setting: *civil society*. This chapter rests on an understanding of civil society that challenges self-abnegating politicians who slip into thinking of citizenship and government as contrary to one another and campaign on behalf of civil society by campaigning against politics—who insist privatization can cure every social ill. But it also challenges those who think that civil society is a communitarian construct that turns citizenship into some form of identitarian politics and cannot distinguish hierarchical communities of exclusion from free civil associations.

I start, rather, from the view that between the extremes of big government and wholly private commercial markets exists a potential terrain we may call civil society; and that this terrain, bridging public and private, community and individual, power and liberty, can serve to democratize and thus relegitimize government and communitarian identity at the same time that it civilizes and thus tames the marketplace. Civil society as I will describe it here is not an alternative to democratic government but the free space in which democratic attitudes are cultivated and democratic behavior is conditioned. It is not a synonym for the private market but an antidote to commercial selfishness and market incivility.

The idea of civil society itself is hardly novel. In just a few turbo-media years, it has gone in the West from being an esoteric preoccupation of intellectual historians concerned with the influence of Locke, Hegel, and Marx to being a chic catch phrase as ideologically malleable as it is substantively vapid. Stirred in with such terms as *communitarianism, civic republicanism, trust, free markets,* and *civic virtue,* it has helped create a new menu of political choices and a new debate about America's public weal. At the same time it has offered political fare tastier for its novelty than its meaning. Citizens have grounds to feel suspicious of so elastic and apparently empty an idea.

Although some of its proponents argue the term is bipartisan or even transpartisan, it has been seized upon by partisans on both sides of the aisle to serve rather narrower ideological purposes.[1] It has also been used nostalgically to call up a lost era of localism and communal self-government (the Tocqueville paradigm) and to proffer a utopian civic vision to women and men in traditionally authoritarian societies that are moving toward democratization.[2]

Debates about civil society have been inflamed by controversies over the supposed decline in social membership, social trust, and social capital in America that has been debated in the work of Robert Putnam, Francis Fukuyama, Amitai Etzioni, Michael Sandel, William J. Bennett, Senator Dan Coats, and Harry Boyte, as well as this author.[3] If civil and voluntary associations are indeed in decline, if voter turnout is in free fall, and if social trust is in jeopardy in the United States, and if these behaviors are in some fashion constitutive of what we mean by civil society, the repair of civil society obviously becomes a sine qua non of democratic survival. Similarly, if the ideal of civil society provides a justificatory framework for those in transition from autocratic to democratic governments, to understand its character as a form of resistance becomes the sine qua non of democratization. But all such uses depend on a clear understanding of what civil society actually means or ought to mean either as a prescription for the ills of our democracy or as a recipe for democratization elsewhere.

My primary task in this chapter will be to offer a framework for conceptual clarification that elicits some ideational order from the current chaos of usage by distinguishing strong democratic forms of civil society from rival readings. I will then use this clarification to offer some concrete proposals and practical strategies aimed at reestablishing (or, where they already exist, reinforcing) institutions and practices constitutive of civil society in this rich civic sense. Such strategies help re-create a space between big government and commercial markets where citizens can breathe freely and behave democratically without regarding themselves as pas-

sive complainers, grasping consumers, hostile clansmen, or isolated victims—a space, in short, for democratic citizens.

DEFINING CIVIL SOCIETY: THREE MODELS

Defining civil society is a particularly problematic conceptual task, especially for someone who does not share the naive view that facts and values can be easily sorted out and kept in splendid isolation (a point of view
social scientists call *positivism*). Rather, I believe that politics demarcates
a zone that necessarily conflates the actual and ideal and that, as part of
a political vocabulary, civil society has both normative and empirical aspects. It tells us something about how we actually do behave even as it
provides an ideal of how we ought to behave. Attempts to extricate our
ideals from our actual practices usually succeed only in nullifying the
meaning of both. My claim is simply that civil society's ideal normative
meaning as given by certain democratic and civic standards is inextricably bound to the various civic attitudes and practices that surround it in
real life.[4]

In well-established democracies, the idea of civil society has been used
to point back to foundational aspects of democracy—back to an infrastructure which, although perhaps in crisis, has a history and an institutional legitimacy.[5] Here, civil society has been an appeal to what we once
had as a reproach against what now is, an appeal to a program for reviving old institutions. This strategy, even when used by liberal democrats,
often has a nostalgic if not quite a conservative or even reactionary cast,
looking back to earlier ideals for the reform of current practices. This is
why communitarian appeals to civil society may at one and the same time
seem to offer a radical critique of current practices and to call up a conservative ideology rooted in family values and traditional mediating institutions. Civil society, its advocates may be inclined to say, is something to
be retrieved from some imagined (not to say imaginary) but now vanished nineteenth-century world. At the same time, my account suggests
democratizing, even radical, uses for civil society even where the ideal is
drawn from imagined history.

My object, then, is to illuminate three distinct takes on civil society that
can be found within the foundationalist heritage: what I will call the libertarian, the communitarian, and the strong democratic models of civil society. These three models are in turn conditioned by a distinction that can
be drawn between what I understand as a "two-celled" model of social
space and a "three-celled" model. These rather abstract notions are crucial because they are the predicate for a revitalization of the idea of civil

society and hence are the necessary condition for the taming of markets, the civilizing of society, and the democratizing of government.

THE LIBERTARIAN (LIBERAL MARKET) PERSPECTIVE: CIVIL SOCIETY AS A SYNONYM FOR THE PRIVATE SECTOR (THE TWO-CELLED MODEL)

Perhaps the most commonplace understanding of civil society conceives of it as a synonym for the private market sector. This construction reflects the belief that if we are to be truly free, we have to make a radical choice between government and markets. In this interpretation of social space, we can think of our civic world as being divided into two cells and two cells only: two rival and largely incompatible public and private sectors, "them" (public) and "us" (private); the first the domain of the state and its governing institutions, the second the domain of almost everything else we can imagine: from individuals to social organizations, from economic corporations to civil associations. Accompanying this perspective is the conviction that the public sector is defined by power (government *is* coercion!), whereas the private sector is defined by liberty (the market *is* freedom, *is* the condition of privacy and individuality!). As a consequence, any growth in the one must come at the cost of attrition in the other. More government means more power and hence less liberty. The public and the private confront one another in a zero-sum game where any change in one entails an equal and opposite change in the other. More power, less liberty; more private, less public—and vice versa.[6]

As it dichotomizes the people and the government, liberty and power, individuals and the state, and voluntarism and coercion, this classically liberal model ("libertarian" in our modern parlance) leaves no other venue for civil society but the private sector.[7] No large distinctions can be posited between individuals and the "private" civil associations they may constitute, between economic corporations and civil organizations, or between the realm of markets and the realm of culture, ethics, or religion (to take just a few examples). Dualism here yields an implacable (and improbable) opposition between the public and the private that leaves those frustrated with government thinking that privatization is their only option: if you do not like government, downsize and limit it, privatize its civil functions, and leave individuals and their corporations and communities alone to do as they please. On the other hand, if you do not like your chances in the private market, turn to big government as your ally and guarantor.

In the libertarian model, social relations both within the private sector and between the private sector and the state sector feel like contract relations: a series of deals that free individuals or free associations make in the name of their interests and goods and in defense of their liberties.[8] When the individual looks out at government from the privileged sanctuary of the private sector, as she does in the libertarian model, she sees only a fearsome leviathan sometimes capable of serving her interests as a client of government bureaucracies or as a consumer of government services but just as likely to swallow up her liberties whole. "A government powerful enough to give us all we want," President Ford was still proclaiming at the 1996 Republican convention, "is powerful enough to take from us all we have."

Liberties, the prudent libertarian will conclude, must therefore be surrounded by a thick wall of rights. Philosophers looking at such citizens, as they pursue their economic interests and install a defensive parapet of rights to protect themselves against an encroaching state, will see in the citizen little more than an economic animal—*homo economicus*—or the citizen defined as a consumer of government services and as one of the sovereign but passive beings to whom limited governments are accountable. From this point of view, civil associations feel (at best) rather like consumer cooperatives or rights alliances. They permit individuals to protect themselves more efficiently and serve themselves more securely but have little to do with participation, cooperation, or sociability per se, let alone solidarity or community and the pursuit of a commonweal such a community makes possible.[9]

Civil society understood as a surrogate for the private sector presents freedom in a strong sense but sociability in its very thinnest sense. This helps explain why the strategies of privatization being used in the name of democratization in Eastern Europe have yielded results that frequently fail to sustain the civic culture on which democracy depends. Consumers enjoy newly acquired economic power and a novel sense of their rights but do not wear the textured mantle of engaged citizens and, as a consequence, are often ambivalent democrats at best. Thanks to formal institutions, consumers become voters, but voters, satisfied as "clients" of government, do not become citizens in any deeper sense. With shopping and voting deemed interchangeable activities, countries where shopping flourishes get mislabeled as democracies.

By focusing on the consumer who is burrowed into a shell of rights and thus—autonomous, solitary, and egoistic—likely to venture out into the social sector only to get something from a service-station state whose compass of activities must always be kept minimal, the libertarian model of civil society can envision only a rudimentary form of social relations that remains shallowly instrumental: the citizen as client, the voter as customer, the democratic participant as consumer.

By the same token, this libertarian model yields a version of liberty that is hyperindividualistic. That is, it regards freedom as something that is

negative and reactive with a vengeance, always oppositional to government, and likely to survive only where politics and society are marginalized and minimalized. Nor can the libertarian model of civil society serve
to soften relations between individual and state, as many of traditional
sociology's constructions have tried to do (e.g., both the so-called Gemeinschaft and Gesellschaft models put forward by the German nineteenth-century sociologist Ferdinand Toennies). Neither can it respond to
the yearning for community and solidarity that besets modern peoples
living in mobile, postindustrial societies. This thinness accounts for much
of the communitarian frustration that attends thin liberal conceptions of
civil society and can be dangerous to democracy. For it is a basic law of
modern politics that where democratic communities cannot be found to
do the work of solidarity and identity that human beings demand, undemocratic communities that do so will appear. And they will seem irresistible.

THE COMMUNITARIAN PERSPECTIVE: CIVIL SOCIETY AS A SYNONYM FOR COMMUNITY (THE TWO-CELLED MODEL)

The communitarian perspective answers these frustrations but often
without abandoning the idea that society is sharply divided into two domains, one governmental, the other private. However, although they
share the two-celled framework that is liberalism's premise, communitarians do not understand private space as a domain of solitary, rights-bearing individuals or grasping entrepreneurs. Rather, because they assume
that people are embedded in a nexus of communities and tied to one another by bonds that precede and condition their individuality, communitarians envision civil society as a complex welter of ineluctably social relations that tie people together into families, clans, clubs, neighborhoods,
communities, and hierarchies. Where libertarians see a play space for individuals and their voluntary and contractual economic associations,
communitarians discover a zone of interaction, embeddedness, and
bonding.

Communitarians begin with the premise that most human associations
are given ("ascriptive") rather than chosen ("voluntary"). We are born as
Jews or Catholics no less than as males and females; as Persians or Thais
no less than as Caucasians or Asians. We play little part in fashioning the
communities into which we are born, and these communities have for the
most part what we regard as natural rather than instrumental purposes.
And though even the most "natural" associations may have voluntaristic
roots in some ancient time (traditions and ancient communities are also
socially constructed), traditional membership communities are sanc-

tioned by time and tradition in a manner that utilitarian and contractual organizations can never be. Today's artifice may of course become tomorrow's entrenched community, just as today's innovative practice may become tomorrow's hoary tradition. Yet the distinction between the ancient communities we call "natural" and the new associations that seem so obviously "artificial" remains palpable and politically consequential.

That today's natural communities were once artificially constructed does not diminish their conservative political potency as "ancient" and "natural" associations impregnable to today's fashions and popular whims. The Russell, Kansas, or Hope, Arkansas, to which modern politicians appeal as an ancient habitat for the molding of political character and that looks "natural" compared with the contrived metropolises of urban industrial civilization was in truth itself once founded and contrived—an unnatural blight on the "natural" environment it can (say, from a Native American perspective) be seen as despoiling. This is the great lesson of Edmund Burke's account of the "prescriptive constitution," a creation of ancient artifice that for Burke gave England its modern common-law constitution, with its natural resistance to the whims of transient majorities.

If the defining actor of civil society on the libertarian model is the rights-bearing consumer, the defining actor of civil society on the communitarian model is the clansman, tied to community by birth, blood, and bathos. Citizenship here takes on a cultural feel and marks its territory by exclusion rather than inclusion, often specifying anonymous "others" and "outsiders" whose foreignness helps define the excluding (and thus exclusive) community. Inclusiveness is traded away for patriotism, equality for a powerful sense of belonging.

The great virtue today of civil society comprehended as a private and closed nexus of tightly knit communities is that it offers a social glue to otherwise disparate individuals and groups in an ever more anarchic social and economic world. If the sundering of social bonds (Marx) and the rationalization, contractualization, and bureaucratization of social relations (Weber) are the defining features of modernity, communitarian solidarity and fraternity promise to reanchor membership and assuage the uncertainty and psychic isolation that attend life in posttraditional society. Solidarity may, of course, bring with it hierarchy, exclusivity, and conformity, and citizens who identify their social membership with the particularism of one parochial Gemeinschaft may not make very effective democrats. Indeed, in the absence of offsetting or mediating values not generated by communitarianism itself, such illiberal norms as authoritarianism, parochialism, inequality, paternalism, and hierarchy may be a concomitant of communitarianism. They appear as likely—perhaps even necessary—ingredients of the kinds of identity politics that issue out of a deeply rooted communitarianism.

There can, of course, be democratic communities, and a modern document such as Amitai Etzioni's "Communitarian Platform" certainly aspires to a more democratic form of communitarianism, just as Michael Lerner's "Politics of Meaning" tries to offer an egalitarian and just form of Jewish communitarianism.[10] Democracy, however, is neither a necessary nor even a probable attribute of communitarianism per se, and communitarians must constantly work at it and work for it. As they apply standards of justice, equality, and inclusiveness to a social form of intimacy that resists such standards, they risk the weakening of communitarian bonds.

What is dangerous politically about an unvarnished communitarian perspective is that it tends to absorb and assimilate and thus finally to monopolize all public space.[11] When America's "cultural conservatives" make war on consumer capitalism as well as on the thin liberal state, they conjure up old notions of Kulturkampf (Patrick Buchanan's culture wars) and of a colonizing cultural paradigm that assimilates state and private sectors alike. Although liberalism may insist on a high wall between the state and the private sector, demanding a minimalist governing apparatus, it has little interest in governance per se, other than to limit its compass. It may envision free markets as apt surrogates for many functions of government, but its aim is to do away with government rather than to take it over.

Communitarians, on the other hand, seem sometimes to want to subordinate the state and its institutions to a larger community. Civil society is in this perspective the community of all communities, organic and whole, the source of all moral and political authority, including governmental authority. Whereas libertarians worry about state bureaucrats imposing substantive values on free individuals and groups, communitarians fear that the state may be corrosively agnostic and possess no guiding values at all. They may seek cultural safety not in laissez-faire insulation from the state but in a cultural takeover of the state—as Patrick Buchanan and Ralph Reed did in their 1992 and 1996 presidential campaign efforts and as European rightists such as Eric Haider (of Austria's Republican Party) and Jean-Marie Le Pen (of France's National Front) have in their campaign against both libertarian antistatists and welfare state socialists on the Continent. The German experience reminds us that the siren call of community, though attuned to deep needs in the human spirit, can be answered in ways that violate both liberalism and democracy. American communitarians are not always sufficiently alive to the darker side of the yearning for communal identity, though they are for the most part pragmatic democrats, and they operate in the safety of a thin but well-entrenched hyper-liberal regime which probably benefits from their alternative "thick" perspective.

I hope I have shown that although both communitarian and libertarian versions of civil association assume a two-celled model of public and private, they tend in both cases toward a single-celled unitarian integrity. Market liberalism achieves this by downsizing the state until it nearly vanishes ("the best government is no government at all"), leaving behind what amounts to a nearly sovereign private sphere. Communitarianism achieves the same unitarianism by subordinating the state to a larger community which the state must faithfully serve—whether that community is the fatherland, a *Volksgemeinschaft,* or some blood clan writ large (the "Austrian people," the "Scottish nation," the "Bosnian Serb state," or "Christian America").

In addition to the totalitarian temptation that afflicts communitarians, they also must confront the paradox that the natural communities to which they aspire are often in practice realized only in the most artificial manner. Under modern conditions in which the environment for natural community has been undermined by secularism, utilitarianism, and the erosion of "natural" social ties, many communities claiming traditional and natural identities are engaged in a strenuously artificial effort to reconstitute themselves as natural communities they no longer are or can be. Their labors result in contrived "voluntary" associations pretending to be "natural communities." The Ku Klux Klan is no more a "clan" in the sense of an extended kinship association or a blood band than self-consciously hyphenated American identity groups such as Polish-Americans or African-Americans are really Polish or African. American-born Polish- and African-Americans may identify with remembered or reinvented cultural roots in the abstract, but they quickly discern, when they visit the homelands that provide their hypothetical ethnic identities, how remote those identities are from what they have inevitably become— namely, deracinated Americans!

Roots call on memory. But the "memory" appealed to by poets and patriots resisting tyranny can be a tricky faculty. Reconstituting a remembered but historically eroded identity simply does not permit the fashioning of a community in anything like its original form. Indeed, many of the pathologies of modern communitarianism arise not out of the features of real community, but the features of an imitation that, because it only mimics its ideal, is thin and defensive despite its quest for an identity that is thick and self-sufficient. Islamic Jihad is defined as much by its modern enemies as by an Islamic theological essence, just as American Protestant fundamentalism is more reactive to the secular, materialist culture of America than proactive on the model of early Augustinian Christianity or the Puritans' City on the Hill. The pathologies I explore under the rubric of "Jihad" in my *Jihad versus McWorld* are not so much the problems of, say, an Ibo tribesman in the precolonial period as they are the predicament of a cosmopolitan of Ibo origins living among members of other tribes in a commercial, postcolonial city such as Nairobi.[12]

It is understandable that communitarians can be anxious in the face of cosmopolitan disorder and the spontaneous anarchy of radical individualism: for it is those facets of modernity which, after all, they associate with the corruption of their earlier identities.[13] They are more likely to fear creative anarchy and respond favorably to authoritarian orderliness. Such fears will obviously serve neither liberty nor public man.[14] The connections between communitarianism and authority (as well as hierarchy) are not fixed or determinative, but they are well established in practice. This puts the onus to some degree on communitarians. It is up to them to show how the natural tendencies of solidarity and fraternalism toward authoritarianism and hierarchy are to be deflected.

Such linkages suggest why, for some people—often the young, the adventuresome, the creative—communitarianism can feel cloistered and airless: the trap of a small town in which local hierarchies, rigid rules, and too much intimacy forge an inflexible culture of convention and gossip that drives them to flight. The creative friction between cosmopolitan cities and small towns is marked by this tension between self-creation and ascriptive (given) identity. The identity that the deracinated city dweller—long since uprooted from some faintly remembered village childhood—seeks as a home for his yearnings may appear to those still enmeshed in village life as nothing so much as a prison. Thus, village life as portrayed in literature has enjoyed a twin reputation. Depicted through the gentle memories of nostalgia writers such as Thornton Wilder and Dylan Thomas, the village community appears as a remembered sanctuary from the world's dismal urbanity. Depicted by unsentimental realists such as Toni Morrison or Thomas Hardy, it is little more than a death trap.[15]

Michael Oakeshott captures the spirit of the cosmopolitan when he writes of a mobilizing Renaissance world peopled by "younger sons making their own way in a world which had little place for them, of foot-loose adventurers who left the land to take to trade, of town-dwellers who had emancipated themselves from the communal ties of the countryside, of vagabond scholars."[16] Such adventurers strode out across the threshold of modernity into a fledgling urban world that would leave little room for the clan fealty of the Middle Ages. But in leaping from a stolid world of community into the frenzy of deracinated urban life, they prepared the ground for a later communitarian nostalgia. The small "face-to-face" towns they abandoned for a life of urban liberation were to be reconstructed by their great-grandchildren as imagined sanctuaries from ur-banity's plagues.[17]

These manifold portraits of community and cosmopolis may represent literary antipodes, but they are not really as contradictory as they appear. Both reflect the distance traveled from earlier intimate face-to-face com-munities to the elephantine urban civilizations that define modern life for most Westerners and that have raised up the new communitarians as champions of an imagined but mostly vanished way of life. They also ex-plain why the communitarian perspective on civil society is so fraught and ultimately problematic as social policy. For communitarians are call-ing for the restoration of ancient communities whose vanishing is an inev-itable consequence precisely of the modernizing (and postmodernizing) trends they decry and for which they prescribe community as the rem-edy. The world on which they wish to refound a civil society is the world we have lost, and if civil society is to depend upon its restoration, it may be that there can be no civil society.

THE STRONG DEMOCRATIC PERSPECTIVE: CIVIL SOCIETY AS A MEDIATING THIRD DOMAIN BETWEEN GOVERNMENT AND MARKET (THE THREE-CELLED MODEL)

However different their conception of the private, what the libertarian and communitarian models share is a framework that divides social space into two cells, a single public and a single private sphere. My challenge to both rests on a challenge to the two-celled view. It is, I will argue, inad-equate as a description of our actual world of social engagement and in-sufficient as a normative ideal for citizens in search of a reinvigorated do-main of civic activity that is neither as thin and uninspiring as market liberalism nor as thick and glutinous as clannish community. The ten-dency of both libertarians and communitarians to conflate private and civil space (whether in the form of markets or of communities) condemns us to stark political choices that are neither desirable nor realistic. Con-tract associations and kinship communities, as well as their clones and imitations, do certainly represent two kinds of human engagement, but neither offers room for us to play out our relations as neighbors, collabo-rators, and citizens. A far more flexible frame for political and civic de-bate is yielded when we imagine social space as representing at least three distinct spaces.

A three-celled model of social space not only distinguishes public and private, or a state sector occupied by government and its sovereign insti-tutions and a private sector occupied by individuals and their contract associations (the "market"), but separates these two domains from a third that I will call the *civic sector*. The civic sector is defined by those civic communities that qualify as membership communities but are sufficiently open and egalitarian to permit civic participation on a voluntary basis. The parameters of this third civic sector are generously enough drawn to encompass groups that fall short of the ideal—for example, a church that includes those who are "born" into it as well as those "baptized" as adults or otherwise there by choice; or a civic group such as the NAACP that serves the interests of a particular identitarian group even if, as is the case here, its membership is open to all. But the dominant character of the civic domain is given by its nature as a public and open realm (like the state sector) which, however, is voluntary and noncoercive (like the private sector), and its constituent member communities must have some aspect of openness and inclusion. For although it is "private," it partakes of the egalitarianism and nonexclusivity of the democratic public sector; and although it is public, it is neither sovereign nor coercive, and it partakes of the liberty and voluntariness of the private sector. By sharing certain virtues of both the public and private realms, it constitutes a third and independent sector: a perspective I identify with strong democracy and that has many features of what others call the civic republican perspective.

Once we establish the traits that demarcate this third civic sector, we will be in possession of a fresh viewpoint on civil society. For the third sector which is defined by both publicness and liberty, by egalitarianism and voluntarism, models what we seek in the normative ideal of civil society: a domain of citizens who appear neither as consumers of government services and rights bearers against government intrusion, on the one hand, nor as mere voters and passive watchdogs to whom representative governing elites retain some vestigial accountability, on the other. Rather, in the strong democratic perspective, citizens appear as members of civil society because they are active, responsible, engaged members of groups and communities devoted to exploring common ground and pursuing common relations. Civil society's relations are thicker and more rewarding than those afforded by markets or the economic interactions produced by production and consumption, yet they are less solidaristic and imprisoning than those of blood communities.

It is this strong democratic model to which I now want to turn in some detail, for it not only captures the traditional Tocquevillean model of a civic republican civil society as it was historically practiced in America, but also represents a powerful normative ideal for addressing many of the civic defects of our current situation.

The Strong Democratic Three-Celled Model of Civil Society

The three-celled model of civil society rooted in a strong democratic version of civic republicanism is an ideal type. But it also reflects a certain historical and sociological reality. Once upon a time, between the oppositional poles of government and market, state and individual, contract association and community, there was a vital middling choice for America. Though in eclipse today, the powerful imagery of civil society held the key to America's early democratic energy and civic activism. Michael Sandel offers a fascinating account of this traditional civic republican perspective (though with a decidedly communitarian bias) in his *Democracy's Discontent*. Although republicanism scarcely discloses a golden age in our history (after all, it coexisted with slavery and the franchise inequalities of the nineteenth century), it did link liberty, he writes, to "sharing in self-government" understood as "deliberating with fellow citizens about the common good and helping shape the destiny of the political community."[18]

This civic republican perspective posits a third domain for civic engagement which is neither governmental nor strictly private yet shares the virtues of both the public and the private. It provides a space for work, business, and other activities that is focused on neither profit nor services. It also yields a communicative domain of civility that grounds political discourse in mutual respect and the search for common understanding even as it permits the expression of differences and the identification of conflicts.

It shares with government a sense of publicity and a regard for the general good and the common weal, yet (unlike government) makes no claims to exercise a monopoly on legitimate coercion. It shares with the private sector liberty, without being individualistic or anarchic. Rather, it is a voluntary and in this sense "private" realm devoted to public goods. Civil society remains the domain of church, family, and voluntary association, the domain where "belonging" takes place not as a surrogate for freedom but as its condition and training ground.[19] Civil society's middling terms can potentially mediate between the state and private sectors and offer women and men a space for activity that is both voluntary and public. When the government appropriates the term *public* exclusively for affairs of state, the real public (you and me) ceases to be able to think of itself as one (an "us"), and politicians become the only significant "public officials." In this perspective, politics is professionalized and citizenship is transformed into a private occupation. Under such circumstances, it is hardly surprising that individuals feel compelled to withdraw into themselves and claim the identity of narcissistic consumers or exclusionary clansmen.

Without civil society, suspended between big bureaucratic governments that citizens no longer trust (Putnam's problem) and private markets they cannot depend on for moral and civic values (Michael Lerner's or Amitai Etzioni's complaint), citizens are homeless. A free country depends for its liberties first of all neither on formal democratic governing institutions nor on free commercial markets but on a vibrant civil society. Alexis de Tocqueville celebrated the local character of American liberty and thought that democracy could be sustained only through vigorous municipal civic activity of the kind that typified Andrew Jackson's America. He would scarcely recognize America today, where our alternatives are restricted to government gargantuanism and either market greed (the libertarian model) or identitarian parochialism (the communitarian model) and where the main consequence of recent elections seems to be the supplanting of New Deal arrogance by market triumphalism. Both Newt Gingrich's Republicans and Bill Clinton's Democrats have proclaimed the end of the era of big government without having identified clear alternatives to the solitariness and greed of the private sector.

The impact of these theoretical models on concrete policy debates is evident from the health care fiasco of 1993. Health care reform failed in a paroxysm of mutual recrimination. But it was the policy process instigated by the administration itself as much as the enemies of reform that brought the Clinton plan down. For in what became an ever more technocratic and professionalized debate about what reform required in the abstract, the public at large simply went missing. Experts from the government debated experts from the private sector, but the people in whose name reforms were being drawn up were invisible. The merits of the Oregon health plan can be debated, but Oregon got a plan because it took care to make civic debate in specially created civil society institutions such as health parliaments central to the policy-making process. Contrarily, the abyss separating the president and his intended constituents—the missing American public—sealed his plan's doom.

It is not only policy debate but our understanding of what it means to be a citizen and a politician that is transformed by the two-celled model of social space. Without a civil society that occupies a third sector to nourish engaged citizens, politicians, we have observed, turn into public "professionals" out of touch with their constituencies, while citizens are reduced to their privatized and whining antagonists or turned into ungrateful clients of government services they readily consume but are unwilling to pay for. Yet as Harry Boyte and Nancy Kari have insisted, despite the public cynicism of our own times, there is still an appetite for civic engagement that is manifest in local activity throughout America: "For all of our problems and fears as a nation, civic energy abounds . . . a rich array of civic work in many diverse settings is evident across the country."[20] What is missing is the space—both literally and metaphorically—where that engagement can take place and be understood.

When we once define civil society in the context of a third domain, what then does it demand of us? How might it be reconstituted in a fashion that gives citizens and politicians alike a space in which to act that is neither governmental nor commercial? Neither coercive nor private? And time in which to play and deliberate and interact in the face of the time-guzzling demands of production and consumption? Is civic space imaginable that is neither radically individualistic nor suffocatingly communitarian? A civic dwelling place that is neither a capitol building, nor a shopping mall, nor a tribal fireside?

To imagine how a vigorous civic republican civil society might look, we may want to think about the actual domains Americans occupy as they go about their daily business when they are engaged in neither politics (voting, jury service, paying taxes) nor commerce (working, producing, shopping, consuming). Such daily business includes going to church or synagogue, doing volunteer work, participating in a civic association, supporting a philanthropy, joining a fraternal organization, contributing to a charity, assuming responsibility in a PTA or neighborhood watch or a hospital fund-raising society, or joining with neighbors to clean up a local park. From this perspective, our civic engagements are not private activities but nongovernmental public activities; they define the spaces we share for purposes other than shopping or voting. These spaces and occupations share with the private sector the gift of liberty; they are voluntary and are constituted by freely associated individuals and groups. Unlike private sector associations, however, they aim at common ground and consensual (i.e., integrative and collaborative) modes of action. It is in this sense that we can see civil society as public without being coercive, voluntary without being privatized.

A civic republican civil society represents a form of association richer and thicker than contractual market relations but not so binding as kinship or ascriptive relations of the kind that define the ideal Gemeinschaft community. The clansman has all the virtues of the blood brother but also the limitations of the bondsman. The consumer has the virtues of the autonomous freeman but the limitations of the deracinated solitary. Civil society's ideal citizen mediates between these virtues and vices: she is not as steeped in solidarity as the clansman but is far more free; she is less radically autonomous than the consumer but better able to enjoy the comforts of neighborly social relations. Her membership in a panoply of civic associations such as the PTA and the block association may feel more "artificial" than the ties of a natural kinship community, but it may well feel more "natural" than what draws the shopper to a mall or the voter to a polling station.

It is in this civil domain that such traditional civic institutions as foundations, schools, churches, public interest groups, voluntary associations, civic groups, and social movements belong. One thinks of organizations such as American Health Decisions, the Industrial Areas Foundation (from Saul Alinsky to Ernie Cortez), the Oregon Health Parliament, the National Issues Forums of the Kettering Foundation, the Study Circles Movement, policy juries, and deliberative video town meetings (see James Fishkin's work, for example). The media, too, where they privilege their public responsibilities over their commercial ambitions, are better understood as part of civil society than of the private sector. Only when the free space that is civil society goes unrecognized are we forced to treat all civic activity as private activity no different than commerce. This is how certain traditional liberal constituencies concerned with the public environment, public safety rules, full employment, and other social goods lost their status as public interest entities and seemed to reappear as private sector "special interest groups" indistinguishable from for-profit corporations and private associations with far narrower interests.

In sum, the strong democratic civic model of civil society offers a mediation between the thick communitarian and thin market libertarian models of the social world that is both descriptively useful and prescriptively attractive. It yields an understanding of citizenship conducive to civic revitalization and democratic engagement.

The three alternative accounts offered here can be summed up in the following chart:

CIVIL SOCIETY AS		
THICK COMMUNITARIAN	MEDIAN CIVIC	THIN LIBERTARIAN
blood relative	neighbor	stranger
clan	citizen	consumer
Gemeinschaft	civic polity	Gesellschaft
membership	citizenship	contractee/client
VIRTUES = solidarity and inclusion and thickness	VIRTUES = equality and inclusion and openness	VIRTUES = economic liberty and autonomy and personal choice
feels natural	feels conventional	feels artificial
VICE = exclusion and hierarchy	VICE = thinness and arbitrariness	VICE = alienation and loneliness

MAKING CIVIL SOCIETY REAL

There are three obstacles to reestablishing civil society as a third, mediating domain between the government and private sectors: government itself, market dogmas, and the yearning for community that can subordinate liberty and equality to the hunger for solidarity. The first obstacle is the tendency of government to think it is a surrogate for all civic action and that its job is to govern on behalf of citizens instead of facilitating their own self-government. The second is the tendency of market liberals to think that privatization is a synonym for democratization and empowerment and that all civic liberty needs to flourish is for government to get out of the way. The third and last is the tendency of communitarians to yearn for a restoration of the values and value communities of earlier times, and to seek the imposition of such values either by government or by coercive public opinion entities without regard for liberty or diversity.

Ironically, although government itself has so often been seen as part of the problem, it has an opportunity here to be part of the solution. For it not only can behave in a modest and self-limiting manner (as the New Democrats of the Democratic Leadership Council's Progressive Policy Institute propose) but can also participate in limiting the crushing effects of monopoly corporations and what I have elsewhere called "McWorld's" commercial uniformity and cultural homogenization. And it can assure, through its judicial institutions, that we are protected against the side effects on liberty of the communitarian longing for solidarity. The enemy of civil society is in fact neither government nor private corporations per se but bureaucracy, dogmatism, unresponsiveness, totalism, bloat, unaccountability, absolutism, and inertia, wherever they are found. And they are, we have seen, found in the private commercial sector no less than in the government sector, among firms and fraternities no less than in welfare bureaucracies and regulatory inflexibility. Where government is at fault, legislation must help government help itself toward self-limitation and reform; but where the private commercial sector is the problem, government must be the public's ally in curbing commercial and market abuses. Ultimately, government is but an extension of the common power of citizens, and citizens must be allowed to use that common power even as they work to reform that power's dangers and defects.

PRACTICAL STRATEGIES FOR REESTABLISHING CIVIC SPACE FOR CIVIL SOCIETY

A government pledged to give practical support to citizenship and civil society can effectively and legitimately act through legislative initiatives and legislative reform as:

1. a positive facilitator of civil society,
2. a partner of citizens in removing negative governmental obstacles to civil society practices, and
3. an ally of civil society in challenging the private commercial sector and overly zealous communitarian groups where they impact negatively on citizenship.

There is no legislative domain that cannot be thoughtfully reframed by thinking about its requirements from the perspective of civil society. Both Democrats and Republicans have manifested interest in "legislating civil society," the Clinton administration in its ongoing fascination with civil society and the Republicans in the legislative agenda offered by William Bennett and Senator Dan Coats.[21] Some possible programs are more easily enacted than others. I would propose at least six arenas as possible domains of innovative and liberating legislation directed toward the goals referred to earlier. Ideally, legislation in these domains would be low expenditure and high impact. In many cases, it would build on legislative strategies already in place (e.g., campaign finance reform, free TV time for candidates, the use of new telecommunications technologies for the public weal), although in some cases it would envision quite new initiatives. In every case, specific legislative initiatives would aim at reorienting and reconceptualizing the reasoning behind policy goals in ways that downplay government as an end in itself or as a direct solution to social problems, and emphasize its role as a facilitator and instrument of citizens in getting their own public work done.

The pertinent arenas for potential model legislative action in support of civil society include the following:

1. *Enlargement and reinforcement of public spaces*: specifically, retrofitting commercial malls as genuinely multiuse public spaces
2. *Civic uses of new telecommunications technology*: specifically, preventing the commercialization of the new media from destroying their civic potentials; creating a civic Internet and public access cable; keeping advertising and the commercial exploitation of children in check
3. *The global economy from the perspective of production*: protecting the labor market and challenging disemployment practices through programs of corporate responsibility; making corporations responsible members of civil society
4. *The global economy from the perspective of consumption*: protecting justice in safety, environment, and wage policy through a civic consumers strategy that labels and boycotts goods produced in countries and environments without regard for safety, environment, and child labor laws

5. *Enhancement of civic education and civil society*: creating civil society programs via national and community service
6. *The arts and humanities*: treating artists as citizens and citizens as artists through arts education and service programs

These examples of practical approaches to reestablishing or reinvigorating civil society argue for the social realism of the three-celled model of social space and the strong democratic perspective on civil society. They demonstrate that civil society, far from being an esoteric normative ideal or a remote subject of nostalgic memory, has vital political and civic importance in understanding our epoch and developing legislative and corporate strategies to make it more democratic. The theory of civil society has a practice that is both realistic and pragmatic.

NOTES

1. See *New Democrat* 7, no. 2 (March/April 1995), special issue on Civil Society, and George Liebmann's *The Little Platoons: Local Governments in Modern History* (New York: Praeger, 1995) for an account from the left; Senator Dan Coats, "Can Congress Revive Civil Society?" *Policy Review* (January/February 1996), for a view from the right. Also see the new second edition of the classic work by Peter Berger and Richard John Neuhaus on mediating institutions and civil society, *To Empower People: The Role of Mediating Structures in Public Policy* (Washington, D.C.: American Enterprise Institute, 1996 [1977]).

2. Thus Bronislaw Geremek writes, "The concept of civil society appeared fairly late in the annals of Central and Eastern European resistance to communism . . . [appearing] as a program of resistance in Poland during the late 1970s and 1980s." "Civil Society and the Present Age," in *The Idea of a Civil Society* (Research Triangle Park, N.C.: National Humanities Center, 1992), 11.

3. See Robert Putnam, "Bowling Alone: America's Declining Social Capital," *Journal of Democracy* 6, no. 1 (January, 1995): 65; *Making Democracy Work: Civic Traditions in Modern Italy* (Princeton, N.J.: Princeton University Press, 1993); Francis Fukuyama, *Trust: The Social Virtues and the Creation of Prosperity* (New York: Free Press, 1995); Amitai Etzioni, ed., *New Communitarian Thinking: Persons, Virtues, Institutions, and Communities* (Charlottesville: University Press of Virginia, 1995); Michael Sandel, *Democracy's Discontent: America in Search of a Public Philosophy* (Cambridge, Mass.: Harvard University Press, 1996); Harry Boyte and Benjamin Barber, *Civic Declaration—A Call for a New Citizenship: A New Citizenship Project of the American Civic Forum*, an Occasional Paper of the Kettering Foundation (9 December 1994); Harry Boyte and Nancy Kari, *Building America: The Democratic Promise of Public Work* (Philadelphia: Temple University Press, 1996). The charge of "decline" in trust and membership is a controversial one, especially in the form it has been put by Robert Putnam. For the debate, see "Controversy," *American Prospect*, no. 25 (March–April 1996): 17–28.

4. I cannot here develop a philosophical genealogy of civil society. Andrew Arato and Jean Cohen offer a penetrating and broad-ranging account in their *Civil Society and Political Theory* (Cambridge, Mass.: MIT Press, 1992), but at a level of philosophical sophistication that may be daunting to the general reader. An excellent collection of essays that discloses the contours of the European debate is Adolf Bibic and Gigi Graziano, *Civil Society, Political Society, Democracy* (Ljubljana: Slovenian Political Science Association, 1994). Adam B. Seligman's account of the history of the idea (in his *Idea of Civil Society* [New York: Free Press, 1992]) is more accessible but is marred by episodes of uncertain scholarship and peculiar biases against current political debates about civil society, presumably due to his preoccupation with Eastern Europe and his seeming ignorance of the practical political character of the debate in the United States.

5. This is in contrast to transitional societies (say, in Eastern Europe) where the notion of civil society has flourished as a way of talking about samizdat politics and dissent, alluding as much to what is absent in the autocratic societies it critiques as to anything present in the paltry institutions of critics and dissenters. In such societies, it has had a radical utopian cast: what we would ideally like to have is a critique of what we actually do have.

6. When Senator Dole offered Americans the choice of "trusting government or trusting the people," he polarized public and private in just this way, leaving us only with the demonized "them" of public sector government and the glorified "us" of the private sector people.

7. There is considerable confusion nowadays surrounding the term *liberal*. As used in modern ideological quarrels, the "L word" is a synonym for leftist or progressive or welfare statist and is used by conservatives to castigate such "tax and spend" big government types. But in earlier times, *liberal* referred to those who upheld the liberal or private sector against government or statist intervention, and in this usage it more aptly describes conservatives or Republicans with a libertarian, antigovernmental bias. To avoid such complications, I will generally use the term *libertarian* when referring to classical "liberal" strategies of containing government to secure the private realm of liberty and *liberal* in its modern connotation only as a synonym for *progressivism*, as in the "L word."

8. Robert Nozick's conception of beings who "live separate existences" among which "no moral balancing is possible" and whose "voluntary consent" is required for every step taken toward the construction of political relations captures perfectly the attenuated nexus of human relations in the traditional liberal conception. See *Anarchy, State and Utopia* (New York: Basic Books, 1974), preface, ix. This variety of libertarianism has an anarchist tinge to it and, with its Nietzschean overtones, recalls radical works such as Max Stirner's nineteenth-century tract *The Ego and Its Own* (recently edited by David Leopold; Cambridge: Cambridge University Press, 1995).

9. In Eastern Europe after the fall of communism, civil society has commonly been regarded as a synonym for the market: "Civil society can only go hand in hand with a free market economy," writes Russian journalist Sergei Grigoriev; to which Hungarian editor Gyorgy Varga adds, "It is the individual entrepreneur . . . who will lead in the establishment of voluntary associations, philanthropy

and the other patterns of civil society." Both quotes are from "On Markets and Privatization," in *The Idea of Civil Society*, 8.

10. Etzioni, ed., *New Communitarian Thinking;* Michael Lerner, *The Politics of Meaning: Restoring Hope and Possibility in an Age of Cynicism* (Reading, Mass.: Addison-Wesley, 1996); see also Lerner's magazine, *Tikkun.*

11. If Anglo-American liberalism sees civil associations as little more than variations on the contractualist market corporation, European communitarianism has tended to see economic corporations as little more than variations on the natural community—a vision that calls up organic corporatism of the kind imagined by Italian fascist thinkers such as Rocco and Gentile.

12. See my *Jihad versus McWorld* (New York: Times Books, 1995).

13. Thus the conservative, sometimes reactionary face of traditional cultural communitarians. Richard Sennett once celebrated the urban (and urbane) uses of disorder that attend cosmopolitanism. Although he later rued the "fall of public man," Sennett's fallen public man was a cosmopolitan rather than a communitarian. Richard Sennett, *The Uses of Disorder: Personal Identity and City Life* (New York: Knopf, 1970), and *The Fall of Public Man* (New York: Knopf, 1977).

14. Many observers, both professional sociologists such as Peter Berger and political critics such as William Bennett, have linked the crisis in values with the vanishing of order and authority. Robert Nisbet, for example, believed the dimming of community in late Western civilization brought with it a devastating twilight of authority. See Nisbet, *The Twilight of Authority* (New York: Oxford University Press, 1975); Berger and Neuhaus, *To Empower People.*

15. The death trap image is from Michael Lesy's *Wisconsin Death Trip* (New York: Doubleday, 1991). On the dark side, Thomas Hardy offers a disconcerting feel for the intolerance that can define a village community in *Jude the Obscure,* while Toni Morrison's *The Bluest Eye* is unsentimentally savage about the character of the kind of impoverished African-American family that might have once been the subject of nostalgia. See also Sherwood Anderson's *Winesburg, Ohio.*

16. Michael Oakeshott, *On Human Conduct* (Oxford: Clarendon, 1975), 239.

17. Peter Laslett's *The World We Have Lost* (New York: Scribner, 1965) gives a philosopher's idealized and nostalgic account of life in face-to-face village communities in Britain in the sixteenth and seventeenth centuries.

18. Sandel, *Democracy's Discontent,* 5.

19. See Sara Evans and Harry S. Boyte, *Free Spaces: The Sources of Democratic Change in America* (New York: Harper & Row, 1986).

20. Harry C. Boyte and Nancy N. Kari, *Building America: The Democratic Promise of Public Work* (Philadelphia: Temple University Press, 1996), 5.

21. See Senator Dan Coats, "Can Congress Revive Civil Society?" *Policy Review* (January/February 1996): 24.

2

Making Civil Society Work

Democracy as a Problem of Civic Cooperation

William M. Sullivan

Less than a decade after the fall of the Berlin Wall and the end of apartheid—events that seemed part of a worldwide flourishing of enthusiasm for democracy—the bloom is off the rose. "At Hour of Triumph," ran a headline in the *New York Times* in early 1996, "Democracy Recedes as the Global Ideal." The article went on to quote Fareed Zakaria, managing editor of *Foreign Affairs*, who observed that although more countries wear the trappings of democracy—holding elections, for example—this does not always translate into more democracies in fact. How, then, can the United States encourage the growth of democratic societies? Zakaria offered this advice: instead of devoting all its energies to ensuring free elections, "America might do better by promoting civic values like free speech, separation of church and state and property rights."[1] In cases where nations newly emerging from authoritarian regimes lack such civic virtues, the rush to elections may actually be weakening the new states, creating a problem of instability that undermines the legitimacy of democracy in the eyes of their citizens.

In another context, Zakaria had made a similar point in discussing the new prominence of the notion of civil society, a prominence due in major part to the use of the term as a rallying cry by opponents of the now-fallen communist regimes of Eastern Europe. Those struggles for national liberation, beginning with the Solidarity movement in Poland, opposed civil society, understood as the realm of free association, to the control from above exercised by the communist regime. Civil society is usually understood as the realm of those institutions larger than the family yet smaller than the state that form the social fabric of modern societies.

Zakaria criticized a simplistic identification of the notion of civil society with a successful democratic polity. He cautioned that all intermediate associations are not equally conducive to the democratic virtues. While Scouting and professional associations may promote democratic habits, paramilitary militia groups probably do not. "What we want," Zakaria concluded, "is not civil society, but civics—what the Romans called civi-tas; that is, public-spiritedness, sacrifice for the community, citizenship, even nobility. But not all of civil society is civic minded."[2]

Through the sharp contrast he draws, Zakaria is posing a fundamental question that the recent revival of the idea of civil society has only begun to engage. Since 1989 many Western policy analysts and politicians, par-ticularly in the United States, have been working on the assumption that a world of peaceful, cooperative nations has finally appeared on the his-torical agenda. In this optimistic scenario, a civil society of freedom for individual action and association, together with free market economies, equals stable democracy, and democratic nations do not wage war against each other.

Is civil society as such essentially equivalent to democratic citizenship? Or could it be that rights to independent economic activity, private life, and social associations can be established and even to some extent flour-ish without developing a society of popular engagement in public life and a corresponding public accountability of political leadership? The history of the Meji Restoration in Japan, Bismarck's Germany, and some more re-cent East Asian and Latin American societies provides evidence that forms of civil society can exist, and even be developed "from above," under paternalistic or authoritarian regimes. Today, conditions in both Eastern Europe and East Asia raise serious questions about a facile impu-tation of a necessary connection between civil society and market econo-mies, on the one hand, and democratic political regimes, on the other.

CIVIL SOCIETY AND THE PROBLEMS OF DEMOCRACY

In what follows I will try to address this complex and troubled issue of the relation between civil society and the civic ethos of democracy. I will treat civil society as a distinctive kind of social space, one that supports security of person and property, together with individual freedom of con-tract and association. As the experience of nations emerging from author-itarian regimes has highlighted, these are the essential social conditions for the development of a private sphere of life outside direct governmen-tal control. At the same time, the freedoms of civil society rest on certain political goods, especially the maintenance of social peace and civility, as well as the provision of justice under a rule of law. These goods depend on an effective public power, a government and political institutions to enforce respect for the rights and dignity of individuals. Negative examples from various parts of the world amply demonstrate the importance of effective legal government. Civil society cannot long survive ineffective, corrupt, or capriciously despotic regimes.

Modern aspirations, however, go beyond life in a civil society understood in the sense of secure private rights. In the United States and other developed democracies, but also in more and more parts of the world, people demand rights of participation in the direction of common affairs. They aspire to the dignity of citizens who count in the life of their societies. Individuals seek, that is, public standing as contributing members of society to complement their sense of private efficacy and legal equality. In modern democracies, these aspirations have been institutionalized in civic communities enjoying political cultures of active public involvement. The public-regarding spirit of such civic communities is indispensable for shaping those attitudes of citizen responsibility that ensure that representative government functions with a strong sense of public purpose and accountability.

Modern democratic life in civil society thus has a civic core. This is the theme of Parts II and III of this chapter. The argument is that the viability of a society's civil forms depends on the strength of that society's civic content. In modern democracies, civic discipline sustains both increased social cohesion and greater liberty for individuals. By establishing among the citizens themselves a high degree of normative agreement about rights and responsibilities, civic communities can remain resilient and cohesive with far less direct control of individuals than in less internally disciplined societies. In this way civic community supports individual freedom. Thus, while the concept of civil society describes the dimension of free communication and activity that modern civic solidarity makes possible, civil society is not a freestanding dimension of democratic life, nor is it a self-sufficient idea or form of life. In its fully developed forms, it rests on the effective institutionalization of collective responsibility in democratic government.

Today, there is increasing concern in the United States, as elsewhere, that civil society is threatened with decay. Complaints about declining civility mingle with popular and expert worries about low voter turnout, weakened trust in major institutions, evidence of declining voluntary participation, and a diffuse sense that social bonds are unraveling. Surveys suggest that the social trust on which functioning democracy rests is suffering from the effects of growing disparities between the affluent and the poor and a shrinking middle class. There is less agreement, of course, about the causes of these worrisome developments. However, it seems difficult to avoid the conclusion that an increasing sense of economic insecurity, coupled with the perception of widening inequality, is a serious threat to civic community in the United States. The workings of the economic structures of civil society have begun to threaten the moral and political bonds on which its viability depends.

To observers outside the country, these developments appear parallel to those that are loosening the social bond in other democratic nations, trends linked to recent economic changes. For example, John Gray has asked whether the new economic order is not undermining civil society itself through its assault on what he sees as the cultural basis of Western democracy, the long-running mutual reinforcement between capitalism and the "bourgeois form of life with all the security and commitment to career and the status associated with vocation that was so evident in Victorian novels." Especially in the United States, Gray contends, "communal attachments" and "civic engagement" appear as optional extras on "a fixed menu of individual choice and market exchange." The result is social incoherence: "extraordinary technological and economic vitality" amid social breakdown, political withdrawal, and cultural uncertainty—all trends which will undercut the areas of vitality if they are not arrested.[3]

There is a parallel here to the debate carried on in the early 1990s in the Czech Republic between the president, Vaclav Havel, and the prime minister, Vaclav Klaus. Then the issue was whether democratic citizenship can rest on economic liberalization alone or whether it demands a widely shared collective commitment to the well-being of the society as a whole. Havel, drawing on his dissident experience, argued for the primacy of collective moral commitment. Klaus, an economist educated in the West, interested in reform under the Communist regime, and dedicated to monetarist economics, argued to the contrary that the rapid establishment of free markets in land, labor, and capital would itself be the most effective school for educating the citizen body in the principles of Western democracies. It was Klaus's policies that were implemented during the 1990s. But the results have been dismaying. Although economic life in the Czech Republic has begun to recover from its post–Velvet Revolution decline, citizen participation in public life has shriveled as cynicism and distrust have grown. In this case, the very fragility of the emerging democracy serves to underscore the tensions between civil society's economic foundations in the market and the civic morality on which democracy depends.[4]

American society today also seems to be beset by a withdrawal of social engagement at all levels, but most disturbingly on the part of the successful. In this situation it is especially important to clarify the case for the civic basis of the freedoms of civil society. If these civic roots are allowed to decay, the proud freedoms of liberal society will surely wither. Parts IV, V, and VI address this issue. Part IV takes up the question of how to move American society toward a renewed level of civic life by rebuilding civic community at both the national and local levels. Specifically, this part sketches the logic of "public cooperation" as the needed direction for institutional reform. The further questions of who will take responsibility for leading a new movement for national reform, and on what principles such a movement might develop, furnish the themes of Parts V and VI.

The issue of responsibility brings into prominence the great strategic power and importance of the leadership of the nation's dominant institutions. In all spheres this leadership is to a striking degree drawn from members of the "national class." This designates a highly visible and prestigious group of Americans drawn from all parts of the nation who have been shaped by the common experience of meritocratic success through advanced education at highly selective universities. The subsequent careers of these men and women are likewise typically national in scope and cosmopolitan in outlook. Part V investigates the relevance, to these leaders, of the American tradition of the "calling" to public service, asking whether it might again serve to infuse civic purpose into the ethic of achievement. Part VI answers this question by relating the current crisis of civic community in the United States to the ongoing debate over national purpose and the meaning of American democracy.

BUT WHAT IS CIVIL SOCIETY?

The use of the language of civil society by dissidents in Eastern Europe beginning in the late 1970s has since gained momentum, so that the term is frequently invoked not only by intellectuals and journalists but also by politicians, and in Western countries as well. In a sense, the brief recent history of the use of the term *civil society* recapitulates important features of the development of the idea through the eighteenth and nineteenth centuries. As Ernest Gellner has put it in an influential work on the topic, a term "which seemed distinctly covered with dust" became suddenly "a shining emblem" of what was missing but sought after in societies dominated by Communist regimes. Although civil societies of a kind had existed previously under despotic regimes and civic communities had thrived as independent republics in the past, the modern Western European novelty was the successful combination of a stable, self-governing, and self-defending civic community based in a society of private freedom. It was this achievement that the Eastern Europeans wanted to emulate.[5]

The Eastern European use of civil society started out by emphasizing the distinctiveness of those areas of social life that stood outside, or that might at considerable personal cost be removed from, the direct control of the totalitarian state. The dissidents saw civil society as a "parallel polis," an alternative sphere in which a shadow public realm could be developed. Their success, of course, was extraordinary. But because they used the term polemically, sharply opposing the areas the state controlled to all other spheres of social activity, the dissidents came to stress the importance of individual rights and the rule of law as making possible a plurality of free associations while linking the market economy, institutionalized in legal property rights, tightly to their idea of civil society.

The dissidents were thereby recalling the eighteenth-century understanding of the term. During the century of the Enlightenment, civil society ceased to be equivalent to political society, as it had been in the previous century for John Locke. Instead, the conception of civil society was used to draw a line "between political community and civil society to mark off coercive decision-making from free exchange."[6] This distinction laid the basis for that key feature of modern polities, the distinction between private and public spheres. Thinkers such as David Hume and Adam Smith valorized this realm of private property, contract, and exchange as a new kind of social sphere in which individuals could freely establish independent identities and sustain a society of dignity and civility under the protection but not the arbitrary intrusion of the state authority. Of course, the optimistic assessment of civil society by the Scottish Enlightenment did not last long into the European nineteenth century. Thinkers as different as Georg Hegel and Alexis de Tocqueville used civil society in the more restricted, less honorific meaning of the sphere of market exchange and private property.

By the early nineteenth century, Hegel had extrapolated the logic of Smith's theory of market exchange into a critique of civil society. Hegel criticized market-based civil society as a form of competitive interdependence that necessarily generated alienation, inequality, and poverty as well as individual freedom. Civil society's positive potentials for fostering individual freedom could only be realized in a wider kind of ethical solidarity sustained by the family and given embodiment in occupational groupings and functional organizations summed up and maintained by a representative state. Hegel's critique and attempted synthesis provided a kind of anticipation of the logic of the twentieth-century European "social state." It also famously laid the foundation for Marx's more radical dismissal of civil society as a kind of mirage, a system of hidden despotism ruthlessly bending individuals to its impersonal will, subjecting the many to the propertied few, yet decked out as an apparent realm of freedom and choice. The critical legacy has posed the question of whether the unregulated market can undermine and distort the freedom and solidarity sought for civil society as effectively as encroachments of despotic political power, and indeed whether the two may work together toward that end. The debate between Havel and Klaus in the Czech Republic begins to recapitulate this nineteenth-century awareness of the problematic status of civil society in relation to both market and state.

It is misgivings about the institutional matrix of modern societies that have reappeared in the latest civil society debates in Western countries. Here the term has most often been invoked to call attention to the need for solidarity and social responsibility on the part of individuals. "The current wish to return to civil society," writes Adam Seligman, is in the West about the desire "to reassert a social solidarity that would affirm community no less than individuality."[7] For Seligman, there is a moral value at the heart of the idea of civil society. This core value, however, is neither individualism nor voluntarism, but "civility, the mutual recognition of each individual's innate human dignity," a recognition that underlies the idea of individual rights.

This recognition of dignity is in turn rooted in relations of trust, often unconscious but operating in social relationships of all types. The basis of civil society is therefore the "precontractual," tacit, but shared norms presupposed by any more explicit contract or agreement. These social and moral bonds support the individual's "membership in the political community." However, according to Seligman, this necessary foundation of trust is exactly what is under threat today. In Eastern Europe the boundaries of trust are too often confined to particular ethnic, religious, or national groups. There the common bonds of civility are too weak to override more restrictive particularistic loyalties. In Western societies, by contrast, the problem is that this basic social trust has somehow become abstract and is dangerously weak as a support for the social solidarity on which civility depends.[8] Today's much-discussed declines in political participation, social trust, associational life, and civility are symptoms of underlying weaknesses. Seen this way, the recent upsurge of interest in the idea of civil society amounts to a series of efforts to understand and address this underlying problem of civility and social solidarity.

The idea of civil society, then, can be a normative aspiration as well as a claim to sociological description. The core of the concept is the recognition that human societies are grounded on and held together by shared normative understandings and so should be guided by discourse and moral suasion rather than external coercion. Here the values of civil society overlap with ideals of modern democratic citizenship. These themes have received important articulation in the work of Jürgen Habermas, while Andrew Arato and Jean Cohen have developed similar ideas with reference to contemporary social movements.[9] In this view, civil society becomes preeminently the sphere of discourse and deliberation but also of experimentation and struggle among contending views of the good life. This emphasis on the communicative and the normative is important in contrast to those reductionistic theories, also legacies of the Enlightenment, that are much in vogue today in the variants of rational choice theories, the economic model of social action. By emphasizing that human beings are social and therefore moral beings, more than simple creatures of interest or egoistic calculation, the revival of the perspective of civil society can provide an important corrective to technocratic and economistic thinking, especially in areas of social policy, as Alan Wolfe and others have argued.[10] However, as other scholars have noted, by emphasizing the private sphere and its liberties, the idea of civil society can also be interpreted in ways that obscure the necessarily public—and political—dimension of civil freedoms.[11]

The revival of civil society is thus valuable as a reassertion of the idea that modern Western societies are engaged in a collective moral enterprise: that they represent a project propelled in important part by the effort to realize freedom, equality, and solidarity in concrete social and political arrangements. As Michael Walzer has argued, civil society has from its inception been linked to the liberal spirit of tolerant pluralism that began with John Locke's argument for (limited) religious toleration.[12] Historically, the rise of civil society greatly spurred the development of modern ideas of freedom and the good life in which voluntary commitment and association take center position. In this way civil society has served as the incubator of liberalism, both as a public philosophy and as a conception of the good life. Later, the democratic state and the political philosophies of modern citizenship were also historical successors to the idea of civil society and offspring of the same social processes that produced liberalism. It remains unclear whether the revival of civil society discourse will contribute anything importantly new to this tradition of citizenship, as set forth, for example, by T. H. Marshall.[13]

There is, then, a deep tension written into the constitution of modern democratic life. If modern persons are and strive to be autonomous individuals with rights seeking individual fulfillment in the private sphere, they are also members of complex societies organized in part through widely shared, "precontractual" understandings of social membership. Modern identities are thus significantly constituted by the public status of citizenship and the norms that govern the public realm. The question is not whether the promise of individual freedom held out by civil society needs the soil of social membership to flourish. It is clear that it does. Rather, the key questions and arguments center on how much and what kind of social membership, institutionalized in which ways, and animated by what kind of public spirit. These are the issues now reappearing, though often not very clearly, in the debate over civil society.

THE SOCIAL SPACE OF DEMOCRACY: FROM CIVIL SOCIETY TO CIVIC COMMUNITY

Social space is a metaphor for describing the norms and expectations that have developed historically in a particular society or group of societies to guide thought and behavior in everyday life. A social space takes on a distinctive structure according to its criteria for evaluating, interpreting, and reacting to particular events. Because they function as constant references of thought and action, the norms of a given social space structure the lives of the individuals who inhabit it and shape their subjective desires and fears, their very sense of self. Embodied in institutional patterns, these norms anchor individual and group life by providing the standards to which persons hold themselves and each other accountable. As a metaphor, social space can thus make it easier to differentiate one society from another by focusing on the norms that give rise to distinctive patterns of relationship, such as the dominance and subordination common in authoritarian regimes, or the exchange and reciprocity typical of civil societies, or the mutual collaboration toward common ends that distinguishes democratic polities. The metaphor can also clarify the necessary but often overlooked relationship between civil liberties and civic commitments.

Seen as a kind of social space, civil society has two dominant characteristics. First, a modern civil society is a commercial society based on division of labor mediated through market exchange. It is a place in which many individuals are linked through the market in competitive yet interdependent relations. Second, however, a well-developed civil society is also characterized by dense networks of noncommercial association, reaching beyond kinship and ethnic ties through associations ranging from clubs and hospitals, to religious fellowships and scientific societies. Such a social space is defined by particular norms and expectations. Chief among these is the expectation of individual security and opportunity. Its normative form is the rule of law based on the idea of civil rights. The notion of civil rights imposes a moral imperative to respect others' rights as the boundaries of one's own liberty, an imperative that also legitimates individual initiative and makes individuals responsible for their own conduct.

The norm of equal civil rights for all makes civil society a social space in which individuals can choose important aspects of their identities for themselves, including occupation, marriage partner, place of residence, and religious affiliation. At its best, this morality of rights works toward universal applicability, so that all persons are seen as deserving the same opportunities. Civil society licenses individuals to take initiative and to define their own purposes through contracts enforceable at law, including marriage and divorce and property freely traded. At the same time, individuals are also licensed to form associations to pursue common objectives. Hence the range of associational life, from business partnerships to corporations, professional associations, and unions, as well as the whole spectrum of religious, political, cultural, and educational organizations, along with social movements that aim to change or expand the norms of civil society. The basic norms have, through historical struggle, come to have a wider applicability to more classes of persons, to women as well as men, to the less fortunate, and so on, at the same time that they have penetrated more deeply into relationships within the private sphere, as in the case of relations between spouses, parents and children, employers and workers.

Equal freedom and opportunity for all, then, are the moral core of civil society as a social space. But these values depend on a certain disposition on the part of individuals to cooperate and play by the rules of equity. For such a disposition to take root, persons must be willing to trust that unrelated and socially distant others will do the same, which is the rub. Sustaining the level of trust needed to make the rule of law and a pluralism of groups work is notoriously difficult. Typically, groups within civil society discover that they succeed better when their members are united by strong bonds of trust and solidarity. Such groups are said to be rich in *social capital,* understood as the norms and trustful relationships that enable individuals and groups to pursue goals effectively—hence the importance of social classes and racial or ethnic groups in modern societies. However, these bonds, and therefore the enabling effects of social capital, will not necessarily extend beyond the boundaries of the class or group.

For this reason, a complex, pluralistic society such as a modern nation can govern itself by deliberation and consensus only if its norms and institutions somehow bridge the many particular interests. Its social space must embody norms and expectations that generate social capital, sustaining trust and cooperation for goals common to the whole range of civil society. A social space of this kind, developed over time, enables the members of a society to recognize one another as trustworthy and accountable coparticipants in a larger moral project. This expanded understanding of themselves and their fellows in turn greatly enlarges the horizon of what they can do and become. We can call this a "civic culture."

So understood, a civic culture is characterized by social capital of a kind that spans particular interests, easing cooperation for larger goals. The norms of civic culture are not strongly developed in every civil society, but civic culture is the key enabling condition of democracy. The social space of civic culture, embodied in institutions that enable public discussion and cooperation to take place, adds new norms to those that govern relations in civil society. Besides respect for rights and reciprocity, civic culture moves toward the creation of a community of solidarity. This aim at community establishes the terms of public cooperation: what individuals and groups, government and citizens, owe each other and can expect from each other in light of the goals of their common partnership. The social space of civic culture, then, structures a common point of view about what is rightfully "public." Participants in civic cultures in turn develop a sense of self for which common goods realized in the public sphere are critical aspects of individual identities.

The idea of civic culture was first enunciated by classical civic humanism, as in Cicero's influential definition of a commonwealth or *res publica* as "not any collection of human beings brought together in any sort of way, but an assemblage of people in large numbers associated in an agreement with respect to justice and a partnership for the common good."[14] The citizen is thus seen as a bearer of rights, as defined by the "agreement with respect to justice," and also as a member of a community, a "partnership for the common good." So understood, civic membership entails two responsibilities: to maintain the terms of the "agreement" with respect to justice, but also to contribute to the public partnership. The American founding documents embody these aims. Taken together, the Declaration of Independence and the federal Constitution set out the terms of the agreement as well as (in the Constitution's famous Preamble) the goals of the public partnership. Under the impact of the Enlightenment, the documents speak in explicitly universal terms. It is sobering, however, to note that it has required many decades, and a destructive civil war, to establish (and then still imperfectly and precariously) the universal application of the terms of the agreement on "freedom and justice for all," while the dimensions of the public partnership are still hotly disputed.

Recent research has reinforced the claims of civic humanism about the importance of civic commitments for civil life. In his landmark study of Italian regional governments, Robert Putnam developed a set of characteristics, as well as empirical measures, of the kind of social space necessary for "making democracy work." Putnam has argued that the differences between regions in which democratic governments work well and those in which they do not are best accounted for by the presence in successful regions of what he calls a civic community. Civic communities exhibit four important characteristics. The first characteristic is a high level of citizen engagement, and, complementing this, a high degree of political equality so that "horizontal" relationships of reciprocity and cooperation predominate over "vertical" relationships of authority and dependence.

The third feature of civic regions is a high level of tolerance, trust, and solidarity. These features are in turn supported by dense networks of overlapping associational life that nurture skills of cooperation and habits of shared responsibility. The cross-cutting memberships of these associations work to moderate and expand loyalties, further strengthening bonds of trust and reciprocity. The relative strength of social bonds and civic norms determines the extent of a region's cooperative capabilities. In places with strong civic communities, governments tend to be efficient, and the citizens take pride in their governments and identify them as their own. Perhaps most surprisingly, the strength of civic culture turns out to be the best predictor of economic vitality as well.[15] Civic virtues do not in themselves account for economic success. They do, however, explain why civic communities such as the northern Italian regions Putnam studied are able to respond to challenges and opportunities so much more effectively than less civic regions such as the Italian south.

In sum, civic community structures the social space of civil society in public-regarding ways, anchoring individual identity and conscience in shared norms of solidarity, trust, and reciprocity. When these expectations are effectively institutionalized, citizens derive a strong sense of standing and purpose through participation in civic life. While a pluralistic civil society provides opportunities for individuation and creative experiment, sustaining an open society requires public spirit as well as an achievement ethic. As Putnam puts it, the Italian case suggests that because citizens in civic regions enjoy the benefits of community, they are able to be more liberal.[16] The civic capacities of individuals grow through their willingness to cooperate for the sake of an enlarged sense of identity and purpose. It is in this quite realistic sense that democratic citizenship is a moral project, a historically rare and precarious process of collective social practice.

"Happiness," Putnam concludes, "is living in a civic community."[17] In part this is because the abundance of networks and cooperative habits makes things go more smoothly, enabling individuals to accomplish their ends, and to feel secure, more readily. But in significant part it is because individuals experience a sense of meaning and purpose that transcends their particular concerns through belonging to and participating in the larger civic life. Yet, these patterns of civic cooperation are themselves precarious in the face of the many centrifugal forces operating in the modern world. Interdependence becomes harder to attain even as it permits the expansion of areas of private choice.

Drawing on a wide body of social scientific research, Jane Mansbridge has generalized this argument. She summarizes the relevant findings by saying that "successful polities cannot work on the basis of purely private spirit." Particularly in the face of challenges and disruptive events, when great adaptability is needed, the "only feasible solution to collective action problems" is reliance on high levels of social trust and common commitment.[18] These findings are particularly germane as the United States faces the realities of major political, economic, and social changes attendant upon the ending of the cold war and the intensification of global market competition.

THE RENEWAL OF CIVIL SOCIETY: THE IDEA OF PUBLIC COOPERATION

The effects of civic community on the economic and social affairs of nations are the subject of Jonathan Boswell's study, *Community and the Economy: The Theory of Public Cooperation.*[19] Drawing on observations of long-term historical trends, Boswell argues the controversial thesis that the most successful national economies over the long run have not been those with the highest growth rates for any short term but those that have exhibited the most balanced growth and steady economic performance. Boswell's measure of growth is multifaceted, including high employment, low inflation, avoidance of either larger trade deficits or surpluses, the enhancement of a nation's capital assets and physical environment, and at least no worsening of poverty. The smaller European nations, such as the Benelux countries and Scandinavia, rank high on these measures, and for the past half century they have been leaders in the development of "public cooperation."

In polities with high levels of public cooperation, the economic and political spheres operate more as partners than as adversaries. Elements of civic community are thus institutionalized at the level of major national institutions. Equally important, such polities are characterized by high levels of communication among the whole range of sectoral interests: business, labor, but also education, mass media, religious and cultural institutions, as well as government at several levels. The result, Boswell argues, is that the whole becomes more than the sum of its often fractious parts. A synergy develops, produced by practices of "forethought, colloquy, and operational adjustments" among the economic and social groupings involved. Under conditions of public cooperation, competition is often intense, but it is balanced and guided in constructive directions by a sense of shared citizenship.

As in the case of Putnam's civic regions, public spirit is made safe for all to practice by the presence of formal and informal sanctions against its violation. In polities with strong public cooperation, all social participants know that the opportunistic pursuit of all-out interest maximization is likely to lead to negative long-term consequences in the form of increased costs of mutual surveillance, outflanking strategies, and sanctions. As in Tocqueville's famous description of self-interest rightly understood, the participants in public cooperation may begin from strongly self-interested motives, but they rarely continue to be exclusively guided by them. The social, political, and even economic payoffs from these often time-consuming practices of communication and negotiation are impressive. Overall efficiency rises along with social cohesion. Where one might have expected massive government intrusion or takeovers, there is instead "a diffusion of public tasks, as opposed to these being neglected, centrally monopolized or selfishly defined."[20] A diffuse but tough tissue of civic connection grows throughout the anatomy of economy and society.

This outcome speaks directly to contemporary American society's core problem of failing civility and security. According to Boswell, the achievement of public cooperation signals a crucial "upward shift" in a society's capacities for cooperation. Public cooperation, that is, is achieved through the transformation of a situation of fractious political gridlock into a public life of citizenship in which not just individuals but social institutions such as business firms, governmental agencies, and educational and cultural organizations become able and willing to invest their resources and energies in long-term common goals. They are willing to do this, in part, out of calculation, but also because they have come to understand themselves as members of viable national communities. Thus, appeals to utility overlap with appeals to principle and civic membership. The more these overlap, the stronger the push toward public cooperation.

Goals and interests thus can and do change through the experience of participating in common efforts to improve public cooperation. On the other hand, these developments have nowhere been steady, smooth, or complete. The United States, for instance, established important elements of public cooperation during World War II and was able to sustain something of this spirit (along with a variety of organizational linkages in both the economic and voluntary social sectors) into the 1960s, but it has subsequently lost many of its earlier gains. Under the pressures of external economic forces, similar achievements are threatening to unravel in several of the nations previously most advanced in public cooperation.

When it has occurred, the "upward shift" has usually required three things: (1) a favorable history of successful institution building in surmounting past crises; (2) a national emergency that could interrupt business as usual long enough to engage energies toward new collective goals; and (3) not least important, the presence of widely diffused moral understandings that could give support and sanction to efforts at higher levels of economic cooperation and civic community. An important question for the future of American democracy is how the United States appears in the light of these three factors.

RESOURCES FOR RENEWING CIVIC COMMUNITY
IN THE UNITED STATES

The concerns of Boswell's theory of public cooperation are not wholly foreign to discussions of America's present problems of civic engagement and political commitment. On the first count, the history of American democracy can offer encouragement. The nation has several times faced and surmounted potentially fatal crises: slavery and secession in the nineteenth century; transformation into an urban and industrial society on a continental scale at the turn of the twentieth century; then depression, world war, and the burdens of global leadership in the middle of the twentieth century. Each time it was the capacity to cooperate effectively, including institutional innovation, that proved decisive, allowing the United States to achieve significant "upward shifts" in levels of institutional integration, social justice, and national purpose.

The current difficulties stand out strongly against the background of the postwar decades, which saw, under the partial mobilization of the cold war, not only unprecedented economic expansion but also the extension of civil rights across the color line, led by what Putnam has termed the nation's "long civic generation."[21] However, in regard to Boswell's second condition, it is not yet clear that awareness of the current problems of civic engagement amounts to anything approaching the magnitude of a national emergency comparable to the great challenges of the past.

Boswell's third factor, the diffusion of public understandings that support efforts toward higher levels of cooperation, is perhaps most important and at the same time most difficult to address at present. It is noteworthy, however, that Boswell's idea of public cooperation extending into the economic sphere is far from entirely missing from American debate today. On the contrary, it has become widely discussed, but not at the level of national policy, social or economic. Rather, it is in the burgeoning literature on regional economic development that the close connection between public cooperation and "the competitive advantage of nations" has begun to get serious attention. This literature stresses the link between improving economic productivity and developing comprehensive, coordinated economic development strategies for cities, regions, and states.[22] These strategies often focus on investments in human skills improvement and public investment in physical infrastructure, but they can also include investment in social infrastructure such as the family and neighborhood. Yet, applying the lessons of these efforts at the national level has been far less favorable.

Could this be a signal instance of the divergence between the concerns of what Robert Wiebe has termed the "national class"—which directs our major institutions from positions in which the norm is to work instrumentally and top-down, managing or marketing products, services, or policies—and the "local middle class," who must deal more directly with groups on whose cooperation their position depends?[23] In any case, given the urgency of the nation's social and economic problems, this is surely a remarkable omission or failure of learning. So strange is it, in fact, that accounting for the slight attention paid to these themes by national leadership may shed light on why the United States seems caught in a kind of suspended animation in confronting the deterioration of its social fabric.

The curious fact is that, whatever the merits of public cooperation in solving regional economic development issues, most of the nation's political and opinion leaders seem bent upon a revival of old-fashioned laissez-faire at the national level. This policy direction surely serves the immediate interests of powerful constituents of both the political parties, but it is far from obvious that it will serve the general welfare over the longer term. This is particularly so in the face of the ominous reversal of the postwar trend toward income convergence: the endurance, even through years of much-heralded growth in the national economy, of unrelenting job insecurity, rising debt, and stagnating incomes among the traditional middle classes. It is this discrepancy that various observers warn is likely to prove of decisive importance for democracy in the United States. Could it be that the values of the most powerful groups in the American polity, with their strong valence toward unrestricted individual freedom, particularly in the economic realm, are simply inimical to anything like an "upward shift" in public cooperation if it should at all compromise their present advantages?

There is abundant corroborating evidence that this may be the case. First, the secession of the most successful groups from engagement with their fellow citizens into enclaves of private education and private government, while they withdraw support from systems of public provision, does not augur well for developing stronger civic bonds across economic classes or among racial and ethnic groups. Then in the ideological sphere there is the increasing importance of a kind of free-market theory that does more than advocate the value of competitive markets for national well-being. Rather, a series of intellectual currents reminiscent of Gilded Age social Darwinism stresses the desirability of extending market competition into virtually all areas of public as well as private life.

The absolutizing of strategic considerations threatens any objective morality. Most seriously for public cooperation, however, by insisting on the primacy of choice and utility, market imperialism relativizes all loyalties to other persons, as well as commitments to communities or institutions. Breaking faith with employees, after all, has become routine in American business. The current cult of the market as master metaphor for social life subverts the promise of civil society. To the degree that these social and ideological trends come to dominate American life, the possibilities for renewing public cooperation must correspondingly recede.

These tendencies toward unrestrained individualism and market imperialism find resonance in some deeply set features of American culture and experience. But they exaggerate and seriously distort this culture at the same time. Such ideologies are today making it harder to discern the other sources of moral direction that have been especially critical in past crises of the American national project. Therefore, it is important to make the case that because of its narrowness, the current ideology of market imperialism cannot be sustained without severe public disaffection and backlash. Even more important, however, this ideology fails to do justice to a whole aspect of personal identity that Americans continue to value highly: the sense of being not just a maximizer of competitive advantage but also a responsible community member and citizen. But how might such an alternative view be put together?

In America, democracy has been marked by a greater emphasis on individual initiative and voluntary cooperation than in Europe. Unlike the European practice of mediating individual freedom through membership in various functional groupings given public status within a national community (as in the European "social state"), the American pattern has etched the individual more sharply against the moral order, placing almost unlimited responsibility on the individual to live up to social demands to be self-reliant, responsible, and bent upon achievement. These traits are still markedly more prominent among Americans than among citizens of other democratic countries, as Seymour Martin Lipset has recently reminded us.[24] Whereas "white men in America, spreading themselves thin early in the nineteenth century, assumed they could create a democracy without the state," notes Robert Wiebe, "Europeans, congregating in cities late in the century, needed the state to create their democracy." One result has been that while Americans have often distrusted the state, Europeans have invested all kinds of conflicting hopes in it, as the vehicle by which once-subordinated classes could enact their aims. Another consequence of moment has been that whereas Europeans have often thought of rights as collectively based, "Americans saw them as inhering in individuals."[25]

By so emphasizing individual conscience at the expense of authoritative institutions such as the church and state, American culture has tended to evacuate basic value from social institutions as such. The effect has been to reduce the public realm to a heavily instrumental status, as simply a system of many means by which ethically independent persons could pursue their individual purposes. This has helped give civil society a strongly competitive and marketlike ethos: it has been, in David Popenoe's characterization, "a sphere governed by a marketplace for acceptance, and acceptance is a scarce commodity that is allocated through competition; it must be strived for, earned, and maintained, and, hence, is highly conditional."[26] These effects are magnified by the peculiar American understanding of community, according to which community is conceived as the result of voluntary agreements among individuals. Communities are consequently thought of as fragile, not to be taken for granted, and as lacking much vitality of their own. To gain entry to community requires individual effort; a person must show both willingness and the ability to be a part of it. At the same time, this pressure to conform threatens individual autonomy, leaving individuals often of two minds about their participation with others in relationships. Hence, the ubiquity of association is shadowed by its fragility.[27]

On the other hand, this is not the whole picture. When these traits get center stage, it becomes difficult to understand how such a society could function or avoid collapse into anarchy and despotism. In fact, it was just these questions that led Tocqueville to search for other features of American culture that he reasoned must be powerfully present to counterbalance the individualism and voluntarism that Americans of his time, as of ours, so loudly celebrated. Tocqueville was enough of a realist in human affairs that he never seriously entertained the hypothesis that the American social order could be accounted for as the result of some invisible hand orchestrating market exchange among self-seeking individuals. Rather, he argued that it was above all else religious (originally congregational Protestant) morality that made democracy viable by restraining the anarchic tendencies of individualism. Religion was, he famously claimed, the first of the Americans' political institutions. Without it, as recent scholars have argued, the democratic republican society of the United States would have been impossible.[28] Even today, organized religion is the only institution in American society that provides widespread opportunities for the materially less advantaged to develop civic skills, counteracting the otherwise strong correlation of participation in civil society with income, education, and occupation.[29]

The American ethic of achievement has its roots in the originally Protestant doctrine of the calling. This ethic supported Congregational asceticism. But it also directed the individual outward into worldly responsibility, while strengthening both conscience and the ability to cooperate voluntarily. It provided a crucial support for the workings of democracy by giving a seriousness to community service. This made possible those features of American democracy that so impressed Tocqueville: the prevalence of voluntary associations and citizen participation in the state. As a consequence, the American civil society of markets and law developed within a moral magnetic field institutionalized in a unique social context, the distinctly American "political society" of myriad associations. Through voting, serving on juries, and holding local political offices, citizens learned to take responsibility for the common welfare. In the process, Tocqueville argued, individuals developed a stronger sense of identification with the whole. Here he was echoing not only John Stuart Mill but also the tradition of classical political thought, which stressed the essential educative and moral role played by republican institutions of government. Without open political institutions, the notion of the common good would remain vague and feeble at best. Without government, civil society would not long remain civil.

The idea of the calling has played a vital part in reconciling Americans to the demanding moral order of responsibility and achievement. In several important respects, its function within American society is analogous to that of the more institutionalized forms of group membership that have integrated European polities.[30] It was this originally religious notion that held, and to a considerable degree continues to hold, the individualist and the community-regarding tendencies of American culture together. Its social correlates have been work, family life, and public involvements. The nation itself and its historical experience are regularly referred to in terms redolent of the same moral beliefs, as when the United States is described as having a "mission" and a destiny to realize certain ideals.

American men and women, however secularized, continue to guide themselves with reference to something very like the idea of the calling. As in the myriad biographies that Americans devour in large numbers, individuals typically see life as a moral drama with a twofold plot. That is, a well-lived life is understood as first of all a quest, a search that each person must undertake to find that specific task to which that individual has been uniquely called. Second, life is a drama of struggle, a story of temptation and its overcoming, a romance of moral heroism.

As Tocqueville noted, this reverence for the calling overturned an age-old pattern by placing all honest occupations on an equal level and made work and achievement the primary focus of living. Try as one may, it is impossible to discover fulfillment or peace in life by shirking this quest for one's calling—so runs the American creed. This ethic of the calling has provided common understandings that link otherwise diverse and differently oriented individuals. It legitimates toleration for the vagaries of each person's quest. It justifies the need that each of us has to go our own way, leaving home and neighbors if need be, to find and accomplish our unique task. The idea of the calling has even given a distinctive tone to friendship, marriage, and family life for both men and women, since marriage itself has been understood as a valuable calling, which therefore becomes important to the community as a whole. The centrality of the calling has also justified private philanthropy and collective state action to make the wherewithal for pursuing a calling more widely available. Given its enormous importance in American life, the calling seems an essential beginning point in trying to renew concern with the commons.

PROSPECTS FOR CIVIC RENEWAL:
THE KEY ROLE OF THE NATIONAL CLASS

Like many features of American culture, the idea of the calling has been a site of conflict between two rival versions of democracy, an ongoing debate between two competing understandings of its promise, two public philosophies. Both endorse the liberal values of a constitutional order, civil rights, and the rule of law. However, within this shared framework the liberal-individualist variant has valorized competitive individual achievement while stressing the satisfaction of individual preferences and wants. This variant of liberalism construes the purpose of public institutions as simply the provision of a reliable and equitable basis for individual pursuit of privately derived goals with a minimum of external restraint. Jacksonian democracy was perhaps the classic moment for this kind of liberalism, a historical legacy that remains alive in what many Americans consider "conservative" values.

In contrast, the civic republican or reform version of the American creed has emphasized a more positive role for government and for institutions generally. It has stressed the responsibility of individuals to develop their abilities and to apply them to enhance the civic community as a whole—for example, by aiding others in developing their own capacities. This strand of public philosophy received its most eloquent embodiment in what J. David Greenstone has termed "the Lincoln persuasion," though it had origins in Puritan New England and reaches into the twentieth century through the Progressive era, the New Deal, and civil rights reforms.[31] It is this legacy of public cooperation that has been eroding over the past quarter century. But this erosion has been nowhere so noticeable, and so consequential, as among that mobile stratum of professionals, managers, and elites who stand at the helm of America's major institutions.

Much of the experience of today's national class resonates with the influential liberal-individualist version of the calling, the familiar moral imperative to make something of oneself, usually as measured by economic success, always as confirmed by subjective satisfaction. This understanding has been widely popularized in the late twentieth century, of course, as the meaning of that elusive grail called the American Dream. The specialized, meritocratic cadres of the national class are men, and increasingly women, trained at national universities during the postwar era.

Many have come to see themselves as experts. They have learned to conceive of themselves as "problem solvers" who can bring, even to the benighted hinterlands if necessary, the latest technical knowledge—which the public as a whole (it has been widely presumed) is too limited to understand. In their own eyes self-made and cut free from the restricting ties of ethnicity, religion, and locality, many members of the national class think of their callings in terms of deploying their skills, usually in highly remunerative ways, rather than as taking responsibility in the public interest. In the context of the contemporary economy and national government, their careers have less often than in the past led them toward consultation. Thus, they have much less sustained collaboration with citizens not of their class.

The alternative, civic conception of the calling, however, has been quite different. Here the emphasis has been on distinguishing oneself in and through service to the community, particularly through service in government and institutional leadership, but in any case through one's work and participation in the life of one's society. The civic version of the calling has stressed not just the opportunity but also the moral duty to develop one's abilities—but precisely so as to give one's activities a general value, to make a contribution to the community through excellence in activities that are of value to the larger whole as well as to the self. The current popularity of disparaging government service, with the exception of the military, is one indicator of how far the civic understanding of the calling has declined in influence over the past two or three decades.

The liberal-individualist understanding of the calling stresses the individual's autonomy, or choice of task to pursue, while it exalts those who succeed in competitive struggle. As a public value, then, the calling comes to mean equal opportunity, access to the means for self-help, and often sanctions for not working. The civic conception of the calling, on the other hand, holds out wider possibilities as a moral source. The civic conception recognizes the difficulty of pursuing the right calling in the absence of institutions that can sustain and reward concern with public goods. Consistent with its own logic, it insists that both private and governmental institutions, and in particular their leaders, are responsible for creating economic and social contexts in which individuals can identify with the common ends of the society and enact this connection to the whole by seeing their private pursuits, in economic as well as in community life, as ways of supporting the community. In public policy terms, of course, this requires a much more ambitious agenda than the individualist approach. It certainly means that the terms and conditions of work are as much the public's business as its availability, and that the public has a general obligation to expand and upgrade the opportunities for work that can support a genuine calling.

Achieving these goals would require a movement of revitalization involving many Americans besides the national class, in order to spread public cooperation into the economy as well as among the several sectors of civil society and government. And yet, in significant part at least, it is the national class that will determine whether any such renewal of civic spirit will appear in our country. Collectively, they have never been so important or so powerful in American life. The present, though comfortable for the national class in many ways, is also a time of discontent, even of a kind of spiritual danger. The fate of the Russian nomenklatura stands as a glaring example of the fate of modern elites who lose their collective moral bearings and who slip from self-satisfaction into arrogance and finally into a deadening demoralization. Fortunately, the national class is also an inheritor of the American spirit of voluntarism and the characteristic belief that it is always possible to reform, that great things can come of changing hearts and minds.

It is possible that their disgruntled fellow citizens may force some such change, as may be presaged by the reassertion of organized labor. Yet, for the moment at least, much of the impetus for change must come from within the ranks of America's most successful and privileged citizens themselves. It is worth remembering the admonition of a member of what was perhaps the most stunningly successful yet in the end disastrously myopic "national class" in history. Just before the downfall of the Roman republic, Cicero addressed to his fellow senatorial leaders the reflection that

> the abuses of the leading citizens are bad enough; but what is worse is that they have so many imitators. Experience shows that the leading citizens have always dictated the character of a society. Whenever there has been a transformation of morals and manners among the social leaders, the same transformation has followed among the people.[32]

Unsettling thoughts for our time, but surely compelling ones as well.

NOTES

1. Judith Miller, "America's Burden; At Hour of Triumph, Democracy Recedes as the Global Ideal," *New York Times*, 18 February 1996, sect. 4, 1, 5. The quotation is Miller's paraphrase of Zakaria's views.

2. Fareed Zakaria, "Bigger Than the Family, Smaller Than the State," review of Francis Fukuyama, *Trust: The Social Virtues and the Creation of Prosperity*, *New York Times Book Review*, 13 August 1995, 1, 25.

3. John Gray, "After Social Democracy and beyond Anglo-Saxon Capitalism," *New Perspectives Quarterly* (Fall 1996): 42.

4. See Daniel N. Nelson, "Civil Society Endangered," *Social Research* 63, no. 2 (Summer 1996): 345–68.

5. Ernest Gellner, *Conditions of Liberty: Civil Society and Its Rivals* (New York: Penguin, 1994), 1.

6. Michael Walzer, "Liberalism and the Art of Separation," *Political Theory* 12, no. 3 (August 1984): 321.

7. Adam Seligman, *The Idea of Civil Society* (New York: Free Press, 1992), 97.

8. Seligman, *The Idea of Civil Society*, 172, 196.

9. Jürgen Habermas, *The Structural Transformation of the Public Sphere* (Cambridge, Mass.: MIT Press, 1989); Jean Cohen and Andrew Arato, *Civil Society and Political Theory* (Cambridge, Mass.: MIT Press, 1992).

10. See Alan Wolfe, *Whose Keeper? Social Science and Moral Obligation* (Berkeley: University of California Press, 1989), and Amitai Etzioni, *The Spirit of Community* (New York: Touchstone, 1993).

11. For criticisms of this use of *civil society*, see Adam Seligman, "The Changing Precontractual Frame of Modern Society," *Responsive Community* 6, issue 1 (Winter 1995–96): 28–40; and Christopher Beem, "Civil Is Not Good Enough," *Responsive Community* 6, issue 3 (Summer 1996): 47–57.

12. See Michael Walzer, "The Idea of Civil Society," *Dissent* (Spring 1991): 293–304.

13. T. H. Marshall, *Class, Citizenship, and Social Development* (Westport, Conn.: Greenwood, 1973).

14. Marcus Tullius Cicero, *De Re Publica (On the Commonwealth)*, trans. Clinton Walker Keyes (Cambridge, Mass.: Loeb Classical Library–Harvard University Press, 1988), I.39, 65.

15. Robert D. Putnam, *Making Democracy Work: Civic Traditions in Modern Italy* (Princeton N.J.: Princeton University Press, 1993), 87–91, 6–8.

16. Putnam, *Making Democracy Work*, 112.

17. Putnam, *Making Democracy Work*, 113.

18. Jane Mansbridge, "Public Spirit in Political Systems," in *Values and Public Policy*, ed. Henry J. Aaron, Thomas E. Mann, and Timothy Taylor (Washington, D.C.: Brookings Institution, 1994), 146–72, 148–49.

19. Jonathan Boswell, *Community and the Economy: The Theory of Public Cooperation* (London: Routledge, 1990).

20. Boswell, *Community and the Economy*, 73.

21. See Robert D. Putnam, "Bowling Alone: America's Declining Social Capital," *Journal of Democracy* 6, no. 1 (January 1995): 65–78.

22. See, for example, Michael E. Porter, *The Competitive Advantage of Nations* (New York: Free Press, 1990), and Rosabeth Moss Kanter, *World Class: Thriving Locally in the Global Economy* (New York: Simon & Schuster, 1995).

23. Robert H. Wiebe, *Self-Rule: A Cultural History of American Democracy* (Chicago: University of Chicago Press, 1995), especially 141–49.

24. Seymour Martin Lipset, *American Exceptionalism: A Two-Edged Sword* (New York: Norton, 1996).

25. Wiebe, *Self-Rule*, 182–83.

26. David Popenoe, *Disturbing The Nest: Family Change and Decline in Modern Societies* (New York: Aldine de Gruyter, 1988), 332.

27. This logic of individualist community is discussed in Robert N. Bellah, Richard Madsen, William M. Sullivan, Ann Swidler, and Steven M. Tipton, *Habits of the Heart: Individualism and Commitment in American Life*, new edition (Berkeley: University of California Press, 1996 [1985]).

28. This argument has received increasing attention by scholars. See especially Robert N. Bellah, *The Broken Covenant* (New York: Seabury, 1975). As related to the development of the idea of civil society, see Seligman, *The Idea of Civil Society*.

29. Sidney Verba, Kay Lehman Schlozman, and Henry E. Brady, *Voice and Equality: Civic Voluntarism in American Politics* (Cambridge, Mass.: Harvard University Press, 1995), 18–19.

30. E. Digby Baltzell has provided a suggestive account of the role and importance of the Calvinist doctrine of the calling for American public life in his *Puritan Boston and Quaker Philadelphia: Two Protestant Ethics and the Spirit of Class Authority and Leadership* (Boston: Beacon, 1979).

31. J. David Greenstone, *The Lincoln Persuasion: Remaking American Liberalism* (Chicago: University of Chicago Press, 1993).

32. Cicero, *De Legibus (The Laws)*, trans. Clinton Walker Keyes (Cambridge, Mass.: Loeb Classical Library–Harvard University Press, 1988), III, xiii, 495 (translation amended by the author).

3

American Civil Society Talk

Jean L. Cohen

The ubiquity with which the concept "civil society" is evoked in the United States these days as the source of trust, the key to social integration, and the basis of strong democracy is truly striking. After lagging behind international discussions, American interest in civil society has suddenly exploded.[1] Moreover, a particular conception of civil society as "group association" is now hegemonic, at least within the most influential recent American political science literature on the topic and in the rhetoric of an ever-increasing number of politicians at all points on the political spectrum.[2]

The context for the revived interest in civil society today is the crisis of the welfare state and not, as it was in the 1950s, the fear of a totalitarian state.[3] Now it is dissatisfaction with the social and cultural effects of successful, normal, and global, rather than failed, modernization that motivates civil society talk. The renewed interest in the social cement of trust is clearly related to the sense that models of social integration, civic engagement, and associational life that were once taken for granted are being strained by new forms of social diversity, by institutional transformation, and by technical, economic, and cultural change.

Apparently, neither the centralized state nor the magic of the marketplace can offer effective, liberal, and democratic solutions to the problems of "postindustrial" civil societies in a context of globalization. Statist correctives are said to threaten freedom, but social injustice is exacerbated when the state completely abandons the field to market forces: both "reforms" can be socially disintegrative, oppressive, and unjust. Given the political impossibility of continuing the welfare state model in the old way and the undesirability of returning to market magic, it is understandable that the discourse of civil society has become so widespread and so contentious. Welfare state legality has shifted emphasis toward public administration and the courts and triggered calls for revitalizing and protecting both democracy and community. "Civil society" has thus become a slogan for the 1990s because it appears to offer an alternative center for political and economic initiatives. Hence the revival of interest in the cultural conditions of democracy and in the informal modes of socialization that allegedly foster civic virtue and the moral "habits of the heart" necessary to make democracy work. But the idealized, one-dimensional version of the concept that is being revived is hardly up to the task, in my view.

In this chapter, I focus on one of the most prominent and influential recent interventions in the American civil society debate: the neorepublican stance of Robert Putnam and his school.[4] I will demonstrate that "civil society" in this approach has become so reduced that the normative thrust of the concept, particularly its relevance to democracy, is being obscured. The most glaring defect is the omission of the crucial category of the public sphere from Putnam's and most others' conceptualizations. Following Putnam, nearly everyone in the current discussion has come to equate civil society with traditional forms of voluntary association (including "the" family), as already indicated. And nearly everyone assumes that the "intermediary bodies" created by voluntary association and crucial to social integration are in decline in contemporary America—the debate is over the causes of the decline and what to do about it.

I contend that this conceptualization of civil society is theoretically impoverished and politically suspect. When combined with the discourse of civic and moral decline, it undermines democracy instead of making it work, threatens personal liberty instead of enhancing it, and blocks social justice and social solidarity instead of furthering them. Unless this model is corrected, the current revival of the discourse of civil society in the United States will play into the hands of social conservatives who aim to retraditionalize civic life and to substitute local "volunteerism" for the public services and redistributive efforts of the welfare state, as if these are the only options we have.

The conservatives pretend that we can have a vital, well-integrated, and just civil society without states guaranteeing that universalistic egalitarian principles inform social policy regardless of which social institution or level of government carries it out. If civil society discourse is left in this form, we will not be able to articulate, much less resolve, the critical problems facing democratic polities in the coming century. My claim is that it matters very much, both politically and theoretically, *which* concept of civil society we use and seek to foster.

CONCEPTIONS OF CIVIL SOCIETY

In contrast to the narrow view of civil society predominant in contemporary American discussions, nineteenth-century sources offer a rich and multileveled conception. Civil society was understood as a sphere of social interaction characterized by forms of plurality (groups with different worldviews and interests), publicity (civil publics and the media of communication—at that time, print), privacy (a domain of individual self-development and ethical choice), and legality (the rule of law and sets of subjective rights protecting individuality, plurality, and publicity and institutionalizing social differentiation generally).[5]

Twentieth-century European analysts of civil society added three crucial components to this understanding. The first, stressed by Antonio Gramsci, was an emphasis on the cultural and symbolic dimension of civil society and the role it plays in generating consent (hegemony) and hence in integrating society.[6] Gramsci was the first and most important Marxist to abandon the economistic reduction of civil society to political economy and to insist on its autonomy and distinctiveness from the state (political society). His conception is presented in a notoriously confusing terminology, but the idea that runs through all his attempts at a definition is that the reproduction of the existing system occurs through a combination of two practices: hegemony and domination, consent and coercion. These operate through two different sets of institutional frameworks: the cultural and associational forms of civil society, and the legal, bureaucratic, police, and military apparatus of the state. Indeed, his most important category, hegemony—referring to the dominant action-orienting symbols, beliefs, values, identifications, and social constructions of reality—is meaningless without its corollary concept, civil society.

Thus, Gramsci's key contribution to the conceptualization of civil society was his emphasis on its politically relevant cultural dimension: civil society is construed both as a symbolic field and as a network of institutions and practices that are the locus for the formation of values, action-orienting norms, meanings, and collective identities. But the cultural dimension of civil society is not given or natural; rather, it is a site of social contestation: its associations and networks are a terrain to be struggled over, and an arena in which collective identities, ethical values, and alliances are forged. Indeed, competing conceptions of civil society are deployed in a continual struggle either to maintain cultural hegemony by dominant groups or to achieve counterhegemony for subordinate collective actors. Accordingly, no conception of civil society, including Gramsci's own, is neutral but is always part of a project to shape the social relations, cultural forms, and modes of thought of society. Gramsci, in short, has shown us that the discourses and culture of civil society are politically relevant and multiple.

Both the second and third crucial twentieth-century contributions by Europeans to the theory of civil society take up the threads of Gramsci's analysis. At the same time, they dispense with his exclusive focus on class hegemony and with his rather functionalist and monistic approach to civil society's cultural and associational institutions as the expression of one or another class's hegemony. In short, they retain the importance of the cultural and dynamic aspects of civil society stressed by Gramsci while insisting that the abstract norms and organizational principles of modern civil society—from the idea of rights to the principles of autonomous association and free horizontal communication (publicity)—have intrinsic value and are not simply functional to the reproduction of capitalist or any other hegemony. The structures of civil society are what allow for the contestation over hegemony to occur.

One major contribution on this terrain, made by Alain Touraine, Alberto Melucci, and others, was the emphasis on the dynamic, creative, and contestatory side of civil society—informal networks, initiatives, and social movements as distinct from the more formalized voluntary associations and institutions and from class organizations (parties, unions).[7] Recognition of this dimension allows one to articulate and shift between two perspectives: civil society as a dynamic, innovative source for thematizing new concerns, articulating new projects, and generating new values and collective identities; and civil society as institutionalized civic autonomy. It also allows one to see how in its dynamic capacity (collective action), the institutional shape of civil society as well as the polity can be targeted in struggles over democratization.

The other key contribution I have in mind is the communicative, deliberative conception of the public sphere developed primarily by Jürgen Habermas and his followers.[8] The category of the public sphere was already present in eighteenth- and nineteenth-century understandings of civil society, but its normative weight and its role in mediating between the particular and the general were not clarified until relatively recently.

In civil publics people can discuss matters of mutual concern as peers, and learn about facts, events, and the opinions, interests, and perspectives of others. Discourse on values, norms, laws, and policies generates politically relevant public opinion. Moreover, through its generalized media of communication, the public sphere can mediate among the myriad minipublics that emerge within and across associations, movements, religious organizations, clubs, local organizations of concerned citizens, and simple socializing. There are of course differentiated and institutionalized civil and political publics, weak and strong.[9] Liberal democracies link these in a variety of ways, depending on the relative strength of the liberal and the democratic norms in the particular conception of the public sphere. On any liberal democratic conception, however, discursively generated public opinion is meant to influence the debates within political and legal publics proper (legislatures, constitutional courts) and to bring under informal control the actions and decisions of rulers and lawmakers (the principle of responsiveness). Openness of access and parity of participation (equal voice) is the regulative ideal underlying every institutional arrangement claiming democratic legitimacy. All citizens affected by public policy and laws should have the right to participate and to articulate their views, and all participants should be able to do so on equal terms.[10]

The concept of the public sphere thus brings together the normative and the empirical, the universal and the particular. It is, in my view, the normative core of the idea of civil society and the heart of any conception of democracy. Indeed, the political legitimacy of modern constitutional democracies rests on the principle that action-orienting norms, practices, policies, and claims to authority can be contested by citizens and must be discursively redeemed. As Claus Offe has recently argued, unconstrained critical discourse in the public sphere (secured by rights) is the form of institutionalized "distrust" that is crucial to maintaining trust—belief in legitimacy—in constitutional democracies.[11]

I would defend an even stronger claim: the deliberative genesis and justification of public policy in political and civil public spaces respectively are *constitutive* of the modern form of democracy. I will elaborate more on this aspect of civil society later. For now, suffice it to say that without the concept of the public sphere, the discourse of civil society will remain hopelessly one-sided and analytically useless because it will not be able to explicate the complex articulation between social and political institutions.

As already indicated, voluntary association is an important aspect of a vital civil society. So are the rights protecting personal freedoms of thought and expression, association, privacy, liberty, and diversity.[12] But focusing exclusively on the dimension of voluntary association is impoverishing, to say the least. So is the degeneration of "civil society talk" into rhetoric about the decline of morals and civic virtue. It is also backward looking and politically dangerous. Minus the public sphere, civil society talk all too easily lends itself to projects that have little to do with democratization.

VOLUNTARY ASSOCIATION AND WORKABLE DEMOCRACY

Robert Putnam's claim in his extraordinarily influential book *Making Democracy Work* that democratic government is more responsive and effective when it faces a vigorous civil society is, of course, one that I embrace. He argues convincingly that horizontally organized voluntary associations that cut across social cleavages are more likely to nourish wider social cooperation, to reinforce norms of reciprocity, and thus to "make democracy work" than hierarchical segmental organizations or clientelistic structures.[13] A civic culture of "generalized trust" and social solidarity, peopled by citizens willing and able to cooperate in joint ventures, *is* an important societal prerequisite of a vital democracy.

Nevertheless, Putnam's approach is unsatisfactory, in part for methodological reasons. He reduces civil society to the dimension of voluntary association and construes the latter as the *sole* source of what he calls "social capital." The feature of the social context that matters most to the performance of democratic institutions, on Putnam's analysis, is the presence or absence of a civic culture. The indicators of civicness that he cites are similar to those mentioned in the civic culture studies of the 1950s: the number of voluntary associations, the incidence of newspaper readership (a sign of interest in and being informed about community affairs), electoral turnout, and a range of civic attitudes including law-abidingness, interpersonal trust and general cooperativeness. So far so good.

Indeed, Putnam's historical chapters provide a rich description of the emergence of civicness and what it needed to take root, at least in the north of Italy. Here, in addition to the dense network of associational life and the oaths of mutual assistance sworn by members of associations in the early Communes, Putnam mentions the importance of institutions and institutionalized norms, such as the professionalization of public administration and credible state impartiality in the enforcement of laws, for the maintenance of social trust. Strong and autonomous courts, reliable administrative state structures, and *confidence* that the administration of justice, enforcement of contracts, and legislation would be impartial seemed to be a sine qua non for the networks of civic associations to succeed in generating solidarity outside the bonds of kinship.[14] Thus, on the descriptive level, at least, the charge of reductionism seems inappropriate.

The important concluding theoretical chapter of the book, "Social Capital and Institutional Success," however, *is* open to such a charge. For there, history, tradition, culture, normative orientations, and their transmission over time are analyzed in terms of the concept of inherited "social capital"—defined as the social stock of trust, norms, and networks that facilitate coordinated actions—whereas the *source* of social capital and of its generalization is narrowed down to involvement in secondary associations. We are left with a weak theoretical framework and an unconvincing analysis. Unfortunately, this framework is greatly influencing the American civil society debate.

The crucial chapter on social capital asks how "virtuous circles" generate, generalize, and transmit traditions of civic engagement through centuries of radical social, economic, and political change. Putnam dismisses the classic Hobbesian solution, "third party enforcement." If cooperation for the common good requires trust in everyone's willingness to contribute equally, a "third-party enforcer" such as the state should enable subjects to do what they cannot do on their own—namely, trust one another. But apparently the use of force is expensive, and impartial enforcement is itself a public good subject to the same dilemma it aims to solve: what power could ensure that the sovereign does not defect? Nor, as the new institutionalists suggest, will the best institutional design ensure impartiality even if it entails the participation of the affected parties in defining the rules, the subjection of violators to sanctions, and low-cost mechanisms for resolving conflicts. For the same dilemma apparently obtains vis-à-vis the institutionalist understanding of the state as impartial lawgiver that confronted the state as Hobbesian sovereign—namely, the problem of infinite regress: trust and generalized reciprocity are presupposed for the establishment of the institutions in the first place.

Putnam accordingly turns away from state structures to "soft" sociocultural solutions. Dense networks of civic involvement are both a sign and a source of social capital. Participating in horizontal voluntary associations lubricates cooperation and generates social trust, thus allowing dilemmas of collective action to be resolved.[15] Apparently such participation produces "moral resources" which can be transmitted over generations (inherited) and whose supply increases through use—stocks of social capital tend to be self-reinforcing and cumulative. Inheritance of a stock of social capital renders voluntary cooperation in a community easier and, thus, makes democracy work.[16]

Although Putnam does say that trust has two sources—norms of reciprocity and networks of civic engagement—the former is primarily a function of the latter.[17] Dense networks of associations entail repeated exchanges of what he calls "short-term altruism" and "long-term self-interest"—I help you out now in the expectation that you will help me out in the future. These rational exchanges, and the direct experience of reliability, repeated over a period of time, encourage the development of a norm of generalized reciprocity.

That voluntary association is *evidence* of social cooperation and trust is both undeniable and almost tautological, but why is it construed as the only significant source of social capital? Why are democratic political institutions, the public sphere, and law absent from the theoretical analysis of how social trust is developed? The answer is obvious: once the state is defined and dismissed as a third-party enforcer, once law is turned into sanctions that provide for a certain level of social order but no more, once institutions are dismissed as irrelevant to social trust because their gene-

sis already presupposes social trust, and once a vital civil society is reduced to the presence or absence of intermediate voluntary associations,
no other source of social trust is conceivable.

As others have already pointed out, the theory has many flaws.[18] The
problem as I see it is not that the analysis is society-centered but that it
operates with an overly narrow conception of civil society and a method
that, in turn, leads the analyst to screen out the role of law and political
institutions in fostering civicness as well as the reciprocal relationship of
influence of civil publics on the state and on civil institutions. Indeed, the
failure to include publics and interstitial networks of communication in
the conceptualization of civil society is one of the main drawbacks of the
theory as a theory of democracy. I will turn to these issues later. Let me
first dwell on two difficulties internal as it were to the conceptual and
methodological framework used by Putnam. Since this framework is
being widely adopted, it is worthwhile to spend a bit more time on it.

It is unclear just what is doing the work in the analysis even on its own
terms. Apparently participation in *horizontally* organized secondary associations generates norms of reciprocity and social trust. But we are never
really told why only horizontal as distinct from vertical associative networks produce social capital. Or is it that horizontal association produces
"good" as opposed to "bad" social capital, enabling, say, associated bird-
watchers to develop democratic competence, invest their accumulated social skills and social orientations in other voluntary collective endeavors,
and demand good government, whereas members of the Mafia or the
Catholic Church, with their bad social capital, cannot, as it were, reinvest
it elsewhere? Yet certainly Mafia and Church members belong to dense
networks of interpersonal communication, formal and informal, although
to be sure, the linkages among the unequal agents are vertical. Putnam
seems to be making a more general point: societies characterized by vertical, hierarchical relations of dependency foster defection, distrust, shirking, exploitation, and isolation regardless of the density of their associational networks.[19] But why?

Apparently a vertical network cannot sustain social trust and cooperation because flows of information are less reliable and, more important,
because sanctions that support norms of reciprocity against the threat of
opportunism are less likely to be imposed upward and less likely to be
acceded to if imposed. Linkages between agents of equivalent status and
power are what generate (good) social capital; linkages of unequal agents,
in asymmetric relations of hierarchy and dependence, do not.

But this is not a very satisfactory explanation—too much is left untheo-
rized. Do the aims and substantive values of the association play any role
here? Would it matter for the impact on civicness that a horizontally organized association of peers has political aims that are either illiberal or

antidemocratic? What if the group has an instrumental attitude to its internal organizational structure? Or, conversely, would it make any difference if an organization that is hierarchically structured and internally authoritarian has democratic and/or liberal aims?

Putnam is aware of these issues. In a footnote he states that not all associations of the like-minded are committed to democratic goals or organized in an egalitarian fashion. We are accordingly urged to consider other civic virtues, such as tolerance, when we try to weigh the consequences of any particular organization for democratic governance.[20] Implicit in this statement is an argument for "congruence" between the structure and goals of civil and political-democratic institutions: both, it seems, should be organized in an egalitarian fashion and embrace egalitarian democratic principles.

Yet how odd to leave such a crucial and hotly debated issue to a footnote and to implicit rather than explicit argumentation! Much too little is said about why the equal status of members matters vis-à-vis the creation of social capital. I suspect that the issue is handled this way because the most obvious argument cannot be made without considerably complicating the theoretical framework: namely, that perhaps what develops interactive abilities and *democratic competence* within an association is participation as an equal in the exchange of opinions and in collective *deliberations* over associational affairs—that is, *voice* in the association's internal *public sphere*. Hierarchical, authoritarian associations such as the Mafia can easily generate skill in strategic action; the Catholic Church can generate loyalty. But I suspect that only associations with internal publics structured by the relevant norms of discourse can develop the communicative competence and interactive abilities important to democracy.

I agree with Nancy Rosenblum that the plurality and multiplicity of civil associations with guaranteed exit possibilities does indeed have "moral effects" vis-à-vis fostering and maintaining a liberal, tolerant, and civil society. I also support her argument against state-induced full congruence between the structure of civil associations and political institutions: the danger of paternalism and Gleichschaltung is all too obvious.[21] But I am also convinced that democratic as distinct from liberal competence cannot be learned in hierarchical settings. Moreover, I suspect that the presence of democratically structured associations is what renders benign the effects of membership in hierarchical, authoritarian groupings on the overall societal community. If *all* the myriad associations of civil society were structured like the Mafia, I doubt that either democratic competence or even liberal tolerance among citizens would be widespread. I would thus like to maintain that *voice*, over and above loyalty (altruism) or chances to exit, is what matters most here.[22]

Without the normative concept of the deliberative public sphere understood as a core principle of civil society, however, such arguments cannot
be made, much less tested. Unfortunately, the concept of social capital, as
deployed by Putnam, steers us away from the dimension of voice, placing
too much emphasis, in my view, on the dimensions of loyalty, trust, and
virtue. Consequently, the advantage of horizontal over vertical structures
remains unclarified.

This brings me to the second set of "internal" difficulties deriving from
the exclusive focus on voluntary association and the use of the concept of
social capital. Curiously, Putnam fails to say just what generalizes the social trust produced within voluntary associations. How does intragroup
trust become trust of strangers outside the group? Why does the willingness to act together for mutual benefit in a small group such as a choral
society translate into willingness to act for the common good or to become politically engaged at all? Indeed, is the interpersonal trust generated in face-to-face interactions even the same thing as "generalized
trust"? I don't think so.

Let me be clear here. I do not doubt that trust lubricates cooperation
or, more important, that general abstract *norms* of reciprocity allow the
reconciliation of self-interest and solidarity. I am not convinced, however,
that the trust that emerges within particular associations is sufficient for
producing "generalized trust" or, in the language I prefer, belief in the
legitimacy of institutionalized norms, acceptance of the universalistic
principles of reciprocity and society-wide social solidarity, and confidence that these will orient the action of both powerful elites and average
citizens. What is very odd is that Putnam offers no mechanism for explaining how these emerge.

I believe that the use made of the concept of social capital is at fault.
Obscuring more than it illuminates, this concept allows one to avoid the
difficult task of showing that the particular trust built up between specific
individuals in one context can be transferred without further ado to other
contexts, to strangers, or to society at large. In short, prior to the issue of
what generalizes social capital is the question of whether "inherited social capital" is the right concept to use for *six* rather different things: interpersonal trust, social solidarity, general norms of reciprocity, belief in the
legitimacy of institutionalized norms, confidence that these will motivate
the action of institutional actors and ordinary citizens (social solidarity),
and the transmission of cultural traditions, patterns, and values.

The metaphor of social "capital" allows the theorist to finesse the generalization issue and to blur these distinctions by suggesting a false analogy between direct interpersonal social relations and economic exchanges
in a market. Capital accumulated in one context can of course be invested
in another place: it can easily be saved, inherited, and exchanged regard-

less of its particular form because there is a universal equivalent for it—money—and an institutional framework for the exchange—the market economy. As the medium of exchange and the universal equivalent for all forms of wealth, money solves the generalization issue. Impersonal contractual market relations are possible because money in a market system substitutes for direct communications in the coordination and integration of actions.[23] Of course, even the market presupposes *confidence* that the value of money is backed up by the banking system and that contractual obligations are recognized and enforced by states.

Interpersonal trust, on the other hand, is by definition specific and contextual—one trusts *particular* people because of repeated interactions with them in specific contexts in which reciprocity is directly experienced. Interpersonal trust generated in face-to-face relationships is not an instance of a more general impersonal phenomenon. Nor can it simply be transferred to others or to other contexts. Indeed, it is entirely possible that without other mechanisms for the generalization of trust, participation in associations and membership in social networks could foster particularism, localism, intolerance, exclusion, and generalized mistrust of outsiders, of the law, and of government. Without other mediations, there is no reason to expect that the forms of reciprocity or trust generated within small groups would extend beyond the group or, for that matter, that group demands would be anything other than particularistic.

The argument that repeated interaction games within small-scale face-to-face groups of strategic calculators can generate universal norms of law-abidingness or reciprocity is unconvincing. Repeated interaction within a group may help generate local norms of reciprocity between members, because each learns gradually to expect that the other will cooperate.[24] Interpersonal trust involves not only the experience of reliability of the other but also the moral obligation of the trusted person to honor the trust bestowed upon her and the mutual expectation that each understands this principle and will be motivated internally to act accordingly. For interpersonal trust to turn into generalized reciprocity or to foster general law-abidingness, however, the universalistic normative expectation itself would have to be presupposed *as a norm* in a wide variety of contexts. The *obligatoriness* of reciprocity and law-abidingness and the motivation to act accordingly require something more than the repetition of sets of strategic interactions. In short, for impersonal, general trust of strangers to be conceivable and warranted, other factors would have to mediate.[25] The principle of reciprocity would have to be institutionalized on the one side, and the aspiration/motivation to be trustworthy would have to become part of one's identity, as it were, on the other. Thus, the analysis does not escape the problem of infinite regress.

To see what role institutions play here, one would have to understand law and the state not just as a third-party enforcer. At the very least the two-sidedness of law—law as sanction *and* law as institutionalized cultural values, norms, rules, and rights—would have to be theorized. Only then would it be possible to reflect on the role of law and rights in substituting *universalistic* norms as functional equivalents for personalized trust, and in substituting confidence in abstract institutions (backed up by sanctions) and belief in their legitimacy, purpose, and particular norms for direct interpersonal ties. For example, legal norms of procedural fairness, impartiality, and justice that give structure to state and some civil institutions, limit favoritism and arbitrariness, and protect merit are the sine qua non for society-wide "general trust," at least in a modern social structure.[26] So is the expectation that institutional actors will live up to and enforce the norms of the institutional setting in which they interact. Rights, on the other hand, ensure that trust is warranted insofar as they provide individuals the opportunity to demand that violations of legitimate reciprocal expectations be sanctioned.

It makes little sense to use the category of generalized trust to describe one's attitude toward law or government. One can only trust *people*, because only people can fulfill obligations. But institutions (legal and other) can provide functional equivalents for interpersonal trust in impersonal settings involving interactions with strangers, because they, as it were, institutionalize action-orienting norms and the expectation that these will be honored.

What Emile Durkheim once called "professional ethics" does indeed have an effect on "civic morals." If one knows one can expect impartiality from a judge, care and concern from a doctor, protection from police, objectivity and veracity from a journalist, concern for the common good from legislators, and so on, then one can develop confidence (instead of cynicism) that shared institutionalized norms and cultural values will orient the action of powerful others. But confidence of this sort also presupposes public spaces in which the validity of such norms and the fairness of procedures can be challenged, revised, redeemed, or reinforced through critique.[27] As already indicated, the presence of public spaces within and across associations, and the existence of society-wide uninstitutionalized publics that elaborate and test the generalizability of norms in which all citizens can participate, are at the core of any conception of a democratic civil society.

The point here is that Putnam's narrow theoretical framework prevents him from articulating these complex interrelations. Nevertheless, even with its flaws, *Making Democracy Work* was open to a more sophisticated interpretation. After all, the book traces the effects of institutional reform in Italy: the devolution of important powers from a centralized state to newly created regional political public spaces, closer to the populace and open to their influence. Moreover, many of the vital elements of a richer society-centered analysis were at least mentioned in the text. In claiming that dense networks of civic engagement generate greater trust, participation, and stronger democracy, Putnam implicitly relies on the concept of the public sphere even if he lacks the categorical framework to account for the interstitial, transactional, open-ended flows of communication that transcend the associational enclaves in which they originate.[28] Although Putnam misinterprets his own data, his research suggests that well-designed political institutions are crucial to fostering civic spirit because they provide enabling conditions—a political opportunity structure—that can become an incentive to civil actors to emerge and a target of influence for them once they do.[29] The path not taken in the theoretical chapter of this book was nonetheless made available.

The recent work on civil society in the United States is all the more disappointing in this regard. Far from broadening the analytical framework, the new research is guided exclusively by the methods and categories of that final chapter. "Civil society" is cast in very narrow terms. As I already indicated, it is the link of the reductionist conception of civil society to the discourse of civic decline that makes this approach ambiguous, and so prone to ideological misuse.

AMERICAN CIVIC AND MORAL DECLINE?

In a series of recent articles, Putnam and his associates have argued that low electoral turnout and declining membership in political parties in the United States are part of a much wider phenomenon: the gradual disappearance of American social capital.[30] Given the alleged centrality of social capital to civic engagement and effective, democratic government, its erosion is presented as a serious cause for alarm.

The most widely publicized findings from Putnam's research show stagnant or declining levels of aggregate associational membership beginning in the second half of the twentieth century. "The downward trend is most marked," Putnam has written, for certain kinds of traditional secondary associations—"for church-related groups, for labor unions, for fraternal and veterans' organizations, and for school-service groups."[31]

These findings would not be so alarming if functional equivalents for the old groups were emerging. But according to the research, they have not. "Countertrends" such as the emergence of new mass-membership organizations (e.g., the National Organization for Women) and the explosion of interest groups represented in Washington (e.g., the American Association of Retired Persons) are only apparent, for these groups are really "tertiary," "mailing-list" organizations rather than "secondary" associations. The latter are characterized by face-to-face interactions and direct horizontal interpersonal ties of people who actually meet one another, whereas the former involve abstract impersonal ties of people to common symbols, texts, leaders, and ideals and not to one another.[32] According to the theory of social capital, associational membership should increase social trust. But apparently membership in tertiary groups does not yield the kind of social connectedness that generates social capital.

Compared with the civic generation born between 1910 and 1940, the postwar baby boom generation that matured in the 1960s and all those that followed are disturbingly "postcivic." Indeed, the phenomenon of decline is generational, all other factors having been controlled for.[33] What caused this decline, if we assume that it is real?

Putnam says that the decline was caused by the arrival of TV, a new medium of communication that became prevalent while the 1960s generation was maturing. Television viewing is the only leisure activity that inhibits participation outside the home, coming at the expense of nearly every social activity. Analyzing General Social Survey data from 1974 through 1994, and controlling for factors such as education, age, and income, Putnam found that TV viewing is negatively correlated to social trust, group membership, and voter turnout.[34] People who watch too much TV are no longer neighborly; they do not socialize, join clubs, or form the sorts of secondary associations that would foster civic orientations. Television, in short, has privatizing and stultifying effects. Apparently the culture industry is finally having the effect so feared by its critics: the transformation of American civil society into a mass society.[35]

I do not find this account persuasive. First, other analysts show that not all the data on civicness point to decline. In a recent major study, Sidney Verba and his colleagues do not find that the falloff in voter turnout is part of a general erosion in voluntary activity or political participation.[36] They report increases in certain forms of civic activism such as membership in community problem-solving organizations. Some older types of associational membership and activities have even been expanding, both numerically and qualitatively. Moreover, different loci and sorts of social activity may serve purposes similar to those of traditional forms of secondary association.[37] Putnam's research screens out such innovations in social connectedness.

Equally important is the phenomenon of "shifting involvements" noted many years ago by Albert O. Hirschman.[38] The political engagement of contemporary citizens is episodic and increasingly issue-oriented. Membership in political parties, labor unions, and traditional voluntary associations may have declined, but the willingness of Americans to mobilize periodically on local and national levels around concerns that affect them cannot be deduced from this fact. The new action repertoires invented by civic and political actors cannot be assessed adequately by criteria derived from older forms.[39]

Indeed, to discount the new types of association, mobilization, and public engagement of the 1960s and 1970s, simply because they differ from traditional secondary associations, makes little sense. These allegedly uncivic generations, and their successors, created the first consumers' movement since the 1930s, the first environmental movement since the turn of the century, public health movements, grassroots activism and community organizing, the most important feminist movement since the pre–World War II period, the civil rights movement, and innumerable transnational nongovernmental organizations and civic movements—all of which have led to unprecedented advances in rights and social justice.[40]

This highly civic activism is not the product of disassociated individuals mobilized by direct mailings or glib leaders. It draws instead on myriad small-scale groups different in kind from Putnam's preferred intermediary organizations but most certainly involving face-to-face interpersonal interaction and oppositional public spheres, as well as more generalized forms of communication. In other words, the forms of association out of which mass mobilizations emerge nowadays might not involve organizations with official membership lists, but they can and often do involve discussion groups, consciousness-raising groups, self-help groups, and the like that are continuously cropping up and disappearing but surely are signs of the ability to connect and act in concert. Moreover, top-down and bottom-up forms of political mobilization are not incompatible.[41]

Why is all of this dismissed or ignored? If one starts from the assumption that only a certain form of secondary association is the source of social capital, then obviously if it wanes, the conclusion of overall decline is unavoidable—it is an artifact of the method. But the normative structure and identity of society have different manifestations in different contexts and epochs. The real question is why certain forms of civic activity appear when they do. Surely the "political opportunity structure" afforded by the state and "political society," legal developments, the level and type of organization of economic life, along with the nature of other dimensions of civil society, would have to be analyzed, including, to be sure, the form and impact of the mass media, to arrive at an answer.[42]

If one does not screen out "functional equivalents" for traditional forms of voluntary association at the outset, then the relationship of new media of communication to new forms of collective action and engagement could be analyzed along with their (alleged) potential to undermine old ones. Indeed, if the analyst had the normative concept of the public sphere at his disposal, the "two-sidedness" of all mass media would be apparent. Generalized forms of communication, from the printed word to radio, television, and now cyberspace, do not necessarily displace or degrade interpersonal communication.[43] Nor do they perforce "privatize" or block civic engagement. They could even foster it by enabling the extension of communications and networks beyond local contexts.[44] The media of communication are, along with law, important mechanisms by which the "particular" and the "universal," the local, the national, and international (meanings, norms, and issues), are interrelated. Even media that have little claim to be interactive, such as TV, might foster discussion about the content of what is broadcast, despite the fact that reception may initially be private. Interactive media can of course do more. In short, there is no zero-sum relation between deliberation and mass media, between direct face-to-face discussion and indirect communication. Moreover, generalized media of communication are themselves institutions subject to the norms of the public sphere and hence are open to critique if access to them or their functioning violates these norms. Let me return once more to this concept to clarify what is at stake here.

THE MISSING PUBLIC SPHERE

The Normative Model

The normative understanding of the civil public sphere as analyzed by Habermas refers to a juridically private (nonstate) "space" in which individuals without official status can communicate and attempt to persuade one another through argumentation and criticism about matters of general concern.[45] Ideally, participation in discussion is universally accessible, inclusive, and freed from deformations due to wealth, power, or social status. Argumentation and critique involve the principles of individual autonomy, parity of discussants, and the free and open problematization of any issue that is of common concern, including the procedural principles guiding discussion. As already indicated, public discussion also has the important political purpose of controlling and influencing the formation of policy in the juridically public institutions of the state.

The historically new type of civil public analyzed by Habermas is "liberal" in that sets of rights necessary to secure the autonomy of civil communication (freedoms of speech, press, assembly, association, and communication) together with those dimensions of individual autonomy it presupposes ("privacy rights") constitute the public and private domains of modern civil society and serve as limits to state power. Legally distinct from the state, this sphere and its members have a critical argumentative relation to the polity rather than a directly participatory one.

From the point of view of democratic theory, the public sphere provides the only possible setting in which all concerned can participate in the discussion of contested norms and policies. Collective will formation occurs through the medium of unconstrained communication, with the civil public itself becoming the critical authority vis-à-vis the genesis of power and the legitimacy of norms. But it is also the level, as already indicated, at which public opinion can form and attempt to influence policy formation by thematizing and debating issues of general concern. The civil public is thus "democratic" insofar as the representative political public sphere (the legislature) is supposed to be open to the influence of civil society—the issues, debates, and opinions contested and developed in the latter ought in principle to be among those that are taken up by the former. The modern state administrative apparatus is to be checked, supervised, and controlled not only by the rule of law but also by a public sphere that penetrates the state in the form of legislatures. The civil, politically oriented public, rooted in the communication processes of civil society, presumably has a communicative connection to the legislatures and thereby serves as the most important mediation between the citizenry and its elected officials in a constitutional democracy. This communicative influence, along with the sanction of the vote, keeps political elites responsive and, as it were, representative.

It should be clear from this account that conceptual analysis of representative constitutional democracies implies a distinction between civil and political publics. The former are "weak" yet relatively unconstrained publics in which deliberation and expression predominate over the chance or pressures to "decide." Civil publics exercise influence and symbolic power. The latter are "strong" publics, involving not only deliberation but also decisions backed up by state sanctions. Although decision making in political publics (legislatures) takes place also through compromise and voting, deliberation (attempts to persuade the interlocutor through argument) presumably plays a central role in the democratic process of arguing for and justifying policies and laws. Needless to say, most publics can be placed on a continuum between weak and strong, discursive and decisional.

Criticisms of the Normative Model

Four lines of criticism have been directed at this normative understanding of public space. First, it has been argued that the concept of the *liberal* public, which emphasizes rational speech, deliberation, and argument along with the separation of public and private, is naive vis-à-vis mechanisms of persuasion. Even worse, it entails exclusion, hierarchy, and inequality.[46] Second, liberal democratic parliaments do not now, and never did, even minimally satisfy the conditions of rational deliberation and persuasion through argument. Instead they are dominated by party discipline and/or back-room negotiation and interest compromises that reduce public deliberation to mere show.[47] Third, state intervention into all spheres of society and neocorporatist arrangements have allegedly obliterated the autonomous space between state and civil society so that instead of indirectly controlling the political public sphere, civil publics have disappeared.[48] Fourth, the massification, commodification, and industrialization of culture, especially evident in the new electronic media, have transformed social communication, making individual responses passive, privatized, and susceptible to manipulation through advertising and propaganda techniques.[49] Thus, the space for a critical, autonomous, and influential civil public sphere is also destroyed from within.

Although only the last argument can be found in Putnam's work, perhaps all of these concerns led him to omit the concept of the civil public from his analysis of civil society. Perhaps. But this would make sense only if the criticisms were fully persuasive, and in my view, they are not. Moreover, without the concept of public space, civil society talk cannot link up with democratic theory. Let me address these criticisms, focusing primarily on the first and the last, to clarify my argument.

1. The fact that exclusion from the public sphere has operated through differences in class, gender, ethnicity, race, and so forth, does not alter the normative core of the concept. Democratic legitimacy and the ideal of the public sphere as the central context of participation are tied up with the potential for inclusion. Thus, legal guarantees and mechanisms facilitating equality of access—such as public education, affirmative action, provisions for child care, policies supporting and destigmatizing alternative cultural forms of expression, and civil, political and social rights—become all the more necessary in light of the critique of exclusion and of particularistic standards for inclusion.

The claim that the ideal of rational argument constitutively favors a particular gender, class, or race while silencing and privatizing others is also unconvincing and even condescending. Certainly if dominant groups enshrine a particular form of discourse, style of argumentation, or understanding of what is appropriate rhetoric or body language in public speech, they can indeed silence people who are not de jure excluded, yet who differ from those who have previously had privileged access to the public sphere. But this would clearly be a deformation of the normative principles of public discourse rather than their expression. Moreover, these principles are presupposed and invoked when particularistic standards for inclusion are challenged, and even when struggles for cultural hegemony are engaged in.

To be sure, one must take into account the performative dimensions of speaking—the rhetorical, dramatic, expressive, and gestural aspects—and their role in persuasion. One must also acknowledge the group-specific distribution of styles of communication and inequalities that attach to these. But to do so would eliminate neither the normative ideal of the civil public nor the importance of rational-critical debate in those parts of it that involve politically oriented discussion.

Instead, acknowledgment of these points should lead to the following conclusion: the issue of access/exclusion can be defused if one abandons a unitary conception of the public sphere in favor of a pluralistic model. In other words, the principles of publicity in a modern society imply the pluralization of public fora in the sense of cultural, civil, and political publics. The weight of the various aspects of speech can vary accordingly. Once one grasps that there is an elective affinity between the principle of publicity, a multiplicity of public spaces, and a plurality of types of publics, one can parry the charge of constitutive exclusiveness.

Two types of pluralization are involved here: functional and segmental. Functionally distinct publics are necessarily specialized. The publics of science, art, religion, the academic disciplines, politics, law, and so forth, are examples. Each such public is structured by the norms of the respective enterprise. The style of communication, standards regarding what counts as a good argument, and so on, vary accordingly.

Segmental pluralization has a different logic. This refers, first, to the multiplicity of publics that develop in the milieu of voluntary associations, social movements, clubs, and the like, that are not functionally differentiated yet are limited in purpose and scope. There can be as many such civil publics as there are groups that generate issues of common concern to their members. Their style of communication can also vary enormously. But another mode of publicness is relevant here. I have in mind the nonspecialized, civil, "public of publics" that allows for the communicative interaction of members of different functional spheres or social groups. It is crucial to see that alongside the myriad publics of a differentiated and pluralist society there are general civil publics—society-wide fora of public communication that, though incapable of decisional power, can influence political publics specialized in decision making as well as the more specialized civil publics.

It is possible to theorize the porousness of partial and general publics vis-à-vis one another in two ways. If one draws on the insights of network analysis, it is possible to see publics not only as enclaved within associations or specific milieux, but also as interstitial: as sets of communicative interactions that ease transitions between specific domains by decoupling actors from the pattern of particular relations and understandings embedded within any given network.[50] As such, they serve crucial bridging functions between distinct network realms.[51]

One can also draw on the concept of a more abstract, general public sphere of readers, listeners, viewers, and now cyber-communicators scattered around the national (and international) society to articulate what it is that brings together the participants in partial publics and constitutes them as more generalized fora (i.e., the mass media). These publics enable socially distant interlocutors to come into contact impersonally, formulate collective orientations, and form alliances in the effort to exercise political influence. They also allow members of partial publics to understand themselves as part of a larger public and as contributing to "public opinion" in general.

I will return to the relation of the mass media to general society-wide publics of publics in my response to the fourth objection. My point here is to show that when interpreted in terms of multiplicity and plurality, the concept of the public sphere need not be associated with exclusion or silencing. Rather, it is the "site" where power asymmetries between partial publics get thematized and challenged. But one must not forget that new media of communication also become sites for new forms of inequality, exclusion, and contestation. Struggles over access to them, and over control of the production and dissemination of communications that they facilitate, indicate that the relation between technologies of communication, publicity, and participation is complex and worth serious attention. In short, every new form of exclusion and control linked to new media triggers struggles for inclusion, hegemony, and democratization.

2. and 3. The second and third objections to the normative conception of public space can be dealt with together. The claim that decisions in legislatures are made through bargaining and voting is convincing only if one concludes that deliberation and the imperative to give reasons before one's legislative peers and to the civil/electoral public are thereby irrelevant. For even if the norms of argumentation do not inform the actual motives of participants who may be simply self-interested or acting strategically, they nonetheless have a steering effect on the course of debates. Legislators are forced or induced to argue in terms of the public interest and to justify their policy choices in terms that others can accept. This has important effects on what can be said and done. Jon Elster has referred to this fact as the "civilizing force of hypocrisy."[52]

State interventionism and corporatist trends are undeniable. Certainly the control function of civil publics loses its meaning in relation to bureaucratic and corporatist processes that are closed to scrutiny and do not involve deliberation. Nevertheless, the norms of publicity create legitimation problems for both state interventionism and corporatist interest representation.

Unlike the apparently spontaneous results of the market, state action calls for explicit justification. Although neocorporatist arrangements reduce some of the demands on the state, they trigger challenges by all those excluded from such arrangements. Demands for the democratization and publicization of bargaining processes and for the justification of outcomes in terms of the public good proliferate precisely where neocorporatism is the strongest.

Even the return to neoliberal economic policies and the displacement of state and corporatist action onto the voluntary sector of civil society does not reduce the increasing social scrutiny of the arrangements, decisional processes, and apparent self-limitation of states. Instead, the effects of state action and inaction, of institutional design and redesign, on civil society become thematized and subject to legitimation demands according to the criteria of the public sphere. Indeed, this is what the civil society debate is all about.

4. I have already indicated that Putnam's exclusive focus on those aspects of the media that privatize and trivialize is misleading. So is the thesis that the amount of time spent with such media is both a sign and a cause of the erosion of social capital. Such an assessment revives the old saw that the quality of culture and of public communication declines with its "democratization" (i.e., "massification")—a claim raised every time a new technology further extended communications to the "masses."

Nevertheless, it is worth taking a closer look at the arguments regarding what Frankfurt theorists once called "the culture industry" to see what is really at stake here for democratic theory.[53] The main claim is that democratization of culture and communication, through new technologies such as TV, is allegedly pseudo-democratization of something that is no longer either culture or real communication. When Putnam complains about the privatizing effects of the media, what he implies is that the public sphere is deformed and the critical and civic orientations of citizens are undermined. Accordingly, the reasoning civil public splits into a minority of experts and a mass of consumers. As Adorno and Horkheimer already maintained, in such a context political communication approximates advertising. Propaganda—the advertising and selling of political leaders and policies—presupposes, and is required by, already passive, privatized audiences. Under these circumstances, what is called "public opinion" is no longer of any normative weight. Instead of being the product of a public debate among peers, it is simply a statistical aggregate of singly solicited and privately expressed individual opinions, typical of survey results.

This is a serious argument that would have disastrous results for democratic theory and civil society if it were fully compelling. For even if the existence of a public sphere outside the legislature can be shown to exist (my reply to arguments 2 and 3), liberal and democratic claims regarding political publicity would be undermined if the mass media eliminated the reasoning critical public. Neither the increased range of the media nor the multiplication of chances to have access to them would make any difference if, owing to structural factors, they undermined critical reasoning. If, in other words, one could sell a candidate to the voters on the basis of advertising techniques, irrespective of the positions she or her party argue for in the legislature, it would be meaningless to claim that legislative debates have a rational function or that the civil public has a control function. There would be no possibility for the public's self-enlightenment through the general airing of views in the media if issues and concerns were prepackaged on the basis of extrinsic considerations such as the maximization of profit or the power of political entrepreneurs.

If one does not assume that technologies of the mass media are intrinsically privatizing, then such media can undermine critical reasoning publics in two ways: through direct state control and censorship or through the commodification and industrialization of cultural life. State control and censorship of societal communication always involves a negative sanction and is linked to fear. Yet the state's ability to streamline society and culture is limited: only by terroristic means and the clear abandonment of liberal democratic principles can competitive cultural forms be eliminated.

Commodification of cultural life and the "industrial" production of culture operate through the positive sanction of profit. On the one hand, they imply competition and the possibility that genuine creators and real debates and not only cultural or political hacks could be rewarded by market success. But it is also true that the big media entrepreneurs prestructure the markets and vastly reduce competition. Nonetheless, the industrial producers of culture never have the field fully to themselves, as thriving countercultures show. Indeed, the penetration of competing messages through the appropriation of autonomous and popular culture indicates the existence and influence of public opinion even on the supreme expression of the culture industry: TV. Creativity does seem to occur at the margins. Conflicting imperatives of journalistic ethics and network interests, the difficulty of integrating competing political, economic, and aesthetic interests in broadcast networks, the hostile response of everyday communication to attempts at direct manipulation and to the degradation of programming (e.g., excessive violence), and the development of alternative media technologies all indicate the existence of countertrends. Thus, it is important to note both the homogenizing and privatizing logic of commercialized and industrialized mass media as well as important countertendencies.[54] Much depends here on the institutional supports and strategies behind the countervailing tendencies. But these in turn depend on which normative model of the media one operates with when one devises such strategies. Empirical studies should be guided by a normative preunderstanding of how the media and civil public should interrelate. It is this dimension that is missing from Putnam's analysis.[55] Without it, one cannot begin to address the questions of what laws should govern mass communication; what principles ought to orient the professional code of journalism; what is the best mix of commercial (private), public (nonprofit, nongovernmental), and state-run media; or what methods of funding can best foster the political and economic independence of cultural institutions along with their openness to the variety of interests, associations, and cultural orientations of civil society. In short, the political questions crucial to a democratic theory of civil society cannot be raised. Absent a normative conception of publicity, one tends to screen out the two-sided potential of all media, assume a sort of technological determinism regarding allegedly intrinsic effects of the media, and then translate questions of institutional design, institutional ethics, and appropriate public policy into laments about moral decline and incantations about voluntarism.

CONCLUSION

I do not doubt that the old sorts of associations that fostered civicness for certain segments of the population are disappearing. Nor do I want to claim that functional equivalents are flourishing and that there is nothing to think about. Assuredly some social, economic, and structural changes have undermined the traditional shape of civil society and rendered some of the old avenues of participation and influence obsolete. We may well be in a political context now in which *institutional redesign* of various aspects of the political (and economic) system is necessary to strengthen new sorts of civil sociality. It is not necessary to choose between an institutionalist and an associationalist path to the creation of social trust. These can be mutually interdependent and reinforcing. But where to look and what is to be done will only be obscured by backward-looking analyses focused on reviving old forms of association that may no longer be appropriate.

An approach that omits law, rights, and the public sphere from the conceptualization of civil society has no conceptual means to counter the thesis that legalization itself—in particular, the expansion of personal rights, entitlements, and public freedoms—actually causes the disintegration of civil society and civic capacities.[56] The step from here to the moralizing values discourse of social conservatives is not a large one. But it takes us farther and farther away from the real issues that a civil society discourse can and should raise.

I have argued in this chapter that a narrow conception of civil society obscures and miscasts important problems, not that these problems do not exist. Without question the welfare state paradigm, corresponding forms of legalization, and established modes of civic engagement, political participation, and social integration are all in crisis today. But the dichotomous thinking that opposes civil society to the state, duties to rights, custom to code, informal to formal socialization (as the source of trust), and status to contract leads to an overhasty conclusion of social decapitalization and a set of false policy choices.

If we had a richer concept of civil society at our disposal, the discovery of the erosion of one type of civic institution would not have to lead to a claim of general civic decline. Given a different method, functional equivalents for older forms of associationalism could become visible, along with new types of civic action targeting an altered environment of civil, economic, and political institutions. The question of whether the political public spheres, including the party and electoral systems, are sufficiently receptive to new forms of civic engagement aimed at influencing them could then be addressed. This in turn could point to consideration of the role of government in encouraging or blocking civic participation and renewal.[57] Crucial questions regarding how the state, law, and professions should prestructure the terrain such that the autonomy of civil society, the vitality of civil publics, and civicness are strengthened could be raised. Attention could turn to the institutional structure of the state and its impact on and receptivity to organizational initiatives and public expression in civil society. This concern should be at the center of democratic theory.

Such considerations do not replace a societalist analysis with a state-oriented one. Rather, if we had a rich conception of civil society that included the civil public sphere, we could fruitfully consider the reciprocal lines of influence between it, the state, and the economy. This perspective could point us to an important range of questions begging for serious research. For example, what is an optimal relation (or division of labor) among the state, civil society, and the market under contemporary conditions? What institutional reforms or redesigns are necessary to accomplish the material goals of the welfare state without destroying incentives for individual and group initiative or responsibility? How would the principle of subsidiarity apply when issues of efficiency, democratic values, social justice, and social autonomy are raised? What type of federalism can encourage democratic participation and citizen initiative without feeding into parochialism and local intolerance?

What legal paradigm could guarantee the basic rights of civil society without sacrificing public to private autonomy? What conception of constitutionalism could protect the plurality of forms of life within civil society from intolerant majorities without privatizing or reifying "difference"? Are there ways to institutionalize civil publics so as to protect professional ethics in a wide arena (from medicine to journalism) from the corrupting influence of money? Indeed, how can the media of communication, which are crucial to the generalization of norms of reciprocity, be more receptive to civil input without allowing the power of money to control the agenda of debate and to silence others? How, in short, does the unequal distribution of income affect civicness? Finally, what effect do structural factors such as the flight of real capital and the ever more prominent role of money in politics have on the vitality of civil and political institutions? The problems plaguing American civic culture at the end of the twentieth century are not due to lack of consensus about the ideals of our political system or some general moral decline. Rather, they are attributable to the sense that our country is run by a political-economic elite, whose special interests (greed and power) block needed institutional reforms and exercise a negative corrupting influence on the institutional and professional ethics that are indispensable to a well-functioning democracy. To address these questions we must drop the rhetoric of moral and civic decline.

NOTES

1. For an analysis of the international discussion, see Jean L. Cohen and Andrew Arato, *Civil Society and Political Theory* (Cambridge, Mass.: MIT Press, 1992), 1–26.

2. Senator Dan Coats, "Re-funding Our 'Little Platoons,' " *Policy Review: A Journal of American Citizenship* 75 (January/February 1996): 25; Bill Bradley, "America's Challenge: Revitalizing Our National Community," *National Civic Review* 84, no. 2 (Spring 1995): 94. For more references, see Theda Skocpol, "Unraveling from Above," *American Prospect*, no. 25 (March/April 1996): 20–21.

3. Gabriel Almond and Sidney Verba, *The Civic Culture: Political Attitudes and Democracy in Five Nations* (Princeton, N.J.: Princeton University Press, 1963), is the most important example of the pluralist approach to civil society in the postwar period.

4. Robert D. Putnam, *Making Democracy Work* (Princeton, N.J.: Princeton University Press, 1993); Robert D. Putnam, "Bowling Alone: America's Declining Social Capital," *Journal of Democracy* (January 1995): 65–78; Robert Putnam, "Bowling Alone Revisited," *Responsive Community* 5, no. 2 (1995): 18–33; Robert Putnam, "The Strange Disappearance of Civic America," *American Prospect*, no. 24 (1996): 34. The other important intervention in this debate is that of communitarian political theorists who gather around the journal *The Responsive Community: Rights and Responsibilities*. The main figures of the neocommunitarian movement are Amitai Etzioni, a professor of sociology at George Washington University; William Galston, a political philosopher and professor at the University of Maryland, and until recently a domestic policy adviser to President Clinton; Mary Ann Glendon, a

Harvard law professor; and Michael Sandel, a Harvard professor of political science. Their journal, edited by Etzioni, sees itself as the voice of a new movement for communitarian values.

5. Cohen and Arato, *Civil Society and Political Theory*, 346.

6. Antonio Gramsci, "State and Civil Society," in *Selections from Prison Notebooks* (New York: International Publishers, 1971), 206–77. See also Perry Anderson, "The Antinomies of Antonio Gramsci," *New Left Review* 100 (November–January 1977): 5–78; and Cohen and Arato, *Civil Society and Political Theory*, 142–59.

7. Alain Touraine, *The Voice and The Eye* (Cambridge: Cambridge University Press, 1981); Alberto Melucci, "The Symbolic Challenge of Contemporary Movements" *Social Research* 52, no. 4 (1985): 798–816; "The New Social Movements: A Theoretical Approach," *Social Science Information* 19 (1980): 199. See also Cohen and Arato, *Civil Society and Political Theory*, 492–564.

8. Jürgen Habermas, *The Structural Transformation of the Public Sphere* (Cambridge, Mass.: MIT Press, 1989). See also Craig Calhoun, ed., *Habermas and the Public Sphere* (Cambridge, Mass.: MIT Press, 1992).

9. On the distinction between civil and political publics, see Cohen and Arato, *Civil Society and Political Theory*. On "weak" and "strong," see Nancy Fraser, "Rethinking the Public Sphere: A Contribution to the Critique of Actually Existing Democracy," in *Habermas and the Public Sphere*, ed. Calhoun. One must think of the distinctions between civil, weak, political, and strong publics as a continuum. Weak publics are relatively speaking more deliberative and open to fewer constraints on deliberations. Strong decisional publics are more constrained both qualitatively and quantitatively (time for deliberation is shorter). A consciousness-raising group in a feminist movement is an example of a weak uninstitutionalized civil public open to all sorts of statements and reasoning. A jury is an example of an institutionalized civil public that is "strong" in the sense that its deliberations lead to politically binding decisions. A parliament is an even stronger institutionalized political public, legislating for the whole of society. For another way of distinguishing between the various constraints on different sorts of publics, see John Rawls, "The Idea of Public Reason" in *Political Liberalism* (New York: Columbia University Press: 1993), 212–54.

10. This way of conceptualizing the public sphere precludes granting legitimacy to any group or institution claiming to embody or represent the public, endowed with the authority to define what is a matter of public concern. Moreover, the line between public and private, along with the question of who is to be included in the public, cannot be decided once and for all.

11. Claus Offe, "Trust and Knowledge, Rules and Decisions: Exploring a Difficult Conceptual Terrain" (paper delivered at "Democracy and Trust" conference at George Washington University, 7–9 November 1996).

12. For a discussion of the importance of personal privacy rights in particular, see my "Redescribing Privacy: Identity, Difference and the Abortion Controversy," *Columbia Journal of Gender and Law* 3, no. 1 (1992): 43–118; and "Is There a Duty of Privacy? Law, Sexual Orientation, and the Construction of Identity," *Texas Journal of Women and the Law* 6, issue 1 (Fall 1996): 47–129.

13. Putnam, *Making Democracy Work*, 173–75. Putnam knows that all networks

and associations mix the horizontal and the vertical but insists nonetheless that the basic contrast between horizontal and vertical linkages, between weblike and maypolelike networks, is reasonably clear. But isn't it possible for people to belong to both sorts of organizations? Does Putnam insist on full congruence between civil and political institutions? For a critique of this idea, see Nancy Rosenblum, "Democratic Character and Community: The Logic of Congruence?" *Journal of Political Philosophy* 2, no. 1 (1994): 67–97.

14. Putnam, *Making Democracy Work*, 128, 147. I use the word *confidence* advisedly. What is at stake is analytically distinct from interpersonal trust (i.e., the trust of concrete individuals). Confidence that the administration of justice will be impartial, or that the legislative process is fair, responsive, and representative, rests on the shared understanding that the principles of impartiality, fairness, equal concern and respect, and so forth, have been institutionalized as norms and that these are internalized by the institutional actors as well as those subject to these institutions. It is thus possible to lose trust in a particular lawmaker or judge without losing confidence in the legal system or the legislative process as a whole. Their legitimacy rests on the belief that generally they function in a manner appropriate to their institutionalized norms.

15. Putnam, *Making Democracy Work*, 165–66; Putnam, "Bowling Alone," 67.

16. Putnam, *Making Democracy Work*, 167, 176–77, 182.

17. Noted by Margaret Levi, "Social and Unsocial Capital: A Review Essay of Robert Putnam's *Making Democracy Work*," in *Politics and Society* 24, no. 1 (1996): 47; Putnam, *Making Democracy Work*, 171–74.

18. Alejandro Portes and Patricia Landolt ("The Downside of Social Capital," *American Prospect*, no. 26 [May/June 1996]: 18–21) have stressed the circularity of the argument, while Sidney Tarrow ("Making Social Science Work across Space and Time: A Critical Reflection on Robert Putnam's *Making Democracy Work*," *American Political Science Review* 90, no. 2 [1996]: 389) points to the confusion of the indicators with causes of civicness. Levi ("Social and Unsocial Capital") has noted the sloppiness of the definitions, which makes it almost impossible to differentiate between social capital, interpersonal trust, and generalized reciprocity, as well as the absence of a definition of trust in Putnam's work. Skocpol ("Unraveling from Above") notes the one-sidedness of the society-centered analysis to the neglect of other important actors, most notably government, and factors such as the structure and nature of the state. Although I agree with these criticisms, we must beware of overcorrecting here. The society-centered analysis is itself a corrective to one-sided, state-centered approaches. What we need is a model broad enough to capture both dimensions.

19. Putnam, *Making Democracy Work*, 177.

20. Putnam, *Making Democracy Work*, 221, footnote 30.

21. See Rosenblum, "Democratic Character and Community."

22. See Albert O. Hirschman, *Exit, Voice, and Loyalty: Responses to Decline in Firms, Organizations, and States* (Cambridge, Mass.: Harvard University Press, 1981 [1970]), for the concept of "voice."

23. See Jürgen Habermas, *The Theory of Communicative Action* 2 (1981): 113–99, on this point.

24. James Coleman, *Foundations of Social Theory* (Cambridge, Mass.: Harvard University Press, 1990), 251, 273, shows that under the assumption of rational action, norms *can* arise, but he gives no argument about the emergence of norms in general. Nor does he address the deeper issue of how values (standards used to evaluate evaluative standards) emerge. I do not believe this can be answered within a rational choice framework. Putnam's work suffers from the same deficiency.

25. On the concept of warranted trust, see Mark Warren, "What Should We Expect from More Democracy? Radically Democratic Responses to Politics," *Political Theory* 24, no. 2 (1996): 241–70.

26. "Civil society" was understood as a sphere of social interaction distinct from the economy and state, characterized by voluntary association, civil publics and the media of communication, and sets of subjective legal rights. The rule of law and the autonomous administration of justice were central to civil society because although the latter creates itself spontaneously, it cannot on its own institutionalize or generalize its norms and orientations ("habits of the heart"). A legal system and a legal culture committing practitioners to the norms of impartiality are crucial to the process by which the particularistic goals and projects of associated individuals within civil society could be informed by, made compatible with, or generalized into the universalistic principles of modern constitutional democracies.

27. As Offe has recently put it in a brilliant analytical paper on trust, democratic citizens build "generalized" trust on the basis of what they know about institutions and their ability to orient action, not on the basis of what they know about political elites (whom they in fact do not know). See Offe, "Trust and Knowledge, Rules and Decisions," 23.

28. For an excellent discussion relating network analysis and the idea of interstitial links to the concept of the public sphere, see Mustafa Emirbayer and Mimi Sheller, "Publics in History: A Programmatic Statement" (unpublished manuscript filed with the author).

29. Nadia Urbanati, "The Art of Tolerance," *Dissent* (1993): 573.

30. Putnam, "Bowling Alone," "Bowling Alone Revisited," "The Strange Disappearance of Civic America" (see note 4).

31. Putnam, "Bowling Alone," 72.

32. Putnam, "Strange Disappearance," 35; "Bowling Alone Revisited," 71.

33. Putnam, "Strange Disappearance," 35–43.

34. Putnam, "Strange Disappearance," 46–48.

35. It is bizarre to present the adult generation in the 1950s as the paragon of civicness or the 1950s and early 1960s as an era of the generalized social trust that makes democracy work. This period was the heyday of McCarthyism (hardly noteworthy for generalized trust), institutionalized racial segregation, and exclusion of women from a wide range of economic and political institutions and associations (hardly a model of cross-cutting plurality), a pervasive ideological (and economic) movement to push women out of the labor force and into the housewife role with all its attendant "volunteerism" (something that did not exactly foster egalitarian gender norms).

Civil privatism and authoritarian cultural and social conservativism would seem a more apt characterization of that period than civic virtue. Indeed, if voluntary association was alive and well in the 1950s, this is proof that it does not suffice to render a political culture civic or to generate generalized trust or active egalitarian participation in public life. Moreover, I suspect that economic expansion and the impact of the New Deal had a good deal more to do with the effectiveness of government than the vitality of the Elks Club did. Or one could say that if trust was widespread under such circumstances, perhaps it was unwarranted and naive, based on the attitude "my country right or wrong," as opposed to a mature civic patriotism. See Alan Wolfe, "Americans' Civic and Moral Beliefs," *National Commission on Civic Renewal Newsletter* 1, no. 1 (Spring 1997): 2.

36. Henry E. Brady, Kay L. Schlozman, and Sidney Verba, *Voice and Equality: Civic Voluntarism in American Politics* (Cambridge, Mass.: Harvard University Press, 1995), 68–91.

37. Michael Schudson, "What If Civil Life Didn't Die?" *American Prospect*, no. 25 (March/April 1996): 17–18.

38. Albert O. Hirschman, *Shifting Involvements: Private Interest and Public Action* (Princeton, N.J.: Princeton University Press, 1982).

39. Sidney Tarrow, *Power in Movement: Social Movements, Collective Action and Politics* (New York: Cambridge University Press, 1994), and others have argued that social movements can produce lasting effects on political culture by legitimating new forms of collective action and by establishing a permanent place for issues on the public agenda that remain alive even in a general context of demobilization. See also my article, "Strategy or Identity: New Theoretical Paradigms and Contemporary Social Movements," *Social Research* 52, no. 4 (1985): 663–716. For an interesting albeit controversial recent discussion of the relation between movements and state forms, see John Dryzek, "Political Inclusion and the Dynamics of Democratization," *American Political Science Review* (September 1996): 475–88.

40. Schudson, "What If Civic Life Didn't Die?" 20.

41. Nor is there any incompatibility between direct and more mediated forms of communication. Ties to common leaders, texts, symbols, and ideals can inform and foster horizontal styles of association and interpersonal interaction by providing points of reference for discussion and for mobilization when the time comes. Skocpol, "Unraveling from Above," 25, points to the Christian Coalition as a successful example of a secondary association that melds top-down and bottom-up styles of political mobilization.

42. Skocpol, "Unraveling from Above," 23.

43. Pippa Norris, "Does Television Erode Social Capital? A Reply to Putnam," *Political Science and Politics* 129, no. 3 (1996): 476–79, convincingly shows that the data do not permit one to claim that civic and political disengagement vary unambiguously and positively with the sheer amount of TV that one watches. What matters more is the content of what one watches. Given the diversity of channels, programs, and choices, from *Nightline, 60 Minutes, CNN World News, NPR, Meet the Press,* and C-Span to the information available now on the Internet, it might even be the case that Americans are as a whole better informed about national and international issues than ever before.

44. Norris, "Does Television Erode Social Capital?" 475–76. The problem of disentangling the direction of causality that plagues all cross-sectional survey analysis is not resolved regardless of how one comes down on this issue. It is not clear whether those who are already actively involved in public life turn to the news networks for more information or whether tuning into TV news or reading about public affairs encourages people to become more active in public affairs and civic life. Either way, the charge that television is the root cause of the lack of trust in American democracy is unproven and implausible.

45. Habermas, *Structural Transformation of the Public Sphere*, 1–26. Habermas developed his conception through an analysis of the forms of social intercourse and the institutional self-understanding of the bourgeois public sphere as it emerged in eighteenth-century Europe.

46. See Fraser, "Rethinking the Public Sphere," and Iris Marion Young, *Justice and the Politics of Difference* (Princeton, N.J.: Princeton University Press, 1990), chapters 4 and 6.

47. This is originally the argument of Carl Schmitt. See Cohen and Arato, *Civil Society and Political Theory*, 201–54, for a summary and reply.

48. Cohen and Arato, *Civil Society and Political Theory*, 201–54.

49. The classic example of this critique is that of the older Frankfurt School. Max Horkheimer and Theodor Adorno, *Dialectic of Enlightenment* (New York: Herder & Herder, 1972), 120–67.

50. Emirbayer and Sheller, "Publics in History," 19, citing Harrison White, "Where Do Languages Come From? Part 1," *Pre-Print Series*, Lazarsfeld Center for the Social Sciences, Columbia University 4 (1995); and H. C. White, "Network Switchings and Bayesian Forks," *Social Research* 62 (1996): 1055.

51. Emirbayer and Sheller, "Publics in History," 19.

52. Jon Elster speaks of the "civilizing force of hypocrisy" in "Arguing and Bargaining over the Senate at the Federal Convention," in *Explaining Social Institutions*, ed. Jack Knight and Itai Sened (Ann Arbor: University of Michigan Press, 1995), 16. Elster summarizes the "goods" that deliberative democracy in public spaces yields in the following list: it reveals private information, lessens or defeats the impact of bounded rationality, forces or induces a particular mode of justifying demands, legitimizes the ultimate choice, is desirable for its own sake, makes for pareto-superior decisions, leads to better decisions in terms of distributive justice, generates a larger consensus, and improves the moral or intellectual qualities of participants.

53. Horkheimer and Adorno, *Dialectic of Enlightenment*, 120–67.

54. Indeed, one might note that today the autonomy and integrity of civil publics and personal communication are explicitly asserted and institutionalized as public norms, and they are better protected by law and courts than ever before. Certainly First Amendment protections for public, political, and personal expression are incomparably stronger now than they were in the 1950s, as are legal protections of personal autonomy rights. What is needed now is reflection on how to make these principles effective in the public sphere.

55. For an interesting effort at developing a normative analysis of the tasks the media ought to fulfill, see Jürgen Habermas, *Between Facts and Norms* (Cambridge, Mass.: MIT Press, 1996), 377–79.

56. This is the thesis of conservative communitarians. See Mary Ann Glendon, *Rights Talk* (Cambridge, Mass.: Harvard University Press, 1991). See also Michael Sandel, *Democracy's Discontent* (Cambridge, Mass.: Harvard University Press, 1996).

57. For an argument that governmental structures greatly affect civil society's capacities, see Dryzek, "Political Inclusion and the Dynamics of Democratization."

PART TWO

GOVERNMENT AND CIVIL SOCIETY

4

Is There Civic Life beyond the Great National Community?

William A. Schambra

Given the mounting flood of news articles, television programs, political addresses, academic seminars, and national commissions devoted to the contemporary condition of civil society, one might think its prospects are bright indeed. Certainly the entire discussion has come a long way from the time and place I first encountered it, as a young research assistant at the American Enterprise Institute (AEI) in the late 1970s. There, almost lost amid the swarms of prominent economists and political scientists, a handful of scholars had begun to explore the possibility of meeting human needs not through government, and not through the market, but rather through what they called "mediating structures"—family, neighborhood, church, ethnic and voluntary association, and other social institutions that mediated between the individual and the state.

Although AEI was considered a conservative think tank, it was by no means obvious that this was a peculiarly conservative idea. To be sure, Robert Nisbet, who had alerted us to the centrality of "intermediate associations" for human well-being in his landmark *The Quest for Community*, was clearly of the right.[1] But that was not so clear with sociologist Peter Berger and antiwar cleric Richard John Neuhaus, whose *To Empower People* had been the first serious exploration of the utility of mediating structures for delivering public services.[2] And former George McGovern speechwriter Michael Novak clearly hoped at the time that mediating structures would become the vehicle for a revitalized *left*—one that would, as he put it in *The Rise of the Unmeltable Ethnics*, "turn toward the organic networks of communal life . . . family, ethnic group, and voluntary association in primary groups."[3]

Ideological classification of this tiny band of scholars was additionally complicated by the fact that they professed equally a profound skepticism about conservatism's romance with the marketplace and rugged individualism, on the one hand, and about liberalism's infatuation with the state, on the other. Neither ideological position, they insisted, took adequately into account the small, humble civic institutions in between state and individual—institutions through which the American people had traditionally lived their daily lives and directed their own affairs, sharing benefits and burdens, constructing and passing on to their children their moral and spiritual values, and enjoying a sense of belonging, purpose, and meaning. Indeed, insofar as most of our political energies were drawn either upward to the state or downward to the individual, they feared for the future of that fragile but vital middle zone of our national life.

What I first encountered in the 1970s as a clunky, arcane sociological term has today bedecked itself in the far more glamorous garb of "civil society" and found its way onto the covers of major news magazines. Even U.S. senators are celebrating the virtues of that realm between state and individual, where, as Bill Bradley put it so eloquently, "Americans make their homes, sustain their marriages, raise their families, hang out with their friends, meet their neighbors, educate their children, worship their god."[4]

Yet it is difficult for partisans of mediating structures simply to take pleasure in all this attention, for, as is usually the case, to be big news, it has to be bad news. Civil society's prospects are, apparently, not so bright after all. The headlines tell us that American citizens today are massively alienated from their public institutions, refusing even to vote, much less to involve themselves actively in public affairs. They are so absorbed in enjoying and defending their individual rights that they have turned their backs altogether on any sense of civic or moral responsibility. People are no longer engaging themselves in civic associations but instead are "bowling alone."[5]

We are now in the midst of a furious debate among social scientists about the magnitude of this decline in our civic vitality, or indeed about whether in fact there has been a decline at all. Wherever one finally comes down on this empirical question, though, there can be no dispute that our civic institutions face an uphill struggle for survival against a number of powerful intellectual and social trends today. And the prime suspects among potential civic corrosives are pretty much the same ones discussed by that small band at AEI back in the 1970s—namely, the marketplace, on the one hand, and the state, on the other.

In this chapter I shall consider first the relationship between the marketplace and civil society, noting that there is indeed friction between the two realms, but arguing that this friction or tension, fully intended by the architects of our national political life, has been by and large healthy and invigorating. The relationship between state and civil society, on the other hand, has not been so healthy. That is because the state has, over the course of the twentieth century, attempted to arrogate unto itself the community-building functions once considered the exclusive province of civil society. A substantial federal government is, by itself, not incompatible with civic health, as the Founders understood. But a federal government that sets out explicitly to build a great national community by absorbing the authority and function of all lesser communities is another matter altogether.

CIVIL SOCIETY AND THE MARKETPLACE

Contemporary liberals enjoy chiding conservatives about their failure to acknowledge any tension between civil society and the marketplace, with its attendant characteristics of individualism and materialism. To be sure, the purely libertarian strand of conservatism may not concern itself much about this friction. The same, however, cannot be said about Robert Nisbet conservatives.

"Unfortunately, it has been the fate of [civic] institutions and relationships to suffer almost continuous attrition during the capitalist age," Nisbet noted in *Quest*.[6] The marketplace produces and celebrates a materialistic individualism that inevitably distracts the citizen from his civic obligations and erodes the authority of family, church, and neighborhood, he warned. Capitalism's tendency to produce a "sand heap of disconnected particles of humanity,"[7] or "enlarging masses of socially 'free,' insecure individuals,"[8] left citizens easy prey to the state's embrace, he cautioned, and so it was "absurd to suppose that the rhetoric of nineteenth-century individualism will offset present tendencies in the direction of the absolute political community."[9] Here is one conservative with no illusions about the tension between civil society and the marketplace.

The important thing about this tension in the American context, however, is that it was very much part of the design of our nation's Founders. Believing that the only legitimate government was one that secured the individual's "unalienable rights" to "life, liberty, and the pursuit of happiness" outlined in the Declaration of Independence, James Madison, Alexander Hamilton, and other leading Federalists were reluctant to leave such rights to the tender mercies of the small, homogeneous states of the time, in which popular majorities easily formed behind schemes of oppression and abuse of minority rights.

The Founders' answer to this dilemma, as Martin Diamond taught, was to establish through the Constitution the world's first large, modern, commercial republic.[10] Here, the marketplace could be counted on to give rise to an endless variety of occupations and economic interests (*Federalist* 10's famous "multiplicity of interests"), thus making far more difficult successful collusion in schemes of oppression.

Commerce requires large markets, and large markets require "a great extent of territory"—sufficiently great that its orderly administration demanded an energetic national government. This national government would serve as a sentinel of individual rights against potentially abusive local majorities, intervening forcibly when necessary, but more generally accomplishing this purpose through the upbuilding of a vigorous, continent-wide commercial infrastructure, which would diversify and fragment potentially oppressive local majorities.[11]

The Founders understood full well that commerce brought with it strong and not altogether attractive tendencies toward self-interested individualism and materialism, which would in turn diminish the authority of traditional, local civic communities. But for the Federalists, commerce's vice was also its chief virtue. Small communities powerfully animated by cohesive ideological or religious sentiments, they had learned from history, were precisely those most likely to be violators of the individual rights whose protection was the first object of government. By "multiplying the means of gratification" and "promoting the introduction and circulation of the precious metals, those darling objects of human avarice and enterprise," as Hamilton put it in *Federalist* 12, government would ensure that the lives of its citizens were animated more by the relatively peaceful and subdued self-interested pursuit of material prosperity than by the sort of religious or philosophical zeal that had traditionally been fatal to human rights.[12] Did the Founders understand that there would be a tension between civic virtues or civil society and the marketplace? Absolutely—and they made the most of it.

America might long ago have been dissolved into Nisbet's "sand heap of disconnected particles of humanity" had the commercial republic been the sole impulse behind the American founding. Happily, though, another critical element was contributed by the Anti-Federalists—public figures such as Richard Henry Lee, Patrick Henry, Mercy Warren, and Melancton Smith, who, as Herbert Storing suggests, are "entitled to be counted among the Founders."[13]

These political theorists were by no means persuaded that a large, commercial republic was desirable, or even possible. Taking their cue from Montesquieu's *Spirit of the Laws*, they insisted that republicanism was possible only with public-spirited or virtuous citizens, who would willingly put aside matters of self-interest for the sake of the public good. They must be imbued with the "love of the laws and of our country" and "exhibit a constant preference of public to private interest."[14] Such a rigorous standard of civic virtue, however, could only be maintained in a small, intense community, in which citizens readily sensed their oneness with each other, and where public affairs were immediately accessible and understandable. For binding together such intense communities, the Anti-Federalists insisted, nothing was more important than rigorous moral or religious codes: "without the prevalence of Christian piety and morals, the best republican Constitution can never save us from slavery and ruin," one wrote.[15]

All of these critical republican features, the Anti-Federalists understood, would be radically compromised by the large commercial regime. A large, distant federal government would be too remote and alien for people to involve themselves in its affairs. Commerce would corrupt civic virtue and distract people from dutiful commitment to the public business. "As people become more luxurious, they become more incapacitated of governing themselves," noted one.[16] And commerce diminished the strong moral and religious bonds that were critical for the virtuous republican community. Mercy Warren feared that Americans might be destined for the disastrous path taken by the Europeans: "Bent on gratification, at the expense of every moral tie, they have broken down the barriers of religion, and the spirit of infidelity is nourished at the fount."[17]

Clearly, the sort of small, virtuous republic championed by the Anti-Federalists was inconceivable on the continental scale of the Federalists' plans, and so they pressed hard at the Constitutional Convention for mitigation of the radically nationalist scheme proposed originally by Madison, John Randolph, and others. As a result of their efforts, we were bequeathed a strong national Constitution that nonetheless imposed many decentralizing limitations on the reach of the national government, thereby leaving the management of the critical, everyday affairs of civic life to the states, localities, and civil associations.

Insofar as America has enjoyed a vital and active civil society for much of its history, we probably owe it less to well-known statesmen such as Madison or Hamilton than to the far more obscure Anti-Federalists. Although our civic institutions have always been a far cry from the rigorously virtuous republics they envisioned (the Federalists enjoyed reminding them that even at the time of the Founding, such virtuous republics were nonexistent), the barriers against nationalist centralization that they managed to build into the Constitution secured enclaves within which local civil and public associations flourished, nurturing at least attenuated versions of the qualities so important to the Anti-Federalists, including civic virtue, public-spiritedness, religious faith, and intense involvement in and devotion to community.

No one understood better than Alexis de Tocqueville the complex coexistence of Federalist large-republicanism and Anti-Federalist small-republicanism in American life, from which emanates the ongoing tension between market and civil society. According to Tocqueville, Americans had "forcibly reconciled" those "two theoretically irreconcilable systems."[18] There was no name for the government that resulted—it was a kind of "incomplete national government,"[19] which combined the "various advantages of large and small size for nations."[20]

America was destined to be prosperous, Tocqueville understood, because it was a large, commercial republic, giving "free scope to the unguided strength and common sense of individuals."[21] This led to some by-now familiar problems: it is "always an effort" for the commerce-minded to "tear themselves away from their private affairs and pay attention to those of the community," thus permitting the public business to languish or to gravitate into the hands of a distant and potentially oppressive state.[22] Furthermore, commerce's "love of comfort" threatens to erode the moral and spiritual capacities of individuals; its aims are "petty," but "the soul clings to them; it dwells on them every day . . . in the end they shut out the rest of the world and sometimes come between the soul and God."[23]

But Americans had found ways to counter these tendencies, Tocqueville suggested, through their traditions of local self-government and civic association—traditions preserved constitutionally by the rearguard skirmishing of the Anti-Federalist small-republicans. American lawgivers had wisely "given each part of the land its own political life so that there would be an infinite number of occasions for the citizens to act together and so that every day they should feel they depended on one another."[24] Within "each part's" political life, citizens were bound closely to one another by strong families, tightly knit neighborhoods, active voluntary and fraternal groups, and vigorous churches. Through these small, local, human-scale associations, Americans not only achieved a sense of belonging and connectedness, but they also involved themselves directly in solving the most important human problems. As Nisbet noted, echoing Tocqueville, "the social problems of birth and death, courtship and marriage, employment and unemployment, infirmity and old age were met, however inadequately at times, through the associated means of these social groups."[25]

Thanks to the small-republican impulse, Tocqueville understood, citizens were thus fully engaged in creating their own public life and in solving their own social problems, and so were unlikely to succumb to the temptation merely to immerse themselves in the self-interested pursuit of material gain. Moreover, their ability to construct, within each locality, a coherent and powerful moral and spiritual community—a community reinforced by the mutually supportive teachings of churches, schools, associations, and neighborhoods—made unlikely the spiritual and moral decline threatened by an untrammeled marketplace.

For Tocqueville, the "forcible reconciliation" of "two theoretically irreconcilable systems" was absolutely central to the survival of America. When he inquired into the "main causes tending to maintain a democratic republic in the United States," he listed first the "federal form . . . which allows the Union to enjoy the power of a great republic and the security of a small one."[26]

The two systems or principles would always be in tension, according to Tocqueville, each threatening to consume or overwhelm the other. In his own time, for instance, he feared that the states and localities were inordinately powerful and posed a challenge to the union. The real danger, however, he foresaw for the future, when a centralizing national government might threaten to swallow up the local institutions so important for civic life.[27] But for all its messiness and occasional tilts toward the excess of one principle over the other, Tocqueville understood, America had found a realistic way to extract the best of the two principles while minimizing their vices, in the event giving us a polity that preserved both liberty and community.

As we look back today at our history, a century and a half after Tocqueville's American tour, can we not agree with him that the tension between the local civic life preserved by the Constitution's small-republican features and the national market created by its large-republican features has been, by and large, healthy and invigorating, each element moderating the worst aspects of the other? Not according to a significant strand of America's literary tradition, of course, which would have us believe that America's ethnic and religious communities are hopelessly and unprecedentedly narrow-minded, stultifying, moralistic, and oppressive. But any fair-minded analysis would have to conclude that American associative life, for all its occasional excess, is vastly more tolerant and open than the village life of traditional societies.

For that, we must thank the national commercial republic, whose penetrating networks of trade and finance permit no local community to seal itself off completely from the moderate habits and values of the outside commercial world. Commerce compels shopkeepers to befriend "outsiders" who might become customers, tempers ideological and religious zeal with the awareness that one has to go to work in the morning, and gives rise to huge, diverse urban centers, to which embittered writers may flee and where they may write (commercially successful) novels about the oppressiveness of Main Street. Those who warn darkly that "civic renewal" will instead reduce America to a distinctly uncivil, balkanesque collection of bitterly warring ethnic and religious factions forget that *our* civil society has been thoroughly tamed and subdued by the commercial regime within which it is embedded and by whose sober, stolid values it is permeated.

Likewise, for all the jeremiads about the terminal civic and moral decline of the American republic, surely our churches, neighborhoods, and civic associations have over time managed to temper and moderate the harshest aspects of the marketplace's self-interest and materialism. Generation after generation, Americans have been taught that there are obligations beyond mere personal gain and the pursuit of wealth—obligations to family, community, and faith—and have behaved accordingly. When, as is often the case, they organize themselves to protect their families and communities against the harshest and most disintegrative aspects of the marketplace, we celebrate their display of courage and public-spiritedness. It is no accident that one of America's most beloved movies, *It's a Wonderful Life,* should relate the tale of a communitarian Bedford Falls refusing to dissolve itself into the self-interested commercial riot of Potterville.

But is it not the case, as some scholars suggest today, that the market has assumed such an unprecedentedly virulent, global form that it threatens to destroy civic community once and for all? That is possible, of course, but a certain skepticism creeps in when we consider all the *preceding* unprecedentedly disruptive forms the market is alleged to have taken over the past two centuries. Indeed, Thomas Bender points out in *Community and Social Change in America* that the "technology destroys community" theme is an old and familiar canard in scholarship's account of the American experience.

After surveying American historical texts, Bender wryly observes that if they "are placed in serial order, they offer a picture of community breakdown repeating itself in the 1650s, 1690s, 1740s, 1780s, 1820s, 1850s, 1880s, and 1920s," each work treating the change in its particular era as "*the* great change in which the scales were decisively tipped in favor of modernity."[28]

We are entitled to wonder with Bender, "How many times can community collapse in America?"[29] And we are entitled to share his conclusion that, for all the historical variations in the relationship between community and marketplace (or, in his terms, Gemeinschaft and Gesellschaft), "American social history refutes the notion of community collapse."[30] Today, as in Tocqueville's time, we may conclude with Bender, it is possible to enjoy a "humane urban life" built upon "a complex balance of gemeinschaft and gesellschaft that is itself grounded upon appreciation of both of these patterns of social relations."[31]

The interplay between the large commercial republic and the small, civically virtuous republic, like all human contrivances, has not always and everywhere worked well. Individual lives *have* been stunted by oppressive local communities. Families and communities *have* been ripped asunder by commerce. And the system has experienced larger episodes of profound and tragic breakdown. James Madison had hoped that the spread of national commercial institutions and values into the southern states would open up and moderate insulated local custom, putting an end to the slavery at the heart of those "virtuous" small republics. Instead, the insularity, as well as the power, of the slaveholding states grew, until they mounted an armed challenge against the principle of national union.

Even after a bloody civil war, the tightly knit "small republics" of the South persisted in the massive violation of the rights of minorities, necessitating an ongoing effort by the national government to vindicate those rights. The tremendous moral authority of the struggle for civil rights, however, derived precisely from its ability to appeal to the Founders' unfulfilled promise of protection for "certain unalienable rights," and the Federalists' national government has been a potent, if not always steadfast or successful, instrument of enforcement. Furthermore, the spread of modern business and market values into what has come to be known as the "New South" may yet, albeit belatedly, vindicate Madison's hopes for the ameliorative effects of commerce on that region.

Nonetheless, in light of this history, it is small wonder that discussion of the virtues of local government and civic institutions should send up storm signals within the African-American community. That is why it is necessary to remind ourselves constantly that the small-republican impulse must always be checked by the large-republican impulse and that, as the Federalists planned, the national government must be prepared, even in decentralizing times, to protect the rights of minorities against overbearing local majorities.

Without claiming more than is appropriate for any human device in this broken and imperfect world, the interplay between Federalism's national commercial republic and Anti-Federalism's small, virtuous republic has given us a healthy and vigorous, if not always coherent or tidy, national political life. Within the clash of "irreconcilable systems," we have managed to sustain a remarkable degree of material prosperity and individual freedom, on the one hand, and civic vitality and moral community, on the other. Yes, there is a tension between civil society and the marketplace—and it has been good for the Republic.

CIVIL SOCIETY, THE STATE, AND THE GREAT NATIONAL COMMUNITY

The same, however, cannot be said for the relationship between state and civil society, at least as it has evolved in the course of the twentieth century. Whereas the state and the community-building impulse were held in balance during our early political history, at the beginning of this century, an attempt was made to resolve the tension and bring the two harmoniously together. This "fateful combination of widespread quest for community . . . and the apparatus of political power that has become so vast in contemporary democratic societies" is, as Nisbet suggested, "the single most impressive fact in the twentieth century."[32] It has certainly had ominous implications for American civil society.

This effort to marry the two impulses originated with American progressive liberalism at the turn of the century. Whereas the crisis of the Civil War had come about because the small-republican impulse had become too powerful, the Progressives understood themselves to be dealing with the opposite problem: national trends after the late 1800s were threatening to overwhelm the small-republican impulse.

The decentralized, self-governing, civically vital way of life within America's "island communities" (as Robert Wiebe aptly describes them) was doomed, according to theorists such as Herbert Croly, Walter Lippmann, Richard Ely, Charles Horton Cooley, Edward Alsworth Ross, Robert Park, and John Dewey, and public figures such as Theodore Roosevelt. In their view, the irresistible forces of modernity were beginning to sweep away the boundaries that historically had contained and preserved our island communities. Modern means of transportation and communication—the railroad, telegraph, telephone, and high-speed press—had breached the small town's borders, ending its isolation and opening it up to the influences of the larger world. Technology had given rise to vast corporate giants whose operations reached far beyond the jurisdiction of any single state or city. Great cities had sprung up, populated by aggregates of isolated, disconnected individuals, rather than by tightly knit neighbors. Immigration added millions more people from threateningly alien cultures to these already forbidding metropolises. Political control all too often passed out of the hands of town meetings, into the grasp of what were described as corrupt, boss-driven political machines. Citizenly duty seemed to have been lost in the stampede for wealth, a stampede that was legitimized by new doctrines of emancipated individualism.

In short, the forces of modernity had precipitated a crisis of community and civil society in America: the small town and its civic virtues had been shattered. As Lippmann described it, modernity had forever and permanently "upset the old life of the prairies [and] destroyed village loyalties."[33] Although it was pointless, in the Progressives' view, to try to preserve or restore the civic and moral ethos of the small town (*that* had been the failed Populist response), it was now possible to move to a new and higher form of community: the great, national community.

The essential instrument of this new and higher form would be a far more powerful and active national government than had theretofore characterized our political system. In Croly's famous formulation, the Jeffersonian values of "community of feeling and . . . ease of communication" could now be established within the nation as a whole, using the Hamiltonian instrument of a vigorous central government.[34] Or, as Tocqueville might have understood it, the sense of community once thought possible by the Anti-Federalists only within the small republic would now be reestablished on a national scale, through the energetic government established by the Federalists.

The central government, for instance, could tame through regulatory measures those great and disruptive concentrations of private wealth, the corporations, thereby turning them into "express economic agents of the whole community," as Croly put it.[35] The government would also become "expressly responsible for an improved distribution of wealth" and would begin to alleviate, through the progressive income tax and social welfare programs, the inequalities of wealth that might imperil the sense of national oneness.[36] A vigorous program of "Americanization" would serve to integrate diverse immigrant populations into a single, coherent people. "Scientific management" and other new developments in the social sciences held out the promise that enlightened, bureaucratic administration could order and direct toward public purposes the chaotic popular masses. (As sociologist Charles Horton Cooley put it, the era demanded "a comprehensive 'scientific management' of mankind, to the end of better personal opportunity and social function in every possible line.")[37]

Behind these specific developments and programs, however, lay a larger moral purpose: the creation of a genuine national community that could evoke from the American people a self-denying devotion to the "national idea," a far-flung community of millions in which citizens nonetheless would be linked tightly by bonds of compassion, fellow-feeling, and neighborliness. In Croly's words, there would be a "subordination of the individual to the demand of a dominant and constructive national purpose."[38] A citizen would begin to "think first of the State and next of himself,"[39] and "individuals of all kinds [would] find their most edifying individual opportunities in serving their country."[40] Indeed, America would come to be bound together by a "religion of human brotherhood," which "[could] be realized only through the loving-kindness which individuals feel . . . particularly toward their fellow-countrymen."[41]

The catalyst of the national community, the articulator of the "national purpose," in the Progressive view, was to be the president—the galvanizing, unifying voice of all the American people. The president's is the "only national voice in affairs," Woodrow Wilson argued.[42] He alone could unite and inspire the people by combining their many views into one, coherent whole: "The voices of the nation unite in his understanding in a single meaning and reveal to him a single vision, so that he can speak . . . the common meaning of the common voice."[43] From the "bully pulpit" of the executive office, the president would summon from the American people the self-sacrifice, public-spiritedness, and compassion that the national community required.

This vision of national community reached its apotheosis in World War I. Suddenly, the Progressives discovered the awesome capacity of war to nurture public-spiritedness and national oneness, and to legitimate the accretion of power to the central state. Dewey would speak appreciatively afterward of the "social possibilities of war."[44] Lippmann noted approvingly that "the war has given Americans a new instinct for order, purpose, and discipline" and served to "draw Americans out of their local, group, and ethnic loyalties into a greater American citizenship."[45] Richard Ely insisted that "after the War we must 'carry on' and gather the fruits of the splendid accumulation of energy which has been engendered during the War . . . from top to bottom cultivating that social cement of mutual loyalty which makes working together a joy."[46] Liberalism would never forget the wonderfully unified national selflessness of 1917–1918. Henceforth, in times of peace, it would search diligently for the "moral equivalent of war," a kind of war that would energize the national community without the actual spilling of blood.

What would all these developments mean for the humble, local institutions of civil society? Clearly, the new philosophy of national community suggested dramatic changes in the way everyday civic life was to be conducted and experienced. Whereas before the public business had been well within the grasp of the average citizen, easily comprehended and managed by everyday folk wisdom and common sense, now public affairs had allegedly been so complicated by modernity that the average citizen could no longer hope to understand or manage them. Among the more promising "social possibilities of war" foreseen by Dewey, however, was that the public would now come to realize the centrality of the expert for the management of its affairs. The "one phase of Prussianism, borrowed under the stress of war from the enemy, which is likely permanently to remain, is systematic utilization of the scientific expert," Dewey remarked. Indeed, this "social mobilization of science is likely in the end to effect such changes in the practice of government—and finally in its theory—as to initiate a new type of democracy."[47]

In this new democracy, Dewey believed, broad public education in the social sciences would teach citizens, in Timothy Kaufman-Osborn's formulation, "the radical insufficiency of the maxims of everyday conduct," as well as that "the roots of most problematic situations do not lie within the jurisdiction of the locality and hence that their commonsense analyses of those situations are unreliable."[48] The good citizen now accepted his "inescapable dependence upon those trained in the expert methods of the social sciences" and graciously deferred to the experts who alone knew how to manage the complexity of modern public life.[49] As city management advocate Henry Bruere put it, "citizens of larger cities must frankly recognize the need for professional service in behalf of citizen interests. . . . Even efficient private citizens will evidence their efficiency by supporting constructive efforts for governmental betterment."[50]

For the Progressive elites, "governmental betterment" meant reforms in governing systems that all but assured deference to the new professionals by structurally elevating public affairs out of the average citizen's reach. Historian Samuel P. Hays points out that decentralized, localized ward and precinct systems of representation, which had "enabled local and particularistic interests to dominate" and had assured that elected officials "spoke for . . . those aspects of community life which mattered most" to the average citizen, now gave way to at-large, citywide systems of voting and representation, which handed over governance to corporate and professional elites possessed of an enlarged, scientific, rational view of governance.[51]

As Hays suggests, structural revisions such as the short ballot, initiative, referendum, recall, and city manager system that familiarly present themselves as prodemocratic, antimachine reforms, might in fact be better understood as methods to subvert and undermine the smaller civic associations through which common citizens had previously expressed themselves, so that the enlightened elites might rule. In Hays's formulation, the earlier, decentralized system "involved wide latitude for the expression of grass-roots impulses and their involvement in the political process." The Progressive vision, by contrast, "grew out of the rationalization of life which came with science and technology, in which decisions arose from expert analysis and flowed from fewer and smaller centers outward to the rest of society."[52] As E. A. Ross bluntly put it, "removing control farther away from the ordinary citizen and taxpayer is tantamount to giving the intelligent, farsighted, and public-spirited element in society a longer lever to work with."[53]

The triumph of Progressive structural reform would mean, in essence, that citizen involvement in public affairs was reduced from active, intense, face-to-face problem solving on a daily basis, to passively casting a lonely, solitary ballot once in a great while, for a handful of offices. ("Probably no voter should be called upon to vote for more than three men in a year, even as a maximum," suggested Richard Ely.)[54] That ballot would be aggregated with vast numbers of other solitary votes into a

mandate for an elite corps of professional experts, who would now conduct the real business of public life.

Clearly, this new reliance on rational, scientific principles and institutions to create a national community prompted serious doubts about religion, traditional morality, and their local civic manifestations, which
tended to be fragmenting, parochial, and divisive. E. A. Ross complained
that America had been peculiarly plagued by "thousands of local groups
sewed up in separatist dogmas and dead to most of the feelings which
thrill the rest of society." The remedy was the "widest possible diffusion
of secular knowledge" among the many, which "narrows the power of
the fanatic or the false prophet to gain a following," plus university training for the few, which "rears up a type of leader who will draw men together with unifying thoughts, instead of dividing them, as does the sect-
founder, with his private imaginings and personal notions."[55] James
Nuechterlein notes that the Progressives at the *New Republic* were particularly contemptuous of the Roman Catholic church, considering it "the
champion of obscurantism and the enemy of modern intellectual progress. It committed the great sin of 'looking for truths in the past' and
stood stubbornly 'against most effort to advance scientific knowledge.' "[56]

Indeed, many of the Progressives understood the new social sciences
and their seeming capacity to reorder society into a coherent and orderly
whole to be a secular evolution from or substitute for religion, a realiza-
tion of the Kingdom on Earth—to recall Croly's formulation, a "religion
of human brotherhood." Sociologist Albion Small considered his discipline "a science . . . of God's image," "the holiest sacrament open to
men," teaching that "we live, move and have our being as members one
of another" (rather than as children of "our heavenly Father," as taught
by discredited conventional Christianity).[57] John Bascom argued that "a
theology which seeks the regeneration of society in ignorance of social
laws is doomed to failure," while a government that grasped such laws
was "a surrogate for the churches and voluntary societies."[58] Progressives
generally shared Bascom's view that traditional, local civic institutions—as he put it, "rambling, halting voluntaryism"—based on traditional moral principles could only obstruct and delay the creation of a
new, sleek, streamlined, rational centralized order.[59]

Was it in fact true that, at the dawn of this century, a crisis on the order
of the Civil War had arrived in America because, as sociologist Robert
Park put it, "the old forms of social control represented by the family,
the neighborhood, and the local community [had] been undermined and
greatly diminished" by irresistible modern forces?[60] This is, of course, one
of the many precedents of today's claim of an unprecedented crisis of
community advanced by some contemporary scholars. Given the strong

links between the Progressive movement and the organization of the American historical profession, it is perhaps not surprising that today we should be left with the impression that the Progressive era was the *real* crisis of American community. Nonetheless, we are well armed against such claims by Bender's critique of the "crisis of community" industry in American scholarship, and so we should treat this interpretation of the era with considerable skepticism.

It is surely clear, however, that the Progressives seized on one of the periodic imbalances in the interplay between Federalist and Anti-Federalist impulses to advance a political order they considered a vast improvement over the old civil society's "rambling, halting voluntaryism." As Robert Nisbet argued, Progressivism's desire to create a national community through bureaucratization, rationalization, centralization, and the centripetal moral impulse of the national idea bespoke an active hostility to civil society's intermediate associations, which Progressives worked to destroy by shifting function and authority upward to the national state and its elite corps of experts. American civil society was not so much dead as in need of euthanasia, in the Progressives' view, to clear the way for a vastly superior order that overcame the tension between and brought harmoniously together the Anti-Federalist small-republican impulse with the Federalist large-republican impulse within the great national community.

The implications of the Progressive program for civil society and genuine self-government were not lost on prescient observers at the time. Presidential candidate Woodrow Wilson sounded the alarm: "What I fear . . . is a government of experts," he noted in his 1912 Labor Day address in Buffalo.

> God forbid that in a democratic country we should resign the task and give the government over to experts. What are we if we are to be [scientifically] taken care of by a small number of gentlemen who are the only men who understand the job? Because if we don't understand the job, then we are not a free people.[61]

Wilson's campaign for a decentralist alternative to an expert-led national community left us what Fred Siegel and Will Marshall describe as "liberalism's lost tradition."[62] Before his first term had ended, though, Wilson would himself succumb to the charms of the Progressive project and the "social possibilities of war." After a hiatus in the 1920s, this project would be brought to political power by Franklin D. Roosevelt's New Deal, and then pursued relentlessly throughout the rest of the century by a succession of powerful, energetic, progressive liberal presidents.

THE REIGN OF PROGRESSIVE COMMUNITY

Indeed, every great liberal president of the twentieth century following Wilson made the cultivation of the national community the central goal of his administration, expanding the power and reach of the national government and calling on Americans to put aside self-interest and local allegiances on behalf of the national idea (often invoking the moral equivalent of war). The explosion of government power during the New Deal, for instance, proceeded behind FDR's call in his first inaugural address for Americans to "move as a trained and loyal army willing to sacrifice for the good of a common discipline." We must be "ready and willing to submit our lives and property to such discipline," he insisted, and pledge that "larger purposes will bind upon us all as a sacred obligation with a unity of duty hitherto evoked only in times of armed strife."[63]

Samuel Beer notes that, for all the debate about the intentions and impact of the New Deal, nonetheless "in creating among Americans the expectation that the federal government could and should deal with the great economic questions and that the nation could and should bear the consequent burdens, the achievement of the New Deal was close to revolutionary." (Beer brings an insider's perspective: as a young speechwriter for FDR, he notes, "I vividly recall our preoccupation with persuading people to look to Washington for the solution of problems.")[64]

Within the Roosevelt administration, the most coherent expression of this centralizing tendency was the drive for national planning. (The drive's slogan, "We planned in war, why not in peace?" harked back to the glorious centralizing years of World War I.) Nurturing a sense of national oneness, as much as a return to prosperity, was the planners' highest ambition. As *New Republic* editor George Soule put it in the final sentences of his 1932 paean *A Planned Society*, "[I]nstead of being baffled and burdened by . . . social forces, we shall be at work, through society, mastering our life and creating it as a whole. We shall have a warm and active bond with our fellows."[65]

Roosevelt was quite lucid about his intention to bring to a national scale America's traditionally localized sense of civic community. To his neighbors at Hyde Park, he explained that the "drastic changes in the methods and forms of the functions of government" followed from the fact that "we have been extending to our national life the old principle of the local community." All Americans, he affirmed, must now think of themselves as neighbors: "The many are the neighbors. In a national sense, the many, the neighbors, are the people of the United States as a whole."[66] Roosevelt adviser Rexford Tugwell suggested that this homely metaphor captured perfectly the "general direction" of the New Deal, beneath its "multifarious and confusing" details: "It is a march renewed, as a nation, to landmarks which in our earlier pioneer neighborhoods stood always plain. Common neighborliness. Common decency. In a recent talk to his neighbors at Hyde Park, the President made that plain."[67]

Looking back almost wistfully from the early 1960s at the Depression years, Harry Girvetz noted that Americans had indeed been "imbued with a spirit of mutuality [and] a sense of common purpose" and had "discovered a sense of community and developed the kind of social conscience that produced the New Deal." So far had we tumbled from this sense of national community by the 1960s, however, that Girvetz would suggest "we need a moral equivalent to depression."[68]

Henry Luce and the editors of *Life* magazine shared Girvetz's alarm, and so in 1960 they asked a series of major public figures to propose ways to restore America's flagging sense of mission and togetherness. Published as a volume with the title *The National Purpose* (the subtitle—this is 1960—was "America in Crisis: An Urgent Summons"), the perspectives were typified by Clinton Rossiter's view that America must develop a "profound, inspiring, benevolent sense of mission." But, he continued:

> if we choose greatness . . . we choose effort—the kind of national effort that transcends the ordinary lives of men and commits them to the pursuit of a common purpose, that persuades them to sacrifice private indulgences to the public interest, that sends them on a search for leaders who call forth strengths rather than pander to weakness.[69]

As if responding to the call for such an inspiring, unifying leader, John F. Kennedy stepped forward and issued his stirring summons to America to put aside self-interest on behalf of national purpose: "Ask not what your country can do for you—ask what you can do for your country." Concrete accomplishments aside, Kennedy promised to make us feel as a nation that we were together, united, "moving again." "These are times that appeal to every citizen's sense of sacrifice and self-discipline," he announced during the campaign of 1960. "They call out to every citizen to weigh his rights and comforts against the common good." The presidency, according to Kennedy, "must be the center of moral leadership—a 'bully pulpit' . . . for only the President represents the national interest." He must be "willing and able to summon his national constituency to its finest hour . . . to demand of them the sacrifices that would be necessary."[70]

Liberalism's national community project reached its modern zenith, however, in Lyndon Johnson's Great Society (it would have been more accurately named the Great Community). Again, there was the familiar explosion of federal government activity, justified by an equally familiar rhetoric: "I see a day ahead with a united nation, divided neither by class nor by section nor by color, knowing no South or North, no East or West, but just one great America, free of malice and free of hate, and loving thy neighbor as thyself."[71] America, Johnson insisted, must "turn unity of interest into unity of purpose, and unity of goals into unity in the Great Society."[72]

At the heart of the Great Society, Johnson believed, was the presidency, whose task was to forge among the American people a sense of national community. "As I conceive it," he noted, "a President's first role and first responsibility is to help perfect the unity of the people."[73] It was "one of the great tasks of political leadership to make our people aware . . . that they share a fundamental unity of interest and purpose and belief."[74] Thus, he pledged his presidency to "[keeping] us pulling together, keeping our ranks closed, keeping us loving our brother and our fellow man."[75]

Johnson hoped to perfect American unity in part by launching an all-out war on poverty, calling citizens to a passionate, unified effort behind this great national crusade. "We will not win the war against poverty until the conscience of the entire nation is aroused," he insisted.[76] The effort to eradicate poverty would erect a "standard of service [that] will decrease the isolation of men from each other and will increase the deep feeling of community and concern that are the sinews of a large and great democracy's strength."[77] Naturally, the metaphor of a *war* on poverty was chosen quite deliberately: war "evokes cooperation [and a] sense of brotherhood and unity." The "military image" of the war on poverty would "rally the nation" and "sound a call to arms which will stir people . . . to lend their talents to a massive effort to eradicate the evil."[78]

Hidden beneath this summons to a passionate embrace of national community, however, another Great Society trend was running in a dramatically different direction. The "professionalization of reform," Daniel Patrick Moynihan noted in 1965, was quietly taking political initiative out of the uncertain hands of the public and passing it instead into "the hands of the administrators and the professional organizations of doctors, teachers, social workers, therapists, counselors and so forth." Because huge numbers of professionals "were involved in various aspects of social welfare and reform," he noted, "they would tend to have their way." Beyond that, though, "as professionals in a professionalizing society, they are increasingly *entitled* to have their way. That is how the system works." An elite corps of professionals organized into vast, gleaming bureaucracies would now run a burgeoning array of programs without undue interference from citizens or "clients" because "professionals *profess*. They profess to know better than others the nature of certain matters, and to know better than their clients what ails them or their affairs."

Unhappily, Moynihan conceded, the price of this professionalization was apt to be a "decline in the moral exhilaration of public affairs." (So much for "stirring the conscience of the nation" or creating a "deep feeling of community and concern.") Just when the civil rights movement had "at long last provided the youth of America with a moral equivalent of war," professionalization would mean "this kind of passion could seep out of the life of the nation."[79] But this was a small price to pay, in Moynihan's view, as we began to tackle social problems that seemed to require technical professional expertise more than moral exhilaration or popular passion.

The Progressive vision, of course, had always sought to conceal its icy reliance on apolitical, scientific expertise beneath the legitimating cloak of a fiery political summons to national community. But would Americans so readily acquiesce in leadership by experts were the cloak to begin to slip away? The Great Society would raise this question more forcefully than any other version of this century's progressive project. Had Moynihan been listening carefully to the era's rumblings among the "youth of America" and elsewhere, he might have been less sanguine about our willingness to acknowledge that professionals are "entitled to have their way" in public policy simply because they "profess to know better than others." Indeed, he might have been shocked at the "passion" this casual and self-serving assumption of the Great Society elites was about to provoke and introduce into the life of the nation.

Before we turn to the Great Society's difficulties, however, it might be useful to reflect for a moment on the progressive project's impact on the vitality of American civil society over the course of this century—that is, to return explicitly to the question of the relationship between state and civil society. About the adamant hostility of the progressive elites toward small, civic institutions and their "rambling, halting voluntaryism," there can be little doubt. While extolling the glories of the centralized, rationalized, secular national community, those elites have, for some eighty years, relentlessly hammered civic institutions for being notoriously and hopelessly backward, partial, parochial, reactionary, and riddled with irrational myths and prejudices. Such backwaters of reaction stubbornly cling to obscure and retrograde notions of traditional morality and religious faith, rather than bowing sensibly to the authority of scientifically credentialed professionals and experts, who alone can exploit the potential of modernity. It is no surprise that Progressivism should have worked steadily throughout this century to transfer authority and function away from civic institutions into the hands of bureaucratic, secular elites.

To be sure, a quick head count suggests that this century has seen no shortage of new civic associations. Theda Skocpol triumphantly points to this as proof—in the face of the unremitting hostility of the progressive elites—that state and civil society are perfectly compatible.[80] But a hasty look at *quantity* cannot begin to measure the dramatically diminished *quality* of civic association and membership over this century. Where once, as Nisbet put it, "the social problems of birth and death, courtship and marriage, employment and unemployment, infirmity and old age were met . . . through the associated means of these social groups," these tasks have today largely been transferred into the hands of centralized bureaucracies. Responding to this trend, many of our largest civic associations now seem designed chiefly to lobby for favors from those bureaucracies, maintaining "grassroots" membership lists chiefly to increase clout in Washington. Indeed, many civic groups have themselves become bureaucratic, secular, and expert-driven as they have evolved into state-funded "service delivery vehicles"—in the meantime, relegating citizens (now mere "volunteers," annoyingly underfoot) to trivial supportive and symbolic roles.[81]

Clearly, taking out a membership in *this* sort of civic association is a far cry from the immediate, everyday involvement in public affairs that civic groups once made possible. Occasionally signing a mass-produced form letter to a legislator or stuffing envelopes for a fund drive are radically diminished versions of the citizenship that once meant direct engagement in making and carrying out public decisions about the most significant human matters. Our progressive elites would have no problem with the new, "civic lite" associations. Humble petitions to the authorities and sentimental volunteerism pose no challenge to the "entitlement" of experts to run our affairs.

"Civic lite" is nicely illustrated by the PTA, which typifies, Skocpol accurately argues, many of the large civic associations launched earlier this century. Did the impulse for the PTA well up from parents and neighborhoods, demanding more say in the education of their children? Precisely the opposite: it was launched in 1897 by two inside-the-future-Beltway Progressives who were determined to bring the new, enlightened, expert-driven science of "child culture" to benighted parents. The PTA must always "begin its activities from the school as a center," Julian Butterworth noted in *The Parent-Teacher Association and Its Work* (1929), because "here the most progressive educational thinking in the community is apt to be taking place. Sooner or later the school is likely to expose the limitations of out-of-school experiences [read: reactionary parental influences]." Should parents even be allowed to make *suggestions* about running the schools? "The obvious danger . . . is that parents may go too far," Butterworth cautioned. "They may insist their point of view be adopted, when the professional officers with their greater insight may realize that it is neither feasible nor sound. . . . Decision concerning the suggestions is a technical job that should be left to the teachers and supervisors."[82]

In short, far from posing any challenge to the growing power of the progressive elites, the PTA and other such organizations were shrewdly organized by the elites themselves to project their expertise and authority into the remotest schoolhouse, town hall, and parlor. Indeed, properly structured and manipulated, "civic lite" associations could themselves be useful in eroding parochial loyalties and building up instead allegiance to the national community. Writing in the midst of the gloriously unifying days of World War I, Richard Ely observed that "our Councils of Defense, our Red Cross Societies and other patriotic organizations are a magnificent beginning of that cooperation which embraces the entire nation. . . . They are bringing us together and organizing America as a nation."[83] Once Ely and his friends have been permitted to tamper with and recalibrate the gauge of civic vitality, Skocpol should have no problem demonstrating the compatibility of state and civil society.

Given the manifest intentions of the progressive elites, it should not be surprising that their state has, over this century, posed a threat to genuine civic vitality far more formidable than the market. The market, after all, understands itself to be altogether different from and in tension with civic community. The progressive state, by contrast, claims to be able to perform civil society's critical community-building function *better than civil society itself,* and so feels entitled to absorb the authority and functions of its institutions. It promises to deliver a vastly superior version of community—no longer confined to contemptible ethnic and religious backwaters, but rather now spread over a grand, national stage, coherently coordinated by credentialed, social scientific professionals.

The problem with a vision that seeks to conceal the rule of a dispassionate, bureaucratic, scientific elite beneath a passionate summons to national community—all the while denigrating the traditional sources of community—would come to light in the course of the 1960s and 1970s.

THE DECLINE OF THE NATIONAL COMMUNITY IDEA

If a central theme runs through the diverse currents of dissatisfaction and unrest that marked the 1960s, it would have to be the loss of faith in the idea of national community that lay behind progressive liberalism, and a radical disenchantment with the elites whose rule it had once legitimated. As Theodore White noted in his account of the presidential election of 1968, the period was dominated by a "general sense of breakdown— breakdown of control of old instruments, . . . breakdown of leadership uncertain of its purposes and unclear in its language, breakdown, above all, of ideas and dreams that once made America a community."[84]

Instead—and in spite of six decades of progressive warfare against "parochial" civil institutions—there appeared once again a yearning for the intimate, face-to-face, participatory community to be found in small groups, family, neighborhood, church, and ethnic and voluntary association. The Anti-Federalist small-republican impulse apparently had not, after all, been subsumed into and satisfied by the Federalist state.

The New Left, for instance, insisted that the Great Society was, in spite of its claims, radically anticommunitarian, characterized by (in the Port Huron Statement's formulation) "loneliness, estrangement, [and] isolation."[85] This was inevitable in a society governed by what they now described as a massive, distant, alienating bureaucracy, linked closely with giant business concerns in that unholy alliance the New Left came to call "corporate liberalism." Federal social programs were not expressions of national community but rather cynical devices for "regulating the poor," as Francis Fox Piven and Richard Cloward put it.[86]

As an alternative, the New Left offered "participatory democracy." A society organized according to that principle would devolve major political and economic decision making to small, tightly knit local groups, within which people would "share in the social decisions determining the quality and direction of their lives."[87] Wini Breines observes of the New Left that "a basic if rarely articulated purpose of the movement was to create communities of equality, direct democracy and solidarity. In bold contrast to the values of competition, individualism, and efficiency, the movement yearned for and occasionally achieved the community it sought."[88] As Greg Calvert of the Students for a Democratic Society (SDS) put it, "while fighting to destroy the power of the loveless anti-community, we would ourselves create the community of love—the Beloved Community."[89]

The rejection of the national community and the impulse toward smaller, more intimate communities also characterized the Black Power movement of the 1960s and 1970s, and the subsequent flowering of similar movements centered on ethnic identity and community control that it inspired. According to Stokely Carmichael and Charles Hamilton in *Black Power*, blacks should begin to "recognize the need to assert their own definitions, to reclaim their history, their culture; to create their own sense of community and togetherness." Local social institutions such as the schools and police should not be run by white liberals downtown but by blacks in the neighborhood: "We must begin to think of the black community as a base of organization to control institutions in that community." With the celebration of black culture and morality in their own schools and other public places, a "growing sense of community" at the neighborhood level would be further encouraged.[90]

So powerful were these new doctrines that Senator Robert Kennedy seized on them for his electoral challenge to Johnson's Great Society. He

argued in *To Seek a Newer World* that the nation's slums could be transformed only through "new community institutions that local residents
control, and through which they can express their wishes." He called for
a "decentralization of some municipal functions and some aspects of government into smaller units, no matter what the race or economic status of
the governed." This would, he noted, move us "toward [Jefferson's] vision of participating democracy," an objective that had otherwise become
"increasingly difficult in the face of the giant organizations and massive
bureaucracies of the age."[91]

Perhaps the most politically potent expression of dissatisfaction with
the national community in the 1960s and 1970s, however, came from the
opposite end of the political spectrum—from lower-middle-class, blue-
collar neighborhoods, usually connected to the older industrial cities of
the North and East, usually heavily ethnic (of Southern and Eastern European origin), Democratic, and Catholic. As they saw it, the national government seemed to have launched a massive assault—through cold, bureaucratic edict or equally cold judicial fiat—against the traditional
prerogatives of locality and neighborhood to define and preserve their
own ways of life. Suddenly, they could neither pray in their local schools,
nor indeed count on sending their own children *to* the local school because of compulsory busing, nor ban from their community forms of expression or sexual conduct that they considered offensive, nor define the
conditions under which abortion might be proper, nor even enforce the
most rudimentary forms of civil order under the police power.

The most spectacular expression of this discontent came, of course,
from George Wallace, who insisted that people were "fed up with strut-
ting pseudo-intellectuals lording over them . . . telling them they have not
got sense enough to run their own schools and hospitals and domestic
institutions." Consequently, Wallace explained, there had been a "backlash against the theoreticians and bureaucrats in national government
who are trying to solve problems that ought to be solved at the local
level." His answer to this was "States' Rights and local government and
territorial democracy."[92]

Describing the deeper impulses behind the white ethnic revolt, Michael
Novak in *The Rise of the Unmeltable Ethnics* suggested that ethnics had historically been the primary victims of progressive liberalism's effort to
eradicate particularist allegiances on behalf of one vast homogenized, rationalized, bureaucratized national community. Now they had made a
dramatic and forceful "turn toward the organic networks of communal
life . . . family, ethnic groups, and voluntary associations in primary
groups."[93]

THE POLITICAL ECLIPSE OF NATIONAL COMMUNITY

Beneath the variety of intellectual currents of revolt during the 1960s lay this central truth: progressive liberalism's intention to eradicate "parochial" loyalties and allegiances on behalf of the great national community had failed miserably. That failure became ever more conspicuous during the 1970s and 1980s, when the nation's political landscape reshaped itself to accommodate this truth, along with the groups that had been roused to an angry political revolt over the assault on their "organic networks."

Indeed, after 1964, *no one* would again win the presidency by boasting about building a Great Society, a great national community, in America. *No one* would again call proudly and forthrightly for a shift of power to Washington and away from the local organic networks. Indeed, every president from 1968 to the present has placed at the center of his agenda the *denunciation* of centralized, bureaucratic government, along with promises to slash its size and power and to reinvigorate states, small communities, and civil society's intermediate associations.

Thus, President Richard Nixon complained that "a third of a century of centralizing power and responsibility in Washington has produced a bureaucratic monstrosity, cumbersome, unresponsive, ineffective." He proposed a New Federalism in which "power, funds, and responsibility will flow from Washington to the State and to the people," through block grants and revenue sharing.[94] During the presidential campaign of 1972—even after he had presided over four years of dramatically *expanding* government programs—Nixon would nonetheless insist that the "central question" of that election was "Do we want to turn more power over to bureaucrats in Washington . . ., or do we want to return more power to the people and to their State and local governments, so that people can decide what is best for themselves?"[95] Similarly, President Gerald Ford characterized his programs as an effort to "return power from the banks of the Potomac to the people in their communities."[96]

During this period, Republican presidential hegemony would be interrupted but once, by an "outsider" Democrat who insisted that the Republicans had, rhetoric notwithstanding, permitted the federal government to become too large and inefficient. What was needed, Jimmy Carter insisted, was an engineer's savvy to trim it down to size. Thus, his schemes for government reorganization, zero-based budgeting, and sunset provisions were aimed at proving government could "serve basic needs without proliferating wasteful, bloated bureaucracies." Cultivating his image as a man steeped in the moral and religious traditions of a small southern town, Carter promised a new emphasis on local community: "the only way we will ever put the government back in its place is to restore the families and neighborhoods to their proper places," because they can "succeed in solving problems where governments will always fail."[97] Neighborhood activist Father Geno Baroni was brought into the government to establish an agenda for the reinvigoration of local community.

Carter, of course, eventually drifted away from his pledge to reduce government and restore the prerogatives of families and neighborhoods. Faced by shrinking popularity, he resorted to what almost amounts to a self-caricature of liberalism's "moral equivalent" ploy. In his now infamous "malaise" speech, Carter declared, "We are the generation that will win the war on the energy problem and in that process rebuild the unity and confidence of America" (as if shivering in an underheated home, remembering to turn out the lights, or sitting in endless queues at gas stations would somehow restore our faith in the central government and sense of national oneness).[98]

Americans were not particularly pleased to be told that they suffered from "malaise," nor were they up for a "war" that simply masked yet another expansion of federal power, in this case the nationalization of energy supplies. Thus was Carter replaced by this century's most consistent and eloquent critic of federal power and spokesman for reinvigoration of local community. Ronald Reagan promised an end to the state of affairs in which "thousands of towns and neighborhoods have seen their peace disturbed by bureaucrats and social planners through busing, questionable education programs, and attacks on family unity." He called instead for "an end to giantism, for a return to the human scale . . . the scale of the local fraternal lodge, the church organization, the block club, the farm bureau," and he pursued it through budget reductions, block grants, a program of private sector initiatives, and a (new) New Federalism.[99] His successor George Bush, in turn, followed Reagan in explicitly rejecting liberalism's project of national community, proclaiming instead a vision of "a nation *of* communities, of thousands of ethnic, religious, social, business, labor union, neighborhood, regional, and other organizations, all of them varied, voluntary, and unique," which would stand as a "thousand points of light" in America's struggle to solve social problems.[100]

Republican ascendancy in the 1990s was terminated when President Bush not only failed to reduce government but actually acquiesced in its expansion through significant tax hikes. His victorious opponent—like Carter, draping himself in the traditional values of a small, southern town, albeit called Hope rather than Plains—swore that he had gotten the message about his party's traditional allegiance to big government.

Proclaiming himself a "New Democrat" by way of shorthand for this political epiphany, Bill Clinton pledged to end welfare as we know it, get tough on crime, and "reinvent" government. He raised questions about reliance on big government and suggested a return to "organic networks." As he noted, "our problems go way beyond the reach of government. They're rooted in the loss of values, in the disappearance of work and the breakdown of families and communities." Problems will be solved, he continued, only when "all of us are willing to join churches and other good citizens . . . who are saving kids, adopting schools, making streets safer."[101] After an early, politically disastrous feint to the left with a centralizing, bureaucratic plan for health care reform, Clinton won reelection when he remembered that "the world of today has moved away from big centralized bureaucracies and top-down solutions; so has your federal government."[102]

All of these quadrennial political promises to the contrary notwithstanding, of course, the power and authority of the federal bureaucratic apparatus continued to grow throughout these years. The point, however, is that such growth came increasingly to be treated as aberrant and illegitimate—the product of "uncontrollable entitlements," "gridlocked" government, "iron triangles," or bureaucratic inertia—even by the presidents under whom such growth continued. After 1968, they seldom affirmed in Lyndon Johnson's ringing tones the centrality of the federal government in American life, or suggested that its purpose was to pull us together into a cohesive, national community.

What explains an erosion of the idea of national community so severe that even the Democratic party itself now hesitates to speak up for it? In part, it must be noted, the moral momentum of national community is extremely difficult to sustain. The project strains to create artificially, at the level of the entire nation, a sense of mutuality and oneness that appears readily and naturally only at the level of the family or local civic community. This transfer may be possible in times of crisis, when the threat to the nation is sufficiently obvious that people do, indeed, feel obliged to pull together as one. The United States has experienced its share of such crises since the turn of the century—the Great Depression, World War II, the cold war—and liberalism has used them to maximum effect, to construct an ever more powerful central government. When real crises are not available, liberal presidents must turn instead to moral equivalents, reviving the language and symbolism associated with periods of national cohesion. A war on poverty, however (to say nothing of a "war on the energy problem"), is but a pallid substitute for the real thing. Today, with the end of a long and exhausting cold war, Americans seem distinctly unwilling to rally around the "national idea."

With the moral foundations of the liberal project thus eroding, its programmatic superstructure—a massive, centralized federal government—is left in a peculiarly exposed and precarious position. No longer understood to be the instrument of high national purpose, the federal government comes to be seen instead as a distant, alienating, bureaucratic monstrosity. To put it in the context of Moynihan's "professionalization of reform," once the aura of moral legitimacy lent by the spirit of national community has dropped away from the federal apparatus, citizens awaken to the fact that public life has been removed from their grasp and transferred into the hands of distant elites who presume they are "entitled to have their way" due to their professional expertise. Moynihan may have thought that the American people would quietly acquiesce in this arrangement, forgoing the "moral exhilaration of public affairs." But our politics since the 1960s has shown that, once the central logic of progressive liberalism is thus laid bare before us, we reject it resoundingly, and insist that public affairs be given back to us because *we*, not the experts, "know better."

Thus we arrive at the contemporary condition of public opinion captured so well in James Davison Hunter and Carl Bowman's exhaustive survey of American political culture, *The State of Disunion*. The American people, they find, are radically dissatisfied with their national institutions and governing elites, believing them to be "out of touch," "incompetent," "unconcerned with values and morality," "irreligious," and generally evidencing an "imperious disregard for the concerns of ordinary citizens."[103] (The elites, it should be noted, return the favor, being generally "dubious about, if not dismissive toward, traditional middle-class morality," uncomfortable with religion, and "most likely to reject bourgeois family life.")[104] Only the institutions closer to home—states, local communities, and churches—are held in high regard, Hunter and Bowman remark, and so there is strong public sentiment for shifting authority away from the national government, back to the localities. "Tocqueville observed that democracy works best when it is local," they conclude, and so "democratic processes and the institutions that sustain them also have greater legitimacy as they become local."[105]

The Anti-Federalists, of course, would not have been surprised by any of these developments. Once we had begun to experience the yearning genuinely to be in charge of our own affairs again, the small-republicans could have told us, naturally we would return to the idea of community that finds expression in small, participatory groups such as family, neighborhood, and ethnic and voluntary associations—in short, we would turn again to civil society. As the Anti-Federalists had insisted two centuries ago, genuine self-government and a communitarian sense of belonging and purpose are possible only within such small, tightly knit groups, not spread over a vast continent. Progressivism's attempt to use the Federalists' central government to re-create at the national level the Anti-Federalists' small republic, they could have told us, was destined to fail.

The final assessment of the relationship between state and civil society will not, of course, be rendered by theorists speculating about their philosophical compatibility or by social scientists tallying the number of civic organizations with headquarters in Washington. That assessment will be made by the American people themselves, reacting to the specific form the relationship has tangibly taken within the political practice of this century. Given the political trends of the past thirty years and down to the present, the assessment seems to be in—and it is not favorable to the state. The progressive state has not, apparently, delivered on its promise to create a form of community superior to those contemptible backwaters of reaction, local civic institutions. To secure genuine community and self-government, evidently we still need civil society.

THE FUTURE OF CIVIL SOCIETY

As we consider the prospects for civil society's future, it is easy to share the pessimism so widespread among social and political commentators today. For the first sixty years of this century, the progressive project sought with some success to delegitimate our civic institutions and transfer their functions upward to centralized, credentialed bureaucracies. Those they did not destroy, they corrupted, seducing many of them into taking on the centralized, rationalistic, bureaucratic trappings of corporations and governments.

Over the succeeding thirty years, the American people have evinced a strong desire to reverse this process and bring authority back to the civic institutions closest to home. Nonetheless, most of the governing authority remains in the hands of the central institutions that, as Hunter and Bowman suggest, enjoy the least legitimacy, while the far more legitimate local civic institutions remain dramatically less powerful. For thirty years, our national political leadership has acknowledged this problem and promised to do something about it. But so far, and with some notable exceptions, very little by way of actual return of governing authority to civic institutions has in fact been accomplished.

Whenever these sorts of reflections lead me to the brink of despair, I recall some of the extraordinary individuals with whom I have had the privilege to work in Milwaukee's inner-city neighborhoods: Bill Lock, who turned a shuttered factory given to his church into a thriving small business incubator; Gerald Saffold, who brings former gang members and drug addicts into his "Unity in the Community" Choir, filling an abandoned VFW hall with gospel music; Brother Bob Smith, whose Messmer High School imparts both character and competence to inner-city teens; Cordelia Taylor, who established a community-based elder care facility in her former home and is now turning the entire block into a senior village; Deborah Darden, who helps AFDC mothers in a public housing project restore a strong spiritual atmosphere for their children.

While scholars and experts in well-appointed conference rooms fret and tussle over the fate of civil society, these Milwaukeeans are actually *rebuilding* civil society—and under circumstances the experts would say are absolutely prohibitive. Major businesses have long since left their neighborhoods; they have watched government programs come and go without leaving a trace; and they are still waiting for their invitation to join the latest coalition or collaboration or alliance formed by the big, downtown nonprofits. Yet in the midst of what we might see as desolation—long after all the experts have thrown up their hands and fled—these grassroots leaders are rebuilding strong families, vigorous neighborhoods, and powerful churches and voluntary associations.

Here, under the least hospitable circumstances imaginable, civil society is being reborn, one block, one neighborhood at a time. Tocqueville would have had no problem recognizing the common ingredient of success running through these diverse efforts: each is designed to turn passive clients or victims into genuine citizens, through a rigorous call to personal responsibility, self-discipline, civic-mindedness, and faith. The Anti-Federalists would have acknowledged that these are precisely the sorts of small, faith-based, virtue-cultivating civic communities that are essential to the survival of democracy, and that they had worked so hard to protect. Robert Nisbet would have seen that, far from being pleasant little voluntary societies gathered "merely to be together," these groups are literally saving lives and souls on a daily basis, and so are squarely in the old tradition of civic associations engaging themselves with the most urgent problems of human life. Finally, Robert Woodson would remind us that these remarkable undertakings in Milwaukee are by no means isolated instances but can be found in various forms throughout the inner-city neighborhoods of this nation—wherever citizens have given up on the hollow promises of the progressive state and have turned instead to the untapped resources of their own neighborhoods.[106]

When the problem of civic revival seems hopelessly abstract or complicated or daunting, perhaps the place to start is with this simple question: What can we do to help these grassroots initiatives flourish and spread? For their leaders are the *true* experts on civil society. They are civic trauma specialists, able to breathe life back into civic institutions that had long since been left for dead.

Here, an agenda readily presents itself. Much of it has to do with removing the obstacles thrown up against such upstart local challenges by the jealous bureaucracies left behind by the failed progressive project. We can dismantle the credentialing regimes that serve chiefly to protect the prerogatives of those who "profess to know better"; strike down laws and regulations that impede start-up businesses, schools, and community initiatives; and lower the barriers against the involvement of faith-based organizations in meeting human needs. Beyond that, we can connect such groups to sources of finance through broader organizations such as community development corporations and help them rebuild order and security in the neighborhood through community-oriented policing. We can begin to convert public assistance to vouchers, so that citizens may escape the hulking prisons of the educational and social bureaucracies and instead engage themselves with their own community institutions, which still cultivate the competence and character they know to be the paths out of poverty.

Around this sort of decentralist, community-building agenda, it might be possible to rally significant elements of both conservatism and liberalism. Among conservatives, for instance, the "mediating structures" approach has grown considerably in influence since its humble beginnings at AEI. As Peggy Noonan cast about for ideas for George Bush's acceptance speech in 1988, for instance, she happened upon an account of the "mediating structures" concept, and concluded, "it was all there, I read and thought, This is Bush; this is what he means." Prosaic "mediating structures" was soon transmuted into a poetic presidential vision of a "nation of communities," composed of a "thousand points of light."[107]

More important, though, is the substantial clout brought to the concept today by the growing influence of the so-called "religious right." While their pronouncements are invariably misunderstood to mean that they wish to establish a rigorously Christian version of the national community—and while they are occasionally prone to utterances that fuel this misunderstanding—in fact they wish only to defend their small, local, virtuous "republics" against progressivism's corrosive secular ethos and its aggressive national agents. Their ongoing insurgency brings enormous political heft to the small-republican impulse within conservative circles.

The small-republican conservatives will have to contend internally, of course, with the perennial skepticism of the libertarians. When *National Review* editor Frank Meyer first encountered Nisbet's defense of intermediate associations, he wondered why we would want to exchange the "all-powerful totalitarian state" for the "subtler, quieter tyranny of 'customarily' imposed community."[108] Echoing this view, David Brooks at the *Weekly Standard* professes to be "taken aback" by conservative enthusiasm for "orderly, coherent, authoritative moral communities."[109] All of which is simply to say that within the conservative camp will be played out once again the old tension between the Federalist impulse toward commerce, individualism, and secularism and the Anti-Federalist impulse toward community, civic virtue, and faith.

The truly heartening news is that within contemporary liberalism, there is a growing skepticism of the progressive project of national community and a turn toward the "organic networks of community life" that Novak had once hoped might become the foundation for a revitalized left. Michael Sandel acknowledges that the "nationalizing project that unfolded from the Progressive Era to the New Deal to the Great Society" has become "politically vulnerable because it does not rest on a sense of national community adequate to its purpose." In the future, he continues, "a more promising basis for a democratic politics . . . is a revitalized civic life nourished in the more particular communities we inhabit."[110] Harking back to Woodrow Wilson's "lost liberal tradition" of decentralization, a small but influential group of communitarians and "New Democrats" now pledges to work to "revitalize economic self-reliance and self-government by returning power from large institutions to people . . . and from the national government to more accessible and accountable institutions, whether they be local government agencies or community organizations."[111]

Their version of the Anti-Federalist impulse will have to contend internally with the towering, bureaucratic empires of "service providers" left behind by the old progressive project, which still retain enormous power even as they have lost legitimacy after the decline of the idea of national community. (They simply refuse to believe that the American people will not someday rally again to the "one big idea" that, Mario Cuomo maintains, is "the heart of the matter"—that "this nation is at its best only when we see ourselves, all of us, as one family.")[112] All of which is to say that within the liberal camp will be played out a relatively new tension between Roosevelt's statist doctrine of centralized, bureaucratic national community and Wilson's preference for decentralized, localist community.

As should be evident, these political developments leave room for some very interesting new alignments, as increasingly influential elements of both left and right now acknowledge the urgent need to protect the middle range of human existence against the tendency of our politics to gravitate either upward to the state or downward to the individual. Within that middle range, Bill Lock, Cordelia Taylor, Brother Bob Smith, and thousands of other grassroots leaders around the country are working every day to re-create civil society—not because they are sentimental and kind-hearted volunteers, but because they know that unless they heed God's call to them, lives and souls will be lost, and revitalized civic institutions are the only tools they have found that make a difference. If we can look beyond old alliances and antagonisms and keep ourselves focused on supplying the civic trauma specialists with the material, political, and spiritual support they need, then the prospects for the future of American civil society will indeed be bright.

NOTES

1. Robert A. Nisbet, *The Quest for Community* (Oxford: Oxford University Press, 1971).

2. Peter Berger and Richard John Neuhaus, *To Empower People: The Role of Mediating Structures in Public Policy* (Washington, D.C.: American Enterprise Institute, 1977).

3. Michael Novak, *The Rise of the Unmeltable Ethnics: Politics and Culture in the Seventies* (New York: Macmillan, 1972), 273.

4. Senator Bill Bradley, "America's Challenge: Revitalizing our National Community," Address to the National Press Club, 9 February 1995, 2.

5. Robert D. Putnam, "Bowling Alone: America's Declining Social Capital," *Journal of Democracy* 6 (January 1995): 65–78.

6. Nisbet, *The Quest for Community*, 238.

7. Nisbet, *The Quest for Community*, 241.

8. Nisbet, *The Quest for Community*, 245.

9. Nisbet, *The Quest for Community*, 245.

10. This account of the political theory of the Federalists is drawn from the teachings of Martin Diamond. See especially Martin Diamond, *As Far as Republican Principles Will Admit*, ed. William A. Schambra (Washington, D.C.: American Enterprise Institute, 1992).

11. Alexander Hamilton, James Madison, and John Jay, *The Federalist Papers*, ed. Jacob E. Cooke (Cleveland: World, 1961), 56–65.

12. Hamilton et al., *The Federalist Papers*, 73.

13. Herbert Storing, *What the Anti-Federalists Were For* (Chicago: University of Chicago Press, 1981), 3. This account of the political theory of the Anti-Federalists relies heavily on Storing's teachings. An earlier version of this synthesis of Federalist and Anti-Federalist thought may be found in William A. Schambra, "The Roots of the American Public Philosophy," *Public Interest* 67 (1982): 36–48.

14. Baron de Montesquieu, *The Spirit of the Laws*, trans. Thomas Nugent (New York: Hafner, 1949), 34.

15. Charles Turner, quoted in Storing, *What the Anti-Federalists Were For*, 23.

16. Turner, quoted in Storing, *What the Anti-Federalists Were For*, 21.

17. Quoted in Storing, *What the Anti-Federalists Were For*, 22.

18. Alexis de Tocqueville, *Democracy in America*, trans. George Lawrence (Garden City, N.J.: Doubleday, 1969), 118.

19. Tocqueville, *Democracy in America*, 157.

20. Tocqueville, *Democracy in America*, 161.

21. Tocqueville, *Democracy in America*, 413.

22. Tocqueville, *Democracy in America*, 671.

23. Tocqueville, *Democracy in America*, 533.

24. Tocqueville, *Democracy in America*, 511.

25. Nisbet, *The Quest for Community*, 54.

26. Nisbet, *The Quest for Community*, 287.

27. Nisbet, *The Quest for Community*, 668–74.

28. Thomas Bender, *Community and Social Change in America* (Baltimore: Johns Hopkins University Press, 1978), 51.

29. Bender, *Community and Social Change*, 46.

30. Bender, *Community and Social Change*, 145.

31. Bender, *Community and Social Change*, 148.

32. Nisbet, *The Quest for Community*, vii.

33. Walter Lippmann, *Drift and Mastery* (Upper Saddle River, N.J.: Prentice Hall, 1961), 81.

34. Herbert Croly, *The Promise of American Life* (Cambridge, Mass.: Harvard University Press, 1965), 61–62.

35. Croly, *The Promise of American Life*, 372.

36. Croly, *The Promise of American Life*, 209.

37. Quoted in Jean B. Quandt, *From the Small Town to the Great Community: The Social Thought of Progressive Intellectuals* (New Brunswick, N.J.: Rutgers University Press, 1970), 139. Quandt's book is an underappreciated resource for understanding the role of the idea of community, and especially of the "great community," in the thought of the Progressives.

38. Croly, *The Promise of American Life*, 23.

39. Croly, *The Promise of American Life*, 418.

40. Croly, *The Promise of American Life*, 406.

41. Croly, *The Promise of American Life*, 453.

42. Woodrow Wilson, *Constitutional Government* (New York: Columbia University Press, 1908), 68.

43. Woodrow Wilson, *Papers*, ed. Arthur S. Link (Princeton, N.J.: Princeton University Press, 1978), XIX: 42.

44. John Dewey, *Character and Events: Popular Essays in Social and Political Philosophy*, ed. Joseph Ratner (New York: Holt, 1929), II: 551.

45. Walter Lippmann, "Integrated America," *New Republic*, 19 February 1916, 62, 64.

46. Richard T. Ely, *The World War and Leadership in a Democracy* (New York: Macmillan, 1918), 151.

47. Dewey, *Character and Events*, 552–53.

48. Timothy Kaufman-Osborn, "John Dewey and the Liberal Science of Community," *Journal of Politics* 46 (1984): 1157.

49. Kaufman-Osborn, "John Dewey and the Liberal Science of Community," 1158.

50. Quoted in Samuel Haber, *Efficiency and Uplift: Scientific Management in the Progressive Era, 1890–1920* (Chicago: University of Chicago Press, 1964).

51. Samuel P. Hays, "The Politics of Reform in Municipal Government in the Progressive Era," *Pacific Northwest Quarterly* 55 (October 1964): 161.

52. Hays, "The Politics of Reform," 169.

53. Edward Alsworth Ross, *Principles of Sociology* (New York: Century, 1920), 268.

54. Ely, *The World War and Leadership in a Democracy*, 94–95.

55. Ross, *Principles of Sociology*, 422.

56. James Nuechterlein, "The Dream of Scientific Liberalism: The *New Republic* and American Progressive Thought, 1914–1920," *Review of Politics* 42 (April 1980): 175.

57. Albion Small, *The Meaning of Social Science* (Chicago: University of Chicago Press, 1910), 277, 295.

58. Quoted in J. David Hoeveler, Jr., "The University and the Social Gospel: The Intellectual Origins of the 'Wisconsin Idea,' " *Wisconsin Magazine of History* 59 (Summer 1976): 288, 289.

59. Hoeveler, Jr., "The University and the Social Gospel," 292.

60. Robert E. Park and Ernest W. Burgess, *The City* (Chicago: University of Chicago Press, 1967), 107.

61. Woodrow Wilson, *A Crossroads of Freedom: The 1912 Campaign Speeches* (New Haven, Conn.: Yale University Press, 1956), 83.

62. Fred Siegel and Will Marshall, "Liberalism's Lost Tradition," *New Democrat* (September/October 1995): 8–13.

63. Franklin D. Roosevelt, *The Public Papers and Addresses of Franklin D. Roosevelt*, ed. Samuel I. Rosenman, 13 vols. (New York: Random House, 1938–1950), 2, 14. Perhaps the best account of the Roosevelt administration's reliance on the war metaphor to mobilize the population is to be found in William E. Leuchtenburg, "The New Deal and the Analogue of War," in *Change and Continuity in Twentieth-Century America*, ed. John Braeman, Robert Bremner, and Evert Walters (Columbus: Ohio University Press, 1964), 81–143.

64. Samuel Beer, "In Search of a New Public Philosophy," in *The New American Political System*, ed. Anthony King (Washington, D.C.: American Enterprise Institute, 1978), 8. Perhaps because of his personal involvement in crafting the New Deal's rhetoric, Professor Beer is by far the most thoughtful analyst of its community-building aspects, which, as he notes, found their initial expression in the earlier writings of Herbert Croly. See especially "Liberalism and the National Idea," in *Left, Right and Center*, ed. Robert A. Goldwin (Chicago: Rand-McNally, 1967), and "The Idea of the Nation," *New Republic*, 19 and 26 April 1982, 23–29.

65. George Soule, *A Planned Society* (New York: Macmillan, 1932), 283.

66. Roosevelt, *The Public Papers and Addresses*, II: 342.

67. Rexford Tugwell, *The Battle for Democracy* (New York: Columbia University Press, 1935), 72. Theda Skocpol concedes that the New Deal was characterized by at least a stab at the rhetoric of national community, when it called for action "in the name of values of neighborliness that would bring the whole nation together in response to the emergency." She concludes, however, that such rhetoric was half-hearted and quickly abandoned, and ultimately condemns the New Deal for failing "to legitimate new national welfare programs in communal terms" or to "offer a sustained vision of new state actions as expressions of *public* interests and the well-being of the national *community*" (emphasis hers). She also insists that such failures should not stop modern liberals from pushing for an "*expansion* of community, regional, and national planning and . . . an explicit legitimation for a *broader*, rather than narrower, public sphere in U.S. capitalism and American society" (emphasis hers). Writing in the early 1980s, she does not provide any clue about how such an expansion of government planning in the name of national community might fit in with a vigorous civil society. Theda Skocpol, "Legacies of New Deal Liberalism," *Dissent* (Winter 1983): 37, 38, 39, 42, 43.

68. Harry K. Girvetz, *The Evolution of Liberalism* (New York: Collier, 1963), 330–31.

69. In *The National Purpose*, ed. Henry R. Luce (New York: Holt, Rinehart, & Winston, 1960), 82.

70. John F. Kennedy, Speech to the National Press Club, January 1960.

71. *Public Papers of the Presidents of the United States: Lyndon B. Johnson, 1963–1964* (Washington, D.C.: Government Printing Office, 1965), 1371.

72. *Public Papers of the Presidents of the United States*, 797.

73. *Public Papers of the Presidents of the United States*, 943.

74. *Public Papers of the Presidents of the United States*, 729.

75. *Public Papers of the Presidents of the United States*, 450.

76. *Public Papers of the Presidents of the United States*, 628.

77. *Public Papers of the Presidents of the United States: Lyndon B. Johnson, 1966*, 435.

78. Lyndon B. Johnson, *The Vantage Point* (New York: Popular Library, 1971), 74.

79. Daniel P. Moynihan, "The Professionalization of Reform," *Public Interest* 1 (Fall 1965): 6–16.

80. Theda Skocpol, "The Tocqueville Problem: Civic Engagement in American Democracy," Presidential Address to the Annual Meeting of the Social Science History Association, New Orleans, 12 October 1996, unpublished manuscript.

81. See John McKnight, *The Careless Society: Community and Its Counterfeits* (New York: Basic Books, 1995).

82. Julian P. Butterworth, *The Parent-Teacher Association and Its Work* (New York: Macmillan, 1929), 48–49, 61–62.

83. Ely, *The World War and Leadership in a Democracy*, 106–7.

84. Theodore H. White, *The Making of the President 1968* (New York: Pocket Books, 1968), 518.

85. "Selections from the Port Huron Statement," in *How Democratic Is America? Responses to the New Left Challenge*, ed. Robert A. Goldwin (Chicago: Rand McNally, 1971), 6.

86. Frances Fox Piven and Richard A. Cloward, *Regulating the Poor* (New York: Pantheon Books, 1971).

87. *How Democratic Is America?* ed. Goldwin, 7.

88. Wini Breines, *Community and Organization in the New Left, 1962–1969: The Great Refusal* (New York: Praeger, 1982), 27.

89. Quoted in Breines, *Community and Organization in the New Left*, 48.

90. Stokely Carmichael and Charles V. Hamilton, *Black Power: The Politics of Liberation in America* (New York: Vintage Books, 1967), 53, 37, 39.

91. Robert F. Kennedy, *To Seek a Newer World* (New York: Bantam Books, 1968), 53, 54, 58. For an illuminating discussion of Senator Kennedy's largely unremarked Jeffersonianism, see Michael J. Sandel, "The Politics of Community: Robert F. Kennedy versus Ronald Reagan," *Responsive Community* 6 (Spring 1996): 14–27. Sandel quotes Kennedy's observations to a rural Minnesota audience: "Bigness, loss of community, organizations, and society grown far past the human scale—these are the besetting sins of the twentieth century, which threaten to paralyze our capacity to act."

92. Quoted in John J. Synon, *George Wallace: Profile of a Presidential Candidate* (Kilmarnock, Va.: Ms, Inc., n.d.), 59, 77, 83.

93. Novak, *The Rise of the Unmeltable Ethnics*, 321.

94. *Public Papers of the Presidents of the United States: Richard Nixon, 1969* (Washington, D.C.: Government Printing Office, 1970), 637–38.

95. *Public Papers of the Presidents of the United States: Richard Nixon, 1972,* 997.

96. Quoted in Henry J. Schmandt et al., "CDBG: Continuity or Change?" *Publius* (Summer 1983): 7.

97. *The Presidential Campaign 1976,* 2 vols. (Washington, D.C.: Government Printing Office, 1978), I: 708–9, 714.

98. *Public Papers of the Presidents of the United States: Jimmy Carter, 1979* (Washington, D.C.: Government Printing Office, 1980), 1238.

99. Ronald Reagan, "Let the People Rule," Speech to the Executive Club of Chicago, 26 September 1975, manuscript.

100. Quoted in Peggy Noonan, *What I Saw at the Revolution* (New York: Random House, 1990), 311.

101. Bill Clinton, 1994 State of the Union Address. Alan Brinkley would observe of Clinton's speech that he was "trying to reclaim from the right a moral language that liberals have—in recent years, at least—largely abdicated. He was continuing the effort . . . to rescue liberalism from the symbolically barren, socially fragmented world it has inhabited for a generation, and to link it to a popular yearning for values and community." Brinkley, "At Last, Maybe a Vision," *New York Times,* 27 January 1994, 21.

102. Bill Clinton, "Commencement Address at Penn State University," 10 May 1996.

103. James Davison Hunter and Carl Bowman, *The State of Disunion: 1996 Survey of American Political Culture, Summary Report* (Ivy, Va.: In Medias Res Educational Foundation, 1996), 25–28.

104. Hunter and Bowman, *The State of Disunion,* 47–48.

105. Hunter and Bowman, *The State of Disunion,* 22.

106. Robert L. Woodson, *The Triumphs of Joseph: How Today's Community Healers Are Reviving Our Streets and Neighborhoods* (New York: Free Press, 1998).

107. Noonan, *What I Saw at the Revolution,* 311–12.

108. Frank S. Meyer, *In Defense of Freedom: A Conservative Credo* (Chicago: Regnery, 1962), 141.

109. David Brooks, "'Civil Society' and Its Discontents," *Weekly Standard,* 5 February 1996, 18.

110. Michael J. Sandel, "America's Search for a New Public Philosophy," *Atlantic Monthly* 277 (March 1996): 74.

111. "The New Progressive Declaration," in *Building the Bridge: 10 Big Ideas to Transform America,* ed. Will Marshall (Lanham, Md.: Rowman & Littlefield, 1997), 23–24.

111. Mario Cuomo, Address to the Democratic National Convention, 28 August 1996 (www.dnc96.org/day2/draft08.html). For other contemporary arguments on behalf of the national community idea, see especially Alan Brinkley's contributions to Alan Brinkley, Nelson W. Polsby, and Kathleen M. Sullivan, *New Federalist Papers* (New York: Norton, 1997). Brinkley urges us to remember that, in addition to the Tocquevillean tradition of local community, there is "also a larger vision of community that . . . transcends localism and parochialism. . . . The idea of national

community is, in fact among the oldest and most powerful in our history" (95). Similarly, Nicholas Lemann suggests that America's racial divisions will not be healed without a return to that "larger vision": "It is during the times when there has been a strong sense of *national* community that [racial] problems have been addressed. . . . The ghettos, and race relations in general, are the one area in American domestic life where . . . the vocabulary of crisis and national responsibility is not in the least trumped up." Nicholas Lemann, *The Promised Land* (New York: Knopf, 1991), 352–53.

5

Civic Infrastructure in America

The Interrelationship between Government and the Voluntary Sector

Steven Rathgeb Smith

For those who worry about the condition of America's civil society, the fate of membership organizations that depend on local volunteers is a matter of particular concern. Robert Putnam has reported that over the past few decades, the growth of the nonprofit sector has not been primarily in traditional membership groups such as the Elks or the PTA. Instead, growth has been concentrated in advocacy and service provider organizations linked to the state.[1] Some critics charge that this trend has led to a deterioration of voluntarism and civic engagement. Many nonprofits, these critics say, never become an integral part of their communities. Instead of assisting and empowering ordinary citizens, they concentrate power and resources in the hands of paid staff and "credentialed elites." And as a result, the indictment concludes, these groups have been sadly ineffective in resolving social problems, especially those connected with urban poverty.[2]

In this chapter, I examine the changing character of nonprofits in the postwar period, with a special emphasis on service providers. I consider why the government has encouraged the formation and expansion of these groups, and whether they have indeed supplanted networks and organizations that rely on direct volunteer involvement. I also ask how reductions in state support are affecting nonprofits and the communities they serve.

More generally, this chapter addresses the civic infrastructure of local community as it relates to the provision of social welfare and health services. Although *civic infrastructure* is subject to different definitions, I will use the term to refer to the network of public and voluntary associations in a community and their capacity to address social problems. The rise of nonprofit service agencies in the postwar period, funded extensively by government, altered the civic infrastructure. More recent shifts in federal policy, including welfare reform and devolution, raise new questions about local civic infrastructure in the United States.

THE DATA

This chapter is based on research on two types of community organizations. The first type consists of nonprofit service providers, often funded by government through contracts or grants. These agencies include AIDS service organizations, soup kitchens, community development corporations (CDCs), homeless shelters, day care centers, and child welfare agencies. Usually these providers are incorporated as 501(c)(3) tax-exempt organizations, allowing individuals to receive a tax deduction for cash and in-kind contributions. Data on these organizations have been obtained from several sources, including historical data on trends in government social and health expenditures, case studies of nonprofit service providers, and archival data from government and nonprofits.

The second type of organization is represented by community partnerships and coalitions—a mixed organizational form with many different varieties. Some partnerships are created through a formal contractual agreement between government and nonprofit organizations. Other partnerships are complicated arrangements involving the public, nonprofit, and for-profit sectors. For example, many school systems have affiliated foundations that raise money from corporations and individuals.

The partnerships most responsive to present concerns about fostering voluntarism are those that depend primarily on volunteers rather than paid staff. These partnerships have proliferated rapidly in recent years as a strategy to create a more efficient, coordinated response to public policy issues, including economic development, maternal and child health, teenage pregnancy, and drug and alcohol abuse. Good examples of these initiatives are the Atlanta Project, started by former president Jimmy Carter to revitalize Atlanta; empowerment zones funded by the federal government, local businesses, and private foundations to rebuild distressed communities; and the Fighting Back program, an alcohol and drug abuse prevention program in fourteen cities, funded by the Robert Wood Johnson Foundation.

My research in this area is based on an ongoing analysis of community partnerships designed to prevent crime and substance abuse. I have conducted in-depth case studies of more than forty partnerships and coalitions. In addition, I have interviewed relevant government and nonprofit personnel involved with partnership programs around the country.

In the next section, I examine the changing character of nonprofit associations in the postwar period; a subsequent section describes the more recent emergence of community partnerships and coalitions as a favored strategy to address social ills. I conclude with a discussion of the implications of the trends in voluntarism and nonprofit associations for public policy toward the voluntary sector.

THE POSTWAR TRANSFORMATION OF THE NONPROFIT SECTOR: THE CHANGING AMERICAN WELFARE STATE

Prior to the 1940s, some nonprofit service agencies in the United States received cash or in-kind assistance from government. This aid tended to be small-scale, with little government oversight or monitoring. Many service providers were opposed to accepting government funds, viewing their mission as private and separate from government.

World War II altered the government-nonprofit relationship. The federal government became less reluctant to fund nonprofit organizations, and in turn, these organizations became less resistant to the idea of accepting public money. In response to the imperatives of the war, federal funding of defense-related research at large nonprofit research universities rose sharply. After the war, government support for defense- and energy-related research continued to rise.[3] Diversification also occurred: in the late 1940s and 1950s, the federal government inaugurated several new grant programs in education, mental health, developmental disabilities, public health, and child welfare.

Federal support for nonprofit organizations was provided in several ways other than direct grants. For example, the GI Bill offered financial assistance to individuals, spurring greater access to and demand for higher education. Other federal initiatives helped nonprofit organizations with their capital needs. The federal Hill-Burton Act of 1946, for example, provided hundreds of millions of dollars to nonprofit (and public) health organizations for renovation and new construction. Federal grant-in-aid programs to the states offered funding for efforts to improve regulations and standards for health and welfare services. The federal government also offered direct technical assistance to nonprofit organizations and state and local governments to reform and upgrade their programs.[4]

At least initially, the change in nonprofit revenues and programming was not particularly dramatic: during the 1950s, most nonprofit health, educational, and welfare organizations remained dependent on fees, endowment income, and donations.[5] Fee income was especially important as a revenue source: universities depended on tuition; social welfare agencies relied on client fees; and hospitals depended primarily on a mix of private insurance payments and income from patients. The importance of donations as a source of support varied tremendously from one organization to the next. Social welfare agencies often received small cash and in-kind donations from individuals and funds from the United Way—or the Community Chest, as it was known in the 1950s. But the Community Chest typically supported the established community agencies such as the American Red Cross, the Boy Scouts and Girl Scouts, the YMCA, and family service agencies. These agencies were founded in the nineteenth century or the early part of the twentieth century; few agencies founded in the postwar period, such as community programs for the developmentally disabled, received Community Chest funds.

The universe of service agencies was still relatively small by today's standards, and even long-standing nonprofit agencies had meager budgets—often less than $50,000 for agencies founded in the nineteenth century. Most nonprofit service agencies continued to see themselves as separate from the public sector. Except for selected child welfare agencies and service agencies in some urban areas such as New York City, nonprofit agencies served few publicly funded clients. They played a niche or residual role in the service system, providing counseling for families and children, recreational programs for youth and adults, transitional shelter, and emergency assistance. Individuals needing intensive or long-term assistance were usually served by public agencies: state hospitals and schools for the mentally ill and developmentally disabled; training schools for juvenile delinquents. Cash assistance for the poor was provided by county welfare departments, and public housing by state and local housing authorities. With respect to health care, the situation was more variable. But many regions of the country, notably the South and West, had networks of public hospitals serving the poor and the working classes. Elsewhere, nonprofit community hospitals predominated.

In short, a community's response to social need involved a sizable effort from the public sector and a specialized response by nonprofit service agencies. The public sector served the poor and disadvantaged and prevented the nonprofit sector from being overwhelmed with demand for its services. The capacity of nonprofits to sustain their operations without significant public funding depended on the willingness of the public sector to shoulder the responsibility for the poor, albeit inadequately in many areas.

The War on Poverty and Beyond

This public and private mix of service faced growing criticism in the late 1950s and early 1960s. Researchers charged that state hospitals and state schools were dehumanizing institutions that deprived the residents of their basic human rights,[6] and that nonprofit service agencies neglected the poor and minorities in favor of the middle class and the wealthy.[7] A number of studies suggested that the civic infrastructure of local communities (i.e., the combined efforts of public agencies, nonprofit service agencies, and individual citizen volunteers) was hampered in its response to social need by scarce resources, untrained staff, and political opposition from local leaders.

These studies, combined with additional research from national foundations and the federal government, created a political climate conducive to the major buildup of the federal social role in the 1960s and 1970s. For the most part, the War on Poverty and other new federal health and social welfare initiatives were implemented through new and existing nonprofit service providers at the grass roots. Programs as diverse as Head Start, community mental health centers, and programs for at-risk youth were primarily nonprofit programs funded by the federal government, either directly or through grants and contracts administered by state and local governments. Federal regulations and the new funds also provided incentives for state and local governments to increase their contracting with nonprofit social and health organizations. Although some contracting was with existing organizations, many new contracts were with entirely new nonprofit organizations created either by government officials or by local advocates in response to the availability of government funds.

Federal funding stimulated the growth of nonprofit service agencies and related advocacy organizations through several avenues other than direct contracting. Higher levels of cash assistance for the poor and disadvantaged allowed many people previously excluded from agency programs to pay for various services (sometimes the cash assistance went directly to the agency). New eligibility for services such as health care spurred greater demand for the services of nonprofit providers. The new federal programs also encouraged the growth of national advocacy organizations such as the National Association of Community Mental Health Centers, and of state associations such as the Massachusetts Council of Human Service Providers, which then pushed for more funding of nonprofit service agencies.

One important characteristic of the new nonprofits needs to be stressed: these organizations were providing services that were for the most part unavailable prior to the 1960s. Examples include community residential programs for the developmentally disabled, outpatient services for the chronically mentally ill, home care, shelters for domestic violence victims, and innovative intervention programs for abused children. At the same time, many of these nonprofits represented a form of privatization, assuming societal responsibilities that had once been carried out by public institutions such as state welfare agencies or state hospitals.

The new service providers differed in important respects from traditional nonprofit organizations. For example, the older nonprofits tended to have large boards of directors, composed of community leaders. The boards of the newer agencies were more diverse but smaller, and members were often recruited for their interest in a particular service, such as mental health, rather than for their links to the local community. To be sure, the thousands of nonprofit organizations created through government grants and contracts provided an enormous number of opportunities for private citizens to be board members and donate cash and in-kind goods. Yet few organizations had a general voting membership made up of local citizens, and the structure of the newer agencies did not promote extensive community ties. Moreover, public funding encouraged these groups to focus their attention on government policy—for example, influencing government rate setting and regulatory procedures—and not the cultivation of local support.

Some nonprofit service providers offered new roles for volunteers— from staffing hot lines to ministering to AIDS victims to distributing food at emergency shelters. Nonetheless, such agencies were in a minority.[8] National advocacy groups were either small, staff-driven organizations or larger membership organizations that lacked the face-to-face contact characteristic of community associations such as the PTA. The same can be said of state-level advocacy groups, which emerged as an important force in state politics on a host of new policy issues: the environment, domestic violence, home care, and drug and alcohol abuse prevention and treatment. Some of these groups were affiliates of national organizations such as the Sierra Club, whereas others were state-specific but very interested in national-level policy concerns.

A Change in Direction

The growth of federal social spending halted in the late 1970s as many scholars and politicians started to question the direction of the welfare state in the United States and other advanced industrial countries. The high inflation and unemployment of the late 1970s created profound doubt about the future of the world economy and inevitably focused attention on government expenditures as a possible cause of the economic troubles of countries in North America and Europe. The oil shocks of this period prompted additional concerns.[9]

Worries about the American welfare state contributed to Ronald Reagan's victory in 1980 and gave him the opportunity to win passage of the Omnibus Reconciliation Act (OBRA) of 1981, which inaugurated the first major wave of devolution of federal policy. The OBRA reduced federal spending for social programs, deregulated many federal grant programs, and consolidated many categorical federal social and health programs into block grants.[10] In the ensuing years, federal spending for many social programs such as housing declined, although federal health care spending escalated sharply.[11]

The number of nonprofit organizations continued to rise despite devolution and federal cutbacks. The reasons are varied: after initial federal cutbacks, state and local governments substituted for lost federal revenue; nonprofit organizations generated alternative revenue through fund-raising, higher fees, and entrepreneurial activities such as real estate development and partnerships with for-profit organizations; and many agencies "absorbed" the cuts through lower salaries, longer queues for service, and fewer personnel.

Paradoxically, the cuts in the public sector and the concomitant demand for greater accountability for the expenditure of public funds provided new opportunities for nonprofits. States closed public facilities and transferred responsibilities to nonprofit agencies. Some states shifted management responsibility for services such as child welfare and mental health to third-party, nonprofit (and in some cases, for-profit) management organizations. Government at all levels also responded to emergent public problems such as hunger, homelessness, and AIDS primarily through nonprofit organizations funded by the state. As in the postwar era, many of the new organizations provided services that did not previously exist. Meanwhile, the political ferment surrounding the Reagan cuts and his devolution policies prompted many groups to organize and petition the state. Some of these organizations wanted direct funding, but many were issue- or cause-related and simply wanted to influence government policy. Individual citizens took their cue on forming a nonprofit organization from government and public policy.[12] Overall, the competition for public and private funds increased sharply, since the number of nonprofits outstripped available resources.

The scarcity of public and private charitable funds has encouraged nonprofit service organizations to tap fees and commercial activities (affinity cards, gambling, and for-profit subsidiaries) as sources of revenue.[13] Nonprofit housing developers such as community development corporations cobble together funding from many sources—bank loans, tax credits for investors, local government bond money, and private donations—to build low-income housing. Nonprofit hospitals operate for-profit home care agencies. Museums rely on gift shops and blockbuster shows to generate revenue and memberships. The ability of nonprofits to tap new sources of public and private revenue is a major reason for the continued escalation in the number of tax-exempt, charitable 501(c)(3) organizations—from 322,000 in 1982 to 546,000 in 1992.[14]

The impact of public policy on the nonprofit sector is particularly evident in the transformation of the United Way. The United Way was created in the early part of the century by local agencies as a strategy to fundraise efficiently in the community through one unified, annual campaign. The money raised from the campaign was distributed to member agencies. This remained the basic structure of the United Way until the 1980s, when local chapters experienced pressure to change their operations in response to the cutbacks and devolution of the Reagan years. With fewer public resources available to address social need, at least some local citizens expected the United Way to compensate for government cutbacks. Greater public scrutiny of the United Way's giving practices followed. It turned out that United Way's allocation procedures favored larger, established agencies such as the American Red Cross, the Boy Scouts and Girl Scouts, and the YMCA. Few of the new agencies, such as AIDS service agencies, received funding.

The mismatch between United Way allocation patterns and the funding priorities of the new service providers and their advocates led to a push for a change in United Way practices. Over time, United Way chapters have responded with donor choice and program-related funding, although the implementation of these programs varies greatly from one locality to another. Donor choice allows contributors to designate the agency that is to receive their donation—a significant departure from past practice, in which all the money raised in a campaign was placed in one pool and distributed to member agencies according to a formula. (Until the 1980s, member agencies simply received an allocation that grew incrementally every year, depending on the success of the annual campaign.) Program-related funding is a new practice for identifying priority service areas. For example, a United Way chapter may decide that children and youth services are its main priority; as a result, programs outside this service category will be deemphasized and receive either no funding or a reduced allocation. Established United Way agencies such as the American Red Cross have lost substantial funding under this new allocation arrangement.

Foundation policy has also been affected by the changes in federal policy. For many years, foundations at both the national and local levels provided discretionary, operational funding to arts organizations. Museums, opera houses, and symphonies that received a foundation grant possessed great discretion regarding the purposes to which the money would be devoted. During the 1960s and 1970s, the government also provided hundreds of millions of dollars in grants to the arts through the National Endowment for the Arts and the National Endowment for the Humanities.

As a result of devolution and federal funding cutbacks, foundations are besieged with requests for funding, with the frequent expectation that they will substitute for reductions in government support. The response of foundations is similar in many respects to that of the United Way: more program-related funding, less discretionary funding, and more connection to high-priority local needs. Whereas a local foundation might have given a million-dollar unrestricted grant to a local museum twenty years ago, it will now tie the grant to the willingness of the museum to use the money for a special program for disadvantaged youth. To be sure, foundation funding is not exclusively devoted to these programs, but the shift is substantial, especially at the local level.

Another ripple effect of changing federal policy on nonprofit associations is evident in housing policy. Starting in the 1930s, the federal government created an elaborate, far-flung network of locally based public housing authorities that were responsible for most government-sponsored low-income housing. In contrast to the situation in many European countries, most of this low-income housing was built by for-profit companies rather than nonprofit housing agencies.[15] In the 1980s and 1990s, the federal government retreated almost completely from the production of low-income housing. As a result, the responsibility for creating low-income housing shifted to nonprofit agencies. Habitat for Humanity is a national organization with hundreds of local chapters. Although Habitat refuses to accept direct government grants, it nonetheless receives substantial in-kind support, such as donations of land and materials, from government. Other types of housing organizations, such as community development corporations, have built thousands of housing units using direct government grants and money from private investors who took advantage of federal tax credits for low-income housing.

One last example of a complex public-private relationship is Delancey Street, a nonprofit drug rehabilitation program that refuses direct government aid. Delancey Street has received much-deserved praise for its success in turning around the lives of longtime drug addicts. Yet Delancey Street depends for its success on a close working relationship with local correctional personnel and is able to pick its niche within the overall service system because the public sector (or other nonprofits funded by government) focuses on individuals who do not fit within the Delancey Street model.

In sum, the growth of voluntary service agencies during the 1980s and

1990s has been linked to federal policy, either directly or indirectly. The unanswered question for the future concerns the impact on the nonprofit sector of the current wave of devolution, which is substantively different from the one before: the cutbacks are more extensive; state and local governments have greater discretion in spending money; and for-profit organizations are likely to compete aggressively with nonprofit service organizations for public funds. Consequently, many nonprofits that successfully weathered the 1980s and 1990s may find themselves severely pressed financially, with many closures and mergers possible.

The last fifteen years is also a story of the growth of collaborative initiatives at the local level that rely on volunteers to plan local services and respond to social needs. The hope is that these collaborative programs—often called community partnerships or coalitions—will overcome the fragmentation and inefficiency of current public and private services. The next section examines these programs and their relationship to government.

NEW FORMS OF VOLUNTARISM IN THE AGE OF DEVOLUTION: THE CASE OF COMMUNITY PARTNERSHIPS AND COALITIONS

Robert Putnam's work on social capital suggests that local voluntary associations as diverse as bowling leagues and the PTA are critical to well-functioning communities, effective government, and citizen satisfaction with government.[16] Like Alexis de Tocqueville, Putnam suggests that nonprofit organizations can have a stimulative effect on civic engagement and citizen empowerment: voluntary associations create active citizens who then demand effective government; over time, government policy makers respond to citizen demands, creating even higher levels of citizen engagement and satisfaction.

James S. Coleman and Glenn C. Loury also stress the importance of social capital, although they tend to focus on the contribution of family, relatives, and community broadly defined to helping achieve positive outcomes for youth and families. Coleman and Loury prefer to view social capital as a bottom-up phenomenon that is not directly amenable to public policy intervention. Creating cooperation through public programs is an elusive, ultimately futile goal.[17]

John McKnight emphasizes the importance of community associations as vehicles for citizens to take control of their community and their lives. McKnight and his colleague, John Kretzmann, have popularized a "community assets" approach to social change and addressing social need that relies on mapping assets in the community and taking advantage of these assets rather than depending on government funds and programs.[18]

The work of Putnam, McKnight and Kretzmann, and others has attracted widespread attention from policy makers, scholars, and citizens in part because it offers a diagnosis for what many people regard as the deterioration of local communities and their civic infrastructure (which includes local voluntary associations, local government services, and the overall quality of life), especially in urban areas. One sign of their influence may be found in the extensive efforts now under way to rebuild communities through partnerships and coalitions.

Although their specific approaches differ, partnerships and coalitions share four key underlying assumptions related to voluntarism and civic infrastructure. First, it is hoped that partnerships—by generating voluntarism, consensus, and more extensive community networks—will create new resources to address social problems. This assumption itself has a number of additional components. Implicit in the "new resources" argument is the view that government has crowded out voluntarism and charitable donations; thus, when the scope of government is reduced, the voluntary sector will be freed from its restraints, prompting a new wave of voluntarism and charitable giving. This assumption also suggests that the community will give more money to various service programs if citizens can agree on an integrated, coordinated approach to services. The community, in other words, has been holding back on its giving and voluntarism.

Second, serious social problems such as drug abuse and crime are viewed as evidence of a community's apathy and, in the worst cases, social disorganization. By stimulating voluntarism, partnerships can have a direct impact on remedying social problems. The assumption is that voluntarism changes community norms through greater person-to-person contact and thus will have a measurable positive impact on the community.

Third, partnerships offer an opportunity to problem-solve and cooperate, thus creating more integrated, efficient local services. This assumption reflects an underlying concern that communities are rife with factions and fragmentation, blocking attempts to provide effective public and private services.

Fourth, the voluntarism of coalitions is viewed as critical to forging cooperation. Individuals are motivated by their desire to help their community rather than by purely professional considerations.

In short, partnerships "work" by building civic infrastructure, which will then have a positive impact on public policy problems affecting local communities: more community connections create more empowered citizens, who demand more and better services and create a sense of community ownership. The latter changes the norms of behavior of the community, so that inappropriate behaviors are not tolerated and voluntarism and charitable giving are encouraged and rewarded.

These themes were echoed during the presidential summit on voluntarism, held in Philadelphia in the spring of 1997, which emphasized the value of voluntarism and community service. Similarly, the Points of Light Foundation, an organization started with the support of President George Bush, is leading a national movement to "Connect America" at the grass roots through voluntarism. These initiatives share an enthusiasm for voluntarism and a skepticism toward government action. It is through voluntarism that citizens will rediscover their communities.

In the next section, I argue that the distinction between government and voluntarism, and the related dichotomy between government and community, is untenable. Rather than separate and apart, government is inextricably connected to the ability of these largely volunteer programs to sustain themselves. In this sense, government can support and facilitate voluntarism. At the same time, it is clear that government involvement does not guarantee the success of community renewal efforts, and that in some cases such involvement may have certain undesirable effects.

Community Partnerships and Government

Most community partnerships are voluntary associations or organizations with relatively few staff members; this is true even for partnerships with major federal or foundation funding.[19] The structure and auspices of these partnerships vary substantially. Some coalitions are formally incorporated as nonprofit 501(c)(3) agencies, whereas others constitute a department within city or county government. Some partnerships are informal associations lacking any legal status, or subsidiaries of a larger nonprofit organization such as a United Way chapter or other civic organization.

Ideally, coalitions and partnerships are designed to bring together individuals and organizations in the community to define the community's needs, devise effective solutions, find the necessary resources, and create more efficient services through the cooperation of public and private organizations. Because coalitions depend on voluntarism, their programmatic success hinges on their ability to mobilize volunteers, create cooperation, and maintain volunteer interest and involvement. The nature and extent of government involvement will significantly affect their chances of success in each of these areas. This becomes clear if we consider partnership membership, staff support, organizational structure, and program priorities.

Membership

Most partnerships welcome and encourage participation by any member of the community or relevant target area. In practice, individuals from government or representatives of service providers funded by government are very prominent in coalitions. For example, drug and alcohol abuse prevention efforts naturally attract the interest of many local government agencies: the police, the housing authority, the schools, the community development agency, the mental health authority, and the mayor's office. The staffs of many nonprofit service providers receiving government funds also take a keen interest in partnership operations. These individuals have an expertise in a policy or program area and resources to devote to active coalition participation, unlike many community members with full-time jobs unrelated to substance abuse. Often the leadership of partnerships is provided by local government personnel or service providers receiving public funds.

The dependence of partnerships on local government and private service providers is particularly evident in the informal coalitions without major resources or paid staff. These coalitions rely on the willingness of people to volunteer. The lack of paid staff to mobilize community members or resources for extensive programming means that most volunteers are public and private professionals whose concern with drug and alcohol abuse is part of their regular jobs. Usually, they can receive release time for attending a coalition meeting. However, the lack of resources and complete dependence on volunteers creates organizational fragility; these informal coalitions are thus prone to closure, merger, and long periods of inactivity.

The involvement of local government in partnerships extends to their boards of directors and executive committees. Boards of directors are required for coalitions with 501(c)(3) status. Executive committees are common in informal coalitions or in coalitions that are part of a larger public nonprofit organization. In some cases, city or county government appoints the members of a board of directors or executive committee. Often government officials are members themselves.

The characteristics of local government and its programmatic agenda shape coalition operations. Problems affecting local government such as scarce resources, departmental fragmentation, turf battles, and weak leadership profoundly influence the development and ultimate success of coalitions. In communities with charismatic, powerful local government leaders, coalitions can realize many benefits: volunteer mobilization, government resources, and access to donors and key public and private lenders. More typically, though, coalitions are only one organization among the many seeking the support of the mayor, the city council, or the city manager. In these situations, coalitions can suffer from the inattention of local government, especially after the initial start-up phase.

More indirectly, partnerships often adjust their goals and program priorities to the constraints and priorities of local government. For example, a partnership may craft its priorities to fit the preference of local government officials for school-based prevention rather than policy-oriented advocacy. Thus, an alcohol abuse prevention program might concentrate on developing school assembly programs rather than lobbying for restrictions on alcohol advertising or the location of liquor stores. Or a partnership might emphasize crime prevention if the chief of police is a major player in the coalition.

Alternatively, government mismanagement, arbitrariness, or lack of interest can affect the agenda of a partnership. Volunteers quickly get discouraged and fall away if they believe that local government will be unresponsive to their concerns. And the cooperation built by partnership members can be shattered by the intrusion of government personnel into the sometimes complicated and intricate relationships among partnership volunteers. This can occur with government personnel from outside the local partnership, such as federal grants administrators or municipal government officials who are not part of local professional networks.

Staff Support

In coalitions affiliated with city or county government, staff are often government employees. Many informal coalitions are directed by personnel from local government agencies. Other coalition staff frequently have a connection to local government, including previous work experience in local government or employment with private service providers with government contracts. In general, voluntarism in the partnership depends on capable local government officials who provide support, guidance, and sometimes resources.

Organizational Structure

Partnerships exist along a continuum, with informal, loose associations at one end and formal, freestanding organizations with tax-exempt 501(c)(3) status at the other. The middle of the continuum contains partnerships that are part of a larger lead agency, such as city and county government or a nonprofit organization. These partnerships are not separately incorporated and rely on a lead agency as their fiscal agent to receive a grant. The significant differences in the orientations of these groups derive from the fact that they need to be very concerned with the agendas of their parent agencies.

Partnerships located within city government have certain advantages and disadvantages that other partnerships do not. These partnerships can use the legitimacy of city government to grab the attention of the local community and move quickly to attack an identified problem. The use of city government to manage a grant can ease the burden of grant compliance and fiscal accountability, a particular problem for new partnerships with scant fiscal resources.

The location of a partnership within city departments such as neighborhood services and community development can promote innovation in addressing social problems and engaging citizens in municipal decision making. For example, a partnership in Hampton, Virginia, Hampton for Youth, established several novel, effective prevention programs and reached out to city residents to integrate them more fully into the municipal planning process on substance abuse and related issues. The partnership is a department of city government.

The placement of a partnership within city government is not without its risks. Partnerships can fall victim to city politics. Mayors or city council members can use a coalition to achieve their own political purposes, including assistance with reelection. There may be pressure on coalitions to emphasize programs favored by the mayor and other leaders. City rules and regulations on hiring and budgetary matters can hamper the ability of a coalition to move quickly to take advantage of new funding or program opportunities.

Partnerships located within local government may also be less aggressive than other types of partnerships in seeking new funds or private funds, because some coalition staff may be long-term government employees who will keep their jobs even if a grant expires or private funds are not forthcoming. Some foundations or businesses may be reluctant to contribute to a government program. These constraints on fund-raising prompt some coalitions to separate from the local government and incorporate as tax-exempt nonprofit organizations, giving them the opportunity to obtain donations from individuals, foundations, and the United Way.

Partnership Program Priorities

Partnerships are a form of voluntary action in which individuals come together to conduct needs assessment, planning, and priority setting. Their ability to be successful—and attract and retain volunteer members—hinges on the willingness of local government to respond positively to coalition initiatives. For example, a coalition might identify an after-school mentoring program as an urgent need in the community. Before it can address this need, however, the coalition must gain the cooperation of other key local public agencies—the school system, the county youth bureau, and perhaps the police. Local government—the city manager's office, for example—can encourage these sometimes turf-conscious groups to work together to develop the mentoring program. Gaining cooperation among local agencies is particularly difficult for the informal partnerships and coalitions, because they do not have any political power or influence. Indeed, they usually have only their network ties, which may or may not be characterized by goodwill and trust. Even when goodwill exists, though, it is rarely sufficient to force local agencies to act if they are reluctant. The difficulty of moving ahead and obtaining adequate cooperation is a major factor in the instability of informal coalitions: without a paid leader and evidence of success, these coalitions can easily dissolve.

Freestanding 501(c)(3) coalitions share similar problems. They are usually set apart from the regular human service delivery system. Thus, they lack formal authority, although local officials may appoint their board members and participate as members of the coalition. Tax-exempt status allows the coalitions to raise private funds and may offer them greater control over their fate than if they were part of a larger public or private organization. But complete separation without any ongoing tie to local government agencies carries the risk of alienation and isolation. In this era of diminished resources, this may be a difficult long-run strategy. Policy makers and foundation officials are interested in supporting service integration and consolidation rather than a proliferation of new agencies, however worthy.

The Importance of the Federal Role

Theda Skocpol argues that the national government was crucial in providing the opportunity for the creation of voluntary associations during the nineteenth and early twentieth centuries.[20] The experience of the last several years indicates that the federal government was equally critical in stimulating the growth and proliferation of community partnerships. The current difficulties of many partnerships in sustaining their volunteer activities reflect the direct and indirect consequences of the changing federal role in social and health policy.

First, the federal government provides direct funding through various programs specifically for collaborative activity. The Community Partnership program of the federal Center for Substance Abuse Prevention (CSAP) has funded more than three hundred collaborative initiatives in the last several years; this funding engaged literally thousands of volunteers around the country in efforts to prevent substance abuse. Most recently, CSAP has provided grants for partnerships to collaborate with each other.

The federal Department of Housing and Urban Development (HUD) is funding dozens of empowerment zones and enterprise zones in cities throughout the country. Receipt of this money requires local grantees to involve community residents and engage volunteers in formulating strategies to address community needs.

Second, the federal government uses its convenor/facilitator role to promote collaboration directly and indirectly. For example, the federal government provides seed grants to local volunteer initiatives with the expectation that local public and private funding will be forthcoming to sustain the partnership.

Federal funding cutbacks can undermine the stability and survival of partnerships and other comprehensive community initiatives. Already, many worthy coalitions and partnerships funded through federal grants have closed operations because of their inability to replace federal funding with local public and private funds at the expiration of their federal grants. In addition, reduced federal funding entails the transfer of at least some program costs to local governments, creating a fiscal squeeze that hampers the ability of local officials to respond to partnership priorities. A constrained local government weakens the incentive for community residents, professionals, and other concerned citizens to participate in voluntary activity to address local needs. Further, cutbacks in programs to distressed neighborhoods can increase the skepticism and mistrust within these communities, making it more difficult for coalitions to enlist residents in the work of the partnership.

Federal grants are particularly crucial in sustaining partnerships and coalitions because one of the underlying assumptions of the community-building movement—that private dollars would flow into partnerships once they were established—has proven to be incorrect. Even very successful partnerships with broad-based community support and involvement are not able to generate significant dollars for their operations, either as a complement to federal dollars or as a substitute for federal grants.

Community partnerships provide evidence for Skocpol's view that national nonprofit organizations can provide top-down encouragement to local voluntary associations. For example, a national advocacy group—Community Anti-Drug Coalitions of America (CADCA)—has received sizable foundation and federal grants to provide technical assistance to local partnerships. CADCA also advocates before Congress for more federal funding of community partnerships and fights to preserve federal funding threatened by cutbacks. Other national organizations, including the National Prevention League, are supportive of the partnership movement.

Federal grants to community partnerships are, to be sure, not problem-free. They can distort the operation of local partnerships, moving them away from their original mission. A very large partnership budget, bolstered by federal funding, can set off a scramble for money that creates tension and controversy within the partnership and the larger community. Many federal grants are accompanied by technical assistance that is often inappropriate and ill-advised, undermining the efforts of partnership volunteers to forge consensus and cooperation.

Nonetheless, federal grants and policy play an important direct and indirect role in facilitating the growth and development of community partnerships. They contribute to the invigoration of the civic infrastructure of local communities by offering citizens an opportunity to volunteer and participate in organizations committed to resolving social problems and improving the overall civic character of the community.

RETHINKING NONPROFIT ASSOCIATIONS AND CIVIC INFRASTRUCTURE

The sharp increase in nonprofit organizations in the postwar period was fueled by government funding and public policy. The emergence of service agencies receiving direct government contracts, and the growth of community partnerships, demonstrates that government can support and facilitate increased citizen involvement in nonprofit organizations. Citizens can actively volunteer through involvement on the board of directors or in direct service capacities.

Yet the effects of government funding are complex, and its consequences for voluntarism are not always predictable. For example, social and health agencies receiving government funds tend to be staff-driven organizations, despite their volunteer boards of directors. As we have seen, moreover, many of these agencies also tend to focus their attention on government policy, neglecting the development of extensive community networks and ties. Government regulations governing nonprofit programs can often be complicated and alienating, making it difficult for citizen volunteers to participate actively in the oversight and implementation of those programs.

The comprehensive community initiatives such as coalitions and partnerships also illustrate the difficulty of generalizing about the impact of government policy. Although these initiatives often strive to involve local citizens and build social capital, they are often, in practice, dominated by local professionals who staff other public and private service agencies. Even though partnerships and coalitions may create new networks of cooperation, social support, and voluntarism in the long term, they often face great difficulty in sustaining member participation, especially in communities without long-standing norms of cooperation and voluntarism.

To be sure, voluntary organizations and groups without extensive government funding do exist. As Robert Wuthnow observes, self-help groups represent an increasingly common form of associational activity.[21] Other informal associations include local planning committees, ad hoc committees, and various types of church-related groups. For the most part, these informal associations are not legally incorporated and rarely employ paid staff. Consequently, they are usually absent from various data sets on the nonprofit sector. Although they are undeniably an important source of voluntarism, it remains to be determined whether such informal networks help promote greater citizen participation and social support within communities.

In any event, these informal groups do not have the resources to make a significant impact on social and health problems. They would need to enlist other organizations such as state and local government, foundations, or business to provide resources or political support for their program agenda. Self-help organizations and informal associations are not an alternative to government-funded service agencies: they do not have the resources to address social need in an extensive way, and their social networks are not necessarily conducive to building community-wide civic infrastructure.

CONCLUSION

The complex interplay between the nonprofit and public sectors in the postwar period suggests several lessons for social scientists and policy makers.

To a large extent, the debate about the future of government and civil society has been dominated by an either-or theme: policies should support either government or the voluntary sector. An additional distinction is often drawn to divide the voluntary sector between truly voluntary organizations at the grass roots and nonprofit agencies receiving government funding, with the latter identified as part of the overall government social welfare establishment. Emphasis is placed on how nonprofit agencies influence government, as was evident in the 1997 congressional debate over proposed restrictions on the lobbying activities of these organizations.

But the impact of nonprofit organizations on public policy is only one side of the dynamic relationship between government and the voluntary sector. This chapter has focused on the return arrow: the effect of government on nonprofit organizations and voluntarism. The findings I have described here have a number of implications for current thinking on the welfare state, voluntarism, and civil society.

First, the prevailing view of America's "exceptionalism" with respect to its reliance on the voluntary sector needs to be rethought. The extensive direct and indirect government support for nonprofit service providers suggests that America's distinctiveness in the postwar period may lie in its use of nonprofits as a policy tool to achieve public purposes.[22]

Second, supporters of the current wave of devolution and decentralization of federal policy to local governments and community organizations often argue that this shift will stimulate voluntarism. Their prediction of a substitution effect is based upon a paradigm of separate sectors. However, to the extent that we are guided by the substitution paradigm, we risk overstating the capacity of local communities to respond to social need without government support. This is not to suggest that extensive government funding is the salvation for nonprofit organizations; as noted, public funding (and accompanying regulations) can have many unintended and negative effects on nonprofit organizations.[23] However, we need to recognize that building a healthy voluntary sector requires a positive role for government.

To be sure, many nonprofit organizations also emerge in response to government failure. Recent faith-based grassroots programs to address poverty and unemployment are good examples. But these programs are quickly overwhelmed if they are forced to confront an array of social needs without government help in such basic areas as income maintenance, transportation, and health care, even if this help is indirect. These programs also depend for their successes on diverse public and private service options that allow the matching of individuals to appropriate programs. This array of services needs ongoing public support.

For policy makers, scholars, and nonprofit staff and volunteers, the challenge posed by devolution and the great contemporary interest in civil society is to construct a framework to balance a role for the state in building and sustaining local civic infrastructure with protections against undue intervention by the state in affairs of nonprofit organizations or individual citizens.[24] New options exist for staff and volunteer positions in nonprofit service agencies, but the sustained commitment necessary to build a healthy civic infrastructure is undermined by high staff and volunteer turnover, arbitrary regulations, and periodic fiscal crises. The alternative is not to jettison the state in favor of purely private initiatives but to craft a new balance between public and private responsibility.

To attain this balance, several practical strategies need to be pursued. First, government policy should be designed to bolster the capacity of nonprofit organizations to develop civic infrastructure.[25] Many government programs are already striving to achieve this goal by building into their regulations and funding policies incentives for nonprofits to collaborate with local public and private organizations and to create and strengthen their community connections.

Second, in the age of devolution, many public initiatives to support the development of civic infrastructure will have to be undertaken by state and local governments. State government should be cognizant of the need to help support the fiscal capacities of local and regional governments: without an adequate resource base, municipal policy makers will be unable to respond effectively to the needs of nonprofits in their community. Additionally, state governments should nurture and support the growth of statewide and regional associations representing nonprofits. These organizations can be a source of crucial technical assistance and support for local groups, enhancing their ability to foster voluntarism and supportive social networks in the community. These statewide associations can also help with leadership development.

Third, even grassroots organizations dependent primarily on volunteers must rely either directly or indirectly on government for their ability to build lasting bonds of cooperation. Neighborhood crime-watch groups need a police department that can respond to their concerns. PTA chapters will falter if the public schools are broke and the education wanting. Absent a vital public sector, voluntarism will not flourish.

Finally, the postwar expansion and evolution of nonprofit organizations demonstrates the complexity of community and ways to build or rebuild community. If we as a society are committed to creating a more vibrant and healthy civic infrastructure, we need to examine ways in which local nonprofit organizations—from social service agencies to unions to churches—can become more connected to their community, broadly defined. This challenging task will require new approaches by nonprofit organizations to governance, membership, and community support. Nonprofits across the country are in the midst of experimenting with new approaches. As we learn more about their strategies, we can begin to provide more guidance and support to nonprofit organizations, government, and citizens building local civic infrastructure.

NOTES

I would like to thank Arthur Evenchik and Michael Shalev, as well as the members of the Scholars' Working Group of the National Commission on Civic Renewal, for comments on an earlier draft of this chapter. Financial support from the Aspen Institute, Join Together, the Robert Wood Johnson Foundation, the Graduate School of Public Affairs at the University of Washington, and the Center for Philanthropy at the Sanford Institute of Public Policy at Duke University is gratefully acknowledged.

1. Robert D. Putnam, "Bowling Alone: America's Declining Social Capital," *Journal of Democracy* 6 (1995): 65–78. For studies linking the growth of voluntary associations to the government, see Robert H. Salisbury, "Interest Representation: The Dominance of Institutions," *American Political Science Review* 78 (1984): 64–76; E. James, "The Nonprofit Sector in Comparative Perspective," in *The Nonprofit Sector: A Research Handbook,* ed. Walter W. Powell (New Haven, Conn.: Yale University Press, 1987), 397–415; Steven Rathgeb Smith and Michael Lipsky, *Nonprofits for Hire: The Welfare State in the Age of Contracting* (Cambridge, Mass.: Harvard University Press, 1993); Jack L. Walker, "Interests, Political Parties, and Policy Formation in American Democracy," in *Federal Social Policy: The Historical Dimension,* ed. Donald T. Critchlow and Ellis W. Hawley (University Park: Pennsylvania State University Press, 1988), 141–70. Others regard the formation of voluntary organizations as the result of market failure (Weisbrod, Hansmann) or the reevaluation of the role of the state throughout the world (Salamon). See Burton A. Weisbrod, "Toward a Theory of the Voluntary Nonprofit Sector in a Three Sector Economy," in *Altruism, Morality, and Economic Theory,* ed. Edmund S. Phelps (New York: Russell Sage Foundation, 1994), 171–95; Henry Hansmann, "The Role of the Nonprofit Enterprise," *Yale Law Journal* 89 (1980): 835–901; Lester M. Salamon, "The Rise of the Nonprofit Sector," *Foreign Affairs* 73, no. 4 (July/August 1994): 109–22.

2. See Peter Berger and Richard John Neuhaus, *To Empower People: The Role of Mediating Structures in Public Policy* (Washington, D.C.: American Enterprise Institute, 1977); Jack A. Meyer, ed., *Meeting Human Needs: Toward a New Social Philosophy* (Washington, D.C.: American Enterprise Institute, 1982); Nathan Glazer, *The Limits of Social Policy* (Cambridge, Mass.: Harvard University Press, 1988); William A. Schambra, "Is There Civic Life beyond the Great National Community?" (chap. 4 in this volume).

3. Don Krasner Price, *The Scientific Estate* (Cambridge, Mass.: Harvard University Press, 1965).

4. Anne Kallman Bixby, "Public Social Welfare Expenditures, Fiscal Year 1992," *Social Security Bulletin* 58, no. 2 (Summer 1995): 65–73.

5. Smith and Lipsky, *Nonprofits for Hire*; Ruth Margaret Werner, *Public Financing of Voluntary Agency Foster Care: 1975 Compared with 1957* (New York: Child Welfare League of America, 1976); John R. Seeley, *Community Chest: A Case Study in Philanthropy* (Toronto: University of Toronto Press, 1957).

6. Erving Goffman, *Asylums* (Garden City, N.Y.: Anchor, 1961).

7. Richard Cloward and Irwin Epstein, "Private Social Welfare's Disengagement from the Poor: The Case of Family Adjustment Agencies," in *Social Welfare Institutions: A Sociological Reader,* ed. Mayer N. Zald (New York: Wiley, 1965), 623–44; Alfred J. Kahn, "The Social Scene and the Planning of Services for Children," *Social Work* 7, no. 3 (1962): 3–14.

8. Putnam, "Bowling Alone," and Peter Dobkin Hall, unpublished correspondence, 1996.

9. Rudolf Klein, "Self-Inventing Institutions: Institutional Design and the U.K. Welfare State," in *The Theory of Institutional Design,* ed. Robert E. Goodin (Cam-

bridge: Cambridge University Press, 1996), 240–55; Theodore Geiger, *Welfare and Efficiency: Their Interactions in Western Europe and Implications for International Economic Relations* (Washington, D.C.: National Planning Association, Committee on Changing International Realities, 1978); Organization of Economic Cooperation and Development (OECD), *The Welfare State in Crisis* (Paris: OECD, 1980).

10. Michael F. Gutowski and Jeffrey J. Koshel, "Social Services," in *The Reagan Experiment: An Examination of Economic and Social Policies under the Reagan Administration*, ed. John L. Palmer and Isabel V. Sawhill (Washington, D.C.: Urban Institute Press, 1982), 307–28.

11. Bixby, "Public Social Welfare Expenditures," 67–68.

12. For further discussion of the reasons for the creation of nonprofit organizations, see Smith and Lipsky, *Nonprofits for Hire*, chap. 3.

13. Reid Lifset, "Cash Cows or Sacred Cows: The Politics of the Commercialization Movement," in *The Future of the Nonprofit Sector*, ed. Virginia Hodgkinson et al. (San Francisco: Jossey-Bass, 1989).

14. Independent Sector, *Nonprofit Almanac: 1995–96*, 37.

15. Arnold J. Heidenheimer, Hugh Heclo, and Carolyn Teich Adams, *Comparative Public Policy: The Politics of Social Choice in Europe and America*, 2d ed. (New York: St. Martin's, 1983), chap. 4 ("Housing Policy").

16. See Putnam, *Making Democracy Work*, "The Prosperous Community," and "Bowling Alone."

17. James S. Coleman, *Foundations of Social Theory* (Cambridge, Mass.: Harvard University Press, 1990); Glenn C. Loury, "Why Should We Care about Group Inequality?" *Social Philosophy and Policy* 5 (1987): 249–71.

18. John L. McKnight, *The Careless Community: Community and Its Counterfeits* (New York: Basic Books, 1995); John P. Kretzmann and John L. McKnight, *Building Communities from the Inside Out* (Evanston, Ill.: Center for Urban Affairs and Policy Research, Northwestern University, 1993).

19. In the early to mid-1980s, the drug crisis exploded in cities and communities across the country. The Reagan administration declared a "war on drugs" with a highly publicized media campaign. In response, many community anti-drug and crime coalitions were established. One early coalition was the Ad Hoc Group against Crime in Kansas City, Missouri, established to address crime in the late 1970s. The Ad Hoc Group decided to combat the drug problem in 1985 through marches, protests, and other confrontations designed to rid neighborhoods of drug dealers and unsavory landlords.

As coalitions proliferated, they attracted more support from government agencies and private foundations. Congress passed the Drug Free Schools Act in 1986, providing money for local school districts to prevent drug and alcohol abuse and establish local coalitions. Subsequently, the federal Office of Substance Abuse Prevention (now called the Center for Substance Abuse Prevention, or CSAP) in the Department of Health and Human Services created the Community Partnership Demonstration Grant Program. Since the program's inception in 1989, the CSAP has awarded more than $300 million in grants to more than three hundred coalitions and partnerships around the country. Coalitions against drug and alcohol abuse also receive funding from the Robert Wood Johnson Foundation and, to a lesser extent, from other foundations and state and local governments.

20. Theda Skocpol, "Civic Engagement in American Democracy," testimony prepared for the National Commission on Civic Renewal, Washington, D.C., 25 January 1997.

21. Robert Wuthnow, *Sharing the Journey: Support Groups and America's New Quest for Community* (New York: Free Press, 1994).

22. This point is explored by Martin Rein, "Is America Exceptional? The Role of Occupational Welfare in the United States and the European Community," in *The Privatization of Social Policy?* ed. Shalev, 28–43.

23. Smith and Lipsky, *Nonprofits for Hire.*

24. See Jean L. Cohen and Andrew Arato, *Civil Society and Political Theory* (Cambridge, Mass.: MIT Press, 1992); Joshua Cohen and Joel Rogers, eds., *Associations and Democracy* (London: Verso, 1995).

25. Jeffrey L. Pressman, *Federal Programs and City Politics: The Dynamics of the Aid Process in Oakland* (Berkeley: University of California Press, 1975).

6

The View from Quincy Library

Civic Engagement in Environmental Problem Solving

Mark Sagoff

On their own initiative, about twenty residents of the northern Sierra Nevada, including environmentalists, timber industry representatives, and local officials, held a series of meetings beginning in 1993 at a library in the logging town of Quincy, California. This diverse group hoped to develop a plan for managing the surrounding Plumas and Lassen National Forests—and, in the process, to overcome a long history of contention and mistrust. (They chose to meet at a library, it was said, so that the participants could not scream at one another.) "After fifteen years of fighting . . . the idea that we would sit in one room and recognize each other's right to exist was a new one," observed Michael Jackson, an environmentalist in what became known as the Quincy Library Group.[1]

Like other members of his community, Jackson knew that Native Americans had used fire periodically to remove undergrowth and to thin dense stands of cedar and pine, allowing a few surviving trees per acre to become old and great.[2] Over the last half century, however, a strict policy of fire suppression, together with logging of some of the old growth, had turned the forests into thickets of thin trees and combustible underbrush—a tinderbox. The prospect of a horrendous conflagration concentrated the minds of citizens who might otherwise have remained in "perpetual struggle and gridlock."[3] Because of inaction and indecision by governmental authorities, they had nowhere to turn but to each other. After months of negotiation, when the members of the Quincy group announced their agreement on a management plan, one environmental activist noted that deliberation succeeded where litigation had failed. "We are in a new era," she said.[4]

Across the United States, and especially in the West, hundreds of citizen associations like the Quincy Library Group bring together environmentalists and their adversaries in face-to-face collaboration to manage shared resources. The more inclusive these associations become—for example, by engaging public officials or representatives from national business and environmental organizations—the more democratic are their deliberations and the more legitimate their results. This chapter examines the "new era"—or at least the new hope—that the rise of civic environmentalism creates. The current "winner-take-all" system of confrontation and litigation may be yielding, at least with respect to localized resources, to more deliberative and representative—and therefore more democratic—decision making.

SCIENCE AS A SURROGATE

The Quincy Library Group might be seen as a long-delayed response to the expectation with which Congress in the nineteenth century encouraged settlers to migrate to the West. By giving settlers land in modest plots—usually about 160 acres—the Homestead Act of 1862 and the land acts that followed sought to build a Jeffersonian democracy of small freeholders throughout the region. These landowners were supposed to form associations patterned on town meetings to settle controversies that might arise among them. In refusing to allow public rangeland to be fenced, Congress in 1885 perpetuated the hope that settlers could collaborate to manage the pastoral commons. "It was a noble idea," writes Karl Hess, a scholar of the social history of the West. "It was the expectation that every citizen would be a stakeholder in an experiment of direct, hands-on democracy."[5]

Over most of the West, however, the climate conspired with everything else to doom this hopeful experiment. Herds of cattle require enormous tracts of land—sometimes a hundred square miles—where forage grows slowly. Farms of modest size cannot succeed with only sixteen inches of rain a year. By the end of the nineteenth century, timber, cattle, railroad, and mining "barons," after concentrating their economic and political hold on western land, plundered places and ravaged resources that Congress had hoped associations of farmers, tradesmen, and other small landowners would protect. Theodore Roosevelt spoke for the conservation movement by demanding that corporations "be so supervised and regulated that they shall act for the interest of the community as a whole."[6] The sparse citizenry and the inchoate local government of the

West, however, could hardly challenge mining, timbering, and grazing barons who created jobs and brought in money.

By the 1870s, Congress had become aware that cut-and-run timbering practices had created horrendous problems of disease, fire, and erosion in many areas of the northern and western forests. The "tragedy of the commons" played out even more dramatically on the range, where enormous herds of cattle quickly grazed off the prime forage.[7] At the turn of the century, one federal official observed flocks of sheep and cattle

> passing each other on trails, one rushing in to secure what the other had just abandoned as worthless. Feed was deliberately wasted to prevent its utilization by others. . . . Transient sheepmen roamed the country robbing the resident stockmen of forage that was justly theirs. . . . Class was arrayed against class—the cowboy against the sheepman, the big owner against the little one—and might ruled more often than right.[8]

"Faced with the failure of hands-on democracy on the western range," Karl Hess writes, "a new vision of the West arose from the ashes of the old—a vision of a federal range governed by scientifically objective and politically neutral government agencies." The growing power of the timber barons (Weyerhaeuser practically owned Washington State) lent urgency to the formation of the Forest Service, which, along with the General Land Office and, somewhat later, the Grazing Service, was to manage western public land in the public interest. Conservationists believed that professionals in agencies, not politicians in Congress, could be trusted to determine on neutral, rational grounds what the public interest required. "Reflecting the will of the people, these agencies would be manned by men and women steeped in the value of public service and thoroughly trained in the science and technology of land management, use, and conservation."[9]

Conservationists such as Gifford Pinchot, the founding chief of the Forest Service, argued that in the absence of centralized control, public or private, competition among thousands of cut-and-run operators, each trying to beat the others to market, would destroy the resource base. In harmony with the Progressive movement, these conservationists believed the government should retain control of public lands rather than cede them to corporate oligopolies. "If scientific management in fact required large organization," writes policy analyst Robert Nelson, "then the public sector was preferable to the private sector, or so it seemed to many Progressives. Rather than create one or more new Weyerhaeuser-type empires, Progressives preferred to create the Forest Service instead."[10]

Pinchot and his successors fought on two fronts—first, against large corporations and second, against politicians who might make a pork barrel out of the West. To keep corporations at bay, Pinchot railed against the "vast power, pecuniary and political, [of the] . . . railroads, the stock interests, mining interests, water power interests, and most of the big timber interests."[11] After Pinchot retired, the Forest Service continued to attack timber practices on private land. "Laissez-faire private effort has seriously deteriorated or destroyed the basic resources of timber, forage, and land almost universally," the Forest Service reported in the 1930s. The private sector "has felt little or no responsibility for the renewal of the resources on which its own industries must depend."[12] This was not entirely fair. By the 1950s, millions of acres in tree farms, as one expert noted, received "more intensive forest management than . . . most of the publicly owned lands."[13]

To keep public lands out of the pork barrel, conservationists followed Presidents Theodore Roosevelt and Woodrow Wilson in trying to free agencies from political oversight and control. Conservationists, according to historian Samuel P. Hays, preached a "gospel of efficiency" asserting that "social and economic problems should be solved, not through power politics, but by experts who would undertake scientific investigations and devise workable solutions."[14] Hays writes, "The crux of the gospel of efficiency lay in a rational and scientific method of making basic technological decisions through a single, central authority."[15] Experts using "technical and scientific methods," it was argued, "should decide all matters of development and utilization of resources, all problems of allocation of funds. Federal land management agencies, rather than the parties themselves, should resolve conflicts among livestock, wildlife, irrigation, recreation, and settler groups."[16]

Why should land management agencies rather than the parties themselves resolve conflicts? The question had an obvious answer at the time. Few held out much hope that the processes of representative democracy would flourish amid the "pressure politics" of the Gilded Age. The shootout at the OK Corral in 1881 illustrated the alternative dispute resolution (ADR) and stakeholder arbitration techniques then available. More to the point, conservationists believed that the truth and objectivity of science offered a sounder basis than majority (or mob) rule for determining the public interest. The objectivity of science was supposed to put political decisions above class and faction. The conservationist movement, an analyst writes, believed that a "sense of political community may be regenerated by the adoption of science as the common language of discourse, bringing about an end to irrationality, rivalry of power, and authoritarianism."[17]

Today, nobody utters the words *scientific management* and *centralized planning* except pejoratively, calling up images of Five-Year Plans, Chernobyl, North Korea, and the like. And indeed, scientific management led directly to, among other things, the insect-infested dying forests that surround Quincy Library. Yet, in the early 1900s, Congress had to decide whether to transfer the great resources of the West to empire builders—the railroads, Weyerhaeuser, and a few other major corporations—or to keep its options open by retaining control of public lands.[18] What population existed in the relevant landscapes had all it could do to keep rudimentary law and order. Congress created the Bureau of Reclamation (1902) and the Forest Service to manage natural resources scientifically in the public interest (call it communism if you like) as the only alternative to establishing private empires and baronies in the western states and territories.

If deliberation means discussion of the substance of proposals rather than jockeying for influence, if it means adducing considerations that others can understand as reasons rather than logrolling for results, one could as plausibly look for deliberation among scientists and professionals as among the representatives of the people. For these reasons, scientific management seemed to conservationists to be a good enough surrogate for democracy.[19] At the time, how but by some appeal to "objective" science could the government manage western resources in a manner consistent with the public interest? Local communities of diverse stakeholders and libraries in which to meet hardly existed within national forests or public rangeland prior to World War II. Even if scientific expertise and professional judgment amounted to reading the entrails of chickens, no one offered a better way to determine the public good.[20]

THE ILLUSION OF THE IDEAL ADMINISTRATION

The twenty or so citizens who met at Quincy Library did not convene to protest a Forest Service decision. Rather, they came together as a result of Forest Service indecision. The Service, according to a local newspaper account, had become "a weakened, disoriented agency that used to run the national forests. Today, the forests are run by judges, by environmentalists working through the Clinton administration, and by the timber industry working through Congress."[21] Quincy Library Group organizer Michael Jackson explains that

> because no one knows how to manage the forests, all sides in Congress hack away at the Forest Service. The Republicans attack science, recreation, and implementation of wildlife protection. The Democrats go after roading and other natural-resource budget items. The result is a shrinking agency that spends much of its time wondering when the next blow will fall.[22]

In its heyday before the Second World War, the Forest Service had the benefit of savvy political leadership. Legislation enacted in 1897, moreover, gave the Forest Service a clear and politically feasible mandate—namely, to secure water flows and "to furnish a continuous supply of timber."[23] With this mandate, the Forest Service derided the views of preservationists such as John Muir. "The object of our forest policy," Pinchot wrote, "is not to preserve the forests because they are beautiful . . . or because they are refuges for the wild creatures of the wilderness . . . but the making of prosperous homes."[24] In Pinchot's time scientists and experts knew something; they spoke with moral certainty born of scientific objectivity, and it hardly mattered if what they knew wasn't so.[25]

After World War II, in the rapidly growing new West, hunters, fishers, skiers, and preservationists came into conflict with miners, loggers, grazers, farmers, and developers. Environmental organizations, such as the Sierra Club, as well as industry, recreational interests, and other groups, built up their own staffs of scientists, economists, and other experts to challenge the Forest Service on its own professional grounds. The agency meanwhile had become inbred; its chiefs, always appointed from within the agency, lacked the political savvy of Pinchot. The Forest Service lost ground figuratively and literally after the war: against its howls of protest, preservationists managed to carve several wilderness parks from the national forests.

To block further attempts to turn forests into parks, the Forest Service prodded Congress to enact the Multiple-Use Sustained-Yield Act of 1960, a vague document instructing the Service to manage "the various renewable surface resources of the national forests so that they are utilized in the combination that will best meet the needs of the American people."[26] Although the agency believed that this amorphous delegation of legislative authority would increase its power, it had the reverse effect. Such an indeterminate delegation, as Louis Jaffe once wrote, yields only controversy and litigation "when results do not comport with one or another individual's concept of what the 'public interest' requires. Thus, paradoxically, the more vague a delegation, the more likely the charge that the agency has failed to fulfill its congressional mandate."[27]

When Congress provides an agency, such as the Forest Service, with no instruction more precise than to regulate in the public interest, it creates not legislation but legislators. Congress similarly delegates its legislative powers to others when it sets an impossible goal—that the workplace shall be hazard-free, for example—and then modifies it with a weasel word, such as "to the extent feasible."[28] Chief Justice William Rehnquist, reviewing the Occupational Safety and Health Act, described the phrase "to the extent feasible" as one of many examples of "Congress simply avoiding a choice which was both fundamental for purposes of the statute and yet politically so divisive that the necessary decision or compromise was difficult, if not impossible, to hammer out in the legislative forge."[29]

He implored the Court to invalidate the vague and precatory laws which support today's regulatory state. These statutes, he said, "violate the doctrine against uncanalized delegations of legislative power."[30]

What is wrong with uncanalized delegations of legislative power? Critics of the administrative state sometimes offer the pseudo-sophisticated reply that agencies to which Congress fails to give a clear political mandate will be captured by the industries they are supposed to regulate. Other critics, including those associated with public choice theory, argue even more cynically that bureaucrats will feather their own nests—for example, by endorsing on "neutral" and "scientific" grounds whatever policies bring more money or more power to the agency. If putting out fires brings in money, then science requires the suppression of fires; if further studies attract big bucks, then more research is required. Although there is something to be said for these familiar criticisms, agencies acting even with the best intentions lack authority to make the political trade-offs Congress delegates to them. As a result, little more may be expected from these agencies than regulatory rigor mortis, paralysis by analysis, and an endless loop.

During the 1960s and 1970s—years in which it enacted the nation's basic environmental statutes—Congress acted consistently with the conservationist premise that policy should be professionalized rather than politicized. The National Environmental Policy Act of 1969 (NEPA), for example, hailed at the time as "an environmental bill of rights,"[31] in fact reiterated the conservationist faith that the agencies could spin scientific straw into political gold if they gathered enough of it.[32] The statute told the agencies to "[u]tilize a systematic, interdisciplinary approach which will ensure the integrated use of the natural and social sciences and the environmental design arts in decision-making which may have an impact on man's environment."[33] If a single scientific discipline failed to make an agency sufficiently diverse, democratic, or deliberative, perhaps a whole passel of different disciplines—including the social sciences—would do.

No matter how many scientific specialists—ecologists, for example, as well as foresters—an agency brought on board, the NEPA-mandated Environmental Impact Statements (EISs) it prepared quickly became the targets of litigation. In a representative case, *National Resources Defense Council (NRDC) v. Morton,* an environmental group forced the Bureau of Land Management (BLM) to produce not one (as it planned) but 212 major EISs for the areas for which it granted grazing rights.[34] Ranchers appealed, arguing that the NRDC, which hoped "to run them off the range," had colluded with the BLM, which saw that "its budget allotments would be greatly strengthened"[35] to pay for the EISs. The ranchers then turned to their senators, who held posts on key committees overseeing the land use agencies, to protect their interests from any action the BLM might eventually take.

An "Iron Triangle"—the inevitable result of the overdelegation of legislative authority to the executive branch—now defines environmental policy making as a three-cornered tug-of-war. At one vertex of this triangle, the administrative agencies, such as the Forest Service or the BLM, try to promulgate policies. At the next vertex, the special interests, including industry and national environmental groups, challenge any policy they do not like, often taking the agency to court. At the third vertex, members of Congress intervene with the agency to obtain policies their constituents or contributors desire. Any decision taken at one of these vertices will be appealed and probably blocked at another—and eventually the dispute will wend its way through the judicial system, the fourth corner, as it were, of this infamous triangle. The Iron Triangle as surely sinks public policy as the Bermuda Triangle sinks ships—and equally well serves the public interest.[36]

If Congress had either leased the Lassen and Plumas forests to Sierra Pacific Industries or designated them as wilderness, the good people of northern California would have lived with the results. In a democracy, citizens are supposed to accept and comply with a statute the legislature enacts even if they do not agree with it. Problems arise in the environmental area, however, because legislation is either too ambiguous or too aspirational to dictate policy, leaving the real decisions to the agencies and derivatively to the courts. The citizenry more often than not must get along with no decision at all—just indecision, starts and fits of policy in one direction or another, contradictory statutes, and endless litigation. The Forest Service would fiddle with further studies, the locals thought, even while the Sierras burned.

Torn in opposite directions by well-heeled environmental and industry lobbies, each with its own credentialed scientists and special friends in Congress, the agencies have become Push-Me-Pull-You's utterly unable to make the hard political choices Congress delegates to them. The appearance of civic environmental associations, such as the Quincy Library Group, has an ironic quality in this context. The very political choices civil society pays Congress to decide have come back full circle to civil society again.

THE SOLACE OF SCIENCE

Almost a century ago, the Forest Service enjoyed both a clear political mandate and a solid scientific consensus among experts about how to achieve it. Congress told the Service to protect water flows and to maximize the sustained yield of timber. Foresters and other professionals knew (or thought they knew) how to do these things. Today, when the Forest Service has no instruction more determinate than to "best meet the needs of the American people," what role can science play in agency decision making? It must play an even greater role, one might say, because the agency has to rely on science to determine its ends as well as the means it uses to achieve them. The alternative to scientific management would seem to be pressure politics; then there would be no role for science.

Speaking to a meeting of American foresters in the 1970s, economist John Krutilla declared that the Forest Service must base policy on science or endure "indignities at the hands of one or another group insisting that the national forests satisfy their mutually incompatible demands."[37] Recommending his own discipline of resource economics, Krutilla announced that the agency's goal must be "to manage the national forests in order to maximize benefits"—that is, "to pursue economic efficiency."[38] Robert Nelson aptly comments, "Krutilla argued that the time had come to make good on the original promise of Gifford Pinchot, who preached only scientific management."[39]

Economists such as Krutilla preached the "gospel of efficiency" throughout the 1970s, arguing as scientists that the public interest lay in maximizing social utility. Seizing on this opportunity to add another level of bureaucratic review to stifle regulatory actions, Ronald Reagan, upon becoming president in 1981, issued an executive order requiring a cost-benefit justification of all major regulatory actions, except as prohibited by law.[40] Administrative agencies obediently hired economists to pour the old political wine into new bottles, labeled "costs" and "benefits," from which to decant the public interest.

Seeing their own opportunity in this alchemical project, national environmental organizations hired economists able to demonstrate scientifically that the policies they favored resolved a "market failure" and thus were economically efficient. Krutilla himself authored a number of spectacularly innovative analyses to demonstrate that the costs of economically promising projects, such as the proposed Hell's Canyon dam, actually exceeded the benefits.[41] Traditional combatants carry on venerable political, moral, and ideological battles as if the outcome depended on identifying "externalities," accounting for "existence values," finding the right "discount" rates, or correctly "pricing" safety, health, and ecosystem services. Economists apply the measuring rod of money to opposing political, moral, and religious beliefs and opinions simply by asking how much people are willing to pay for particular policy outcomes. Thus, disputes over the direction of public policy are transformed into data for cost-benefit analysis.

Attempts by economists and other professionals to place public policy

on a scientific and objective footing, however, have made agency decisions only the more vulnerable to "pressure politics" and therefore to revision and reversal. One reason for this is obvious: all sides to a political
controversy can hire their own scientists and economists to refute the
other fellow's experts. Nobel laureates tend to cost so much that only industry can hire them, but there is hardly an interest group, however modest, that cannot afford to enlist reputable expert witnesses to testify at administrative hearings and then in court. Scientists outside a regulatory
agency second-guess everything it says or does, so that the agencies must
employ blue-ribbon science advisory boards or commission National Research Council studies to vouch for their objectivity.[42] Too often cost-benefit analyses, climate models, toxicological studies, and other projections
cancel each other out, while scientific analyses and economic assessments
fracture along traditional political fault lines, eroding public confidence
in science.

By the 1970s, the public recognized that science simply could not answer many of the questions regulators asked of it.[43] Hume's edict about
inferring an "ought" from an "is" became a commonplace caution to policy makers against mixing "facts" and "values." The tendency of newer
"policy sciences" beginning in the 1960s to extend their reach to the
"trans-scientific"—that is, to normative and political questions—aroused
public suspicion, which turned to hostility as "the best and the brightest"
led the nation into the tragedy of Vietnam. Meanwhile, the business of
science—the competition for grants, the constant claims to "paradigm
shifts" that adorn proposals, and the millions of dollars wasted on "big
science" fiascoes such as the International Biology Program—led to public skepticism about the honesty, objectivity, and neutrality of expertise.

Chastened by the public's distrust, some scientists have become cir-
cumspect, qualifying their claims to the point of making them vacuous or
abandoning "relevant" science altogether. Others find themselves preoccupied with policing the boundaries between "real" and "junk" science.
As journalists have taken up the science beat, moreover, debates between
experts have become routinized, presented like theater or restaurant reviews, as matters of taste, or reported like sports events, as competitions.
The press tends to "balance" every assertion with an equal and opposing
one, however implausible. While science has plainly added much to the
store of human knowledge, it has also made us aware of how much we
do not know.

As more people attend college and observe scientists in their university
habitats, they are less likely to venerate science and more inclined to
judge scientific claims for themselves. When the public does seek to judge
for itself, however, it finds less and less in these claims that it can understand. Local knowledge (e.g., of tinderbox conditions in the forests near

Quincy) often bears no relation to scientific models (e.g., concerning "forest succession," "climax communities," or "sustainable yields"). As the models become more mysterious, the assumptions more arcane, the mathematics more hairy, expert opinion loses relevance to public concerns. Sheila Jasanoff notes, "The gap between what experts do and what makes sense to people accounts for a massive public rejection of technical rationality in modern societies."[44] Not science itself but the conservationist faith that it can always be our guide has led to disillusionment—to the widespread belief, as Jasanoff reports, that "science, far from being part of the solution, may in fact be part of the problem."[45]

THE MISCHIEFS OF FACTION

One does not have to look long at the history of the Forest Service to see what James Madison described as the "mischiefs of faction." The single-issue strategies of many lobbying groups routinely "gridlock" policy in the Iron Triangle.[46] For these groups, conflict provides the principal method to deal with issues and to mobilize support. Deliberating with others to resolve problems undermines the group's mission, which is to press its purpose or concerns as far as it can in a zero-sum game with its political adversaries. Anything less than demonizing opponents—for example, negotiating with them in good faith—would disarm and demobilize one side in comparison with the others. When an interest group joins with its enemies to solve a problem, it loses the purity of its position; it ceases to be a cause and becomes a committee.

After many years, the strife of factions around the Iron Triangle has become professionalized. It benefits the lawyers, lobbyists, and expert witnesses who serve in various causes as mercenaries, but it produces no policy. If the crumbling Plumas and Lassen forests go up in flames carrying away the habitat of species as well as that of human beings, as they surely will absent a management plan, environmental groups can celebrate their victory: they will have thwarted the timber industry. The timber industry can savor its victory in having kept the area from becoming a designated wilderness. Like the dead trees that hang upon each other in the forest, interest groups hold each other up in the Iron Triangle, each sustained and supported by its holy war against the forces of evil on the other side.

Political theorists suggest two strategies for dealing with the mischiefs of faction. First, neoconservatives believe that these mischiefs arise whenever public bureaucracies offer vast returns to interest-group badgering and bargaining. Instead of engaging in productive or constructive activity themselves, interest groups will invest resources to wrest favors—"rents" in the technical lingo—from government. The public ownership of resources, as Friedrich Hayek has said, leads to the "domination of government by coalitions of organized interests" and the growth of "an enormous and wasteful apparatus of para-government" needed to placate, reward, and defend against various interest groups.[47]

As if to illustrate Hayek's point, the Forest Service for many decades has subsidized the timber industry by selling timber from national forests at below the cost of administering the sales.[48] Several think tanks, from the Cato Institute to the Progressive Policy Institute, have recommended that the Forest Service budget for road building—another subsidy to logging—could be cut for a savings of about $0.6 billion over five years. At the same time, preservationists recognize the value of habitat restoration, watershed protection, and other maintenance (including fire suppression) that the Forest Service provides. Environmentalists may see in the Forest Service a way to deal at public expense with fire, disease, protection of exotic species, hikers in distress, game management, and many other problems associated with preserving wilderness areas.

Neoconservatives argue that if the government got out of the business of land management, interest groups would get into it, devoting their resources to accomplishing what they want rather than to fighting each other for governmental largess. John Baden and Richard Stroup, for example, have proposed that national forest lands "be put into the hands of qualified environmental groups such as the Sierra Club, the Audubon Society, and the Wilderness Society."[49] They point out that when these groups own land, they are quick to make deals with industry—for example, by leasing mineral rights in return for revenue they can use to purchase even more ecologically sensitive areas for preservation. According to newspaper reports, members of the Quincy Library Group argue that "small-patch logging and thinning will eventually return at least the drier parts of the forests to the open, brush-free state, dominated by large trees, that the first settlers found."[50] If the Sierra Club owned the forests, it might come to the same conclusion. At any rate, it would become responsible for solving the problems that plague the forests—disease, fire, undergrowth, and so on—rather than merely pressing its concerns.

Privatization is not the only strategy to avert the mischiefs of faction. Among liberal theorists, Joshua Cohen and Charles Sabel have described a system of federalism "with multiple centers of decision-making, including central and local decision-makers, and separate spheres of responsibility for different units."[51] Laws that prohibit nuisances or torts—for example, laws controlling pollution—may be administered centrally, since everyone has the common-law right to be free of trespass. Representative citizen groups and stakeholder councils, however, are best situated to respond to problems arising in their communities not related to civil, political, or personal rights. Cohen and Sabel also note that deliberative associations seeking to manage localized resources have much in common. For this reason, these problem-solving groups should be networked, so that they can learn from each other's efforts.

Beginning in the early 1970s, the Forest Service encouraged this kind of federalism by bringing the views and interests of local user groups into its decision-making process. In 1972, the agency initiated its Inform and Involve program, which served as a model for other agencies eager to engage stakeholders in policy debate and discussion. The National Forest Management Act of 1976 called for public participation in the preparation of the long-term forest plans it required.[52] Officials in the Department of Agriculture prodded the Forest Service fully to implement the participatory mandates of the law.[53] A cadre of foresters tried to tease out the public interest by talking with the public; indeed, the Forest Service became preoccupied with public outreach and engagement.

During this period, the Forest Service brought together stakeholder groups, thus preparing the way for the one that met a decade later at Quincy Library. Carmen Sirianni and Lewis Friedland, who work with the Civic Practices Network, point out that "some forests developed programs characterized by genuine dialogue and consensus-seeking among various user groups, and staff began to nurture deliberative regulatory cultures to complement and modify a professional ideology based on the scientific management of the land."[54] In response to the NEPA, the Forest Service redoubled its efforts to solicit public "input" into its EISs and policy decisions.[55]

In the decade-long process to prepare an EIS for areas to be given wilderness status, Sirianni and Friedland report, the Service "involved fifty thousand people in providing input into the scope of the EIS, seventeen thousand in workshops," and many thousands more who sent in comments. Over two decades, the Forest Service has engaged communities of stakeholders throughout the West in "deliberative, consensual and other face-to-face" discussions, including "intensive workshops to clarify and classify different user values" and "weekend retreats to build trust and empathy among traditional opponents."[56] These traditional opponents, when dealing face-to-face with each other, start considering reasons rather than stating positions and thus move from mobilizing support to solving problems.

Often with the encouragement and assistance of the Forest Service, the Environmental Protection Agency (EPA), and other agencies, hundreds of citizen associations now exercise responsibility in managing forests, wetlands, rivers, lakes, wildlife, and other natural assets.[57] Examples include the Henry's Fork Watershed Council and the Sawtooth Wildlife Council in central Idaho, in which diverse community interests are resolving public land issues in Custer County. Similarly, the Idaho Conservation League is trying to find common ground with ranchers in managing the spectacular Boulder–White Clouds wilderness area.

Researchers at the University of Colorado have inventoried more than a hundred voluntary, collaborative associations organized in the West to manage the drainage areas of particular rivers. The citizen groups have convened, according to a recent report, because "current Federal water policy suffers from unclear and conflicting goals, and a maze of competing agencies and programs."[58] With names like the "San Pedro Watershed Alliance," the "Mugu Lagoon Task Force," and the "Eagle River Assembly," these civic environmental groups respond to "the inability of government agencies to resolve problems in the watershed and the desire of watershed residents for more input and control in managing resources."[59]

Rather than simply seeking "input" for a decision that agency experts are to make, the Forest Service can ask these stakeholder councils to make the decision themselves, once they have been offered scientific information and advice. As long as individuals trust their representatives in negotiations with delegates of opposing groups, they are bound to accept the outcome as equitable or as the best that could be achieved. They are likely to challenge the same outcome if reached by an administrative process on the basis of technical or scientific considerations. The challenge may be successful, moreover, if it can muster opposing scientific opinion.

Science cannot determine the public interest. A bureaucracy may implement clear political goals, but it is hopeless when it tries to resolve what are essentially political disputes. The public itself, through a representative and deliberative process, must make out where its interest lies. Unlike the Iron Triangle, where pressure is the only political principle, local stakeholder councils, properly constituted, can be places, as Cohen and Sabel write, "where practicality in the form of problem-solving meets political principle in the form of deliberation."[60]

Management strategies worked out by deliberative and representative citizen groups, of course, become targets of criticism by those who seek to advance a principled position—for example, to permit or to prohibit logging on all public lands—which they believe reflects the best available science. Thus, any consensus-based compromise reached by those trying to resolve an impasse will be "attacked by environmentalists, timber and mining groups, and other backcountry users as providing too much or too little wilderness protection."[61] Despite the obstacles it confronts, however, the Forest Service, along with other regulatory agencies, has continued to experiment with a democratic method—a deliberative and representative process—which might restore a sort of political legitimacy to its actions. Such developments have prompted Robert Gottlieb and Helen Ingram to hail the emergence of a "new environmentalism"—a "grassroots, community-based, democratic movement that differs radically from conventional, mainstream American environmentalism, which always had a strong nondemocratic strain."[62]

In an article entitled "Land-Use Democracy," ecologist Aldo Leopold wrote in 1942, "One of the curious evidences the 'conservation programs' are losing their grip is that they seldom have resorted to self-government as a cure for land abuse. . . . [We] have not tried democracy as a possible answer to our problem."[63] Instead of trying democracy, the nation has generally maintained Pinchot's faith (to quote Julia Marie Wondolleck) "that scientifically trained land managers will be able to acquire the appropriate information with which to . . . reach outcomes that advance the public's interest." Whether a forest should be mined, timbered, hunted, roaded, or designated as wilderness, however, is a political not a professional judgment, which an agency must hide under the cloak of technical analysis. Wondolleck writes, "Like the emperor's new clothes, however, this technical cloak now hides little and . . . the masses are not quiet about what they see."[64]

COMMUNITY SURVIVAL IN PLACE

The Quincy Library Group was born of desperation. Decades of litigation had tied loggers, environmentalists, and public officials in knots—a legal Laocoön from which no one could break loose. Through a series of administrative appeals and suits challenging nearly every timber sale during the 1980s, local wilderness advocates such as Michael Jackson and Linda Blum had forced logging companies, notably Sierra Pacific Industries, to cease most operations, depressing the economies of Quincy, Loyalton, and other communities near the Plumas and Lassen National Forests. When a timber sale did go through, a local newspaper reports, the driver of the truck carrying the big logs was likely to make a detour to pass under Jackson's office window "taunting the environmental litigator with the sight of another fallen giant, before stopping for a celebratory beer on the town's main street."[65] In 1986, things got scary. Angry laid-off workers made threatening remarks at public meetings, and store owners displayed yellow ribbons in solidarity with the industry. Wilderness advocates gave as good as they got. "We blamed and ridiculed our neighbors," Jackson recalled. "There was sugar in the tanks of logging equipment. And they responded in the normal way, including gunshot wounds to windows."[66]

Ten years later, these adversaries found that face-to-face meetings in search of a compromise plan gave each side more than it could gain by struggling against the other. In spite of their earlier acrimony and mutual distrust, environmentalists, loggers, foresters, and public officials united in seeking what the leader of a prominent ecological restoration project in northern California has called "community survival in place."[67]

How did these opponents manage to find common ground? First, they had to solve a problem rather than sustain a lobby. Second, they had arrived at an impasse detrimental to all. Unable to attract any attention from national environmental groups, local activists such as Linda Blum had to act single-handedly to stop logging by filing administrative appeals of specific sales. "That meant driving deep into the forest to review every logging site and writing lengthy documents," said Blum, an environmental consultant in Quincy. "As a grassroots activist, I couldn't keep it up. It wasn't sustainable activism."[68] Logging companies found they could not pay their hundreds of employees in the area, thus upholding the local economy, and still litigate against these diehard environmentalists. Neither side expected that the Forest Service would address the situation, for its interest plainly lay in budgeting for further scientific studies, not in resolving the conflict. Everyone involved in the community around Quincy had come to his or her wit's end, and no one outside the community offered much hope or help.

Third, many of these people knew each other and deeply regretted the social animosity that had torn the community apart. "It is easy to take the moral high ground when you don't live in these communities," said Tom Nelson, a Sierra Pacific Industries forester, who joined the Quincy group. "It is tougher when you have to face these people every day."[69]

Fourth, the threat of a fire in the crumbling forests demanded an effective unified response from traditional combatants. The regime of regular burning adopted by Native Americans had produced the park-like old growth that illustrates the calendars issued by the Sierra Club and other wilderness organizations.[70] When the Lassen National Forest was first surveyed in 1908, trees more than thirty inches in diameter dominated more than 70 percent of the land.[71] At about that time, however, the newly created Forest Service instituted fire prevention as part of its scientific management of the forests. (Fire suppression also brought enormous amounts of money into Forest Service coffers.) Gifford Pinchot wrote in 1917 that "the work of a Forest Ranger is, first of all, to protect the District committed to his charge against fire. That comes before all else."[72]

In an eighty-year effort costing many billions of dollars, Smokey Bear nearly eliminated forest fires in many areas of the West. Partly as a result, in Idaho, California, and other western states, deadwood and brush blanket the floors of forests, and small trees in dense stands compete for water and light. "Such forests in the typical case have become economically less productive, subject to disease and insect infestation, aesthetically unattractive, and ironically now also prone to new and much greater fire hazards," writes Robert Nelson.[73] The conflagrations that ravaged Yellowstone in 1988 were no accident. "They were partly a result of a century of federal fire policy that has sought to eliminate fire from the western landscape but instead has merely changed its time and place."[74]

To relieve the tinderbox conditions in the surrounding forests, local environmentalists, including Jackson and Blum, along with industry foresters, revived a plan that national environmental groups, including the NRDC, the Sierra Club, and the Wilderness Society, had supported ten years earlier. It allowed timber companies to emulate the results of periodic fire by thinning small trees and clearing deadwood and undergrowth, while leaving larger trees untouched. "If I thought this forest could survive without being cleaned up, I would support zero cut," Jackson said. "After 150 years of pounding this is not a normal ecosystem. We've got 50 years' worth of work to get back to a natural cycle."[75]

On 10 July 1993, the Quincy Library Group presented its management plan at a town hall meeting attended by about 150 individuals representing every view, interest, and position in the surrounding communities. The attendees approved the plan nearly unanimously. In 1994, when a huge blaze in neighboring Loyalton destroyed spotted owl habitat, local activists including Blum saw no alternative to the Quincy plan. "It wasn't loggers versus owls that was the unresolved issue," she said. "It was owls versus fire."[76]

The Quincy Library Plan covers about 2.5 million acres which it seeks to return to the condition that existed in previous centuries, when periodic fires pruned away dead and small trees, leaving old growth—twenty to thirty huge trees per acre—to dominate the forest floor. Today, according to observers, fire suppression and other policies have turned the forest into "a thicket of 1,000 or more small trees per acre, with dead ones on the ground or leaning against the living trees." In this context, "the fear is that even small fires will quickly grow to catastrophic, landscape-scale conflagrations that will destroy all trees and habitat."

The plan puts about a million acres of roadless forest into wilderness and other protected status—including 148,000 acres of roadless, old-growth forest now designated by law as timberland. In response to the threat of catastrophic fires, the Quincy Library plan proposes that in the remaining 1.6 million-acre managed area, loggers each year would clear forty thousand to sixty thousand acres of leaning dead trees, some young trees, and deadwood on the ground. All larger trees (those more than thirty inches in diameter) would be protected. The plan also allows ten thousand acres within the managed area to be logged in selected small patches yearly, with a resulting rotation cycle in which each acre would be logged once every 175 years.[77] According to newspaper reports, the plan "limits the size of cuts to 2 acres at most, and takes 30 percent of the most sensitive of the 2.5 million acres off the timber base, including salmon habitat not yet protected by any recovery plan."[78] The group believes that the permitted harvest will allow enough work for loggers to sustain the local economy while at the same time helping turn the forest back to its "presettlement" state.

Having reached a deliberative consensus on this strategy among traditional combatants in northern California, the Quincy Library Group had to convince the Forest Service to implement the plan. But this proved impossible. Wayne Thornton, the Forest Service supervisor of the Plumas National Forest when the Quincy group was formed, correctly surmised that national political groups that dominated the Iron Triangle—and to whom the Service was beholden—did not share the problem-solving spirit of the participants. "Every time I looked at them, I saw almost shadows looming behind them of larger constituencies," said Thornton, who attended some of the library meetings. And it was not clear that "these individuals were doing what these larger constituencies wanted."[79]

Nor was it clear that the Forest Service was eager to find a solution. Critics suggest that increased funding for the Forest Service pays mostly for environmental impact and other scientific studies. Because studies can always be questioned, extended, confirmed, disconfirmed, and so on, getting the science right promises to become an eternal occupation. This is especially true when each side in a controversy earnestly believes that its position reflects the best available science. Paralysis by analysis seemed the only prospect. And so, the members of the Quincy Library Group, following perhaps a lesson they had learned in high school civics, decided to go to their representatives in Congress.

THE POLITICS OF ENVIRONMENTAL POLICY

In 1996—three years after they had first submitted their proposal to the Forest Service—members of the Quincy group approached their local congressman, Republican Wally Herger, who converted the plan to legislation. On 9 July 1997, as the Library Group members watched on C-Span, the House of Representatives debated and passed the bill by a 429–1 majority. "We were thrilled by the vote, of course, but the debate touched our hearts," Michael Jackson later testified.

> To see Congressmen Herger and Fazio working together to include Congressman Miller's objectives in our bill reminded us of our own laborious negotiations in the early years. To see resolution, accomplishment, and good

spirits reign for a morning on the floor of the House was soul-satisfying for us and many like us around the country.[80]

The passage of the Quincy Bill in the House, while "soul-satisfying" for local collaborative groups, greatly angered national environmental organizations, such as the Audubon Society, the Sierra Club, and the Wilderness Society, which, along with the NRDC, had earlier supported the plan on which the Quincy group built.[81] The Sierra Club in the meantime had adopted a "zero logging" principle for the national forests and now opposed even the commercial cutting of deadwood to make firebreaks. The Audubon Society described the Quincy plan as "unfair and undemocratic" because it involved a "paradigm shift from national management of national forests to local management."[82] Louis Blumberg, a spokesman for the Wilderness Society, shared the same concern. The Quincy bill "excludes 99 percent of the Americans who have an equal stake in national forests," he said.[83]

Except for the Sierra Club, which opposes all commercial logging in national forests, national groups objected to the Quincy plan not on substantive grounds but because of the precedent it might set. "Just because a group of local people can come to agreement doesn't mean that it is good public policy," said Jay Watson, regional director of the Wilderness Society.[84] The National Audubon Society stated that Quincy-like bills "would allow a relatively small group of citizens to dictate public forest management, rather than agency officials receiving input from the public at large."[85] Michael McCloskey, chair of the Sierra Club, declared the bill was "designed to disempower our [national environmental] constituency, which is heavily urban."[86]

Quincy Library Group members replied that national groups refused to send representatives to their councils. "We begged. We pleaded. They wouldn't come," said Michael Jackson. "What do you do when they won't come? Tell your neighbors we can't meet because they're too busy having cocktail parties down in San Francisco?"[87] Tom Nelson pointed out that Congress was responsible for making the decision. If Congress votes overwhelmingly for the bill and the president signs it, how is democracy slighted? "It is rewarding that a group of local citizens can take their ideas to a local representative and take it through the whole process," Nelson said. "It is how democracy is supposed to work. That is what I learned in school."[88]

Speaking for the Wilderness Society, Blumberg urged the Quincy group—which he described as "only one special interest group"—to wait for the Forest Service to make its determination, however long that might take.[89] The League of Conservation Voters joined the Wilderness Society in defending the Forest Service process. In her letter to Congress, Deb Callahan, league president, wrote, "The Herger bill could have serious environmental consequences that can only be assessed through full public and scientific review."[90] Michael McCloskey of the Sierra Club joined the others in defending the turf of the Forest Service. Brushing aside the years local residents had awaited a decision from the agency, McCloskey said, "When they run to Congress to impose a negotiated agreement on a national forest, they certainly are displacing an agency's process."[91] Michael Yost, a Quincy environmental activist, replied, "After working eleven years with the national environmental organizations and four years with the QLG [Quincy Library Group] attempting to get an administrative solution, the best option is now to seek a legislative solution."[92]

The Quincy Library Plan also had opponents among antienvironmentalists. In 1995, at the height of the Republican ascendancy, Congress had enacted an infamous "salvage rider" suspending many environmental laws. Several members of Congress asked the Forest Service to implement the "rider" by leasing to timber companies areas the Quincy plan put off-limits to logging. Under this pressure, the Plumas National Forest twice offered timber for sale in a large roadless tract the plan protected. The timber companies, honoring the agreement they entered at the Quincy Library, refused to bid on the tract.

After the House of Representatives passed the Quincy Library Bill nearly unanimously, the president announced his strong support, and the Senate put it on its "consent" agenda for quick passage. National environmental groups, however, convinced one senator to put a "hold" on the bill, thus returning the situation at least temporarily to the gridlock where it had languished for the past fifteen years.

To stop the bill for good in the Senate, the National Audubon Society circulated a "Dear Senator" letter defending the normal processes of the Forest Service. "Forest Service employees," the letter said, "are more likely on the whole to act in the public's best interest than local management coalitions, which don't have the national scientific backing of an agency."[93] The Society acknowledged that one of its "respected chapters, Plumas Audubon Society in Quincy, California, is participating in and actively supporting the QLG's legislative strategy." The letter advised the Senate to ignore the position of the local chapter.

> Local forest users can tell us a lot about their forest, like which areas are used by which species or which are most valuable for wood. They are not necessarily equipped to view the bigger picture of, for example, species declines, cumulative impacts, or policy trends. . . . Considering the big picture is the job of Congress, and of watchdog groups like the National Audubon Society.

The local Audubon chapter, stung and surprised by this letter, wrote back that the national office was "unfamiliar with the individuals, expertise and diverse talents which have developed QLG strategies. Also, this rhetoric is, to put it politely, patronizing." The Plumas chapter, which had joined the Quincy Library negotiations from the start, asked, "How can a local chapter of Audubon remain viable when the National office abandons, sabotages or undermines local efforts to improve conservation on the local scene?" The chapter emphasized the specificity of place and the need for place-based solutions to environmental problems. "National folks could better understand the real meaning of 'place' if they would come to the 'places' in question."[94]

Sierra Club Chair McCloskey explained his group's opposition to stakeholder negotiations in a November 1995 memo. "Industry thinks its odds are better in these forums," McCloskey wrote. "It has ways to generate pressures on communities where it is strong, which it doesn't have at the national level."[95] Environmental leaders in Washington joined McCloskey in alleging that rural westerners are easily snookered by slick-talking industry representatives. According to one newspaper report, literature from national groups often refers "to well-intentioned Bambi consorting with ravenous Godzilla, and naive chickens inviting sharp, high-powered foxes into the coop."[96]

Fifty years ago, when the power relations favored logging and other extractive industries, local preservationists were perhaps at a disadvantage. Today, local communities include entrepreneurs of many sorts; for example, from the Sierra Nevadas to the Colorado Plateau, software developers greatly outnumber loggers. Far from holding the balance of economic power, timber and other extractive industries now represent a small and dwindling sector of an economically diverse and urbanized population. According to the *Atlas of the New West*, only a handful of counties remain in which at least 35 percent of the population is employed in mining, logging, farming, or ranching.[97] The "West has moved beyond extracting natural resources to appreciating them in place: mountainsides not excavated for copper or molybdenum; rangeland homes for wolves instead of cattle; and old-growth forests rather than clear-cuts."[98]

National environmental groups remain suspicious of collaborative stakeholder processes for other and deeper reasons than the fear that local environmentalists can be co-opted by industry flaks. More important, people who are willing to listen to each other and to find ways to solve the problems that divide them are likely to defect from the Manichean battles national groups wage around the Iron Triangle. "It is troubling that such processes tend to de-legitimate conflict as a way of dealing with issues and of mobilizing support," McCloskey wrote in his memo. "Instead of hammering out national rules to reflect majority rule in the nation, transferring power to a local venue implies decision-making by a very different majority in a much smaller population."

McCloskey added that there is a good reason national groups do not accept invitations to participate in councils seeking to govern localized resources. If representatives working at the local level sign on to a compromise to resolve a particular conflict in specific circumstances, the national group will be bound to accept it, even though it departs from national principles. "It is psychologically difficult to simultaneously negotiate and publicly attack bad proposals from the other side. This tends to be seen as acting in bad faith." Because the Sierra Club has committed itself on both scientific and ethical grounds to a "zero commercial logging" national rule, it sees little to gain by negotiation or accommodation. "Too much time spent in stakeholder processes may result in demobilizing and disarming our side."[99]

Robert Putnam has argued that battles environmental groups wage in Washington drain the strength of democracy to solve environmental problems in the nation at large. "We are shouting and pressuring and suing," he has written, "but we are not reasoning together, not even in the attenuated sense that we once did, with people we know well and will meet again tomorrow."[100] While recognizing the political clout of organizations such as the Sierra Club, Putnam denies that they build the social trust on which democracy depends. "For the vast majority of their members, the only act of membership consists in writing a check for dues or perhaps occasionally reading a newsletter. . . . Their ties, in short, are to common symbols, common leaders, and perhaps common ideals, but not to one another."[101]

Many commentators compare national environmental groups to pyramids in which paid professional leaders at the top communicate with the mass of members at the bottom only through mailing-list "surveys" that are actually devices for fund-raising. "Even when they do try to communicate and listen," writes environmental consultant G. Jon Roush, "they are still captives of their own organizational goals and needs, with more incentive to compete than to collaborate."[102]

Charles Jordan and Don Snow, who study environmental groups, add, "Without meaning to and despite their many efforts to the contrary, environmental advocates have managed to create a kind of exclusive 'club of conservation.' " Members of this club—who are nearly all white, Jordan and Snow report—include credentialed experts, primarily lawyers and economists, adept at the Washington policy "game," where they have been most successful. They have few personal ties to and little familiarity with the rural places for which they are hammering out national rules. In this conservation club, the technicians clearly dominate; in most of the club's organizations, the grass roots, represented by the dues-paying membership, has but one role: to support the technical leadership with dollars and the sheer numbers that represent the political clout needed by the professionals as they go about the task of effective advocacy.[103]

CIVIC ENVIRONMENTALISM AND CIVIC RENEWAL

Recently, Randal O'Toole, a respected authority on western resource issues, has warned that the environmental movement faces its greatest crisis. "One likely result is that the movement will fragment into two distinctly different movements, one that focuses on preservation and central control and one that focuses on management and decentralization." O'Toole presents this schism as a replay of the historical opposition between preservationists and conservationists. He may fail to see, however, that preservationists and conservationists now hold many views in common.

Preservationists in the tradition of John Muir demand that the federal government protect as much of the nation's landscape as possible from human intrusion. "Research in ecology, fisheries, soils, and other areas," O'Toole comments, "seemed to support the preservationist claim that 'nature knows best.' " A "precautionary principle," moreover, suggests it is perilous to alter nature if science cannot with certainty predict all the consequences that may result.[104]

Conservationists believe that experts should manage nature intensively to maximize the long-run benefits it offers humanity. Like preservationists, however, conservationists favor centralized control of resources—for example, the management of the national forests by the Forest Service. Both preservationists and conservationists, moreover, base their conceptions of land management—their "land ethic"—on what each takes to be the best available environmental science.[105] For preservationists, science involves succession and equilibrium models, feedback loops, stability-diversity associations, and notions of nature as a superorganism that has a "health" or an "integrity" on which we all depend. For conservationists, science yields the principles of silviculture, genetic engineering, and so forth, on which sustainable forestry and agriculture are based. The best available science shows that humanity can prosper, even survive, only if it manages nature intensively (if you are a conservationist) or leaves it alone (if you are a preservationist). Each side, secure in the objectivity of its science, is certain of the rightness of its cause.

"As heirs to their conservationist forerunners' deference to expertise," Gottlieb and Ingram comment, "establishment environmentalists are embarrassed by the lack of scientific sophistication in the grass-roots movements." Thus, a Sierra Club press release urges defeat of the Quincy bill in part because it "ignores the best available science."[106] Appealing, for example, to the theory of forest succession or to various equilibrium models of the order of Nature, environmentalists may argue that the Lassen and Plumas forests will achieve the "climax" condition pictured on Sierra Club calendars if we just leave them alone. Science shows that Nature knows best; all logging—indeed, all commercial activity in the wilderness—is therefore bad on scientific grounds.

Members of the Quincy group, however, cannot see the old-growth forests pictured in Sierra Club calendars for the sticklike, dying trees that they perceive all around them. Their experience confirms what other ecologists believe—namely, that theories of forest succession, equilibrium, and so forth, serve essentially a political purpose, while nature itself (to quote environmental historian Donald Worster) "is *fundamentally* erratic, discontinuous, and unpredictable. It is full of seemingly random events that elude models of how things are supposed to work."[107] From this point of view, one could argue that only selective logging, by thinning trees and clearing out brush, can replace fire-regimes in the ecosystem. It may be too late—it may no longer be possible—to leave the forest alone.

What is most striking about grassroots movements, Gottlieb and Ingram have written, "is their democratic thrust. . . . Instead of embracing expertise, they have developed self-taught experts. . . . They have become organizations of active members rather than rosters of dues-payers on mailing lists."[108] Jordan and Snow add, "While the traditional groups have amassed memberships to underwrite staff experts in law, science, and policy, the grassroots groups are comprised of members who are personally involved in the issues." Jordan and Snow point out the crucial difference. "In the manner in which they establish their base of support and the ways they select issues and strategies, the grass-roots groups are essentially political, while many of their establishment counterparts have become essentially technical."[109] This difference—rather than the historical divergence between conservationists and preservationists—accounts for the schism now dividing environmentalists.

Environmentalists today confront a fundamental choice whether to conceive their movement as political or as technical in its concerns, its program, and its justification. They cannot have it both ways. If environmentalists at the local level engage their opponents in a political deliberation ending in a compromise, this is bound to offend national leaders eager to vindicate the truth of their science-based position against wrongheaded, ill-intentioned, and unscientific beliefs. It is unsurprising that national groups such as the Sierra Club and the Audubon Society reject the political efforts even of their own chapters in the affected regions. Environmental decisions cannot be entrusted to amateurs whose objectivity and neutrality are compromised because they are invested emotionally and economically in the survival of their human communities in place.

Lois Gibbs, who has criticized mainstream environmentalism ever since the Love Canal days, has argued that it is a mistake to think environmental goals can be framed or justified in technical—including economic and scientific—terms. They are political goals arising from competing beliefs, needs, interests, emotions, and ideologies. They are not matters of technical controversy to be settled by a more scientific, interdisciplinary approach. "Efforts to preserve and improve the environment are sure to be set back, if not fail outright, when advocates for the environment forget or ignore the fact that environmental causes are just as political as any other public policy issue."[110]

If environmental causes are political, advocates must seek to persuade or reach some accommodation with adversaries who are regarded as equals in a joint effort of deliberation. This requires all the sides in a controversy to discuss possible ways to solve a problem, each offering considerations the others may regard as reasons to adopt one solution or another. Rather than denigrating one's opponents as motivated by private gain or as befuddled by bad science, one must engage them in a joint project. The alternative is to delegate political decisions to experts—to interdisciplinary teams of economists, environmental scientists, and lawyers—who, as the Audubon letter said, are "equipped to view the bigger picture of, for example, species declines, cumulative impacts, or policy trends."

Deliberative associations, because they bring together representatives of opposing interests, may curtail the mischiefs of faction, but they do not arise as naturally as factions do. Like-minded people get together far more easily than those of different minds. A democracy, then, must take active steps to bring deliberative associations into being, rather than wait, as at the Quincy Library, for them to form as acts of desperation.

As noted earlier, the Forest Service, EPA, and other agencies are indeed involved in bringing stakeholder groups together, forging alliances between former adversaries, and building institutional arrangements in which factions may work together to resolve their differences. Bonnie Phillips, the head of WaterWatch in Seattle and an observer of collaborative groups, understands the difficulty of organizing them, making them work, and assuring their legitimacy. These groups lack a legal foundation; indeed, it is unclear even if political theory is now able to identify their purpose, powers, and limits. "The environmental community has to come up with a set of guidelines and principles about when collaboration is appropriate," Phillips says.[111]

Perhaps the principal problem of political theory today arises from our felt need to reconceptualize democratic deliberative choice in ways that make it more serviceable for practical problem solving. In an article describing democratic experimentalism, Michael Dorf and Charles Sabel recognize that the goal of collaborative problem solving is not consensus. "Its aim, rather, is to change the reasons and evidence produced in public debate, and with them the conditions for participation in civic life, so that our disputatious democracy is made both more effective as an instrument of public problem solving and more faithful to its purpose of assuring the self-determination of free and equal citizens."[112] The history of the Quincy Library Group may present as fair an example as one may find of such an experiment in democratic problem solving.

The Quincy Library Bill Forest Recovery and Economic Stability Act became law on October 21, 1998, when the president signed an omnibus appropriations bill to which it was attached as a rider. California Senator Diane Feinstein, who had shepherded the bill through the Senate a few days before, observed, "It proves that even some of the most intractable environmental issues can be resolved if people work together."[113]

The success of the Quincy group offers a hopeful instance of the Madisonian project of using governmental power to foster cooperative problem solving on the basis of mutual respect. This collaborative approach to problem solving—often local and always practical—challenges the authority of interest groups intent on maximizing their own gains. National mass-membership organizations, along with their special friends in Congress and the industry groups they oppose, own the Iron Triangle as a preserve for professionalism and expertise. The processes of engagement and compromise, in contrast, have restored a sense of civility—even of common purpose—to the communities surrounded by the Plumas and Lassen forests. Traditional adversaries are now on the same side. Michael Jackson describes one sign of the civic renewal his group has achieved. "These days, when people wave at me, they use all five fingers," he said.[114]

NOTES

1. Ed Marston, "The Timber Wars Evolve into a Divisive Attempt at Peace," *High Country News*, 29 September 1997 (http://www.hcn.org/1997/sep29/dir/Feature_The_timber.html). Many of the sources that follow are accessible through the Web site of the Quincy Library Group, at http://qlg.org/public_html/contents/perspectives.htm.

2. Stephen Pyne, *Fire in America: A Cultural History of Wildland and Rural Fire* (Princeton, N.J.: Princeton University Press, 1982), 71, details the extent to which Amerindian populations used fire as a management tool.

3. Marston, "Timber Wars."

4. Jane Braxton Little, "National Groups Object to Grassroots Power in D.C.,"

High Country News, 31 March 1997 (http://www.hcn.org/1997/mar31/dir/ WesternNationalg.html). The article quotes activist Laura Ames, who directs an alliance of forty-five grassroots environmental groups in the Sierras.

5. Karl Hess, "Beyond the Federal Range: Towards a Self-Governing West," lecture presented at the University of Colorado, Center for the American West, 6 November 1997.

6. Quoted in John Milton Cooper, Jr., *The Warrior and the Priest: Woodrow Wilson and Theodore Roosevelt* (Cambridge, Mass.: Harvard University Press, 1983), 83 (from a speech delivered in 1905 in Chicago).

7. See, for example, Marion Clawson, *The Bureau of Land Management* (New York: Praeger, 1971), especially 71–72; and Julia Marie Wondolleck, *Public Lands: Conflict and Resolution* (New York: Plenum, 1988), 20–22.

8. Quoted by Hess, "Beyond the Federal Range," 5.

9. Hess, "Beyond the Federal Range," 5.

10. Robert H. Nelson, *Public Lands and Private Rights: The Failure of Scientific Management* (Lanham, Md.: Rowman & Littlefield, 1995), 230.

11. Gifford Pinchot, *Breaking New Ground* (New York: Harcourt, Brace, 1947), 260.

12. U.S. Department of Agriculture, *A National Plan for Forestry: The Report of the Forest Service of the Agriculture Department on the Forest Problem of the United States* (Washington, D.C.: Government Printing Office, 1933), I: 41. Before World War II, cut-and-run timbering practices, which may have made economic sense when forests seemed to stretch forever, did denude landscapes, causing erosion, flooding, and so on. Only after the war, as Weyerhaeuser and other companies built up plantations for sustained yields, were private lands generally managed at least as well as the public forests. As demand for timber increased, private owners began to have an incentive to change from cut-and-run to "sustained yield" forestry. For discussion, see Nelson, *Public Lands and Private Rights*, Part II.

13. Quoted in Henry Clepper, *Professional Forestry in the United States* (Baltimore: Johns Hopkins University Press, 1971), 291. Although timber reserves have always been more than adequate, Pinchot and his successors harped on the possibility of a "timber famine" to justify the policies, including fire suppression, they believed were necessary for the efficient and scientific management of the national forests. Since private producers handily satisfied demand prior to 1945, the public forests, if harvested, would have glutted the market, driving timber prices beneath costs. While fulminating against private timber companies, the Forest Service secured their tacit support by keeping public timber off the market except in extraordinary circumstances. The national forests, therefore, never contributed more than a small percentage of national timber production before World War II. Harold K. Steen writes that the Forest Service sought to "avoid competing with private enterprise by withholding federal timber until private supplies were exhausted; sell only to meet purely local shortages; protect national forests from fire and other disasters." Harold K. Steen, *The U.S. Forest Service: A History* (Seattle: University of Washington Press, 1976), 113.

14. Quoted in Samuel P. Hays, *Conservation and the Gospel of Efficiency: The Progressive Conservation Movement, 1890–1920* (Cambridge, Mass.: Harvard University Press, 1959), 267.

15. Hays, *Conservation and the Gospel of Efficiency*, 28.

16. Hays, *Conservation and the Gospel of Efficiency*, 28.

17. Eliza Wing-yee Lee, "Political Science, Public Administration, and the Rise of the American Administrative State," *Public Administration Review* 55 (November/December 1995): 540.

18. For discussion, see Terry Anderson and Donald Leal, *Free Market Environmentalism* (Boulder, Colo.: Westview, 1991), chap. 4. These authors contend that cut-and-run timbering practices were economically efficient—as they probably were. It made more sense economically to turn trees to cash and invest the money in other industries than to reforest the land. From a strictly economic point of view, the most "profligate" timbering practices could well have been the most profitable, given the plentiful supply of forested land.

19. Robert H. Wiebe, *Self-Rule: A Cultural History of American Democracy* (Princeton, N.J.: Princeton University Press, 1995), 143. Conservationists, as Robert Nelson has written, elevated "applied science from a practical tool to a new form of religious faith," with all the intolerance for dissent that implies. It is one thing for experts to speak truth to power; it is quite another for experts to wield power themselves. When they do, the tendency is always "to circle the wagons and defend established policy. Science would be enlisted for the defense rather than left free to inquire in any direction." Nelson, *Public Lands and Private Rights*, 51, 53.

20. A wall-to-wall political consensus at the time favored maintaining federal control of western public lands. Big timber interests generally supported policies to sequester millions of acres of public land. Although opposed in principle to the utilitarian ethic underlying scientific conservationism, preservationists, too, could support Pinchot's policies, since the Forest Service kept wilderness areas out of private ownership. Followers of John Muir did not then—as they do now—feel the political strength to demand zero-cut in the public forests; nevertheless, they could count on little cutting anyway, because private forests, which were more economical, sufficed for the nation's needs at the time. Besides, starting with Yosemite in 1872, preservationists had succeeded beyond their expectations in convincing Congress to create several immense national parks. In retrospect, we know that the Forest Service, inadvertently and against its will, preserved a vast natural reserve from which Congress could later carve several more "wilderness" areas.

In the early twentieth century, no one suggested a better way to manage the national forests and other resources than to entrust them to cadres of professionals and experts. Absent an alternative, reformers could honestly endorse the ideals of efficiency, specialization, hierarchy, and expertise on which Pinchot founded the Forest Service. Wiebe comments, "Scientific government, the reformers believed, would bring opportunity, progress, order, and community" (*The Search for Order, 1877–1920* [New York: Hill & Wang, 1967], 107). The belief that land use decisions were justified scientifically allowed agency experts and bureaucrats to make those decisions stick politically. A study of public administration at the time concluded, "These men are not simply useful to legislators overwhelmed by the increasing flood of bills. They are the government" (Leonard White, *Introduction to the Study of Public Administration* [New York: Macmillan, 1926], preface).

21. Marston, "Timber Wars."

22. Marston, "Timber Wars."

23. For discussion of the Forest Reserve Act, see Nelson, *Public Lands and Private Rights*, 46.

24. Quoted by Hays, *Conservation and the Gospel of Efficiency*, 41–42.

25. Pinchot and his politically savvy successors appeased the timber companies, moreover, by keeping production from public lands low, though after the war, the Forest Service had to increase production to meet greater demand. This meant giving the companies far more access to national forests. Before World War II, the Forest Service used both its clear congressional mandate and the shield of scientific expertise to fend off challenges from both industry and preservationist groups, making compromises as needed. Local communities lacked power to question or the expertise to oppose the will of federal agencies.

26. 16 U.S.C. Sec. 531 (1976 ed.).

27. Louis L. Jaffe, "The Illusion of the Ideal Administration," *Harvard Law Review* 86 (1973): 1184.

28. Occupational Safety and Health Act, 29 U.S.C. Sec. 655(b)(5) (1976).

29. *Industrial Union Department, AFL-CIO v. American Petroleum Institute*, 448 U.S. 607 (1980) (the Benzene decision) (Justice William Rehnquist, concurring). The Clean Air Act, to cite another example, instructs the EPA to control air pollution so tightly that even the most sensitive groups are protected from harm with an adequate margin of safety. Laws this aspirational allow Congress to announce the good news—that the air shall be pollution-free—while leaving it to the agency to announce the bad news—namely, that this cannot be done at a price society is willing to pay. 42 U.S.C. Sec. 7408(f)(1)(C).

30. *Industrial Union Department, AFL-CIO v. American Petroleum Institute*, 448 U.S. 607 (1980).

31. For this view, see, for example, Eva H. Hanks and John L. Hanks, "An Environmental Bill of Rights: The Citizen Suit and the National Environmental Policy Act of 1969," *Rutgers Law Review* 24, no. 230 (1970): 230–72.

32. "The most important feature of the Act," according to Senator Henry M. Jackson, its principal author, "is that it establishes new decision-making procedures for all agencies of the federal government." Henry M. Jackson, "Environmental Quality, the Courts, and Congress," *Michigan Law Review* 68, no. 1079 (1970): 1073–82.

33. National Environmental Policy Act 102(2)(B); 42 U.S.C. 4332.

34. *National Resources Defense Council v. Morton*, 388 F. Supp. at 840 (1974).

35. Quoted and cited in Nelson, *Public Lands and Private Rights*, 159–65.

36. Nothing resembling democratic deliberation or even compromise emerges from this zero-sum game. Gridlock is what Karl Hess calls "the brute reality of the iron triangle—the self-reinforcing relations between entrenched special interests, ranchers, loggers, miners, and irrigators, and regulatory agencies . . . and the western congressional delegations who control the agencies' budgets and who rely on the political support of the monied interests to win re-election again and again." Hess, "Beyond the Federal Range," 6.

37. John V. Krutilla, "Adaptive Responses to Forces for Change," paper pre-

sented at the Annual Meetings of the Society of American Foresters, Boston, 16 October 1979, 6; cited and quoted in Nelson, *Public Lands and Private Rights*, 70.

38. John V. Krutilla and John V. Haigh, "An Integrated Approach to National Forest Management, *Environmental Law* 8 (Winter 1978): 383.

39. Nelson, *Public Lands and Private Rights*, 70.

40. Executive Order 12,291, issued 1 February 1981. The Regulatory Reform Bill of 1981, nearly enacted, would have legislated economic efficiency as the goal of all regulation and mandated cost-benefit analysis to determine when a regulation is efficient. Senator John Glenn and Representative John Dingell opposed the bill; except for their opposition, it would have passed.

41. John V. Krutilla, *The Economics of Natural Environments: Studies in the Valuation of Commodity and Amenity Resources* (Washington, D.C.: Resources for the Future, 1985).

42. See Sheila Jasanoff, *The Fifth Branch: Science Advisers as Policymakers* (Cambridge, Mass.: Harvard University Press, 1990).

43. The classic citation is Alvin Weinberg, "Science and Trans-Science," *Minerva* 10 (1970): 209–22.

44. Sheila Jasanoff, "The Dilemma of Environmental Democracy," *Issues in Science and Technology* 13 (Fall 1996): 67.

45. Jasanoff, *The Fifth Branch*, 12.

46. James Madison, *Federalist* 10, in *The Federalist Papers*, ed. Garry Wills (New York: Bantam, 1982), 42–49.

47. F. A. Hayek, *The Political Order of a Free People* (Chicago: University of Chicago Press, 1979), 13, 15.

48. See, for example, Ross W. Gorte, "Below-Cost Timber Sales: Overview," Congressional Research Service Report for Congress, Environment and Natural Resources Policy Division, 20 December 1994.

49. John Baden and Richard Stroup, "Saving the Wilderness," *Reason* 13 (July 1981), 35.

50. Marston, "Timber Wars."

51. Joshua Cohen and Charles Sabel, "Directly Deliberative Polyarchy," *European Law Journal* 3 (December 1997): 325.

52. U.S. Forest Service, *Framework for the Future* (Washington, D.C.: Forest Service, February 1970); U.S. Forest Service, *Inform and Involve* (Washington, D.C.: Forest Service, February 1972).

53. See John Hendee et al., *Public Involvement and the Forest Service* (Seattle: Pacific Northwest Forest and Range Experiment Station, May 1973). See also Rupert Cutler, "Public Involvement in USDA Decision-Making," *Journal of Soil and Water Conservation* 33 (1978): 264–66.

54. Carmen Sirianni and Lewis Friedland, "Social Capital and Civic Innovation: Learning and Capacity-Building from the 1960s to the 1990s," *Change Magazine* 29 (January/February 1997) (http://www.cpn.org/sections/new_citizenship/change.html).

55. These councils established lines of communication between competing groups and laid the foundations "for the kind of town meeting civic culture that was more common in the national and state forests of the Northeast" (Sirianni

and Friedland, "Social Capital and Civic Innovation"). See also Paul Culhane, *Public Lands Politics: Interest Group Influence on the Forest Service and the Bureau of Land Management* (Baltimore: Johns Hopkins University Press, 1981).

56. Sirianni and Friedland, "Social Capital and Civic Innovation."

57. John DeWitt has discussed several of these efforts in his book *Civic Environmentalism: Alternatives to Regulation in States and Communities* (Washington, D.C.: Congressional Quarterly Press, 1994).

58. "Water in the West: The Challenge for the Next Century," Draft Report of the Western Water Policy Review Advisory Commission (Boulder, Colo.: Western Water Policy Review Advisory Commission, October 1997), executive summary.

59. *The Watershed Source Book: Watershed-Based Solutions to Natural Resource Problems* (Boulder: Natural Resources Law Center, University of Colorado, n.d.), 1–23.

60. Cohen and Sabel, "Directly Deliberative Polyarchy," 338.

61. Sirianni and Friedland, "Social Capital and Civic Innovation."

62. Robert Gottlieb and Helen Ingram, "The New Environmentalists," *Progressive* (August 1988): 14.

63. Aldo Leopold, "Land-Use Democracy," in *The River of the Mother of God and Other Essays*, ed. Susan L. Flader and J. Baird Callicott (Madison: University of Wisconsin Press, 1991), 299.

64. Wondolleck, *Public Lands: Conflict and Resolution*, 119.

65. Marston, "Timber Wars."

66. Marston, "Timber Wars."

67. Patrick Mazza, "Co-optation or Constructive Engagement?: Quincy Library Group's Effort to Bring Together Loggers and Environmentalists Under Fire," *The Cascadia Planet*, 9 August 1997 (http://www.tnews.com/text/quincylibrary. html), quoting Freeman House, a founder of Northern California's Mattole Restoration Council, one of the oldest and most respected community-based ecological restoration efforts. House commented on the opposition of national environmental groups to the Quincy Library plan: "I tend to see the national environmental reaction coming from having developed a power base and feeling threatened by these community groups."

68. Quoted by Tom Philp, "Fallout from a Logging Consensus in the Sierra," *Sacramento Bee*, 9 November 1997 (http://www.sacbee.com/news/beetoday/ newsroom/edit/110997/edit03.html).

69. Philp, "Fallout from a Logging Consensus."

70. Pyne, *Fire in America*, 71.

71. Marston, "Timber Wars."

72. Gifford Pinchot, *The Training of a Forester*, rev. 3d ed. (Philadelphia: Lippincott, 1917), 32.

73. Robert Nelson, *A Burning Issue: Why the Forest Service Is Institutionally Incapable of Dealing with the Problem of Forest Fire, and How This Case Illustrates the Need to Abolish the Agency*, working paper for the Competitive Enterprise Institute, February 1998, 15.

74. Nelson, *A Burning Issue*.

75. Quoted in Mazza, "Co-optation or Constructive Engagement?"

76. Philp, "Fallout from a Logging Consensus."

77. Marston, "Timber Wars."

78. Mazza, "Co-optation or Constructive Engagement?"

79. Philp, "Fallout from a Logging Consensus."

80. "Prepared Testimony of Michael Jackson before the Senate Committee on Energy and Natural Resources Subcommittee on Forests and Public Land Management," 24 July 1997 (Federal News Service).

81. The precursor to the QLG plan, called the Conservationist Alternative to the Plumas National Forest Plan, was originally proposed in February 1986 by Friends of Plumas Wilderness, Mother Lode Chapter Sierra Club, Northstate Wilderness Committee, and Altacal Audubon. The Wilderness Society and the Natural Resources Defense Council later provided financial and legal support for the plan.

82. Daniel P. Beard, "Dear Senator," letter from senior vice president of the National Audubon Society, Washington, D.C., 17 September 1997 (http://qlg.org/public_html/Perspectives/audubonposition.htm).

83. Jane Braxton Little, "Critics Fear Quincy Bill Cedes Too Much Federal Power to Locals," *Sacramento Bee,* 5 July 1997 (http://www.sacbee.com/news/beetoday/newsroom/local/070597/local07.html).

84. Philp, "Fallout from a Logging Consensus."

85. Beard, "Dear Senator."

86. Quoted in Mazza, "Co-optation or Constructive Engagement?"

87. Quoted in Mazza, "Co-optation or Constructive Engagement?"

88. Philp, "Fallout from a Logging Consensus."

89. Ed Marston writes, "Louis Blumberg of The Wilderness Society in San Francisco is not impressed by the QLG's impatience: 'We have all spent many years waiting for the Forest Service to make changes. It's slow to change, but to say that because the QLG is unable to have their plan adopted within two years is testimony to a failure of forest planning—I can't buy that. They're only one special interest group.' " Marston, "Timber Wars."

90. Letter of Deb Callahan, president, League of Conservation Voters, to the House of Representatives opposing the Quincy Library Group Bill, H.R. 858, 8 July 1997 (http://www.lcv.org/eyeoncongress/letters97/Quincy.html).

91. Quoted in Mazza, "Co-optation or Constructive Engagement?"

92. Michael Yost, Letter to the Editor, *High Country News,* 24 November 1997 (http://qlg.org/public_html/Perspectives/yost112497.htm).

93. Beard, "Dear Senator."

94. Sally Yost, president, and Sherry Yarnell, conservation chair, Plumas Audubon Society, Quincy, California, letter to Mike Leahy, forest campaign coordinator, National Audubon Society, 24 September 1997 (http://qlg.org/public_html/bill/audubon/pluaud092497.htm). Although the National Audubon Society acknowledged that "environmentalists who are participating in the QLG are legit and have the best of intentions," the Sierra Club published a full-page ad in the *New York Times* (national edition, 24 September 1997, B10) questioning the bona fides of its local members, whom it described as an "industry-picked group."

95. Quoted in Mazza, "Co-optation or Constructive Engagement?"

96. Quoted in Mazza, "Co-optation or Constructive Engagement?"

97. William E. Riebsame and James J. Robb, *Atlas of the New West* (New York: Norton, 1997), 108. In the arid area from the Sierra Nevada forests to the Colorado Plateau, more than half of the income that people earn comes not from wages of any kind but from investments, retirement accounts, and other "transfer" payments. The rural West is now home to "modem" cowboys, highly educated, environmentally aware refugees from urban centers who love the landscape, conduct business over the Internet, and fly in and out of airports in easy reach of nearly every community. Ted Turner epitomizes the kind of rural hick the Sierra Club fears timber companies will co-opt. Quincy, an old logging and mining town where the Forest Service is the major employer, supports an economically and socially diverse population of 10,000 and a growing tourist industry. Instead of logging, one now logs in at Morning Thunder, the upscale bed-and-breakfast, or at other cafés in Quincy which serve cappuccino, latté, and espresso as well as campfire coffee.

98. Riebsame and Robb, *Atlas of the New West*, 10.

99. All quotes from McCloskey can be found in Michael McCloskey, "The Skeptic: Collaboration Has Its Limits," *High Country News*, 13 May 1996. (http://www.hcn.org/1996/may13/dir/OpinionTheskepti.html). McCloskey's memo was also excerpted in *Harper's*, November 1996, 34–36.

100. "Robert Putnam Responds," *American Prospect*, no. 25 (March–April 1996), 27.

101. Robert D. Putnam, "Bowling Alone: America's Declining Social Capital," *Journal of Democracy* 6 (January 1995): 71.

102. G. Jon Roush, "Conservation's Hour—Is the Leadership Ready?" in *Voices from the Environmental Movement: Perspectives for a New Era*, ed. Donald Snow (Washington, D.C.: Island, 1991), 34.

103. Charles Jordan and Donald Snow, "Diversification, Minorities, and the Mainstream Environmental Movement," in *Voices from the Environmental Movement*, ed. Snow, 73.

104. Randal O'Toole, "The New Conservation Movement," http://www.ti.org/enviroihs.html

105. The reverse may also be true: having arrived at a land ethic, they adopt the science that confirms it.

106. Reprinted as a *San Francisco Chronicle* editorial, 23 July 1997.

107. Donald Worster, "The Ecology of Order and Chaos," *Environmental History and Review* 14, no. 1–2 (Spring/Summer 1990): 13.

108. Gottlieb and Ingram, "The New Environmentalists," 14.

109. Jordan and Snow, "Diversification, Minorities, and the Mainstream," 88.

110. Lois Marie Gibbs and Karen J. Stults, "On Grassroots Environmentalism," in *Crossroads: Environmental Priorities for the Future*, ed. Peter Borelli (Washington, D.C.: Island, 1988), 244.

111. Quoted in Marston, "Timber Wars."

112. Michael C. Dorf and Charles F. Sabel, "A Constitution of Democratic Experimentalism," *Columbia Law Review* 98 (March 1998): 288–89.

113. Quoted in Jane Braxton Little, "Forest Plan Is Alive—So Far," *Sacramento Bee*, 17 October 1998, B1.

114. Marston, "Timber Wars."

7

A Historical Model of Women's Voluntarism and the State, 1890–1920

Kathryn Kish Sklar

The history of voluntarism among American women's organizations offers a valuable perspective on debates now taking place about the nature of civil society and its relationship to the state. Do state initiatives limit those of voluntary agencies? Does the expansion of state responsibilities reduce the effectiveness of voluntary groups? Is society best served by leaving the solution of social problems to voluntary associations independent of state authority and control?

These questions have gained compelling resonance today as Americans seek political strategies to address the social and economic changes wrought by an emerging global economy. Should we rely more heavily on voluntary effort and trim the state accordingly? Or should we expect voluntary groups to work closely with formal political institutions? Historical studies cannot answer these present-day questions directly, but by offering models of past options they can illuminate current ones.

This chapter focuses on women's voluntarism during the watershed of American history between 1890 and 1920 known as the Progressive era. These decades witnessed the construction of modern America. Many of our civil associations, much of our political culture, and the basic tenets of what might be called our current social contract emerged during those decades.[1] Drawing on my research on women's voluntary associations, I want to make three points about that era:

1. Traditions of voluntarism and traditions of limited government in the United States between 1830 and 1920 fostered women's associations of extraordinary strength and independence.

2. Between 1890 and 1920 those traditions meant that many social problems associated with rapid industrialization, rapid urbanization, and massive immigration remained unsolved by predominantly male institutions, whether civil or affiliated with the state, offering a fertile field for women's activism.
3. Between 1890 and 1920 women's voluntary organizations added crucial ingredients to the political culture, which, with the aid of the state and of male civil institutions, created an effective new model for addressing social problems. Their partnership with the state was vital to their achievements.[2]

THE STRENGTH AND INDEPENDENCE OF AMERICAN WOMEN'S ASSOCIATIONS

More than any other factor, the separation of church and state accounts for the extraordinary strength and independence of women's voluntary associations in the United States. Like almost everything else in American political culture, the separation of church and state arose from the interaction of formal political institutions and civil associations. Beginning with Virginia in 1776 and ending with Connecticut in the 1840s, all American states broke the traditional ties that had bound church and state together.

Such acts of "religious liberty"—representing the growing importance of religion rather than its demise—were warmly advocated by the burgeoning dissenting denominations, such as Baptists and Methodists, who did not qualify for state funding. In all denominations this process greatly empowered the laity, whose financial donations now took the place of state monies in supporting the ministry and the church, and accordingly put greater control over church affairs into their hands.[3]

The empowerment of the religious laity had the unexpected consequence of empowering women, not only because women constituted a majority of church members, but also because, beginning in the 1820s, women were able to form vigorous pan-Protestant lay organizations, which challenged the authority of ministers and generated an autonomous social agenda. The best example of such an organization before 1870 was the American Female Moral Reform Society (AFMRS). When the national arm of the AFMRS was formed in 1839, it united more than five hundred preexisting locals scattered in the towns and villages of New England and New York. The grassroots vitality of the AFMRS was a response to changing social conditions, particularly changing patterns of family formation and courtship/sexual behavior.[4] The AFMRS had no equivalent in England or Europe, where church and state remained entwined and the female laity enjoyed less autonomy. The nearest British equivalent was the much smaller Ladies National Association for the Repeal of the Contagious Diseases Act, founded in 1869, which attracted a predominantly elite constituency and never achieved the grassroots potency of the American Female Moral Reform Society.[5]

In the depression winter of 1873–1874, another pan-Protestant organization, the Women's Christian Temperance Union (WCTU), emerged to supplant the AFMRS. By 1883 a branch of the WCTU existed in almost every American county. The WCTU reached its height around 1890, when, in keeping with its campaign to "Do Everything," in Chicago alone it maintained

> two day nurseries, two Sunday schools, an industrial school, a mission that sheltered four thousand homeless or destitute women in a twelve-month period, a free medical dispensary that treated over sixteen hundred patients a year, a lodging house for men that had [by 1889] provided temporary housing for over fifty thousand men, and a low-cost restaurant.[6]

Throughout the United States the WCTU provided prodigious social services to local communities and offered women a wide range of leadership opportunities within their communities. By 1896 twenty-five out of a total of thirty-nine "departments" within the WCTU dealt wholly or in major part with nontemperance issues, such as prisons, jails, juvenile welfare, and "the industrial question."[7]

Through the WCTU women became more politically organized in the United States than was the case in any other Western political culture. To maximize their political power, in the 1870s WCTU locals took the shape of congressional districts, and in 1881 the Union endorsed woman suffrage. Although the British equivalent, the British Woman's Temperance Association, like the WCTU, attracted a larger base of middle-class and upper-class women than the suffrage organizations, the British association was a much smaller group, devoted to scientific education about alcohol and lacking the American's "Christian" capacities. British temperance women did not engage in the political activism that carried American women into their village streets and state legislatures. "We have had no wonderful crusade in England—no such baptism of power and liberty," one British woman lamented in 1883.[8]

Thus, by the time women's organizations began to address the social problems of the 1890s, two generations of women's vigorous and autonomous social activism had preceded them. The pattern of women's participation in American public culture was well established. Although they lacked rights as individuals (especially as married persons), they exercised power collectively through women's organizations.[9]

The generation of women who did so much to reshape American public culture between 1890 and 1920 built on traditions of activism that arose from the separation of church and state, but their opportunities for community service were greatly expanded by their increased access to higher education. By 1880 one of every three students enrolled in American institutions of higher learning was female. Three kinds of institutions produced this remarkable result. First, elite women's colleges, such as Vassar, Smith, and Wellesley, began accepting students between 1865 and 1875, providing equivalents to elite men's colleges. Second, state universities, established through the allocation of public lands in the Morrill Act of 1862 and required to be "open for all," made college educations accessible for the first time to large numbers of middle-class daughters in the nation's central and western states. Public universities accepting women by 1870 were Iowa (1855), Wisconsin (1867), Kansas, Indiana, and Minnesota (1869), and Missouri, Michigan, and California (1870). Third, large numbers of women were enrolled in "normal" colleges, or teacher-training institutions; indeed, the chief force driving women's access to higher education between 1830 and 1870 was their employment as teachers in the hamlets and villages of the newly settled West. Well-established schools helped towns attract settlers; good teachers reflected good entrepreneurship.[10]

Though a small percentage of all women in the 1890s, college-trained women in American cities exercised an influence disproportionate to their numbers. Vida Scudder, a Smith graduate, summarized the spirit of their empowerment in 1890: "We stand here as a new Fact—new to all intents and purposes, within the last quarter of a century: Our lives are in our hands."[11] Women's unprecedented access to higher education in the United States by 1880 created a generation of leaders capable of effectively channeling women's activism to meet the new challenges of their modernizing society.

The best-known and most influential flowering of women's public culture in the 1890s was the social settlement movement. Imitating the British example of Toynbee Hall, settlements consisted of middle-class people who took up residence and tried to promote civil institutions in poor, working-class urban neighborhoods. In the United States this movement was predominantly female, and the neighborhoods were populated by immigrants. Led by Jane Addams, founder of Hull House in Chicago in 1889 and author of two widely acclaimed 1892 essays, "The Subjective Necessity for Social Settlements" and "The Objective Necessity for Social Settlements," the settlement movement attracted women college graduates who had few alternatives other than marriage or teaching. Like Jane Addams, most of the movement's other leaders consisted of women who had been born around 1860 and had spent the 1880s searching for work commensurate with their talents.[12]

By 1910 over four hundred settlements had been established in American cities. About three-quarters were founded by women, and 86 percent of the headworkers between 1886 and 1911 were women. In about half all the residents were women, and in another third the majority of residents were women. Settlements varied enormously in their funding, most drawing on private sources, some on organizations such as the YWCA, some on churches. Settlements were the site of tremendous originality, giving birth to new civic institutions, such as the National Association for the Advancement of Colored People, which arose out of the Henry Street Settlement in 1909, and conceiving important public policy innovations, such as the creation of the U.S. Children's Bureau in 1912, which in turn originated the first federal health legislation, the Sheppard-Towner Maternity and Infancy Protection Act, passed in 1920.

Women reformers affiliated with the social settlement movement formed the core of what has been called a "female dominion" of reform.[13] Much of the power of that dominion rested on the support it received from a wide range of women's voluntary organizations, such as the General Federation of Women's Clubs (formed 1890); the National Congress of Mothers (formed 1897, later called the PTA); the National Council of Jewish Women (formed 1893); the National Association of Colored Women (formed 1895); the American Association of University Women (formed 1881); the Daughters of the American Revolution (formed 1891); and the Young Women's Christian Association (formed in 1866, but re-created in the form that we know it in 1894).

One measure of the success of reformers affiliated with the social settlement movement can be found in the support they enjoyed within the woman suffrage movement. This support muted the suffrage movement's defense of suffrage as a right and amplified its advocacy of suffrage on the grounds of the reform agenda that women could accomplish with the vote. For example, a flyer issued by the National American Woman Suffrage Association around 1910, "To the Woman in the Home," advocated votes for women on the basis of their duty to end sweatshop working conditions (see figure 7.1).

The women's dominion covered a lot of ground, ranging from the social welfare institutions that we saw with the WCTU—basically extensions of traditional charitable institutions—to the passage of labor legislation such as minimum wage laws, which, in the quarter century between the passage of the first minimum wage law in Massachusetts in 1912 and the passage of the Fair Labor Standards Act in 1938, applied exclusively to women.[14]

Figure 7.1   Flyer of the National American Woman Suffrage Association
Manuscript Division, Library of Congress

TO THE WOMAN IN THE HOME

How can a mother rest content with this—   When such conditions exist as this?

There are thousands of children working in sweat-shops like the one in the picture. There are
thousands of children working in mines and mills and factories. Thousands more
are being wronged and cheated by Society in countless ways.

IS NOT THIS **YOUR** BUSINESS?

Intelligent citizens WHO CARED could change all this—providing always, of course, that they had
the power of the ballot.

DO **YOU** CARE?

Mothers are responsible for the welfare of children.
This duty as mothers requires that they should demand

VOTES FOR WOMEN!

NATIONAL WOMAN SUFFRAGE PUBLISHING CO., Inc.
PUBLISHERS FOR THE
NATIONAL AMERICAN WOMAN SUFFRAGE ASSOCIATION
505 FIFTH AVENUE   NEW YORK CITY

WOMEN'S VOLUNTARISM AND SOCIAL PROBLEM SOLVING

There is no doubt that traditions of voluntarism and limited government
formed a positive and innovative context for women's organizations in
the United States. The strength of women's voluntarism drew on the
strength of voluntarism within American political culture generally. Yet

these traditions were themselves a fundamental obstacle that prevented American political culture from addressing some of the era's most grievous problems. For women's organizations, the challenge was to reach beyond voluntarism to forge new models of public responsibility involving the state.[15]

One way of assessing the difficulties these organizations faced is to notice the extent to which courts enforced concepts of limited government and prohibited legislatures from responding to civil groups who advocated enlarged state responsibility. For example, after the fledgling American Federation of Labor (AFL) in the early 1880s obtained the passage of a New York law that prohibited the production of cigars in tenements, the New York Appeals Court ruled the law unconstitutional. As head of the AFL, Samuel Gompers concluded that "the power of the courts to pass upon the constitutionality of the law so complicates reform by legislation as to seriously restrict the effectiveness of that method."[16]

Nevertheless, cross-class women's groups, such as the Women's Trade Union League and the National Consumers' League, continued to advocate protective labor legislation and to defend it in the courts. In its 1906 decision in *Lochner v. New York*, the U.S. Supreme Court ruled unconstitutional a New York law limiting the hours of work for bakers. Arguing that women were different from men and deserved different treatment, the National Consumers' League won a landmark Supreme Court decision in 1908 that permitted regulation of working hours for women.

In this and other examples we might consult, the boundaries between "civil society" and "the state" were blurred in the Progressive era, with voluntary associations pushing for the expansion of public responsibility and the formal institutions of the state using their power to resist that expansion. For our purposes, the most interesting feature of this debate was its anchor in traditions of limited government, which defined the terms of the debate and shaped its outcome.

Those traditions and the voluntarist bias in American political culture become even more evident when we compare American women in the social settlement movement with their German counterparts in the decades before World War I. In Germany, the nearest equivalents to social settlements were the women's organizations that ran publicly funded municipal welfare agencies. Yet differences in American and German political cultures meant that these German volunteers occupied a very different position within their own political culture than was the case with the Americans.[17]

Three constraints on German women's voluntarism made it qualitatively different from that of women in the United States. First, the power of the Prussian state and the central German state, constructed in the 1870s and 1880s as a bulwark against the power of the landed estates on the right and socialism on the left, left less space in the political culture for voluntarism generally, especially women's voluntarism. Second, that power was nowhere more visible than in the laws that from 1848 until 1908 prohibited women in Prussia and other German states from participating in "political" activity. Third, the hegemony of the centrist and right-wing goal of curtailing the growth of socialism dominated the voluntarism of most middle-class women and undercut the possibility for cross-class coalitions.

Emily Greene Balch, who like many American reformers studied in Germany in her youth, encountered the laws prohibiting women's political activism in the mid-1890s when she attended a mass meeting addressed by leaders of the Social Democratic Party (SPD). In 1890 the bans outlawing the SPD had been lifted and the party was quickly becoming Germany's largest. The mass meeting was a device for getting around the law that prohibited women's presence at political meetings, she remembered, but "Police sat on a table on the platform with their spiked helmets in their hands. If their helmets were put on, the meeting was thereby closed."[18] Although laws against women's political participation were unevenly enforced and working-class socialist women felt their effects far more harshly than did middle-class reformers, these statutes muted women's engagement in the political life of their communities. Nominally, at least, their actions had to be "above" politics.

In most German municipalities, property qualifications for voting effectively excluded the Social Democratic Party from local elections until 1919. The SPD's continued exclusion from these elections demonstrated the importance of the local municipality as an antisocialist stronghold. Because this was the venue in which most women volunteers worked, their voluntarism was absorbed within an antisocialist agenda. For example, funds for women's social work in Hanover came attached with the proviso that they oppose the "unpatriotic forces" associated with the Social Democratic Party.[19]

In this context there was nothing equivalent to an independent women-dominated social settlement movement. For young middle-class women to leave their homes and reside in urban slums would have been unthinkable. Perhaps the closest institution was Alice Salomon's women's school for social-work training in Berlin (founded in 1908), where some pupils boarded while they learned to become social-work professionals. Although a few of these went on to become paid professionals, most worked as volunteers. Their energies were disproportionately consumed by municipal agencies—agencies that for the most part were publicly funded and dominated by the antisocialist agenda of Germany's centrist parties.

In Germany the woman suffrage movement was less a mainstream than a minority whose patriotism was tainted by the SPD's enthusiastic and long-standing endorsement of woman suffrage. The single largest German women's organization, the Deutsch-Evangelischer Frauenvereine (German Evangelical Women's Union), considered woman suffrage a socialist measure—a view that was confirmed in their eyes when woman suffrage was enacted in 1919 as part of the SPD-dominated Weimar Constitution after Germany was defeated in World War I. The political dynamics of the suffrage movement in Germany meant that it did not become a site for social reform or cross-class mobilization among women.

This comparison between American and German women's organizations suggests that we can best understand voluntarism by examining not only the actions of civil organizations within a political culture, but also the strength or weakness of voluntarism throughout the entire political culture, including the state's tolerance of autonomous voluntary initiatives.

WOMEN'S VOLUNTARISM AND THE STATE

Women's voluntarism in the Progressive era overflows with examples of how their organizations formed partnerships with the state to implement goals that could not be achieved without the power of the state. This paradigm is well represented in the "White Label" campaign of the National Consumers' League, which between 1899 and 1917 sought to improve working conditions in the garment industry.

Three aspects of the campaign's relationship to the state seem especially pertinent. First, league members viewed the state's legislative power as a means to promote their own and their community's welfare. Second, their interactions with the state fostered a partnership in which their joint interests with state officials became more instrumental in women's actions than any formal distinction between civil and state authority. Third, the state's coercive power, especially the power to pass legislation and enforce the law, was crucial to their goal of improved working conditions.

What was the "White Label" campaign? The label was first proposed by a Hull House resident, Florence Kelley, in 1898 when she was interviewed for the position of general secretary of the newly formed National Consumers' League (NCL), a group that unified flourishing local leagues in New York, New Jersey, Massachusetts, Pennsylvania, Illinois, Minnesota, and Wisconsin. Kelley, who already headed the Illinois Consumers' League, submitted a plan of action for a consumers' label that focused on the conditions under which goods were produced in factories. The first league, founded in New York City in 1890, began when working-class women appealed to middle-class consumers about their working conditions in a hat-making firm. Kelley's 1898 proposal identified some factories already worthy of the label, designed the label, created a model contract between manufacturers and consumers' leagues, and devised "a well considered plan for advertising the label." She was hired as the NCL's "inspector and organizer."[20]

Although the NCL and its local leagues included some trade union members, consumers' leagues consisted overwhelmingly of white, middle-class women, and the White Label itself expressed their middle-class concerns. As a symbol, therefore, the White Label is a good example of what Anthony Giddens means in *The Constitution of Society* when he locates the origins of symbolic ideological expressions in specific regions of the social structure. In contrast to Clifford Geertz, who locates the power of ideology in symbols themselves, Giddens argues that symbols are always shaped by the sectors of public life that champion them.[21] The White Label was a white, middle-class device that evoked the symbolism of white trade unions and their efforts to discourage the patronage of non-union shops. The union label was first used in San Francisco in 1869 by cigar makers who sought to discourage the purchase of cigars made by Chinese immigrants and to encourage the purchase of union-made cigars.[22] So, like the symbolic meanings of the union label, the symbolic meanings of the Consumers' White Label were unstable and multiple, embracing issues associated with class, race, and gender.

Shaped like a bow tie with a circle in the middle, the label announced in its center, "OFFICIAL LABEL: NATIONAL CONSUMERS' LEAGUE, REGISTERED NOV. 17, 1899." Its left side stated, "MADE UNDER CLEAN AND HEALTHFUL CONDITIONS"; the other side declared, "USE OF LABEL AUTHORIZED AFTER INVESTIGATION." (For an example of a state variation on the NCL label, see figure 7.2.) To qualify for the label, manufacturers had to submit to an inspection and meet the following minimum standards, as defined in the NCL annual reports:

> The State factory law is obeyed;
> All the goods are made on the premises;
> Overtime is not worked;
> Children under sixteen years of age are not employed.[23]

In the first years of the campaign, Florence Kelley herself performed the inspections.

Antisweatshop campaigns in major American cities in the 1890s appealed to middle-class self-interest by emphasizing the public health threat posed by garments produced in disease-ridden tenements. Middle-class consumers were taught to fear that such garments might import smallpox, diphtheria, or other diseases into their homes. The new germ theory of disease transmission lent credence to this view.[24]

Figure 7.2   White Label, Consumers' League of Massachusetts
Source: Schlesinger Library, Radcliffe College

THE CONSUMERS' LEAGUE

OF

MASSACHUSETTS

4 Joy Street, Boston.

THIS LABEL

Certifies that the goods which carry it have been
made in clean and safe factories under good conditions, and that the manufacturers who use the
label employ no children and give out no work to
be made up outside the factories.

April, 1907

Yet middle-class consumers were not alone in their concern for clean
and healthful working conditions. Such conditions also mattered to workers. Dank air, filthy floors, and stinking toilets were some of the most ob-
jectionable features of sweatshop labor. "The shops are unsanitary—
that's the word that is generally used, but there ought to be a worse one
used," strike leader Clara Lemlish said in 1909.[25] Tuberculosis was common in the garment industry—induced by the long hours and damp air—
and spread rapidly in unventilated rooms, so the quality of air could be a
life-and-death matter to sweatshop workers. Thus, health issues forged a
common bond between consumers and producers in the garment industry—a bond that promoted the league's view that it was speaking for the
welfare of the whole society, not the narrow interests of one group.

Acting as though they believed that the state, too, represented the welfare of the whole society, league members worked closely with state and local officials.[26] The Louisville league exemplified this process in 1902. The league had been formed the previous year following a meeting of the General Federation of Women's Clubs in Milwaukee where the delegates from the Woman's Club of Louisville heard Maud Nathan and Florence Kelley discuss the New York and the National Consumers' Leagues. The Louisville group's minutes reported that "the first work was to urge the purchase of muslin underwear bearing the Consumers' League label. Efforts were made to get Consumers' League label goods in all the leading department stores. An exhibition of these goods was held." Soon thereafter, the minutes report, league members

> assisted in passing the Child Labor Law and the Compulsory Education Law and amending them at many sessions of the Legislature. Cooperated in enforcing both, by working with the truant officers, visiting the homes of truants, and supplying shoes and clothing necessary to return them to school.

Later the league boasted that it "secured the passage of the ten hour law for women, which is the only labor law for women in Kentucky."[27]

In addition to lobbying for the passage of labor legislation, leagues formed especially close relationships with state factory inspectors. In 1901 the Wisconsin League worked closely with the state's only woman factory inspector. Around that time the Michigan league secured the appointment of two women to the State Board of Factory Inspectors, and the secretary of the New Jersey League made factory inspection part of her duties.[28]

In addition to their self-interested concern about garments made in disease-ridden tenements and their presumed shared concern with the welfare of the whole society, two other aspects of the White Label campaign drew league members into close cooperation with public officials: the educative process involved in granting the label's use to specific manufacturers, and enforcement of the label's terms.

In Louisville, as elsewhere, the label campaign ineluctably carried league members into new realms of knowledge about their communities. It did so by raising detailed questions about working conditions that were new to this middle-class constituency as they searched for manufacturers who qualified for the label.

Before local leagues could award the label to local manufacturers, they had to answer a multitude of questions about the work process. Did the manufacturer subcontract to home workers in tenements? Were children employed? Was overtime required? Were state factory laws violated? Were working conditions safe and sanitary? How far below the standard set by the Consumers' Label were their own state laws? Should the state issue licenses for home workers? What was the relationship between illiteracy among child workers and the enforcement of effective child labor laws? Was their own state high or low on the NCL's ranked list showing the numbers of illiterate child workers in each state? Should laws prohibit the labor of children at age 14 or 16? Should exceptions be made for the children of widows? Could workers live on their wages or were they forced to augment their pay with relief or charitable donations? How energetically were state factory laws enforced? How could local factory standards be improved? Such questions, most of which were quite alien to middle-class women in 1890, by 1905 had acquired personal meaning and moral significance for thousands of politically active women.

Most of these questions assumed that the league's goals could not be fully implemented without the coercive power of the state to intervene in the relationship between employer and employee. That coercive power lay beyond their reach as a voluntary association but was crucial to their aims. Indeed, it is not too much to say that their campaign would not have been possible without the state's coercive power as a weapon in their armory. In that sense their own robust intervention in public culture was decisively aided rather than diminished by the power of the state, and the more responsive the state was to their interests, the more actively they promoted their goals.

Another crucial feature of the campaign was the leadership provided by the national organization. Florence Kelley's professional expertise was especially well suited to the campaign, since in Chicago during the 1890s she had become the nation's leading authority on the passage and enforcement of labor legislation for women and children. She drafted, mobilized support for, and as Illinois chief factory inspector between 1893 and 1896 (with eleven deputies, five of whom were required by law to be women) enforced trailblazing eight-hour legislation for women and child workers throughout that large industrial state. Kelley knew how American political culture worked; her father, William Darrah Kelley, served fifteen consecutive terms in the U.S. House of Representatives, 1860–1890, where he became known as "the conscience of the House." Graduating from Cornell University in 1882, she wrote an honors thesis under her father's direction, which was published that year as "On Some Changes in the Legal Status of the Child since Blackstone." While a resident of Hull House, she completed a law degree at Northwestern University. After moving to New York to head the National Consumers' League (a position she held until her death in 1932), she lived in Lillian Wald's Henry Street settlement on Manhattan's Lower East Side.[29]

Soon after moving to the league, Kelley began building local leagues, understanding that the mobilization of public opinion was a crucial part of the process of change within American political culture. In her first five years she created a grassroots movement, spending one day on the road for every day at her desk. Her efforts were rewarded by the spectacular expansion of NCL locals, both in numbers and location. The 1901 annual report mentioned thirty leagues in eleven states; by 1906 there were sixty-three locals in twenty states, with about seven thousand members.[30]

The Massachusetts Consumers' League, one of the strongest and largest locals, described the effects of Kelley's leadership in 1903:

> [She] can travel from one end of the Continent to the other without losing her hold upon local problems in State Leagues the farthest removed from her bodily presence, stirring our zeal and opening new fields for our activity by *letters*, which are prompt and full as if *letter writing* were the chief occupation of her day. Mrs. Kelley gives us service which it is impossible to overestimate.[31]

Florence Kelley was good at what she did. Although from one perspective the dynamics of her efforts might appear to be "top-down," from another they were "bottom-up," especially when compared with the NCL's closest male equivalent, the American Association for Labor Legislation (AALL). The AALL maintained no locals and sought to influence legislation directly through the power of their members' professional expertise. Yet compared with the NCL, the AALL's achievements were minimal.[32]

The NCL's cooperation with "enlightened" businessmen was an important feature of its success. The alliance of large department store owners with its White Label campaign exemplified the tripartite dimensions of its coalitions: they included entrepreneurs as well as reformers and their grassroots supporters. Economically, the campaign aided large producers who could achieve economies of scale in the pricing of their goods and who profited from the more stable workforce attracted by better working conditions. These economic facts of life became dramatically apparent in the partnership that John Wanamaker and his department stores forged with the White Label campaign. One of the league's largest approved manufacturers, Wanamaker originated what became a staple of the campaign—a series of exhibits in which garments bearing the label were augmented by pictures of sweatshop labor compared with pictures of workers producing Wanamaker garments. Wanamaker carried the exhibit to state and international fairs throughout the United States in the decade before World War I. For him the White Label campaign offered a perfect opportunity to give his commercial leadership a moral aura and at the same time consolidate his economic power.

While local leagues and Wanamaker's stores were campaigning for the adoption of the White Label, the NCL carried the crusade into other women's groups, especially the General Federation of Women's Clubs (GFWC). By 1900 the GFWC had grown to thirty-six state federations of more than 2,600 clubs with a membership of more than 155,000.[33] At the federation's Biennial Meeting that year, delegates learned about the White Label campaign, and federation officers "asked the delegates to report favorably to their respective clubs and federations upon the work of the League."[34]

The results, Florence Kelley said in 1901, "are still perceptible at our office in the form of invitations for speakers, requests for literature, and a vast increase in correspondence and in the demand for labeled goods in many diverse parts of the country."[35] At least some of that "vast increase" was generated by a pamphlet circulated by the GFWC's Industrial Committee, which asked questions that directed women into closer proximity to local and state officials: "What is the legal age for employing children in your state? Have you a woman factory inspector? Is there a license law for manufacture in homes? What is the legal working day?"[36]

State federations of women's clubs appointed "standing committees to promote the work of the Consumers' League." Addresses by NCL officers became a regular event at annual meetings in such far-flung areas as South Carolina, Utah, and Washington. Where statewide consumers' leagues existed, they worked in tandem with state federations of women's clubs. "For a time at least," the official historian of the General Federation of Women's Clubs wrote in 1912, "the quickened conscience made the average woman . . . a more intelligent purchaser."[37]

At the height of the campaign's success in 1904, the league had licensed sixty factories. Yet even more significant than this number was the process by which thousands of women were aroused to civil activism because they believed they could influence the course of public policy for the better.

Florence Kelley exemplified the close working relationship that many elite women maintained with the state in the Progressive era, even though they spent their professional lives in voluntary organizations. The relationship between the NCL and the state was a mutually dependent one: without the mobilization of public opinion exemplified by the NCL, it is extremely doubtful that state legislatures and officials could have overcome the cultural and legal obstacles that heretofore had prevented them from intervening in most matters involving employees and employers.

After 1908 the National Consumers' League moved away from the White Label campaign and put its public power to new uses. Working with its local league in Oregon, the NCL sponsored, in *Muller v. Oregon*, a path-breaking argument before the Supreme Court, in which the Court for the first time recognized the validity of sociological evidence. The so-called "Brandeis Brief" was actually written by Brandeis's sister-in-law,

Josephine Goldmark, who was Florence Kelley's chief assistant. In 1917 the league again worked with its Oregon local to establish the constitutionality of hours regulations for men in nonhazardous occupations. Between 1910 and 1923 the league conducted a successful campaign for the passage of minimum wage legislation, which in 1938 became the basis for the adoption of minimum wage provisions in the Fair Labor Standards Act. In this way the NCL's White Label campaign became an opening wedge for more general protections for American wage earners.[38]

How does the White Label campaign illuminate our concerns about the relationship between civil associations and the state? Four conclusions seem relevant. First, the campaign drew women into public life in ways that validated what might be called their "social citizenship" almost twenty years before the passage of the woman suffrage amendment to the Constitution.[39] By confronting large social questions that grew out of but reached beyond issues related to women and children, women demonstrated their value as equals to men in public life.

Second, women's voices "elaborated and made authoritative" (in Thomas Bender's phrase) new forms of power in public life.[40] The campaign created a new "supply" of women's power. The "demand" for that power came from the need within newly evolving liberalism for an ethical buttress to support state intervention in the economic marketplace. The step from concern about women and children to their advocacy of state intervention was an easy one for many women to take.

Third, NCL members provided innovative answers to "the social question." In its component parts, "the social question" included the largest issues then being debated in public life: What do the social classes owe one another? How could civil society affect the marketplace economy? Where should middle-class people stand in relationship to the changes precipitated by massive industrialization, urbanization, and immigration? Where should middle-class people stand in relationship to the often violent struggle between capital and labor? And how might that conflict be mediated by the state?

Fourth, in our own time liberalism has been defined as a set of principles by which practitioners of divergent conceptions of the good can peacefully coexist. But liberalism requires what today's public culture calls a "level playing field." Consumers' leagues and other women's voluntary associations helped create that fictive field.

CONCLUSION

In this chapter I have explored themes arising from the relationship between women's voluntary associations and the state in the Progressive era. During this period, women's activism increased partly as a result of government responsiveness to it. State and civil institutions were interwoven and interdependent. Women's voluntarism was especially strong in the United States because voluntarism was especially strong throughout American political culture. Women's voluntary associations and the state institutions with which they interacted were two sides of the same coin, not two different coins.

We can make several general statements about the relevance of this model of problem solving to the present. First, the model shows that transformative economic change can become an impetus for extensive social and political change. Second, it suggests that the potential for solving social problems lies in a fruitful combination of civil and state initiatives rather than a withering of state initiatives. Third, the model suggests that given the voluntarist biases in American political culture, we will always be debating where the line should be drawn to limit state authority. That debate arises more from the vitality of voluntarism in our political culture than from the power of our state.

At first glance, the Progressive model might make one wonder whether growing government capacity after 1930 undermined the civic vitality of women's pre-1920 activism. But a closer examination reveals this conclusion to be unwarranted. Historians devote much of their energies to analyzing causal relationships among variables. A simple correlation—such as that between civic activism and limited government capacity at one time, and declining civic activism and government with larger capacity at another time—may or may not reflect a causal relationship. In fact, everything we know about women's activism before 1920 leads us to conclude that this correlation is not causal.

Historians have identified a multitude of causes that led to the decline in women's civic activism. The two most important were the end of the suffrage movement with the passage of the Nineteenth Amendment in 1920 and "Red Scare" attacks on women's activism by hyperpatriotic, right-wing groups in the 1920s. Also important was the cultural shift in the psychological construction of women's identity away from a nineteenth-century emphasis on the differences between the sexes to a twentieth-century emphasis on the similarities between the sexes. Whereas the nineteenth-century formulation had encouraged women's collective activism, the twentieth-century formulation discouraged women's group affiliation and instead encouraged various forms of individualism. Growing government capacity empowered women's activism before 1920, but the effectiveness of women's social agenda had already substantially declined before the New Deal of the 1930s. Women's organizations continued, but in the 1920s their agenda shifted away from social justice issues and toward a more narrowly conceived agenda typified by the League of

Women Voters' focus on women's rights (e.g., the inclusion of women on juries) and clean government.[41] After 1950, when married women between the ages of 35 and 55 entered the paid labor force in unprecedented numbers, women's activism declined even further. Thus, causes other than the expanded capacity of government explain the decline of women's activism in the second half of the twentieth century.

Is this decline irreversible? Though historians shy away from making predictions, I would venture to say that new forms of voluntary association will probably emerge within American political culture. Perhaps they will be connected with the global processes that are driving so much contemporary change—massive immigration, for example, or the Internet. They are not likely to be generated by downsizing the state. On the contrary, new forms of voluntary associations are likely to need partnerships with the state to achieve their goals. If American political culture survives the global marketplace now gaining so dramatically in strength, it is likely to do so because those partnerships embody one of the most creative sites in American society.

NOTES

1. Although an extensive literature exists on the Progressive era, much remains to be done, especially with regard to integrating women's activism into our understanding of the larger political culture. A classic is Robert H. Wiebe, *The Search for Order, 1877–1920* (New York: Hill & Wang, 1967). For a bibliography of work completed before 1980, see John D. Buenker and Nicholas C. Burckel, *Progressive Reform: A Guide to Information Sources* (Detroit: Gale Research, 1980).

2. For a more complete discussion of some of these points, see my "The Historical Foundations of Women's Power in the Creation of the American Welfare State, 1830–1930," in *Mothers of a New World: Maternalist Politics and the Origins of Welfare States,* ed. Seth Koven and Sonya Michel (New York: Routledge, 1993).

3. For the separation of church and state, see John D. Cushing, "Notes on Disestablishment in Massachusetts, 1780–1833," *William and Mary Quarterly,* 3d ser., 26 (1969): 169–90; William G. McLaughlin, *New England Dissent, 1630–1833: The Baptists and the Separation of Church and State* (Cambridge, Mass.: Harvard University Press, 1971); and Chilton Williamson, *American Suffrage from Property to Democracy, 1760–1860* (Princeton, N.J.: Princeton University Press, 1960). Historians of American women have been slow to appreciate the impact of the separation of church and state on women's activism between 1830 and 1890. I treat the topic indirectly in *Catharine Beecher: A Study in American Domesticity* (New Haven, Conn.: Yale University Press, 1973; paperback reprint, Norton, 1976).

4. For the AFMRS, see Carroll Smith Rosenberg's widely reprinted article, "Beauty, the Beast, and the Militant Woman: A Case Study in Sex Roles and Social Stress in Jacksonian America," *American Quarterly* 23 (1971): 562–84. Smith Rosenberg focuses primarily on the national branch of the organization. A soon-to-be-

completed study of the local branches is Daniel Wright, "The Moral Reform Movement in the Antebellum Northeast, 1834–1848" (Ph.D. dissertation in progress, State University of New York, Binghamton).

5. For the Ladies National Association, see Judith R. Walkowitz, *Prostitution and Victorian Society: Women, Class and the State* (New York: Cambridge University Press, 1980).

6. Ruth Bordin, *Woman and Temperance: The Quest for Power and Liberty, 1873–1900* (Philadelphia: Temple University Press, 1981), 98.

7. Bordin, *Woman and Temperance*, 97–98.

8. Quoted in Bordin, *Woman and Temperance*, 29.

9. Some definitions of *public culture* and *power* might be helpful at this point. Thomas Bender has defined public culture as "a forum where power in its various forms, including meaning and aesthetics, is elaborated and made authoritative." Thomas Bender, "Wholes and Parts: The Need for Synthesis in American History," *Journal of American History* 73 (June 1986): 126. Definitions of power usually involve the dominance of some people by other people. With regard to women's activism, I prefer to define power as the ability to control the distribution of social resources. In this connection social resources would include knowledge of social problems as well as the financial resources to generate solutions to those problems.

10. For a discussion of changes in the 1860s and 1870s that enabled white, middle-class women to attend college in sufficient numbers to become a sociological phenomenon—"the first generation of college-educated women"—see Barbara Miller Solomon, *In the Company of Educated Women: A History of Women and Higher Education in America* (New Haven, Conn.: Yale University Press, 1985).

11. Vida Scudder, "The Relation of College Women to Social Need," *Association of Collegiate Alumnae Publications*, series 2, no. 30 (October 1890): 2–3.

12. For the American social settlement movement, see my *Florence Kelley and the Nation's Work: The Rise of Women's Political Culture, 1830–1900* (New Haven, Conn.: Yale University Press, 1995), chap. 8.

13. See Robyn Muncy, *Creating a Female Dominion in American Reform, 1890–1935* (New York: Oxford University Press, 1991).

14. For minimum wage as a women's issue, see my "Two Political Cultures in the Progressive Era: The National Consumers' League and the American Association for Labor Legislation," in *U.S. History as Women's History: New Feminist Essays*, ed. Linda K. Kerberg, Kathryn Kish Sklar, and Alice Kessler-Harris (Chapel Hill: University of North Carolina Press, 1995).

15. This argument is more fully made in my "The Historical Foundations of Women's Power in the Creation of the American Welfare State."

16. Samuel Gompers, *Seventy Years of Life and Labor* (New York: Dutton, 1925), I: 194. For more on the *In Re Jacobs* case, see Eileen Boris, " 'A Man's Dwelling House Is His Castle': Tenement House Cigarmaking and the Judicial Imperative," in *Work Engendered: Towards a New History of American Labor*, ed. Avon Baron (Ithaca, N.Y.: Cornell University Press, 1991), 114–41.

17. My comparative discussion draws on Nancy R. Reagin, *A German Women's Movement: Class and Gender in Hanover, 1880–1933* (Chapel Hill: University of

North Carolina Press, 1995); and my own book, *Women Reformers and Social Justice in the United States and Germany, 1885–1933: A Dialogue in Documents*, coedited with Anja Schüler and Susan Strasser (Ithaca, N.Y.: Cornell University Press, 1998).

18. Mercedes M. Randall, *Improper Bostonian: Emily Greene Balch* (New York: Twayne, 1964), 93–94.

19. Reagin, *A German Women's Movement*, 58.

20. See my *Florence Kelley and the Nation's Work*, 306–20.

21. Anthony Giddens, *The Constitution of Society: Outline of the Theory of Structuration* (Berkeley: University of California Press, 1984).

22. On the beginnings of the union label, see Elmer Clarence Sandmeyer, *The Anti-Chinese Movement in California* (Urbana: University of Illinois Press, 1939).

23. National Consumers' League annual reports, 1901–1904. This discussion of the White Label campaign draws on my article, "The Consumers' White Label of the National Consumers' League, 1898–1918," in *Getting and Spending: American and European Consumption in the Twentieth Century*, ed. Susan Strasser, Charles McGovern, and Matthais Judt (New York: Cambridge University Press, 1998).

24. For the emergence of the germ theory in the 1890s, see James H. Cassedy, "The Flamboyant Colonel Waring: An Anti-Contagionist Holds the American Stage in the Age of Pasteur and Koch," *Bulletin of the History of Medicine* 36 (March–April 1962): 163–76; John Duffy, *The Sanitarians: A History of American Public Health* (Urbana: University of Illinois Press, 1990), 179–80; and Judith Walzer Leavitt, *The Healthiest City: Milwaukee and the Politics of Health Reform* (Princeton, N.J.: Princeton University Press, 1982), 101–7.

25. Clara Lemlish, "Life in the Shop," in *New York Evening Journal*, 28 November 1909, quoted in *Out of the Sweatshop: The Struggle for Industrial Democracy*, ed. Leon Stein (New York: Quadrangle, 1977), 66.

26. Most definitions of the state include references to the "welfare of the whole." An example is Bob Jessop's useful definition of the state as "a distinct ensemble of institutions and organizations whose socially accepted function is to define and enforce collectively binding decisions on the members of a society in the name of their common interest or general will." Bob Jessop, *State Theory: Putting the Capitalist State in Its Place* (University Park: Pennsylvania State University Press, 1990), 340. A useful if simply descriptive definition of civil society is Perry Anderson's "network of cultural institutions—schools, churches, newspapers, parties, associations." Perry Anderson, *Considerations on Western Marxism* (London: NLB, 1976), 80.

27. Minutes, Consumers' League of Kentucky, Sophia Smith Collection, Smith College.

28. NCL annual reports, 1901–1904.

29. For more on William D. and Florence Kelley, see my *Florence Kelley and the Nation's Work*.

30. "Secretary's Report," National Consumers' League, *Second Annual Report*, Year Ending March 6, 1901 (New York: NCL, 1901), 14; The Consumers' League of Ann Arbor, *Fourth Annual Report* (1903), 46–47; NCL, *Seventh Annual Report*, Year Ending March 1, 1906 (New York: NCL, 1906), 14.

31. Consumers' League of Massachusetts, National Consumers' League, *Fourth Annual Report* (1903), 37–39.

32. For more on this comparison, see my "Two Political Cultures."

33. Wood, *History of the General Federation of Women's Clubs*, 131–32.

34. NCL, *Second Annual Report* (1901), 15.

35. NCL, *Second Annual Report* (1901), 15.

36. Wood, *History of the General Federation of Women's Clubs*, 147.

37. Wood, *History of the General Federation of Women's Clubs*, 178.

38. For more on this strategy, see my "Two Political Cultures," 36–62.

39. On women's "social citizenship," see Wendy Sarvasy, "From Man and Philanthropic Service to Feminist Social Citizenship," *Social Politics: International Studies in Gender, State, and Society* 1 (Fall 1994): 306–25.

40. Bender, "Wholes and Parts," 126.

41. For the decline in the unity and the social effectiveness of women's political activism after 1920, see Lois Scharf and Joan M. Jensen, eds., *Decades of Discontent: The Women's Movement, 1920–1940* (Westport, Conn.: Greenwood, 1983). For right-wing attacks, see J. Stanley Lemons, *The Woman Citizen: Social Feminism in the 1920s* (Urbana: University of Illinois Press, 1973). For the shifting cultural ground under women's organizations in the 1920s, see Nancy F. Cott, *The Grounding of Modern Feminism* (New Haven, Conn.: Yale University Press, 1987).

PART THREE

TRUST AND CIVIC VIRTUE

8

The Role of Trust in Civic Renewal

Robert Wuthnow

Shortly before a recent national election, a man in his mid-thirties who lives with his wife and two children in suburban Buffalo, New York, expressed his views on American politics. "In order to get elected, you have to promise certain groups that you'll do certain things," he explained. "It'll be the rich people who are going to keep you in office, so you're going to do things for them." He does not trust politicians to look out for people like himself. "The lower class and ethnic groups just get pushed back," he asserted.

Views like this are not unusual. A retired woman in West Virginia offered much the same view of politicians. "They'll say anything to get elected," she observed, "and then they do whatever they feel like." A Korean American in his late twenties expanded on a similar idea. "They're not looking out for you, they're looking out for themselves. They never admit that things are their fault." He added, "I don't feel like voting for anyone."

In national surveys, the proportion of the public who say they have "hardly any" confidence in the people running the executive branch of the federal government rose from 18 percent in 1973 to 35 percent in 1994. Over the same time period, low confidence in the leaders of Congress rose from 15 percent to 40 percent.[1] Surveys also show that other leaders are not exempt from public mistrust. One study asked, "Overall, how much do you trust Wall Street bankers and brokers to do what is best for the economy?" to which only 5 percent responded "a great deal," 28 percent said "somewhat," 32 percent said "a little," and 30 percent said "not at all."[2] Politicians nevertheless seem particularly vulnerable to mistrust.

Another study asked a national sample of Americans to say which people they regarded as least trustworthy: after lawyers, politicians and car salesmen were mentioned most often.[3]

Most people wish it were different. They believe it would be better if they were able to trust their elected officials. As one man (who says most politicians are "welfare pimps") observed, "[Mistrust] is a bad thing, because then people don't participate in the political process; they just wash their hands of the whole thing."

But the problem is not just that Americans are losing faith in politicians and other leaders. According to national surveys, Americans are also less willing now than in the past to believe that *people in general* can be trusted. For example, the proportion responding that "most people can be trusted" fell from 55 percent in 1960 to 34 percent in 1994, while those saying "you can't be too careful in dealing with people" rose from 40 percent in 1960 to 61 percent in 1994.[4] Other evidence points to the pervasiveness of mistrust. A 1995 survey sponsored by the Kaiser Foundation found that only 35 percent of the public thought "most people can be trusted," while 63 percent believed "you can't be too careful in dealing with people."[5] The man from Buffalo put it this way: "People are just out for themselves nowadays. They'll do anything to get what they want. You see people doing bad things to their own family. You see mothers abusing their own children. You just can't trust anybody."

Such statements give ample reason for concern. At face value, they point to growing fears—about crime, hatred, and selfishness—and to rising cynicism about human nature. Viewed more closely, they suggest that Americans are losing the capacity to work with one another, to cooperate and to give each other the benefit of the doubt. Rising levels of mistrust cause observers to wonder whether Americans are indeed "just out for themselves."

The connection between trust and civic health has been examined in two widely read books. In *Making Democracy Work*, Robert Putnam suggests that trust is a kind of social capital that helps democratic institutions to function more effectively.[6] Francis Fukuyama's book *Trust: The Social Virtues and the Creation of Prosperity* argues that trust is good for democracy (not to mention business) because it encourages citizens to band together, forming private voluntary associations of the kind that Alexis de Tocqueville believed were essential to the functioning of a democratic society.[7] Both arguments find support in other studies: people who trust the leaders of major institutions, such as banks, the courts, and nonprofit organizations, are more likely to give time and money to their communities; and people try to reduce risk in the marketplace (e.g., when purchasing a used car or seeking legal advice) by relying on social networks involving acquaintances they trust.[8]

Of course, questions can be raised about the alleged decline in public trust. It may be that surveys are biased, asking people questions that over-simplify their own understandings of trust; this is a possibility I want to examine in this chapter. It may be the case, too, that people have good reasons for exercising caution in their dealings with others. Still, if trust is declining in the United States (as Putnam, Fukuyama, and others suggest), then one of the ways to renew civil society may be to understand better the conditions that facilitate trust and the ones that erode it. Indeed, many such conditions have been discussed, and there is evidence to support claims about some of them. For example, trust in politicians seems to falter at times when national leaders are embroiled in ethical controversies, trust in religious leaders has dipped when some of these leaders were caught in scandals, trust in corporations fluctuates with economic conditions, and trust in people seems to be influenced both by economic prospects and by public fears about crime.[9]

But beyond this, trust is not very well understood. We know relatively little about why some people respond more favorably in surveys to questions about trust than others. We know even less about what they mean when they give these responses. We know virtually nothing about the thinking that underlies more specific views about whom to trust, for what, and in what situations.

The purpose of this chapter is to consider some of the complexity that needs to be taken into account in discussions of trust. I do this not by trying to develop abstract theoretical distinctions but by looking at some of the quantitative data that have previously gone unexamined and by analyzing what people say when they are permitted to speak in their own words about their lives, their friends, their communities, and their civic involvement. My purpose is not to dispute the claims of those who argue that trust is declining or to provide statistical arguments to explain this decline; it is rather to suggest some of the dimensions of trust that would need to be examined if we were truly to understand its place in civic renewal.

One way to gain a better understanding of trust is to look more closely at surveys. Another way is to interview people qualitatively to learn how they talk about trust. The following observations rely on both these methods. I present new results from several surveys that have asked about trust in various ways. I also discuss preliminary findings from a research project in which approximately 150 people were interviewed qualitatively about their civic activities and their beliefs, including some of their views about trust.[10]

WHAT SURVEYS SHOW

The surveys mentioned previously that ask generally about trust in people have been examined in some detail in recent work by Robert Putnam, Eric Uslaner, and others. Putnam shows that higher levels of trust are found among people with higher levels of education.[11] He also shows that whites are more likely to give trusting responses than blacks and that people who hold memberships in voluntary associations are more trusting than nonmembers. Uslaner examines these and other variables using multiple-regression techniques. His findings suggest that the standard survey question about trust can almost be thought of as a measure of optimism: people who have more advantages in life and who are more confident about their futures have more reasons to be optimistic and thus are more likely to give trusting responses.[12] By implication, trust may be declining because many Americans do not feel as confident about the future in terms of economic opportunities as they did a few decades ago. As Putnam observes, it is nevertheless puzzling that trust should have declined over the same period in which education levels have risen. It is for this reason that Putnam and others have pointed to the mass media as a possible source of wider public concern about violence or public mistrust of politicians.

In considering trends in trust, relatively little can be said definitively because of the sparseness of the questions that have been asked, but two interpretations appear to be supported. One is that some of the erosion in trust is directly attributable to political scandals specifically or to declining confidence in public leaders more generally. For instance, National Election Survey questions about trust in people show abrupt declines during the late 1960s and early 1970s when the Vietnam War and Watergate were raising public concern about national leaders. Other surveys conducted in those years show that large numbers actually believed their trust to have been shaken by Watergate. The National Election data also show that some of the decline in generalized trust can be explained statistically by the decline in confidence in government officials.[13] If, as Putnam has suggested, the mass media have had a dampening effect on other kinds of civic involvement, it would stand to reason that political scandals publicized by the mass media might also have had a negative impact on trust.

The other interpretation of trends in generalized trust comes from looking more closely at its relationships with education. Comparing overall relationships between education and trust in the 1973 and 1994 General Social Surveys suggests that little has changed (Pearson correlations, ordinal measures of association, and chi-squares are all virtually the same in the two surveys). However, disaggregating the relationships (by using likelihood ratio chi-squares) shows an interesting pattern. In 1973, the largest differences in trust were between respondents who had not graduated from high school and those who had graduated from high school. By 1994, this difference had shrunk, but that between high school graduates and college graduates had increased. Indeed, high school graduates in 1994 were about as likely to be trusting as those without high school degrees had been in 1973, and college graduates in 1994 resembled high school graduates in 1973. In addition, the 1994 data showed that college graduates were significantly less likely to trust than were respondents with graduate degrees, whereas in 1973 this difference was not significant.[14]

Substantively, these findings suggest a pattern that has been found in other studies of college effects. Higher education appears to be a measure of *relative standing* in the society, more so than a cognitive experience that simply shapes people's attitudes absolutely. As the proportion of Americans with college and postgraduate degrees has expanded, the large number who have high school degrees or less have become more disadvantaged, and their declining sense of their own opportunities appears to be reflected in a lower likelihood of giving optimistic responses to questions about trust. This is not to deny that even the most privileged in terms of education have also become somewhat less trusting. But it does appear that trust has fallen partly because people with the lowest levels of education have become more similar to one another in their views about trust, while there are greater differentials between these people and those with higher levels of education.

A second data set that permits further analysis of trust comes from a 1982 survey in which a representative national sample of adults were asked questions about their perceptions of *themselves*.[15] Among these was a question asking people to rate themselves on a seven-point scale anchored at one end by the word *dependable* and at the other by the word *undependable*. This question is conceptually interesting because, as I shall suggest in discussing the qualitative data, many people's willingness to trust others seems to be a reflection of whether they believe they can trust themselves.

The variables that are significantly associated with describing oneself as dependable are essentially the same as those in other surveys that correlate with saying that most people can be trusted. Being better educated, being white, having an above-average family income, owning one's home, and scoring higher on a self-esteem scale are all associated with higher probabilities of regarding oneself as dependable (as was civic participation, as measured by volunteering to help the poor and writing letters to political officials).[16] I take these findings as added evidence that trust is influenced by personal circumstances. If generalized trust has been declining, it probably has not done so only because people believe *others* are having more difficulties living up to their agreements, or even because their faith in politicians or the police or the criminal justice system has been shaken. It has probably declined partly because people are less confident in their own capacities to hold up their share of the bargain. We shall have more opportunity to consider this possibility in looking at the qualitative data.

The other survey from which I have been able to draw some additional observations is my 1992 national survey of 1,000 Americans who were currently members of small support groups, such as Bible study circles, twelve-step groups, and self-help groups.[17] In this study, respondents were asked to rate their groups on a number of performance items, including "people trusting each other." Because Putnam and others have argued that trust is enhanced when people belong to groups, this question provides a useful opportunity to determine what kinds of group experiences are most likely to be associated with the view that trust is present. It also provides a more specific context in which to ask respondents about trust, compared with questions that ask only about unspecified "people."

In interpreting the results from this study, it is important to bear in mind that different kinds of people may select different kinds of groups, thus bringing with them a differential propensity to rate their groups high on trust. For example, women generally rated their groups higher than men did. This caveat notwithstanding, the results appear to support most of the arguments that have been made in the recent literature on social capital—namely, that more intimate and encompassing interaction is associated with higher levels of trust. Specifically, group members were more likely to give their groups high scores on trust if they attended frequently themselves, if the group met frequently, and if most members attended every time the group met. They were also more likely to rate their groups high on trust if the group included such activities as eating together, singing, praying, and helping people in the community.[18]

The study also suggests a reason that trust may be declining in the wider society. People in heterogeneous groups—especially ones that included diverse political views and mixed religious views—were less likely to rate their groups high on trust than people in homogeneous groups.[19] From this finding, it may be reasonable to suspect that trust among the public at large has suffered as a result of acrimony between political or religious factions; it may also have been influenced by the growing diversity of the population in ethnic identities, lifestyles, and values.

These data also provide help in thinking about the reasons for differences between blacks and whites in surveys about trust. Here, blacks are just as likely as whites to rate their groups high on trust, and this is true whether they are in all-black, mostly black, or more racially mixed groups. The reason for this lack of differences is probably that blacks and whites are in small, intimate groups where they get to know one another and are relatively on a par with other members. In the wider society, those conditions do not prevail.

In sum, the main conclusions that seem to be supported by the various surveys are that opportunities to realize one's expectations are conducive to trust, inequality and disprivilege are not conducive to trust, low perceptions of one's own trustworthiness undermine trust in others, and social interaction appears to enhance trust. These conclusions also demonstrate that trust is always conditional. Nobody trusts everyone all the time. It is thus important to turn to qualitative data to see how people understand the conditions under which they can and cannot trust others.

WHAT IT MEANS TO TRUST

In our qualitative interviews we asked people a variety of questions about trust. For instance, we asked them the standard survey question (whether most people can be trusted or you can't be too careful in dealing with people) and then asked them to explain their answer. We also asked questions about trust in relation to the civic organization in which they were involved (if they were involved) and about their willingness to trust politicians. Our questions, of course, provided the context in which people framed their answers. But we also found that people bring different kinds of mental frames to bear on their own thinking. Indeed, these frames emerge as a helpful way in which to sort out some of the variations in how people seem to understand trust.[20]

As the survey data suggest, people understand trust in conditional terms, meaning that they implicitly or explicitly assume that it is reasonable or possible to trust *if certain conditions are met*. How they frame their talk about trust is usually an indication of what these conditions are. Frames are thus a way to sort out the different kinds of conditions that are believed to be relevant in making assessments about trust. Examining them can provide clues about why trust may be breaking down and possibly suggest some ways in which it can be restored. Some of these frames focus more on the conditions of the person doing the trusting, whereas others identify conditions that characterize the object of trust.

Consider the following statement made by a man who feels that most people can be trusted:

> I feel that before anything can take place constructive, there has to be a trust relationship. I feel if I can be trusted, I can trust other people. Throughout

my lifetime I've found that to be true, that if you are up and above and honest with people, they will return that respect. It's just as easy as if you give a
smile you're going to get one back.

The central condition that this man places on trust is explicit: if I can be
trusted, I can trust others. The focus is on himself more than on some
characteristic of other people. A statement such as this lends credence to
the foregoing suggestion that one of the reasons trust may be declining is
that people are less certain that they can trust themselves—that is, that
they themselves are able to behave in a trustworthy manner. From other
studies, some of the factors that might increase these worries about being
trustworthy include more complicated family schedules that make it
harder to keep appointments or carry out family and community responsibilities, fears about one's economic future rooted in declining incomes
or rising expenditures either in absolute terms or relative to expectations,
and greater uncertainty about values, moral standards, and religious beliefs. Especially if social and cultural conditions have become sufficiently
complex to generate what Kenneth Gergen has termed "multiphrenia"
(the splitting of the individual into "a multiplicity of self-investments"),
it may be harder for people to know whether they are trustworthy.[21]

This man's statement is revealing in another way. When he voluntarily
goes ahead to explain what he means by being trustworthy, he focuses on
being honest and giving people a smile. It is significant that he does not
equate trustworthiness with being dependable—for example, saying that
you need to make good on everything you promise. Thus, being trustworthy is entirely under his own control, rather than being subject to contin-
gencies that might prevent him from fulfilling other people's expectations
of him. He is able to feel that he (and thus most people) are trustworthy
because the only thing required is being honest and smiling.

These seemingly minimal conditions can nevertheless become problematic. In other research, I found that people are not at all sure (or in
agreement) about what it means to be honest.[22] For many, honesty is
largely a subjective self-assessment that says, in effect, you are honest if
you feel that you are honest. In the absence of clearer external standards,
many people feel that they are operating largely within gray areas (especially in business or their professional lives) that make them wonder
whether they are truly honest. In addition, it is important to note that this
man's argument depends partly on his belief that it is validated by other
people's responses to him. That is, he believes that if he is honest and
smiles, then others will behave in a trustworthy and respectful manner
toward him. But if people do not reciprocate this way, his basis for believing that people can be trusted may be undermined.

Indeed, it is revealing to look at what he says next:

> I know through experience that people are going to stretch the truth. This is
> human nature and everyone does it. However, I think that you can build up
> respect where the level is there that this is not going to be a problem. I think
> I have the capabilities to realize when people are trying to pull the wool over
> your eyes. I have no problem confronting people. I try to do it in a tactful
> way that they are not hurt, and I think with some of these abilities I have that
> I have never found it to be a problem.

This statement is an example of what discourse analysts would call a *secondary warrant*.[23] The primary warrant in the argument is that being honest and smiling generally causes people to reciprocate. The secondary
warrant takes account of the exceptions (the fact that counterexamples
can be given). Most people, we found, have secondary warrants that help
buttress their willingness to trust others by, as it were, explaining away
the counterexamples. In this case, the man argues essentially that he is
capable of minimizing these counterexamples. He believes he has good
social skills and thus understands people; he also believes it is possible to
confront them; and he believes that he can to some extent control other
people by confronting them.

A framework like this turns out, then, to depend largely on being able
to focus on one's own trustworthiness, to feel that one is a good judge of
other people, and to believe in one's own efficacy to the extent that other
people's responses can to a degree be controlled. All this depends on implicitly limiting the object of trust ("most people") to those with whom
one has firsthand contact. By implication, strangers or people who are different enough that one's understanding of them may fail are less likely to
be trustworthy. To the extent that strangers come more into one's thinking, trust may decline.

Among the people we interviewed, those who emphasized characteristics of themselves as the condition for trusting others generally fell into
three categories. One category is illustrated by the man we have just been
considering. It is aptly described as a frame that emphasizes *self-knowl-
edge*. Feeling that you are honest, civil, and capable of judging other people are examples of such knowledge. Other people explained that they
knew themselves well enough to know that they could keep their mouth
shut when they needed to or that they would not make a promise they
could not keep.

A second frame emphasizes *personal experience*. For example, a 44-year-
old newspaper editor attributes his being a trusting person to growing up
in a neighborhood where people knew one another and helped one another. He uses a story to illustrate:

> I remember I had a bicycle accident and my parents weren't there. Grand-
> mother was there but she didn't drive. Just going up the street there were six

or seven houses in a row that I could ask anybody in those houses to drive me to the hospital. They all knew my mother and wouldn't have worried about the liability or anything. Part of this, I think, comes from the fact that it was pretty homogenous and that people stayed there for a long time. That gives you a sense of trust in people just from the years when they've been there; they've never done anything wrong, and you've gotten to know them.

This man is fairly reflective about his own reasons for being trusting. He does not generalize from his childhood experience by assuming that virtually everyone he runs into at present can be trusted. Instead, he observes that his experiences shaped him so that he is simply a trusting person. He also employs a secondary warrant to explain why he now believes that most people can be trusted: "I guess I think there's some sort of bell curve because people are reasonably good, reasonably honest, and they're motivated by pretty much the same impulses."

The third frame explains why one is a trusting person by placing trust in a category that makes sense only as a *leap of faith*. Whereas the first two say, in effect, that there are rational reasons that one is able to trust others, this frame implicitly assumes that trust may not be rational (at least not in terms of what one knows about how people behave), but argues that being trusting is still a good way to live. Here is an example. A woman who works as an artist says she trusts most people but emphasizes that she is not naive and that she has been "burned" a few times. She explains the reason for being a trusting person in terms of a faith commitment that causes her to focus on the inner person: "What I'm seeing is what's going on inside that person; I behold the Christ in you, the good stuff that connects us all, that's in all of us. That's where I connect into people." Her distinction between the inner and outer person also provides an explanation for why her trust is sometimes ill founded: "In the past I have not noticed the outward behavior that they're really giving me. I do this with men and it causes problems. So sometimes there has been trust issues that I've missed because of that." Some of the other people we interviewed emphasized religious faith as their reason for being trusting; others defended their leap of faith on pragmatic grounds. They said they were simply happier or found they could get along better if they decided to be trusting.

It is probably worth noting that few of the people who emphasized being able to trust themselves said that this kind of trust had been influenced by participating in civic groups as an adult. Instead, they described their attitude as something they had always had, as a character trait that they had learned as a child, as having been shaped by where they grew up, or as a leap of faith that had been informed as much by negative experiences as by positive ones. This is not to deny that trust can be enhanced by joining civic associations, but it does cast doubt on the idea that trust is caused primarily by such participation (indeed, it suggests that participation is probably more likely among people who grew up regarding themselves as trusting individuals).[24]

In contrast to those who made the condition for being trusting something about themselves, most of the people we talked to focused on conditions that stipulated different kinds of *objects* toward whom they would be more or less trusting. The most common of these conditions was also the most straightforward: people said they would trust others if those others proved to be reliable. In other words, trust was contingent on a rational assessment of someone's *performance* in the past and the likelihood that the future would hold similar performances by that person or by similar persons. For example, one man said a trustworthy person is someone who "walks the walk and talks the talk; somebody whose deeds reflect their words; somebody who when they tell you something, you can take it to the bank. They're dependable, consistent." As a negative example, a lawyer used a former intern as an example of someone who could not be trusted, saying, "He would miss meetings. He wouldn't call up ahead and let you know why. That kind of thing. He wouldn't get things in on time, would always be late and with excuses."

This kind of trust, it should be noted, is highly contingent on the kind of people toward whom one's trust is directed. Whereas a frame that emphasizes the fact that you yourself are a trusting person suggests an inclination to trust most people under most circumstances, this one is more limited. For example, a man talking about his fellow Masons says:

> I can trust these people. Almost invariably, they say, "I'm going to do it," and they'll do it. You don't generally have to call them up and remind them. Nobody has really, that I can think of, that have been any kind of a regular good Mason, would do anything to hurt you or anything.

He is less sure that people in other contexts can be trusted.

People nevertheless have frames that permit them to draw broad generalizations about whom they can trust. The most common of these frames emphasizes that people can be trusted insofar as their performances are reliable, but then stipulates the type of person who should be excluded. Rationality is often the decisive criterion. For example, a volunteer who works with AIDS patients says this: "I know firsthand how it affects the mind sometimes because they will get dementia and different things, so they're not rational sometimes in their thinking. And the next day maybe they'll be back to normal." Another woman explained rationality by saying that her husband hit her with a lamp once, but he was sick and didn't realize what he was doing. She said you can trust people who are in possession of their faculties. In these examples, trust is conditional on objects of trust behaving rationally; exceptions to the rule are understood to have reasons for not behaving rationally.

Another frame that permits people to say they can trust most other people emphasizes *resources*: objects of trust who have sufficient resources to carry through on their promises and to behave reliably are said to be trustworthy; in contrast, people with limited resources should perhaps not be trusted. A 43-year-old woman who manages a small company illustrates this frame by talking about her employees. She says that people in her organization can generally be trusted because it supplies them with the resources they need to fulfill their responsibilities. She generalizes from this example, stating, "If you give people responsibility and try and give them as many tools as you possibly can, they won't disappoint you."

The main alternatives to frames that emphasize reliable performances are frames that emphasize something about the *self* of the person being trusted. These frames come in several variants. One of the most common argues simply that you can trust people better if you know them well. It says nothing about whether these people have performed reliably in the past, only that you know them well enough to assume that they are people of character, people who are somewhat like yourself in their values and their respect for common norms of decency. For example, one man said, "If I'm talking about people in general, like neighbors on an everyday type situation, I think most people are honest. If I'm talking business dealings, I think you really have to cover your butt, because I think there's all sorts of mistrust." He was indicating that special norms prevail in business that may cause people to behave in an untrustworthy manner, but if most people are like his neighbors, then he figures they are honest.

I emphasize the *self*, though, because many people are more specific in what it is about other people that causes them to be perceived as trustworthy. One frame (which was hinted at by the woman who focuses on the "Christ" in other people) draws a distinction between an inner self that is presumed to be more trustworthy and an outer self that may be more calculating, devious, or unreliable. The people who can be trusted are thus ones who have been willing to disclose something about this inner self. For example, the organizer of a gardening club said it was hard for the women in the club to trust one another because they were all strangers, so she hosted a dinner and some other meetings that encouraged them to become better acquainted. But the decisive factor in her mind was that people started disclosing some of their personal problems: "What happened with trust would be the meetings where people would share their problems or concerns or things that they were pleased with and the reception that it would get at the meetings. The problems that they were experiencing were not trivialized at the meetings."

This emphasis on disclosing the inner self means, perhaps obviously, that people are more likely to trust those with whom they have developed some intimacy. As one woman explained, "I think you have to be pretty careful. I feel that you should be able to trust the people you're closest to. It depends, I guess, on your relationship with the people, like your close friends, your family." But focusing on self-disclosure also encourages people to look for cues, even in strangers, that people are disclosing something about their inner selves or their true feelings. For instance, a man who deals mostly with strangers in his business emphasizes that trust depends on the following:

> It's body language sort of stuff. I think it's looking people in the eye. I think it's the tone of their voice, the way they hold themselves. Obviously what they say, whether what they say is something that sounds truthful or not. Whether they tend to exaggerate.

Disclosing deep emotions or personal problems may be important, but truthfulness in general, as this example indicates, is also especially significant. Trust may be based much less on what people do than on what they say. The following example illustrates this point in another context. This is a man talking about why he trusts fellow members of the zoning board: "Because people say what they think. It seems to be aboveboard. I have never seen a situation where there are any hidden agendas."

Even a cursory examination of statements such as these shows that people develop frames in which they think about trust, and these frames are quite varied, depending not simply on how people rationally assess the behavior of those with whom they interact, but also on beliefs about themselves, and about the role of inner selves and feelings and talk, and on leaps of faith and secondary warrants that account for negative cases. Although many people talk about trust in the way that social scientists do (as a rational prediction of how someone else will perform), it is also clear that performance is bracketed in ways that specify the conditions under which it should be emphasized. For other people, trust is much more an assessment of their own character or a statement about their understanding of feelings and inner selves than it is a statement about behavior.[25] I will come back to some of the ways in which these frames may help us in thinking about civic renewal, but first I want to consider how these frames play themselves out in people's comments about politics.

HOW PEOPLE THINK ABOUT POLITICIANS

The extent to which people say they trust holders of public office is contingent on the frames they bring to bear on this question, just as their trust of other people is. As pollsters suggest, the public's willingness to trust politicians depends heavily on their perceptions of whether these office-holders are people of good character who can make good on their promises. But different people obviously judge the same officeholders in many different ways, and these differences cannot be understood entirely in terms of party loyalties or self-interest. Trust of politicians depends greatly on the frames and warrants that the public uses to *interpret* their behavior.

Consider the following statement by a man in his forties who works as an orderly in a hospital and who said he basically trusts the political system. When asked to say why he does so, he remarked:

> We've been bombarded with so much information that is of no substance whatsoever, has nothing to do with how well somebody does their job. It doesn't matter if Bill Clinton ever had an affair. It really doesn't matter. Whitewater doesn't really matter, because it has nothing to do with how well he does his job as president of the United States. So politics as such, it's the sorting out of information and we have too much information at this point. We don't need to know all this stuff.

This man was saying that performance should be the criterion by which politicians are judged. To make this the relevant condition, he specifically bracketed what some refer to as "character" issues as being irrelevant.

Those who bracket character issues so that they can focus on performance still run into problems, of course: elected officials often fail to perform. One of the people who had lost faith in officials for this reason explained his lack of trust this way:

> I have very little respect for elected officials anymore. There are a handful of them that I think highly of, but most of them I see as hacks who are in there to collect a paycheck, get some perks, make some more business contacts, and live off the public teat.

Because he attributed performance failure to officials' incompetence, he was unable to find much about them to praise.

In contrast, a draftsman in his fifties who also remarked on officials' unreliability said he still trusted them, producing the following warrant to excuse their failure to perform up to the public's expectations:

> I think they honestly believe that when they get in there they're going to be able to do all these things for you. My feeling is once they are elected and they're in the office, they learn the reality of those offices and they find out that things aren't as easily done as they think they are. There are compromises that they have to meet, and those compromises in a lot of cases are

completely contradictory to what they had promised the people that voted them in. I think it's a lack of communication then between that elected official and the people that voted for him, in telling them why he had to change his mind or why he had to do something. So we now have the feeling that all politicians lie, when in fact I don't think they all lie. I think they all are hit with the reality of the office that they had absolutely no knowledge of going in.

Like many of the people we talked to, this man denied that his qualified trust in politicians should be taken as incipient cynicism. He said he was merely being realistic in his expectations of what officials could and could not do.

In contrast to the people who focused on performance, others framed their willingness or unwillingness to trust officials mostly in terms of officials' personal characteristics. In doing so, these people did not have to worry as much about whether officials were performing reliably. But they did have to find warrants to explain why they thought politicians were people with trustworthy personal characteristics. Consider the following:

> Usually, you don't get to be a politician without having some kind of a fairly solid reputation for dealing with other people, and you've reached a certain intellectual level that requires a certain amount of commitment and personal integrity.

This statement came from a man who said he learned growing up that most people were trustworthy; he also believes there is a winnowing process in the political system that causes the most capable people to rise to the top. Other people made their trust of politicians conditional on arguments about how hard officials have to work or how much they sacrifice in earnings or privacy. Some people also explained their trust by saying that politicians share their own values or inevitably reflect the values and interests of their constituents.

It is easy to see why mistrust of officials has increased when trust is contingent on having these kinds of frameworks. Indeed, we found that some people were shifting to arguments that were more similar to the ones they used in talking about more intimate relationships. One young woman provided a vivid example by saying she had volunteered to work for a candidate's campaign in order to decide for herself whether she could trust politicians. She concluded that some politicians could indeed be trusted, but she did so only because she had traveled at odd hours with the candidate, observed her "behind the scenes," and heard the woman talk about her personal life. Other people focused equally on biographical details, body language, reports of affairs, and the use or absence of certain words, basing their opinions of officials largely on what these characteristics revealed about the inner self.

WHY IT IS HARD TO TRUST

These observations can be used to offer some tentative conclusions about why it may be harder for people to trust one another and their elected officials. Frames and warrants can be selected from a large repertoire, but they are subject to disconfirmation both by social conditions and by the messages produced by the media or by scholars. The fact that many people make trust conditional on themselves or the objects of their trust being dependable is indicative of the problem. Complex circumstances that make outcomes contingent on much more than good intentions or hard work mean that it is harder to find examples of people who can be trusted.

Those who do not insist on dependability but offer their trust as a leap of faith may be freer from these conditions. Yet the number of people who can justify this leap of faith in terms of religious beliefs (such as the belief that "God will work things out") may be declining in proportion to the growing number of Americans who express doubt about the truth of the Bible or other religious creeds. As one woman replied when asked why she trusted others, "I don't go to church much, but my belief is still intact," thereby raising the question of what would happen if her belief were not intact. Others who root their trust in a leap of faith sometimes argue that it makes sense to do so on pragmatic grounds (objects of trust rise to the occasion). But pragmatic arguments can easily be disconfirmed by contrary experiences. Those who seemed most convinced that trust was a leap of faith had reflected long and hard about the issue, but their numbers were rare—suggesting perhaps that busy Americans often do not take the time to think much about trust.

Other frames may be equally vulnerable to changing social conditions. People who say they trust others because of having been reared in safe environments sometimes recognize that they would take a different view if they had grown up in a different context. Saying that people who behave rationally can usually be trusted becomes more difficult when it is no longer as clear what rationality means. Those who require intimate disclosures of the inner self may limit their ability to trust to the few people they can know this intimately. Projecting the same framework to politicians, they may focus on personal foibles that have little to do with performance in office.

It is worth noting, too, that many of the people we talked to expressed concern about mistrust and yet found ways to negotiate their lives without being immobilized by this mistrust. They did so by relying on other mechanisms, such as laws, regulations, and markets, to minimize risk. For example, the head of a baby-sitting cooperative in New Jersey told us that her co-op had two hundred members, but only eight families regularly used it. The reason, she thought, was that most of the members did not trust the other members well enough to feel comfortable leaving their children with them. Although she tried to build trust by having parties and other "get acquainted" meetings, most of the members said that they did not have time for such activities. Because they enjoyed upper-middle-class incomes, they used for-profit day care centers instead.

In a case such as this, one could say that trust was being redirected from neighbors to for-profit day care centers. But this is not how the woman herself saw it. In her view, trust is "a personal thing." Like many of the people we interviewed, she makes it conditional on knowing something about the private life—the inner self—of another person. It seems better to her to say that people have *confidence* in day care centers.[26] Trust is not at issue; confidence rests on knowing that these centers are licensed by the state, are governed by a number of laws and regulations, and must do their jobs well if they are to stay in business.

What I have said about trust in general is true of political trust as well: people mistrust individual politicians but find other ways to get on with their lives. Some say it is healthy to be skeptical toward politicians because critical questions get raised or because mistrust prevents politicians from assuming too much power. For many of the people we interviewed, mistrust was more of an irritation than a profound complaint because they felt the political system should not be doing very much anyway. Some believed that private volunteer organizations were better suited to solving social problems. Following the 1996 election, during which high levels of mistrust toward the leading candidates were registered, the stock market soared to record highs. Analysts attributed the increases to investors realizing that a divided government incapable of inspiring confidence would do little to upset their expectations.

IMPLICATIONS FOR CIVIC RENEWAL

The foregoing discussion nevertheless suggests that trust is important enough that people are able to talk about it, generally in more complex ways than have been captured in public opinion polls. It demonstrates that trust is not simply a matter of making rational calculations about the possibility of benefiting by cooperating with someone else. Trust cannot be understood except by paying attention to the ways in which it is *culturally constructed*. People draw on cultural repertoires to frame their ways of thinking about trust and to legitimate their arguments, as well as to account for obvious exceptions to these arguments. If trust is cultural, it may well be vulnerable, as social critics have suggested, to the influences of newscasters and campaign managers, and it may depend as much on renewing the ways in which we think about trust as it does on somehow orchestrating social life so that people can more reliably predict how others will behave. Suggestions for thinking about the renewal of trust should include the following.

First, deliberate *repair work* needs to be done to restore trust that has been damaged by broken promises, disrupted relationships, and fragmented self-images. If it is valid to say that being in love means never having to say you're sorry, then it is appropriate to say that trust does mean saying you're sorry. This point is worth underscoring because promises can be broken for so many reasons that it may be easy to avoid taking responsibility for fulfilling them. As one man observed, he gets busy and fails to "follow through" on all his promises; he disappoints people but does not intentionally deceive them. Yet this man also recognized the value of rendering apologies to keep relationships intact. More important than public apologies that may be unpersuasive, though, is the need for situations in which repair work can actually take place. Some of the people we interviewed said their ability to trust others had been restored only by participating in self-help groups that permitted them to overcome anger, develop new interpretations of body language, and talk explicitly about connections between inner selves and behavior. Many of the people who were active in civic organizations said they had to work hard at maintaining trust. Rather than simply happening as people interacted, it required confrontations, staff meetings, bull sessions, phone calls, and mediation.

Second, the fact that trust of others and trust of oneself depend so heavily on the resources and opportunities at one's disposal means that mistrust can only be addressed adequately by including efforts to redress injustice and inequality. It is not enough to blame negative campaign rhetoric or the use of bad language in motion pictures. To focus attention in those directions can in fact be a smoke screen that prevents more serious problems from being understood. African Americans are not less trusting than white European Americans because they watch the wrong kind of television. They are less trusting because they have fewer economic resources to risk and are more in danger of being victims of violent crime. The frames that privileged Americans use to justify their faith in people attest clearly to the importance of social circumstances: those who generalize from their experiences in safe, affluent suburban families need to know that not everyone is able to draw on the same experiences.

Third, it is not enough to argue that trust can be restored simply by getting people to join bowling leagues and other civic organizations. To be sure, there are statistical correlations between joiners and trusters. But the research on small groups indicates that not all forms of social interaction are equally conducive to trust. Moreover, interaction may be the way to generate norms that permit people to work together, but these norms vary enormously from group to group. As one man who trusted the men in his civic association observed, women just weren't to be trusted because they were always talking and expressing their feelings.

Fourth, there needs to be more widespread recognition of the nonrational bases of trust and, indeed, of the competing ways in which rationality itself is culturally constructed. Social scientists who reduce the study of trust to questions about rational choices and who argue that it has nothing to do with moral discourse miss this point.[27] In rational choice theory, trust may mean little more than an expectation that someone will behave in a certain way. From interviews, we learn that people bring moral frameworks directly to bear on their thinking about trust, talking about how it is simply good to trust others, how trust depends on moral character, and how individuals have a moral obligation to fulfill the expectations of those who have placed trust in them. Even if trust is taken as nothing more than an expectation of how someone will behave, it is invariably conditioned by assumptions about one's own honesty, whether promises are morally binding, and how much the behavior of individuals is likely to be shaped by their moral commitments.

Finally, the role of civic organizations in generating trust must be understood better than it has been. Civic organizations do not simply get people together and thus show them that they can trust everyone. They fill in the public spaces, as it were, between the individual and government or other large-scale institutions. In our interviews, people talked about constructing rules within these organizations that served as heuristics for making decisions about trust. Indeed, these rules were often quite explicit. People did not have to rely on implicit norms about whether to trust someone who failed to show up for meetings or who took handouts but did not look for a job. Because these are gray areas, organizations created local understandings about how to regard such activities. Consequently, participants did not have to trust a "generalized other," as it were, but could respond according to the rules they had learned in these organizations. For example, the baby-sitting co-op included detailed information for members about what to expect and what not to expect; the garden club members developed a voucher system to avoid confusion about who owed favors to whom; a homeless shelter adopted a rule that in effect told volunteers to trust whatever clients told them the first time, but to ask more questions on subsequent visits. In these ways, the presence of civic organizations helped define the conditions under which trust could be exercised.

In a larger sense, civic renewal depends on many things besides restoring trust. But civic renewal is unlikely to be effective unless discussions of trust are brought squarely into the picture. Trust is far more complicated than surveys have managed to capture. A movement for civic renewal must pay attention not only to the social conditions that may reinforce trust but also to the ways in which it is understood.

NOTES

1. General Social Surveys conducted by the National Opinion Research Center (NORC) at the University of Chicago.

2. Survey conducted by Yankelovich Partners, Inc., March 1994; results available through Public Opinion Online.

3. *Great American TV Poll #5* (conducted by Troika Productions and Lifetime Television in 1991 among six hundred randomly selected adults).

4. National surveys conducted by the NORC at the University of Chicago.

5. *Trust in Government Survey* (Princeton, N.J.: Princeton Survey Research Associates, 1996).

6. Robert D. Putnam, *Making Democracy Work: Civic Traditions in Modern Italy* (Princeton, N.J.: Princeton University Press, 1993).

7. Francis Fukuyama, *Trust: The Social Virtues and the Creation of Prosperity* (New York: Free Press, 1995).

8. Paul DiMaggio and Hugh Louch, "Embedding Economic Transactions," unpublished paper, Department of Sociology, Princeton University, 1997.

9. Tom W. Smith, "Factors Relating to Misanthropy in Contemporary American Society," GSS Topical Report No. 29 (Chicago: National Opinion Research Center, 1996).

10. Respondents were selected purposively (nonrandomly) to fill a quota design that called for approximately equal numbers of men and women, younger and older people, whites and blacks, and who were involved in a wide variety of civic activities or were in no civic activities and lived in different regions of the country; each interview lasted at least two hours, with some continuing as long as five hours; the questions about trust occupied a relatively small part of the interview; all interviews were transcribed; quotes included here are verbatim.

11. Robert D. Putnam, "Bowling Alone: America's Declining Social Capital," *Journal of Democracy* (January 1995): 65–78; "Tuning In, Tuning Out: The Strange Disappearance of Social Capital in America" (The Ithiel de Sola Pool Lecture, American Political Science Association, 1995), *P.S.: Political Science and Politics* 27 (1995): 664–83; "The Strange Disappearance of Civic America," *American Prospect*, no. 24 (Winter 1996): http://epn.org/prospect/24/24putn.html.

12. Eric M. Uslaner, "Faith, Hope, and Charity: Social Capital, Trust, and Collective Action," unpublished paper, Department of Government and Politics, University of Maryland, 1996.

13. Robert Wuthnow, "The Changing Character of Social Capital in the United States," unpublished paper, Department of Sociology, Princeton University, 1997.

14. In 1973, the proportion who said most people can be trusted was 32 percent among those with less than high school educations, 54 percent among high school graduates, 67 percent among college graduates, and 70 percent among those with graduate degrees; in 1994, the respective percentages were 20, 33, 50, and 62. Using likelihood-ratio chi-squares because they can be partitioned, researchers found the chi-square for the difference between high school grads and those with less education fell from 59.9 in 1973 to 20.3 in 1994 (significant beyond the .05 level with 1 degree of freedom). In contrast, the difference between high school grads and college grads rose from a chi-square of 8.02 in 1973 to 29.6 in 1994 (significant beyond the .05 level), and the difference between college grads and those with graduate degrees rose from a chi-square of 0.2 in 1973 to 5.2 in 1994 (significant at the .05 level).

15. Self-Esteem Survey, conducted by the Gallup Organization in 1982 among a nationally representative sample of 1,484 adults.

16. For the total sample, the mean score (where 1 = dependable and 7 = undependable) was 1.75; mean scores among the following segments of the sample were as follows: high school grad or less, 1.80; some college, 1.70; college grad, 1.63; gave time to help the poor, 1.62; did not, 1.81; wrote a letter to a politician, 1.60; did not, 1.78; Rosenberg self-esteem scale top third, 1.34; middle third, 1.75; bottom third, 2.05; own home, 1.67; rent home, 1.89; white, 1.73; black, 1.86; income, top two-thirds, 1.66; bottom third, 1.86; all relationships significant at or beyond the .05 level.

17. Robert Wuthnow, *Sharing the Journey: Support Groups and America's New Quest for Community* (New York: Free Press, 1994); a copy of the survey instrument is included in the appendix of that book.

18. Among all group members (where 1 = excellent, 2 = good, 3 = fair, and 4 = poor), the mean score for "people trust each other" was 1.52; No significant differences were present for different-sized groups, for groups that had been in existence for different periods of time, or for members who had been involved in their groups for different periods of time, by members' level of education. Significant differences at the .05 level included: attend at least once a week, 1.56; attend every two weeks, 1.71; attend about once a month, 1.71; attend less than once a month, 1.77; group meets more than once a week, 1.55; about once a week, 1.60; every two weeks, 1.62; about once a month, 1.73; less than once a month, 1.89; most members always come, 1.58; most do not always come, 1.75; women, 1.61; men, 1.69; group is sponsored by a church, 1.61; not sponsored by a church, 1.69; group eats together, 1.61; does not eat together, 1.74; group does things for the community together, 1.62; does not, 1.71; group has parties, 1.59; does not, 1.73; group follows a twelve-step program, 1.52; does not, 1.66; group prays together, 1.61; does not, 1.73; group sings together, 1.57; does not, 1.73; group lets people share problems, 1.61; does not, 1.79. Other factors that did *not* show significant relationships with the trust item were: engaging in sports activities together (contrary to arguments about the beneficial effects of bowling leagues), discussing social or political issues, having elected officers, having an agenda or schedule, and

having business meetings (in short, informal interaction was conducive to trust, but formal structure was unrelated to trust).

19. Mean scores on how much people trust each other were as follows: in politically liberal groups, 1.58; politically conservative groups, 1.61; politically mixed groups, 1.67; religiously liberal groups, 1.55; religiously conservative groups, 1.57; mixed or middle-of-the road groups, 1.69; members who had had disagreements with other members, 1.72; members who had not had disagreements, 1.55.

20. For a more general discussion of frames, see Kenneth Burke, *A Grammar of Motives* (Berkeley: University of California Press, 1969), 3–24; Erving Goffman, *Frame Analysis: An Essay on the Organization of Experience* (New York: Harper & Row, 1974).

21. Kenneth J. Gergen, *The Saturated Self: Dilemmas of Identity in Contemporary Life* (New York: Basic Books, 1991), 73–74.

22. Robert Wuthnow, *God and Mammon in America* (New York: Free Press, 1994), chap. 4.

23. On warrants, see Jürgen Habermas, *The Theory of Communicative Action, Vol. 1: Reason and the Rationalization of Society*, trans. Thomas McCarthy (Boston: Beacon, 1981).

24. Our interviews evoked numerous examples in which civic participation had actually made people *less* trusting (or at least more cautious about whom they could trust); for example, members of township committees who said fellow members were so underhanded that it shook their faith in people, or parents who talked about Scout leaders molesting children.

25. This emphasis on the cultural construction of trust is similar to discussions of the ways in which promises are constructed; for example, J. L. Austin, *How to Do Things with Words*, 2d ed., ed. J. O. Urmson and Marina Sbisa (Cambridge, Mass.: Harvard University Press, 1975); and John R. Searle, *Speech Acts: An Essay in the Philosophy of Language* (Cambridge: Cambridge University Press, 1969), 54–71. It is also apparent that everyday language about trust overlaps only partly with the ways in which people talk about promises.

26. This distinction is parallel to that emphasized by Adam Seligman, *The Problem of Trust* (Princeton, N.J.: Princeton University Press, 1997).

27. Russell Hardin, "The Street-Level Epistemology of Trust," *Politics and Society* 21 (December 1993): 505–29.

9

Self-Help Groups, Community, and Civil Society

David Wasserman

Long before scholars were announcing the decline of civil society, they were announcing the decline of community. As Thomas Bender, writing in 1978, observed:

> Modern Americans fear that urbanization and modernization have destroyed the community that earlier shaped the lives of men and women, particularly in the small towns of the American past. Many popular discussions of alienation, anomie, and other supposed evils of modern urban life are extensions of this general worry about community. These popular concerns have been abetted, if not actually stimulated, by the writings of historians and sociologists that are laced with references to the "erosion," or the "decline," or the "breakup," or the "eclipse" of community.[1]

Bender traced these academic pronouncements back to the earliest days of modern sociology, to the 1887 publication of *Gesellschaft und Gemeinschaft*, describing the replacement of the intimate, private, encompassing social network of traditional communities with the impersonal, instrumental, bureaucratic social order of modern cities. Yet, as Bender noted, the intimacy found in traditional communities had not been lost so much as displaced, divorced from locality, transformed to accommodate the mobility and division of labor in modern society. Social scientists such as Claude Fischer and Peggy Wireman have argued that much of the intimacy found in traditional communities reemerged in the social networks formed by urban and suburban residents, especially in the voluntary associations that flourished after World War II.[2]

Given the highly adaptive, protean character of intimate social groups,

231

it seems plausible to view the apparent reduction in associational activity as evidence of transformation rather than decline. Yet the form that intimate social life assumes is hardly insignificant. Older forms of social organization may have important qualities that their successors lack. For example, a critical feature of both the colonial villages described by Bender and the "three-tiered" national organizations studied by Theda Skocpol is their Janus-faced character: they cultivate strong social bonds among their members while integrating them into the larger political society.[3] It is uncertain whether the prevailing forms of association at the century's end maintain this connection between the personal and the political. The question is not whether intimate social life survives, but whether it survives in a form that alters or preserves its distinctive moral and political qualities.

I will address this question by looking closely at one kind of social group that has become prominent over the past fifty years: the self-help/ support group. These groups, typically organized around a stigmatized condition or a traumatic event, have been expanding at a time when other forms of civil association appear to have been declining. Self-help/support groups have enjoyed striking successes both as intimate associations and as agents of institutional change. At the same time, their proliferation has been seen as symptomatic of a growing inwardness and balkanization in American society.

It will be helpful at the outset to locate self-help groups within the taxonomy of relationships used by social researchers. In 1909, Charles Horton Cooley introduced a now-standard distinction between primary and secondary relationships, which he saw as characteristic, respectively, of Gemeinschaft and Gesellschaft. Primary relationships involve general and usually reciprocal concern; secondary relationships, specific, limited, and often unilateral concern.[4] The contrast can be illustrated by obvious examples—for instance, parent-child as a primary relationship, doctor-patient as a secondary.

Writing in 1984, Wireman noted the emergence of an interesting hybrid relationship in the community organizations she studied in postwar American suburbs. These relationships were based on specific, often public purposes, required only limited and clearly defined commitments, but had "the dimensions of warmth, rapport, and intimacy normally connected with primary relationships." They engendered trust, affection, and familiarity but not extended social contact.[5] Wireman took as a paradigm of such relationships the intense but circumscribed friendships that often developed among the active, long-term members of community associations.

Like the community organizations that Wireman studied, self-help groups cultivate relationships that do not fit neatly into Cooley's primary/secondary dichotomy. These relationships, based on mutual disclo-sure and support, are quite similar to Wireman's intimate secondary rela-tionships in their voluntariness, their limited commitment, and their egalitarian and personal character: they too have the "warmth, rapport, and intimacy" associated with primary relationships. In one obvious re-spect, these groups are more intimate than Wireman's, since they are not organized around public projects and issues but around some of the most personal aspects of their members' lives: the traumatic, constricting, or stigmatized conditions they share. But it is not clear what effect their greater intimacy has on the character of these groups or their roles in the larger society.[6] I will address those questions in this chapter, examining the expansion of self-help groups in postwar America and assessing their contribution to the health of civil society.

THE EXTENT OF THE SELF-HELP MOVEMENT

There is evidence of a significant increase in self-help groups in the past twenty years, when voluntary associations in general have supposedly been in decline. Alfred H. Katz, the leading scholar of self-help groups, speculated in 1976 that there were 500,000 groups with as many as seven million members.[7] In 1983, the Department of Health and Human Services predicted that there would be a million self-help groups by 1990. Evi-dence of rapid growth was provided by an exhaustive study of self-help groups in New Jersey in the mid-1980s, which found an annual growth rate of over 8 percent. Groups were forming at twice the rate they were disbanding, with groups unaffiliated with regional or national organiza-tions showing the highest growth rate.[8]

Less dramatic growth is suggested by Robert Wuthnow's 1991 national survey on small groups, which did not attempt to count such groups but asked respondents detailed questions about their participation. The sur-vey found that self-help groups accounted for about one-eighth of small-group memberships: in the adult population as a whole, this figure in-cludes between eight and ten million people. At an average of about twenty people per group, the number of groups totals at least five hun-dred thousand.[9]

The most recent, reliable, and detailed evidence of the growth of self-help groups comes from the Midlife Development in the United States (MIDUS) survey, carried out in 1995–1996 with a random sampling of 3,032 respondents between the ages of 25 and 74. The MIDUS survey de-fined self-help groups as "groups organized and run by people who get together on the basis of a common experience or goal to mutually help or support one another," explicitly excluding groups organized and led by

professionals.[10] On the basis of the survey results, the researchers estimated that there were "approximately twenty-five million lifetime participants and ten million participants in the last twelve months,"[11] confirm-
ing Wuthnow's earlier estimate. More than one of four people aged 25 to
34 are expected to participate in some type of self-help group by their
mid-thirties.[12] The researchers speculated that the number of participants
would have been far higher if groups organized and run by professionals
had been included.[13]

A large proportion of self-help groups formed in the past two decades
are based on mental health and substance abuse problems. Katz reports
that the New Jersey study of self-help groups "found that the largest
number of new groups formed in 1988 were those to help individuals
with mental-health problems; the second largest were for people with
[AIDS] and their family members; the third largest were for relatives of
people discharged from mental hospitals."[14] The MIDUS survey found
that more than one-third of the lifetime and past-twelve-months participants were in groups for substance abuse problems, close to Wuthnow's
earlier estimate of four in ten. A slightly lower proportion were in groups
for eating problems, emotional crisis or life transition, or family support.
A far smaller proportion—less than one in eleven—participated in groups
for individuals with physical illnesses or disabilities.[15] The breadth of
health-related groups is also impressive: "mutual-aid groups of patients," writes Katz, "exist for almost all of the 200 major disease categories analyzed by the World Health Organization."[16]

The principal distinction among self-help groups, first drawn by Katz,
is between "twelve-step" and non-twelve-step groups. The paradigm of
the former is Alcoholics Anonymous (AA); the latter is epitomized by organizations of parents of impaired, afflicted, and victimized children.
Wuthnow's survey suggests that the majority of the people in self-help
groups are involved in the non-twelve-step variety but that many of the
latter have some significant features, such as anonymity and therapeutic
orientation, in common with twelve-step groups.[17] Katz notes, however,
that there are several critical differences between the two types: the former avoid any kind of political involvement; the latter often mobilize for
lobbying and other political activity. Many non-twelve-step groups display both features of the "Tocquevillean" voluntary associations depicted
by Putman, Skocpol, and others: they forge close bonds among members
but also organize them for political action. Typically, groups evolve from
community to outreach or advocacy (Katz's "seven steps"), but some may
begin with political action and turn inward (and some remain resolutely
inward looking and apolitical).

A NATION OF DEVIANTS

The rapid growth of self-help groups among Americans born after World War II has several sources. The vanguard of the self-help movement was formed by people excluded from mainstream society because of their race, ethnicity, illness, impairment, deviant conduct, or minority sexual preferences. Those at the margins have often been the most active and successful at forming affinity groups, finding common ground, and common cause, in the conditions that isolated or estranged them from the larger society. (Not surprisingly, many of the earliest and most effective self-help groups have been based on physical and mental impairment, substance abuse, and minority sexual orientations.) Those groups based on traumatic experiences could be viewed in much the same way, since trauma may isolate and estrange its victims from their more fortunate neighbors, who may stigmatize extreme misfortune as a self-protective measure.

But the ranks of the self-help movement have also been swollen by people who, in an earlier generation, would have fit much more comfortably into the mainstream and who in many respects still do: people who have lost a spouse, relative, or friend; divorced parents and their children; compulsive eaters and smokers. In some cases, support groups have been formed around conditions far more widely accepted than a generation ago, such as single parenthood and interfaith marriage. (Divorce would arguably fall into this category as well.) It is instructive to begin with the periphery, which gave much of the initial impetus to the self-help movement, and then look toward the center.

Erving Goffman reintroduced the notion of "stigma" to describe the categorization and treatment of people who depart from the norm in salient and socially significant ways:

> While the stranger is present before us, evidence can arise of his possessing an attribute that makes him different from others . . . and of a less desirable kind—in the extreme, a person who is quite thoroughly bad, or dangerous, or weak. He is thus reduced in our minds from a whole and usual person to a tainted, discounted one. Such an attribute is a stigma, especially when its discrediting effect is very extensive; sometimes it is also called a failing, a shortcoming, a handicap. . . . By definition, of course, we believe the person with a stigma is not quite human. On this assumption, we exercise varieties of discrimination, through which we effectively, if often unthinkingly, reduce his life chances.[18]

Goffman recognized that the company of similarly stigmatized people could provide comfort and support in the face of such profound exclusion, but he thought it meager consolation. Writing in 1963, he painted a fairly bleak picture of the "half-world" of such marginalized groups:

> Knowing from their own experience what it is like to have this particular stigma, some of them can provide the individual with instructions in the tricks of the trade and with a circle of lament to which he can withdraw for moral support and for the comfort of feeling at home, at ease, accepted as a person who really is like any other normal person. . . . On the other hand, he may find that the tales of his fellow-sufferers bore him, and that the whole matter of focusing on atrocity tales, on group superiority, on trickster stories, in short, on the "problem," is one of the large penalties for having one.[19]

Only six years later, however, in *Odd Man In*, Edward Sagarin heralded the emergence of such groups for "deviant" individuals as a triumph of Tocquevillean voluntary association:

> In recent years America has witnessed the growth of an important social movement. It embodies the idea of open, formal, and structured organizations . . . among people whom society has characterized as deviant—people who are subject to scorn, discrimination, gossip, sometimes pity, and sometimes punishment. . . . That deviant societies should have originated in America may be due to many factors, not the least of which is the country's tradition of associations. For over a century, both foreign- and American-born observers have taken note of what has come to be described as "the proliferation of associations" in "a nation of joiners." . . . [O]ne is tempted to ask not why organizations of deviants appeared at all, but why they did not appear much earlier in the history of America.[20]

Between 1963 and 1969 fell "the Sixties," a period seen in retrospect as a time of social upheaval after the complacency and conformity of the prior decade, a time in which the most marginalized and oppressed groups in American society demanded recognition and equality and in which many people in the mainstream felt at least a fleeting identification or empathy with those groups. It was also a time when the techniques for eliciting mutual disclosure among relative strangers or limited acquaintances were developed in T- and encounter groups and began to spread to a broader population.

To understand the expansion of self-help groups from the most stigmatized groups in society to its mainstream, it is important to recognize that stigma and normality are often matters of degree. Again, we turn to Goffman:

> The most fortunate of normals is likely to have his half-hidden failing, and for every little failing there is a social occasion when it will loom large, creating a shameful gap between virtual and actual social identity. Therefore, the

occasionally precarious and the constantly precarious form a single continuum.[21]

Goffman attributed this continuity to the nature of the prevailing social norms:

> [W]hile some of these norms, such as sightedness and literacy, may be commonly sustained with complete adequacy by most persons in the society, there are other norms, such as those associated with physical comeliness, which take the form of ideals and constitute standards against which almost everyone falls short at some stage in his life. And even where widely attained norms are involved, their multiplicity has the effect of disqualifying many persons. For example, in an important sense there is only one completely unblushing male in America: a young, married, white, urban, northern, heterosexual Protestant father of college education, fully employed, of good complexion, weight, and height, and a recent record in sports. . . . Any male who fails to qualify in any of these ways is likely to view himself—during moments at least—as unworthy, incomplete, and inferior.[22]

Goffman noted that the "common ground of norms can be sustained far beyond the circle of those who fully realize them,"[23] but only by tacit cooperation between those who conform to and those who deviate from the norm. The partially deviant individual must decide whether to regard his deviation as a regrettable departure from his real, mainstream social identity or as an intimation of a real social identity that his participation in the mainstream has suppressed. How the individual perceives and responds to these gaps will depend on the social resources available for integration and segregation.

In the past thirty years, the success of Sagarin's "deviant societies" in creating secure social identities for their members has made the latter option less costly for the individual, if not for society, while the broad dissemination of techniques for mutual disclosure have made that option more feasible. Outwardly normal people can now meet to reveal their "half-hidden failings" under the supervision of committed professionals or the guidance of protocols honed through years of collective experience; they can withdraw partially and conditionally from the larger society without risking pariah status.

The striking extent to which the larger society has come to accommodate groups of the partially deviant and imperfectly normal can be gleaned from the local paper. The Friday "Lifestyle" section of the West Virginia *Panhandle Journal,* for example, is largely taken up with descriptions and meeting times for local support groups: Alcoholics, Food-Addicts, Narcotics, Nicotine, and Overeaters Anonymous; several other addiction groups; a wide array of medical groups, for conditions such as

Alzheimer's, cancer, chronic pain, diabetes, infertility, lupus, and multiple sclerosis; several grief support and mental illness groups; and groups for interfaith couples and single parents. Listings for local events not associated with self-help and support groups take up less than a third as much space.[24] These groups are a far cry from Goffman's sad collections of social outcasts, in their openness, their respectability, and their broad membership. The pillars of the Panhandle community could affiliate without shame with many of these groups, finding support and solidarity among their fellow overeaters, nicotine addicts, cancer victims, or single parents.

Thus, although self-help groups now pervade the American social landscape, they do not have a monolithic character. Certainly the ideologies underlying these groups are often quite different. Sagarin distinguishes conformist groups, such as AA, which seek to control or eliminate a deviant condition, and nonconformist groups such as gay rights organizations, which seek to transform social norms and legitimize their condition.[25] The contrast may be most striking in the attitude of self-help groups toward the classification of their conditions as diseases and to the role of health care professionals in treating them. Some groups reject the disease classification, and the authority that classification confers on health care professionals; others seek to medicalize conditions once seen as ordinary tribulations, idiosyncrasies, or character flaws; some seek to wrest control of their treatment from the medical establishment; others demand recognition by that establishment. It might be better, however, to see these differences in terms of a spectrum rather than a dichotomy, with some groups seeking to eliminate the shared condition through recovery or treatment, and often affirming its stigma in doing so; other groups seeking to remove the stigma, misconceptions, and disabilities associated with the condition, even while attempting to eliminate the condition; and other groups demanding the full acceptance of their condition.[26] Most twelve-step groups, which embrace a disease model of addiction or dependency, fall on the conformist end of the spectrum, whereas many (but by no means all) non-twelve-step groups tend to be, or become, nonconformist. What these diverse groups, with their often conflicting ideologies, have in common is the decision of their members, less constrained in some cases than in others, to emphasize rather than suppress their differences with the rest of society, and to treat those distinguishing characteristics as central to their social identity and as a primary basis for affiliation.

MORAL AND POLITICAL ISSUES RAISED BY SELF-HELP GROUPS

Bender, Fischer, and Wireman regard small groups as evidence of the adaptability and resilience of human community in the face of social change, fulfilling the critical functions of traditional communities without many of their encumbrances. Wuthnow, on the other hand, sees these groups as a palliative, numbing the pain of dislocation and desensitizing people to the loss of the trust, stability, and commitment that were found in (some) traditional communities:

> Small groups make it possible for us to survive, even as market pressures, jobs, and disrupted personal relationships make greater demands on our lives. . . . To their credit, they provide us with small, portable sources of interpersonal support. Their weakness lies in their inability to forge the more enduring bonds that many of us would like or to strongly resist the fragmenting forces in our society.[27]

This debate concerns the social and political adequacy of small groups in general, not the comparative strengths and weaknesses of different kinds of groups. However reasonable Wuthnow's misgivings, they appear to apply equally to self-help groups and to the voluntary associations that flourished after World War II. Veterans' groups, bowling leagues, and Welcome Wagons all functioned as "small, portable sources of interpersonal support" for a highly mobile generation that was separating itself from extended family and traditional community. The appropriate comparison for our purposes is not between self-help groups and the traditional communities of prewar America, then, but between those groups and the voluntary associations of the early postwar years. The contrast is not a simple one between locality and affinity as a basis for social organization, since groups of both types are based on some kind of affinity and are organized at a local level. As I will argue, however, the affinities around which the two kinds of groups are organized give them very different orientations to their host communities.

Postwar voluntary associations were generally organized around some common interest or widely shared set of experiences, which served as a basis for a wide range of social activities. Self-help groups, in contrast, are generally organized around a deviant, disabling, or traumatic condition, and they have an inward-looking, often therapeutic character. These differences are readily apparent in comparing a typical group of each type: the Parent-Teacher Association (PTA) and the Parents of Murdered Children (PMC). The basis for membership in the PTA is a "condition" considered part of the normal life cycle—having children in elementary school—whereas the basis for membership in the PMC is a condition considered abnormal in the extreme, even if it has become distressingly common in some areas. Moreover, the former condition is generally felicitous, the latter deeply traumatic.

Not surprisingly, the kind of affinity the members have affects the character of the group: the PTA organizes bake sales and tutoring programs; the Parents of Murdered Children share their grief and help each other. The extent to which the members' affinity affects the group's orientation becomes apparent if we try to imagine a group that has the membership criterion of the PTA and the inward orientation of the PMC—for example, Parents of Children in Elementary School, who meet to share the tribulations of getting their children through their homework and off to the bus. (The opposite combination is not so implausible: the parents' shared grief might be the backdrop for an array of conventional social activities.) It is true that the PMC does not limit itself to commiseration; members engage in public education and lobbying to protect other parents from suffering similar losses. Nevertheless, this outreach is a response to the traumatic experience that separates the group from the larger community it seeks to protect. What brings the PTA together is something that links its members to their neighbors; what brings the PMC together is something that distances them, and this helps give the PMC a more inward orientation.

If we shift to a comparison of traditional and recent veterans' groups, the differences become less obvious, though perhaps more instructive. The ranks of the American Legion and Veterans of Foreign Wars (VFW) were filled by millions of demobilized veterans of World Wars I and II. The experience of combat in those wars may well have been as traumatic for the combatants as Vietnam was for a later generation, but those wars were popular and successful, and the combatants were welcomed back into the civilian world (or at least that is the prevailing myth, which I will not challenge). Although many of the members of these groups had experienced similar trauma, the groups' focus was not on the trauma, nor on its personal or political implications. Rather, these groups were intensely civic-minded, organizing a broad array of community-wide events at the same time they were lobbying for the specific interests of their members.

In contrast, the Vietnam War was unpopular and unsuccessful, and it was fought by a smaller and less representative group of citizens. The combatants were not welcomed back with ticker-tape parades, and they experienced far more difficulty reintegrating themselves into civilian life. Not surprisingly, they did not rush to join the traditional veterans' organizations, and the organizations they formed for themselves, such as the Vietnam Veterans of America (VVA), had more of the inward-looking character of self-help and support groups, and less of the local, civic-minded character of the traditional groups. Although the criteria for membership in the VFW and VVA may be quite similar—military service in a theater of war—that service helped integrate VFW members, but not VVA members, into their communities.

The broad contrast between the PTA and PMC, and the narrower one between the VFW and the VVA, suggests that contemporary self-help groups do not play the same role in their communities that voluntary associations of the early postwar era played in theirs. The demobilized veterans and their wives, seeking to overcome the isolation they experienced in postwar Levittowns, became avid joiners. But they joined with their neighbors, and the organizations they joined helped cement the bonds of local community. It would be an overstatement to say that the specific criteria for membership in these groups were pretextual—that what the new suburbanites were really interested in was not veterans' issues, new books, or gardening techniques, but a sense of community. Nevertheless, it is clear that these associations pressed the specific interests of their members into the service of local community formation.

In contrast, the members of self-help groups typically emphasize their differences from the larger community, even if they seek reconciliation or reintegration with it. Some are retreating or withdrawing from communities in which they have been demeaned, stereotyped, and neglected. Others enjoy an outwardly far more harmonious relationship with their communities but still feel lonely, isolated, estranged, or incomplete in them. In either case, the self-help groups to which they turn encourage their identification with others like themselves. As Keith Humphreys, a researcher and promoter of self-help groups, observes, even groups based on specific health problems "are not just treatments for [those] problems; they are also small communities in which members make friends and gain a sense of connectedness to others."[28]

This does not mean that all self-help groups see themselves, or are seen by the larger community, as standing in an oppositional or adversary posture. Unlike the intentional communities of the 1840s or the 1960s, self-help groups do not generally mount a direct challenge to the basic tenets or values of the communities in which they are located, and they are often accepted as integral parts of those communities. But the fact that local communities accommodate support groups does not mean those groups play the kind of role in their communities that postwar voluntary associations did in theirs. A new arrival to West Virginia's Eastern Panhandle, looking for a social life in the community, will be directed by the "Lifestyle" section to people who share a specific problem. She will have to be a bit more persistent if she wishes to join a group devoted to a hobby, sport, local issue, or charitable service; the "Lifestyle" section offers her little more opportunity to become involved in the larger community than that offered by the "Personals" column. The preponderance of self-help groups suggests that the community has become a convenient venue for people with hidden affinities to seek each other out, and that what residents share by virtue of common experience and routine interaction has come to matter less than it once did in forming strong social bonds.

To the extent that self-help groups supplant rather than strengthen local community, they raise issues about the social and moral adequacy of the alternative they offer, issues that voluntary associations, with their more modest agendas and social function, do not confront. I will examine two related issues: how does their focus on deviant, stigmatized, or traumatic conditions affect the social and moral quality of these groups, and how does it affect their integration into the larger society? There may be significant costs in making deep personal affinities a primary basis for social association, in elevating similarity over sustained interaction as a basis for mutual concern, and in building political organizations outside rather than through the locality-based structure of American politics.

STIGMATIZED TRAITS AND TRAUMATIC EXPERIENCES AS A BASIS FOR ASSOCIATION

Katz provides an abundance of testimony about the role of groups in overcoming isolation and creating community:

> What I learned, was that I was not alone, and that there was a very special bond between parents of children with any type of medical problem. . . . Talking with others who had cancer also relieved the heavy feelings of isolation and victimization that I had carried during and after my cancer experience.[29]

As Oliver Sacks observes, a person may feel as much kinship with people who share with him a significant medical or sensory condition as he does with people of his own race, ethnicity, or nationality. Sacks describes the encounter between a Scandinavian psychophysicist with achromatopsia (profound color blindness) and a group of Micronesian children with the same condition:

> Though Knut had read the scientific literature, and though he had occasionally met other achromatopsic people, this had in no way prepared him for the impact of actually finding himself surrounded by his own kind, strangers half a world away with whom he had an instant kinship.[30]

Sacks observes that "a similar feeling may emerge for a deaf traveller, who has crossed the sea or the world, if he lights upon other deaf people on his arrival." He also describes a friend with Tourette's syndrome who visited a remote Mennonite village in which the syndrome was so common, and the community so accommodating, that the friend dubbed it "Tourettesville."[31]

As liberating as it may be to find instant kinship with "one's own kind," however, it can also be oppressive and distorting. The self-help movement has made the claim of affinity into a virtual dogma. Thus, Frank Riessman, the director of the National Self-Help Clearinghouse, lists as the first principle of the movement "The Peer Principle—Social Homogeneity," which he describes as follows:

> Members of a self-help group possess social homogeneity; they share a similar condition, whether it is raising grandchildren or being in debt, on welfare, an ex-offender, diabetic, gay or disabled. Members of the group understand each other as no one else can.[32]

But people may have more than one deviant, stigmatizing, or traumatic condition that they share with others, as well as many other bases for affiliation. The maintenance of the "peer principle" requires that one commonality be elevated above all others. Thus, Goffman describes the homogenizing demands imposed by those who seek to forge the aggregate of the individual's "fellow-sufferers" into a cohesive social group:

> The spokesmen of this group claim that the individual's real group, the one to which he *naturally* belongs, is this group. All the other categories and groups to which the individual necessarily also belongs are implicitly considered to be not his real ones; he is not really one of them. . . . If he turns to his group, he is loyal and authentic; if he turns away, he is craven and a fool.[33]

Moreover, because inclusion in the group is based on possession of the stigmatized or traumatic condition, the members' status and strength of affiliation may depend on the magnitude of that condition. People who felt compelled to deny or downplay their deviant conditions to the outside world may feel pressure to emphasize or exaggerate them within the confines of the group. And if the character of their condition is too public or clearly defined to leave much room for distortion, they may still feel a strong temptation to exaggerate its impact on their lives.

The tendency to exaggerate the magnitude and pervasive impact of the shared condition can be seen in the centrality of addiction and codependency in many recovery groups. The group's emphasis on this shared condition often has an imperialistic character, as explanations in terms of addiction or codependency come to annex ever greater regions of the members' lives. In some cases, the pressure to find affinity can be very destructive, as in survivor groups that encourage their members to "discover" a history of horrific abuse behind their present anxiety, anomie, or dissatisfaction.[34]

On the other hand, the diversity in other characteristics among group members may sometimes moderate an emphasis on, and identification with, the characteristic they share. In struggling against discounting and stereotyping, group members may come to appreciate their differences as much as their commonalities. The shared condition may become less salient and less dominant, and members may feel free to cultivate their distinctive qualities.

Moreover, the distorting and coercive tendencies of self-help and support groups must be set against the discrimination and stereotyping their members suffer in their local communities. However strong the pressures of membership in a self-help group, few such groups will be as "encompassing" as many place-based communities. (Those self-help groups that attempt to encompass all aspects of their members' lives often assume a residential character.) The niche that an individual occupies in a local community, whether comfortable or confining, is hard to change without moving on (and difficult even then, if your reputation precedes you). And the niches assigned individuals with deviant conditions in such communities are often confining; much of the appeal of self-help groups comes from the prospect of escaping the outcast or pariah status their members have endured in their neighborhoods or workplaces. The conformity demanded by many self-help groups pales by comparison with the stereotyping inflicted by many more conventional communities.

But this defense of self-help groups implies that their virtues are comparative. People who are pervasively stigmatized in the larger society, relegated to narrow, demeaning roles, have little to lose and much to gain by banding tightly together, and they should have no compunction about doing so. The case for segregation is weaker for people who comfortably inhabit the mainstream most of the time, but find themselves estranged or sidelined by some failing or misfortune. Although it is surely reasonable for the recently divorced or temporarily insolvent to commiserate, it is unseemly for the groups they join to make the same kind of demands on their members and the larger society that are made by groups of people with severe impairments or despised sexual orientations. To do so would be to enact a grotesque mimicry of people vastly more aggrieved and deprived than themselves. It would be far better if the temporarily deviant pressed their brief experience of exclusion and stigmatization into the service of broader social reform, extrapolating from the embarrassment of insolvency to the indignity of lifelong poverty, from the social distancing faced by a divorcing couple to the ostracism faced by a gay couple.

CHOICE AND COMMITMENT

Wuthnow sees two additional moral problems in the trend toward replacing communities based on family or geography with communities based on specific affinities. The first concerns the volitional character of self-help groups and the qualified commitment that they require:

> When people say they are finding community in a small group, and even when they describe their group as a family . . ., they mean something quite different from the connotations that words like "community" or "family" have had in the past. Whether they recognize it or not, their sense of community now means something over which they have a great deal of control. They have chosen to join one particular group, rather than any of dozens they might also have been exposed to, and they may be involved in more than one, certainly if their involvement over a lifetime is considered. . . . Members of the same tribe may gripe about one another, but know they must work out their differences because they have little choice but to live with each other. Small-group members are more likely to recognize that they can move on to another group.[35]

Similarly, Nancy Rosenblum observes:

> [T]hese associations are typically too fluid to create sustained obligations. Members shop around the crowded marketplace of groups. In my desire for "support" I can choose to identify myself as a Jew, a woman, and a professor and join a synagogue group for orthodox women academics; or I can see myself as an adult child of an alcoholic and enter recovery; and I can reshuffle these attributes and change memberships at will.[36]

Such apprehensions about the subversive effects of choice in the formation of communities are reminiscent of the concerns of those who fear the effects of easy marriage and divorce. They raise terribly difficult questions about the psychological, social, and moral value of encouraging or compelling people to accommodate those with whom they have entered into, or found themselves in, close personal relationships. These questions are so difficult just because they are not susceptible to any general answer—the truth depends on often unknown or unappreciated details—and because the interpretation of empirical evidence is so deeply and unavoidably affected by moral commitment.

To be sure, Wuthnow and Rosenblum may exaggerate the extent to which membership in affinity groups results from calculated choice. People who are isolated or estranged by trauma or disability often embrace those with kindred tribulations like lost family—their involvement in a group is passionate and unreflective, not a result of cool appraisal. On the other hand, self-help groups now recruit from many less traumatized and outcast populations, whose members may have a greater capacity to cultivate multiple social identities, serially or simultaneously. Moreover, within the expanding culture of self-help, even people who feel that they have little choice in their *affinities* may enjoy considerable latitude in their choice of affinity *groups.*

A look at the *Panhandle Journal's* "Lifestyle" section reveals that several groups often cater to similar conditions, affording the prospective member a selection of orientations and venues. Thus, a person with a substance abuse problem can choose between the traditional twelve steps offered by Alcoholics, Narcotics, and Nicotine Anonymous, and the Freedom from Bondage to alcohol and chemical dependency offered by the Covenant Baptist Church; a person who has lost a loved one can seek comfort from the grief support group of the Covenant Baptist Church, the Grief Support Network (which meets at several local churches), or the Hospice of the Panhandle (which offers separate groups for those who have lost fetuses, children, and other loved ones; those who have lost family or friends to suicide; and bereaved teenagers). The widest selection is available to people who eat too much; they can join Weight Watchers, adopt the twelve-step approaches of Food-Addicts or Overeaters Anonymous, join Take Off Pounds Sensibly (TOPS), or enjoy "weight loss through the Bible" with First Place, run by the enterprising Covenant Baptist Church. So even for a single stigmatized or deviant condition, there are likely to be several competing groups from which to choose. And that choice may, as Wuthnow fears, attenuate members' commitment.

There is a related concern about the kind of loyalties self-help groups foster. Although people may always be inclined to become friends with those who share with them some salient quality or interest—a passion for narrow-gauge model railroads, a weakness for bad puns, pariah status in junior high school—the loyalties they thereby acquire arise from their friendship, not directly from their affinity. Even when self-help groups do not demand unconditional identification and loyalty, they typically work on the assumption that people who share a stigmatized or traumatic condition have greater potential for friendship with each other than with others, more capacity for mutual understanding and support. In encouraging people with a shared condition to seek out others like themselves, they may discourage them from finding significant relationships in the larger community. And that may have a moral cost.

The experience of learning to care about people with whom one appears to have relatively little in common is one of the most appealing features of a heterogeneous democratic society. There is great moral value in the effort to respect, understand, and join together with people who initially appear very different from oneself; to create commonalities through shared experience, rather than merely to discover them in shared background. The friendships formed among people of different races, ethnicities, classes, or lifestyles are an affirmation that what we do together matters more than how similar we are. The injunction to love one's neighbor is a powerful and demanding one, and it would be regrettable if the self-segregation of similar individuals reduced the motivation and prospects for honoring it.

SELF-HELP AND POLITICAL ACTIVISM

Wuthnow also worries about the narcissism resulting from a preoccupation with the members' shared needs: "[T]he group itself may function more as a place where each individual comes to think about himself or herself than where genuine concern about others triumphs over individual needs."[37] But this apprehension seems to reflect a false dichotomy between concern for self and others, as well as to overstate the narcissism of self-help groups. As Wuthnow himself documents, members of self-help groups engage in a great deal of mutual aid and outreach to nongroup members.[38]

Nonetheless, the question remains whether these groups are able, in Wuthnow's words, "to form the more enduring bonds that many of us would like or to strongly resist the fragmenting forces in our society."[39] Some critics fear that the personal focus of self-help groups diverts their members from the real causes of their afflictions. Thus, Elayne Rapping complains that women's self-help groups tend to medicalize conditions that are better understood in terms of social and political injustice, thereby misdirecting the efforts of their members:

> Women in abusive relationships now are taught that they are suffering from a disease called codependency, as are their equally "sick" partners, rather than being encouraged to look at the unequal economic and political power relationships between men and women that facilitate and enforce the "normalization" of such male abuse. Women who have come to hate and abuse their bodies because they do not resemble fashion models are similarly taught to view themselves as diseased and to turn to a Higher Power to give them strength to resist their addiction, rather than fighting to change social norms and media images that reflect the unequal gender relations through which women become objects of males' desire to own, possess and even violate. . . . To define oneself in terms of an illness is disempowering and diminishing, especially when it serves to take attention away from the large social structures and forces that have led to the "codependency" or "bulimia." . . . The most depressing thing I witnessed in my study of the recovery movement was the way in which its powerful ideology worked to subtly shift the focus of members' lives more and more toward an inward, self-absorbed,

often obsessive and lifelong focus on meetings and rules and steps and traditions; and further and further from a concern with the larger world whose
destructive forces had sent them into meetings in the first place.[40]

Yet many self-help groups that began with an inward orientation have
turned to confront the destructive forces of the larger world. Katz found
that self-help groups frequently evolve into successful advocacy and lobbying groups. For example, the grassroots Pennsylvania Association for
Retarded Children (ARC) engaged in a campaign of litigation and lobbying that helped lead to passage of the Education for All Handicapped
Children Act of 1974 (now the IDEA), one of the most important pieces
of social legislation in the past generation. A similar role was played by
the National Council of Independent Living Centers (NCILC) in the en-
actment of the landmark Americans with Disabilities Act of 1990.[41]

Riessman and Carroll describe a progression in which self-help

> serves as a transitory stage in the process of political engagement. In the self-
> help phase, a group looks inward to develop its resources, methods of cop-
> ing, and broad identity, mobilizing inner strengths. The group may then
> move outward, establish an advocacy stance, and demand change in the ex-
> ternal environment.[42]

The authors take the ARC as a case in point:

> Chapters of ARC were started in the early 1950s as parents' self-help groups.
> Parents got together because they were disturbed by [being told] to institu-
> tionalize their children born with Down's syndrome, spina bifida, and other
> handicaps. . . . Then they started to look at the options for keeping their
> handicapped children at home. They created and paid for educational pro-
> grams until the early 1970s, when their lobbying efforts resulted in legisla-
> tion guaranteeing every child with a handicap a free and appropriate educa-
> tion in the least restrictive environment.[43]

Rapping's concerns about misdirection may have greater force against
the twelve-step groups that she observed, organized around meetings,
rules, steps, and traditions, than against other types of self-help groups,
less inward and ritualized. Although her misgivings are hardly belied by
the activism and militancy that some self-help groups have engendered,
it is clear that the dynamics of commiseration are complex. For many
women, coming to see codependency or compulsive eating as a disease
rather than a character flaw, and as epidemic rather than idiosyncratic,
may well be a significant step toward seeing it as a symptom of oppression or powerlessness. Moreover, by comparing tribulations with others
like themselves, members may come to appreciate the extent to which
their isolation and disability result from their minority status or their lack
of political voice, rather than from anything inherent in their condition.

Finally, the social dynamics of even the most inward-oriented group may help inculcate democratic values and practices. As Rosenblum observes, those groups give members "the experience of reciprocity," help them to "overcome humility and passivity," and "create the expectation that our pain and indignation will not be met with indifference."[44]

Despite Wuthnow's and Rapping's apprehensions, then, many self-help groups appear to galvanize their members into political action rather than lull them into quiescence. But the forms of political activity they promote may differ significantly from those promoted by the postwar voluntary associations.

THE SELF-HELP GROUP AND THE DEMOCRATIC POLITY

Even if many self-help groups raise political awareness and provoke political action, concerns persist about the kind of political involvement they foster. Do the narrow loyalties that many of these groups cultivate contribute to a divisive interest-group politics, or do the internal dynamics and outreach of such groups give their members a broader, more inclusive orientation? What kind of role do these groups play in mediating among individuals, their social groups, and their local, regional, and national governments? We now consider the impact they may have on the political life of the larger society.

First, there is the Tocquevillean question of whether self-help groups prepare their members for, and engage them in, participation in local, regional, and national politics to the same extent that the postwar voluntary associations once did. The leaders in voluntary associations such as PTAs and veterans' groups were closely tied to their host communities, and their activity in these associations may have served as an effective springboard for leadership in, or representation of, the local community. The campaign flyers of first-time candidates for local office typically list service in such associations as a primary qualification. To the extent that self-help groups have a more tenuous or adversarial relationship with their host localities than voluntary associations do, the route to democratic leadership for activists in those groups is less likely to run through local communities, and more likely to involve regional or national coalition building with similar groups. Is there anything less appropriate about this route to political involvement? Isn't a local community as much of a special interest as a stigmatized condition, the representative of a locality as much of a lobbyist as the representative of a self-help group?

One reason why a locality may *look* less like a special interest is that the diversity of interests within it, and the potential for conflict among them, appear to be greater than in a self-help group. But the members of self-help groups, like the residents of localities, may have vast differences in wealth, education, income, and social status. A locality may also look less like a special interest because conflicts among localities and regions are not as sharp or clearly defined as they have been in other periods of American history. But local regional conflicts clearly exist, and they are often acute (city vs. suburb, Rustbelt vs. Sunbelt). Finally, the interests of localities are already reflected in the structure of American local, regional, and national political representation. But the fact that our political organization is historically based on locality hardly makes locality a superior organizing principle. The enormous growth of the federal government and administrative law over the past fifty years reflects the institutional accommodation of political interests not captured by geography.

These considerations are relevant to the cultivation of civic virtue in self-help groups. If group members' interests are not very diverse, those active in such groups may be acting out of barely extended self-interest; they may not learn the peculiar skills of compromise and coalition building that are associated with leadership in more pluralistic groups. On the other hand, affinity groups may cultivate both extended empathy and coalition building, first, by crossing over economic, social, racial, and gender lines, and second, by widening their members' circles of concern. For example, the members of "Quad Squad," a local mutual-aid group for quadriplegics, might form coalitions with people with a wide range of physical disabilities, then extend their efforts to people stigmatized or discriminated against because of mental, behavioral, and social differences. The danger of such concentric expansion is that the affinities will be spurious or exaggerated, as in the codependency movement. But there is no reason to believe that the distortion or deception will be any greater than it has been for local and regional politics, in which many groups have been seduced into party or candidate loyalty against their economic or social interests.[45]

The metaphor of ever-widening concentric circles suggests the prospect of an enlightened interest-group liberalism. But although an interest-group liberalism based on broad social affinities may be more attractive than one based on narrow economic ones, it still has many of the moral and political limitations decried by Theodore Lowi.[46] It still views individuals as confronting the polity primarily as members of groups and confers enormous moral and political authority on the leaders of those groups. Indeed, the emergence of self-help groups into the political arena over the last two decades can be seen as a marriage of traditional interest-group liberalism with identity politics. How we regard this development depends on what we think of the form contemporary liberalism has assumed—whether, for example, we are heartened or disturbed by the ascendancy of antidiscrimination law, protecting oppressed and vulnerable groups, as the primary vehicle of social reform, replacing traditional progressive politics, with its emphasis on economic injustice and its commitment to comprehensive redistribution of social resources. If we regard the recognition and protection of vulnerable groups as a very imperfect but politically expedient means of achieving justice for individuals in a conservative era, we should have a similar ambivalence about the growing political role of the self-help movement.

NOTES

1. Thomas Bender, *Community and Social Change in America* (Baltimore: Johns Hopkins University Press, 1978), 3–4.

2. Claude Fischer et al., *Networks and Places: Social Relations in the Urban Setting* (New York: Free Press, 1977); Peggy Wireman, *Urban Neighborhoods, Networks, and Families: New Forms for Old Values* (Lexington, Mass.: Lexington Books, 1984).

3. Theda Skocpol, "Civic Engagement in American Democracy," testimony presented at the first plenary session of the National Commission on Civic Renewal, Washington, D.C., 25 January 1997.

4. Charles Horton Cooley, *Social Organization: A Study of the Larger Mind* (New York: Scribner's, 1909).

5. Wireman, *Urban Neighborhoods*, 3.

6. Wireman, *Urban Neighborhoods*, 3. Wireman recognized "therapy and encounter groups" as other exceptions to the primary/secondary dichotomy. But, like Robert Wuthnow a decade later, she did not fully appreciate the public dimension of self-help groups. The groups that she described were private and inward looking, too preoccupied with the individual needs of their members to develop the "public response necessary to accommodate the individuals' needs." Wireman seemed to assume that a group could not have both the intensely personal focus of a therapy group and the "essential public and community basis" of the community associations she studied. The recent history of self-help groups, however, challenges this assumption, suggesting that political activism may not only be compatible with, but a natural outgrowth of, the personal orientation of self-help groups.

7. Alfred H. Katz, *Self-Help in America: A Social Movement Perspective* (New York: Twayne, 1993), 1. The 1976 estimate originally appeared in Alfred H. Katz and Eugene I. Bender, *The Strength in US: Self-Help Groups in the Modern World* (New York: New Viewpoints, 1976), 36.

8. Katz, *Self-Help in America*, 66.

9. Robert Wuthnow, *Sharing the Journey: Support Groups and America's New Quest for Community* (New York: Free Press, 1994), 71.

10. Ronald C. Kessler, Kristin D. Mickelson, and Shanyang Zhao, "Patterns and Correlates of Self-Help Group Membership in the United States," *Social Policy* (Spring 1997): 29.

11. Kessler et al., "Self-Help Group Membership," 31.

12. Kessler et al., "Self-Help Group Membership," 32.

13. Kessler et al., "Self-Help Group Membership," 43.

14. Katz, *Self-Help in America*, 2.

15. Kessler et al., "Self-Help Group Membership," 31, 35.

16. Katz, *Self-Help in America*, 86.

17. Katz, *Self-Help in America*, 18–19.

18. Erving Goffman, *Stigma: Notes on the Maintenance of Spoiled Identity* (Upper Saddle River, N.J.: Prentice Hall, 1963), 2–3, 5.

19. Goffman, *Stigma*, 20–21.

20. Edward Sagarin, *Odd Man In: Societies of Deviants in America* (Chicago: Quadrangle Books, 1969), 17, 16, 28.

21. Goffman, *Stigma*, 127.

22. Goffman, *Stigma*, 128.

23. Goffman, *Stigma*, 129.

24. *Panhandle Journal*, 29 August 1997, D4.

25. Sagarin, *Odd Man In*, 21–24.

26. The most striking example of the last may be the Deaf culture movement and the myriad small groups it has spawned, which reject the assumption that deafness is an impairment properly subject to medical correction and see it instead as the foundation of a distinct and equal culture.

27. Wuthnow, *Sharing the Journey*, 16.

28. Keith Humphreys, "Individual and Social Benefits of Mutual Aid Self-Help Groups," *Social Policy* (Spring 1997): 28.

29. Katz, *Self-Help in America*, 14, 16.

30. Oliver Sacks, *The Island of the Colorblind* (New York: Knopf, 1997), 30.

31. Sacks, *The Island of the Colorblind*, 206.

32. Frank Riessman, "Ten Self-Help Principles," *Social Policy* (Spring 1997): 7.

33. Goffman, *Stigma*, 112–13.

34. The temptation to emphasize or exaggerate the pervasiveness of the condition has another source, in the social authority of the group rather than the status of its individual members. The more deeply the condition shapes the perspectives, sensibilities, and social practices of the group's members, the stronger their claim to a distinct culture. It is, for example, the claim of many Deaf people that the condition which sets them apart from the larger society also provides them with the foundations of an alternative culture. To the extent that a group embodies or represents such a culture, it can serve as an arbiter of success and flourishing independent of the mainstream culture that has stigmatized its members. To the extent the group assumes such authority, it plays a role in its members' lives to which few voluntary associations have aspired.

35. Wuthnow, *Sharing the Journey*, 13–35.

36. Nancy L. Rosenblum, "The Moral Uses of Pluralism" (chap. 10 in this volume).

37. Wuthnow, *Sharing the Journey*, 14–15.

38. Wuthnow, *Sharing the Journey*, 323–33.

39. Wuthnow, *Sharing the Journey*, 16.

40. Elayne Rapping, "There's Self-Help and Then There's Self-Help: Women and the Recovery Movement," *Social Policy* (Spring 1997): 60–61.

41. Katz, *Self-Help in America*, 87–89.

42. Frank Riessman and David Carroll, *Redefining Self-Help: Policy and Practice* (San Francisco, Calif.: Jossey-Bass, 1995), 172.

43. Riessman and Carroll, *Redefining Self-Help*, 174–75.

44. Rosenblum, "The Moral Uses of Pluralism."

45. Historically, however, activism on behalf of racial, ethnic, economic, or other minority groups has not been a stepping-stone to national political office in the United States. The champions of ethnic politics have rarely achieved success beyond the municipal level. And unlike Britain and many Western European countries, we have no Labor Party that began by representing the interests of a particular class of citizens and rose to national power.

46. Theodore Lowi, *The End of Liberalism: The Second Republic of the United States* (New York: Norton, 1979), 50–61.

10

The Moral Uses of Pluralism

Nancy L. Rosenblum

"The Moral Uses of Pluralism" refers to the fact that membership in the voluntary associations of civil society can shape individuals in powerful ways. Not all groups have a formative influence on the moral dispositions of members, nor do the social functions of associations necessarily depend on their moral effects. Yet it is reasonable to think that associational life often shapes moral dispositions and that this has direct and indirect consequences for democratic public culture and politics. This chapter focuses on the moral uses of pluralism for citizens personally and individually.[1]

I offer an assessment, a series of cautions, a theory, and a prescription. Part I assesses current claims about civil society and civic renewal, pointing out the range of disagreements these themes provoke. Parts II and III caution against the psychologically and sociologically simplistic assumptions that underlie many claims about the role of associations in civic renewal. Concrete examples in Part II illustrate that the moral valence of associational life is complex and variable. Part III continues in this cautionary vein by pointing out the vicissitudes of moral development and the fact that besides cultivating virtues associations are also vital in tempering and containing vices. The thesis that emerges from this discussion is that the variability and vicissitudes of membership should not be discounted, indeed should inform our judgment of groups and policies toward them. Based on these considerations, Part III outlines a theory of the moral uses of pluralism. Part IV concludes with a summary of considerations for public policy vis-à-vis the voluntary associations of civil society. Overall, this chapter is distinguished by a call to keep the moral uses of pluralism *for individuals* in the forefront of our thinking about *groups*.

CIVIL SOCIETY AND CIVIC RENEWAL: A CRITICAL ASSESSMENT

It is a staple of liberal democratic theory, amply supported by social science, that civil society is both a complementary and countervailing force to government. Constitutionally protected civil liberties, principally freedom of association, ensure the ceaseless formation of groups representing various interests and opinions. With their independent resources of organization and leadership, these groups are able to serve as a check on political authority. At the same time, however, voluntary associations often cater to dark emotional needs, amplify selfish interests, and give vent to exclusionary impulses that James Madison's "mischiefs of faction" does not begin to cover; and so government checks the power private groups exercise over their members. The political relation between democratic government and civil society is reciprocal, and each side operates as both a reinforcing and countervailing power to the other.

In recent years this classic focus on the *political* functions of civil society, on its centrality for political freedom, stability, and legitimacy, has been supplanted by preoccupation with the *moral* effects of associational life. The focus is on the role of civil society in civic renewal.

The idea that liberal democracy requires the conscious reproduction of citizens is nothing new. If it has sometimes taken a backseat in academic moral and political theory, it has had a permanent place in American ideology and institutional design. The sense that the requisite attitudes and civic capacities are not being cultivated is not new, either. Nothing is as common historically as American jeremiads, and we are increasingly adept at marshaling empirical evidence in support of prophecies of decline.

Analyses of decreasing voter turnout (along with the sorry decline of expectation from the standard of the "reasonable voter" to the "rational voter" to Samuel Popkin's minimally "reasoning voter") are just the beginning.[2] Political mistrust, once thought to keep citizens alert to abuses of power, is seen as wayward, and surveys document "pervasive contempt" for major institutions. We have updated data on crime rates and litigation explosions, even on clinical depression, inspiring Robert Lane to call the United States a "joyless polity."[3] Plainly, official "seedbeds of virtue" such as public schools and local government cannot do the work of character formation and community building alone. Associations must compensate for what are seen as either the natural limitations or perverse failings of public institutions. The reproduction of citizens, it is argued, must go on in the "dense" networks of civil society.

But grim surveys of group membership report a decline in "social connectedness," too. We can dissent from this analysis and insist on a broader accounting of the groups that contribute to civic renewal, looking beyond the limiting category of "civic associations." And we should resist calls to reverse the social trends that are identified as sources of membership decline, among them women's participation in the workplace.[4] Still, there is no denying the pervasive *sense* that dis-association is widespread, along with the belief that it is linked to (perhaps responsible for) the decline of "basic values." Once the preserve of conservatives, the claim "that in the modern world we need to recapture the density of associational life and relearn the activities and understandings that go with it" is echoed across the political spectrum.[5]

That said, there is little consensus about either the promises or the failings of civil society. I want to survey these disagreements. They are honest disagreements, deeply rooted, and no project of civic renewal can hope to overcome them. But it is always useful to clarify our disagreements and to acknowledge the critical points where we speak at cross-purposes.

First, there is disagreement about what moral dispositions are vital to liberal democratic citizenship, about the rank order of these virtues, and about which ones are in shortest supply.

The catalog of virtues ranges from modest law-abidingness and habits of cooperation that hold *any* society together, to willingness to work to support one's family, to the self-control to refrain from violence and public shows of disrespect. These moral virtues are designated "civic," often without explanation. Most lists include distinctively political dispositions as well, but the choices vary dramatically: the wherewithal to exercise one's rights, tolerance, more stringent political competencies such as the ones required by democratic deliberation, and, if not full-blown "civic magnanimity," at least a minuscule concern for the common good. Few political dispositions rank high on the lists of both deliberative democrats and communitarians (unless they are civic republicans), to say nothing of civil libertarians. Christopher Beem points out the disjuncture between popular concerns with "the day-to-day virtues involved in neighborliness, self-restraint, and childrearing" and academics' preoccupation with distinctively political virtues.[6] No wonder a shared concern for "civic virtue" can have us talking at cross-purposes from the start.

Given the range of virtues judged wanting, it is hardly surprising that there is little agreement on the second matter: designating which associations do the work of cultivating moral dispositions, or should. *Invocations* of civil society are typically vague and indicate little more than a general thesis in favor of a strong role for mediating institutions as supplements or replacements for the tutorial role of government. Strategies of avoidance are commonplace. The question of identifying formative groups is evaded if civil society is defined very generally as "the realm of concrete and authentic solidarities where we become sociable or communal men and women."[7] Hard questions are also evaded if civil society is defined narrowly in terms of beneficent, internally democratic, civic-minded groups. The question is eclipsed if voluntary associations are seen as epiphenomena, and the whole weight of moral development is placed on the family or on organizations that specialize in the moral education of children.

Consensus about what moral dispositions are vital to civic renewal and which formative groups are promising schools of virtue would not translate into consensus on the third area of contention: the genesis of associations and government's role in creating and sustaining them. These disagreements are famously partisan, but they persist in part because of limited information and genuine uncertainty about the origin and life history of groups.

One view has it that moralizing, socializing groups arise spontaneously, define their own goals, and are accountable only to themselves. Whether the analogy is to free-market forces or organic growth, the process is seen as unplanned and undirected. Associations provide vital mediating functions and may even cultivate specifically civic virtues, but unintentionally, so to speak, and without the guiding hand of the state. On this view, the spillover effects of moral education from one association to another and from there to public life are spontaneous, too.

On another view, however, civic renewal depends on the conscious reproduction of democratic citizens. For censorious advocates of associations as "private boot camps for citizenship," the internal lives of groups should mirror public norms. The logic of congruence demands more than assurance that secondary associations are free of force, fraud, and the most egregious private despotisms. Civic habits are developed through practice, the argument goes, and democratic practices must be brought home to us. We recognize the congruence thesis from Harry Eckstein's work on authoritarian family patterns, Carole Pateman's on participatory workplaces, and feminist writings that represent caring, egalitarian relations in women's groups as the exemplary training ground for democracy (or mothering as a model of empathy and responsibility).[8]

Both positions are consistent with public encouragement of associations and with government subsidy and support. For obvious reasons, advocates of congruence are more inclined to insist on strong government intervention in associational life. Recall that the U.S. Supreme Court found constitutional grounds to intervene in the membership practices of the Jaycees, Rotary, and Boy Scouts. Today, race and gender antidiscrimination law is generally applicable, and due process is the rule if not the practice in most groups. Some advocates of civic renewal would have government go further. If business corporations represent sinister interests, for example, either their political participation should be restricted, or they should be reformed through shareholder democracy or public interest representation on corporate boards. Proponents rarely recommend enforcing strict congruence "all the way down," however. They stop at advocating government favoritism for congregational churches over hierarchic ones, for example, or legally mandating worker control over other forms of management. We normally recognize the hubris of thinking that government can fill the alleged social void and generate moralizing, democratizing groups by incentive or fiat. We also recognize the danger that politics will colonize and courts constitutionalize every aspect of social life.

Finally, there is very basic disagreement when it comes to diagnosing the perceived breakdown of reciprocity between civil society and democratic government. Peter Berger and Richard Neuhaus staked out one position twenty years ago, when they designated America a *mass society* and government an overbearing "Leviathan." From this perspective, the critical need is for mediating institutions to connect people alienated from the social formations in which moral dispositions and communal attachments are developed and the exercise of virtue is tangible. The axiom that "psychologically and sociologically . . . *any identity* is better than none" indicates that a fear of atomism and anomie eclipses any fear we might have about the bad tendencies of groups.

From this standpoint, Joan Didion's description of children in Haight-Ashbury rings truer today, more than two decades after it was written:

> The center was not holding. It was a country of bankruptcy notices and public-auction announcements and commonplace reports of casual killings and misplaced children and abandoned homes and vandals who misspelled even the four-letter words they scrawled. . . . Adolescents drifted from city to torn city, sloughing off both the past and the future as snakes shed their skins, children who were never taught and would never now learn the games that had held the society together.[9]

A contrasting diagnosis finds an *excess* rather than absence of intermediate associations. Liberal democracy is no leviathan; if anything, it fails by being self-effacing. Committed to freedom of association, it is home to every imaginable group—authoritarian, elitist, bureaucratic and hierarchic, sexist, racist, blindly traditionalist, and paramilitary. It is too hospitable to communitarian enclaves—whether Shakers or armed Freemen, bohemian countercultures or walled and gated residential communities. It allows "identity groups" to claim us as their own, attribute obligations to us, and insist that we should feel as if we belong—labeling us traitors and self-haters if we do not. Liberal democracy gives scope to fierce group loyalties that look on democratic dispositions and attachment to the broader community as unwanted, oppressive assimilation. It is inadequately alarmed by the fact that religious principles may be abhorrent and believers piously cruel or homicidal, taxing widespread assumptions about complementarity between religion and "our nation's moral consensus."[10]

On this view, the danger is not atomism or a "missing middle" but the multiplication of groups that amplify a politics of naked preferences and exaggerate cultural egocentrism.[11] Mediating institutions don't mediate. Independent associations, voluntary and ascriptive, balkanize public life. Again, Joan Didion, this time from her book *Miami*:

> In the continuing opera still called, even by Cubans who have now lived the largest part of their lives in this country, *el exilio*, the exile, meetings at private houses in Miami Beach are seen to have consequences. . . . Revolutions and counter-revolutions are framed in the private sector. . . . [T]his particular political style, indigenous to the Caribbean and to Central America, has now been naturalized in the United States.[12]

La lucha is no one's version of democratic politics.

From this perspective, the critical need is to *loosen* rather than strengthen the hold of gripping affiliations so that members have the psychological latitude to look beyond their groups and identify themselves as members of a larger community. Civic renewal requires a stronger assertion of liberal democratic values in both public and private life.

A dose of sociological and psychological realism suggests that both diagnoses have merit. Processes of connection and disconnection go on simultaneously in our wildly pluralist society. Anomie, aggressive self-interest, and powerful solidaristic group attachments coexist. Which is why we are right to look to associations to *integrate* radically disconnected individuals into formative groups; to *chasten* arrant egotism; and to *loosen* the hold of gripping, sometimes coercive subcommunities. Both greater government regulation and greater solicitude for the independence of associational life are needed, and neither can substitute for the other.[13]

Against this background, I will risk further complicating matters by shifting ground and focusing attention on the experience of men and women personally and individually—as we must, if we think that civic renewal turns on our habitual dispositions.

THE MORAL VALENCE OF ASSOCIATIONS

The obstacles to cultivating and exhibiting everything from very basic moral habits such as cooperation to specifically liberal democratic virtues differ from person to person. We know from experience that what we take from membership in any particular group depends on our life history—that is, on the moral dispositions, ideological expectations, and experiences of affiliation we bring to it. Whatever its formal purpose and authority structure, the moral experiences an association provides its members turn in part on the vicissitudes of their own personal moral development. The effect of membership may be to reinforce moral qualities developed in the course of earlier attachments, or to compensate for an absence of liberalizing/democratizing experiences. An association may actively inhibit democratic dispositions and cut members off from other connections, or it may have little or no constitutive effect—democratically organized groups oriented to public affairs can provide political representation and influence political outcomes without significantly shaping their adherents, for example.

So it is difficult to assess the moral valence of associational life, even for willing members. The moral uses of membership are variable and unpredictable, and, with one exception to which I will turn in a moment, few generalizations hold. We cannot shepherd adults into presumptively benign groups, and if we *could* compel association, there is no assurance that model arrangements would effectively influence dispositions in intended ways—not if we begin with people as they really are.

The *systemic* effects of groups on liberal democracy are a different matter. The consequences of undemocratic and illiberal associations for political stability and legitimacy, and for the climate of public life, are the well-studied domain of political science. My concern here, by contrast, is the moral uses of pluralism.

A few illustrations from the terrain of civil society indicate why the moral valence of associational life is often indeterminate.

Consider the 900,000 religious fellowship groups and 250,000 secular support groups in the United States that Robert Wuthnow has made vivid.[14] Do they fuel narcissism or cooperation? They seem to reinforce self-involvement, since members talk mainly about their own lives, the solution to problems is self-transformation rather than collective action, and the measure of virtually any event is how it makes us feel. "Caring" is defined minimally as hearing one another out nonjudgmentally—hardly an onerous responsibility. In any case, these associations are typically too fluid to create sustained obligations. Members shop around the crowded marketplace of groups. In my desire for "support" I can choose to identify myself as a Jew, a woman, and a professor and join a synagogue group for orthodox women academics; or I can see myself as an adult child of an alcoholic and enter recovery; and I can reshuffle these attributes and change memberships at will.

On the other hand, these groups provide the experience of reciprocity. Even if members mainly take turns speaking about themselves, they do take turns, and they are expected to take a turn at encouraging others. These groups encourage members to overcome humility and passivity, which are *not* democratic virtues. And they accustom members to treat one another identically and with easy spontaneity, which is a pretty good definition of civility in everyday life in America.[15] They create the expectation that our pain and indignation at day-to-day unfairness and abuse will not be met with indifference, and thus may cultivate the iota of trust necessary for democratic citizens to speak out about ordinary injustice.

Consider a less subjective example of the complex experience of associational life and its variable moral effects. The 150,000 homeowners' associations around the country are run by elected boards of directors that assess residents, enforce internal regulations, and assign owners votes in proportion to their proprietary share. Do these associations transform neighbors into shareholders preoccupied with efficient management and value, generating an arid "corporate culture" at home? Or should we see homeowners' associations not as cold contractual arrangements but as elective communities based on covenants? They are not antiworldly utopias, obviously, but they do provide the experience of co-ownership of common areas, rule making, and self-governance. In either case, responsibility defined as meeting economic obligations and conforming to the rules of voluntary association is nothing to despise. Restrictions, duly enforced, preserve communal norms, check arbitrariness and caprice, and channel personal conflict, particularly in the areas that produce the greatest tension among neighbors everywhere—parking, children, and pets.

Despite consent to these restrictions, some critics of homeowners' associations would limit their freedom to regulate conduct and property. They object to constraints on personal liberty, but animus is mainly against the moral message these regulations send. When parents explain to their children that they must abide by the prohibition against changing the color of their house, one critic argues, they are delivering an illiberal lesson: "It is conceivable that children raised in [homeowners' associations] may be undergoing a form of differential political socialization. . . . We have a generation in this country that doesn't know you *should be able* to paint your house any color you want."[16]

This is a strange "should" for those who see homeowners' associations as small-scale democratic communities that "could unwittingly provide a mechanism for reversing the anti-community trends of the last century."[17] From this standpoint, participation should be increased by extending the universal suffrage requirement the Fourteenth Amendment imposes on local communities to homeowners' associations, granting votes to all residents, not just owners.

Initial hopes that homeowners' associations would serve as schools of participatory citizenship have been disappointed. On average only 11 percent of members take part in association governance (and 84 percent of residents responding to a Florida survey thought that owner apathy is the biggest problem facing community associations).[18] A different picture emerges, however, if we look at members who *do* volunteer to serve as directors. They rally owners to meetings, orchestrate decision making, engage in negotiations, maintain compliance, and manage conflict. Association boards are incubators for political organizers, and with a typical five-person board of directors, something on the order of 625,000 people have served—more, if we take rotation into account.

The darker side of homeowners' associations as minidemocratic communities, of course, is that they replicate the localism and "NIMBY" ("Not in My Backyard") politics exhibited by zoning boards and school boards everywhere (and condoned by both courts and public opinion). Does this undermine any claim that associations are scenes of civic education? Or is parochialism inevitable in communities capable of reinforcing family values and social norms—the sort of "natural" or "tribal" structure of community David Popenoe says is vital to civic renewal, and for which no "realistic social alternatives" exist?[19]

These characterizations of homeowners' associations are all accurate; the several faces of associational life are not mutually exclusive. For an individual member, the association may operate mainly to increase appreciation for community and self-government. Or an owner may see him- or herself principally as a shareholder/investor in common property, with a stake in good management and a "maintenance-free lifestyle." Or membership can provoke resistance to community, and contrarian insistence on privacy rights, private ownership, and unfettered personal liberty. The moral valence is variable. It is changeable for members themselves over time.

One last bit of terrain: a Montana Militiaman is described as "alive with conspiracies. They whir in his mind and welter in his heart, and they fill him so full of outrage and nervousness that he cannot ever stay still." Should we therefore commend the seventeen states that outlaw paramilitary groups outright? Or should we take some comfort from the fact that this conspiracist is securely ensconced in a remote compound?

One leader believes that it is better to have "kooks and nuts" inside the organization than out of it on their own:

> Out, they're liable to do most anything at any time without anybody knowing it except them. If they decide they want to go out and blow somebody

up, okay, they go out and blow somebody up. But if they're part of a group . . . well, then there's a good chance someone in the organization will know about it and they're going to take steps to bring this person under control.[20]

In *The Racist Mind*, Raphael Ezekiel reports that the "scared, stranded" youths who join white racist groups have typically dropped out of school years before graduation. They have no prospects of work and no attachments. They are not driven by hate to join groups that mirror their beliefs; they are simply available. Sheer lack goes some way toward explaining why membership may be easy for them: "Most strikingly, recruits have little in their heads to *inhibit* their adopting these [Nazi] legends . . . nothing from family or environment got in the way." "The white supremacist movement—for a while, at least—is a lifeline for these kids," Ezekiel observes.[21]

Hate groups and paramilitary associations seem uncomplicatedly loathsome, obstacles to civic renewal. The fact that membership fulfills the "need" for a sense of belonging is irrelevant to moral development if belonging fails to provide some compensatory experience—to cultivate self-worth or to contain aggression. But again, Ezekiel reports that members "derive a degree of self-confidence and dignity from the suggestion that they are engaged in a heroic struggle for the sake of a larger entity, the reborn family of Whites." Many are able to capitalize on their only experience of social union and move on to other, more benign associations.

The life cycle of membership in these groups is typically brief. As one Klan leader on his way out of the movement explained:

> I've let a lot of things slide, you know . . . you put the Klan first. And I'm tired of me suffering, my mother suffering. . . . We don't *own* nothing. We don't *have* nothing. And as you know, most Klan leaders . . . are self-employed or don't work at all.

Another member observed:

> Girls that will put up with this are hard to come by. . . . I thought I had one, this girl here I dated for three years . . . but you know, when she'd want to do something on the weekend I'd say, "Well, we got a rally."

He left for love.

For those who do not experience alternative social pushes and pulls, exit is a matter of anomic drift. Unable to move on to other associations, they decline into chaos and personal disorganization. Unemployed and socially unattached, they are rarely recruited into alternative groups. The dispositions of potential members may make them effectively unavailable for recruitment into benign associations in any case.

I am not recommending hate groups. I use this example to emphasize that the moral uses of association may be negative—to contain viciousness, say. Above all, this example confirms that membership does not occur in a psychological or social vacuum—whether and how experiences of association come together in the lives of individuals is key to the moral uses of pluralism.

We could multiply examples indefinitely. I chose these because accounts of declining associational life give support groups, homeowners' associations, and paramilitary groups short shrift, and because excellent studies document the life cycle of membership and its variable effects. They remind us that if some associations inhibit liberal virtues, not all illiberal settings do—and even those may not be debilitating for all members. Moreover, illiberal associations may actually perform vital moralizing functions for some. The moral valence of membership is neither simple nor predictable.

These examples also set the stage for one thesis about associational life that *is* generalizable: groups normally cultivate what philosopher John Rawls has called "the morality of association." That is, individuals learn to live up to the ideals of their station in social groups and to cooperate in shared purposes. Associations provide an experience of reciprocity and require members to overcome the vices that impede cooperation—partiality, deceit, and graspingness, to name a few. Moreover, simply by the fact that individuals have a suitable place where their contributions are recognized and appreciated, associations normally instill a sense of self-respect.[22] They bolster self-worth and provide a buffer against other slights and failures, some protection against radical self-doubt. The morality of association obtains for virtually *any* association, including groups that will never be infused with the public norms of liberal democracy.[23]

THE MORAL USES OF PLURALISM

Once we highlight the *dynamics* of membership—the interaction between associational life and the vicissitudes of personal moral development—the limitations of standard accounts of civil society as a school of virtue emerge sharply. They provide cautions for thinking about civic renewal that, if taken seriously, point us past disagreement about virtues, venues, and whether too little association or too much of the wrong kind of association is the chief failing. They point the way to a sober perspective on civic renewal, and beyond to prescriptions.

What problems plague standard approaches to civil society that fail to confront the variable moral valence of associational life and the vicissitudes of individual development?

For one, they operate on the unwarranted assumption that the effects of an association on individual members can be predicted on the basis of a group's formal purpose, structure, or ideology. By now the limitations of this assumption are familiar. It fails to notice that the internal culture of most groups is rarely unitary—homeowners' associations, for example, provide ample opportunity for both self-government and proprietary self-concern. It also overlooks the fact that members' moral deficits vary from an absence of basic impulse control to a lack of competence in deliberation on behalf of the common good, and that the roots of moral fragility in each person's case vary from excessive self-interest to anomie. So it really should not be surprising that what works as an effective school of virtue will vary, too.

Another misleading feature of standard accounts is the "transmission belt" model, which says that the moral effects of membership spill over from one sphere to another. The term *mediating* is meant to convey the idea that associations or informal social networks are not just internally cooperative, integrating, and nurturing of their own. Rather, cooperation begets cooperation—larger-scale social connectedness that ultimately benefits democratic public life. This is a doubtful proposition (unregrettably, since the logic of the "transmission belt" applies to vices). After all, it is simply not the case that labor in an authoritarian workplace produces incorrigibly submissive characters, or that observant Roman Catholics are ritualistic, orthodox Jews legalistic, and followers of charismatic ministers enthusiastic in every domain.

In fact, the *experience* of pluralism cultivates a capacity to *differentiate* among spheres and adjust our conduct to them. So even if we are subject to (or inflict) prejudice, arbitrariness, or deference in one domain, we may be able to exhibit an iota of tolerance, say, in public arenas or fairness in hiring. Which is why fear for the effects of association on members' overall disposition and conduct (e.g., liberal suspicion of traditionalist groups) may be exaggerated.

Finally, it emerges from my examples that standard approaches are too quick to say that the business of civil society is to cultivate and diffuse liberal democratic virtues rather than temper and contain illiberal, antidemocratic vices. We should always be open to improvement, but sociologists remind us that deviance is as much a part of social life as the reproduction of norms. Surely it is important that groups provide relatively benign outlets for ineradicable viciousness, intolerance, or arrant self-interest, and that antidemocratic dispositions be contained when they cannot be corrected.

Only a fine line separates the respects in which associations function as "safety valves" from their posing a "clear and present danger." Nonetheless, containment is a crucial aspect of the moral uses of association, and it has a particular role in American democracy.

A permanent feature of voluntary association is the formation of groups based on every conceivable identity and difference, affiliation and exclusion. Despite populist fears, Americans are not opposed to exclusive organizations for themselves: "The plain citizen sometimes wearied of his plainness" and wanted rites as well as rights, ceremonials, titles, exotic regalia, and selective comradeship.[24] Rawls was wrong to think that the plurality of associations "tends to reduce the visibility, or at least the painful visibility, of variations in men's prospects."[25] The whole point is to make them visible. Inevitably, restricted membership groups will be seen as advancing some claim to preference or privilege, and provoke accusations that they are not only exclusive but subversively antidemocratic. Inevitably, they inspire counterpart groups, mirror images of their exclusiveness. Nothing is more common than the American penchant for secret societies and groups formed in reaction, to combat "conspiracies." There are always fresh waves of affiliation and exclusion. As some forms of identity and descent, patriotism and moral superiority are thrown off, others are invented, along every imaginable dimension.

This dynamic is permanent. In part, it is a perfectly understandable response to our public ethos of equal citizenship and equal public standing. Membership is distinguished from citizenship in the United States precisely because the worth of citizens is supposed to be equal and to have nothing to do with individual attributes or contributions. There is thus a limit to the significance citizenship can have for status and self-worth. The dynamic of affiliation and exclusion is permanent, too, because our conceptions of social status are unstable. A newspaper report on the decline of the Loyal Order of Moose in Roxbury, Massachusetts, described the lodge's plan to give up its hats and capes and to attract young men to join by starting up new activities. The difficulty seemed immense even to the hopeful Moose: "If they're already into drugs [and gangs], it'll be hard to get them into the drum and bugle corps."[26]

Exclusive groups that are home to intolerance, viciousness, and defensive self-aggrandizement are ineliminable. Democracy generates them, and freedom of association protects them. Of course, we should fight these impulses in ourselves and challenge their appearance in public life. At the same time, we should recognize their moral uses. Without this dynamic, which operates more freely here than anywhere else, there would be many fewer sources of the "primary good" of self-respect and less containment of irrepressible vices.

By emphasizing the personal uses of association, I have risked complicating an already complex subject. My conclusion, however, is simple. We have plenty of opportunity to observe that nothing in the existence of a plurality of associations per se insures that they actually function as schools of virtue for members personally and individually. The moral uses of association depend, in addition, on making the experience of pluralism available to men and women personally and individually. Very simply, the possibility that membership provides a beneficial experience of cooperation, of moral reinforcement or reparation, or of grim containment, is enhanced by shifting involvements. Unsystematic cultivation of moral dispositions and containment of vicious ones need not be entirely a matter of serendipity, though. There are the sophisticated recruitment efforts of many groups, and there is public policy.

PUBLIC POLICY AND SHIFTING INVOLVEMENTS

Government has a predominantly *enabling* role: to facilitate the experience of pluralism. One way is by creating a climate conducive to the formation of associations. Tax policy plays an important facilitating part here. Government can also create a climate for pluralism by doing as little as possible to inhibit schism within established groups. Courts decline to intervene in the internal disputes of religious associations over leadership, discipline, doctrine, and membership. The same spirit, which is favorable to schism, should guide courts vis-à-vis secular voluntary associations. This is not a matter of favoring novelty and fickleness over establishment and commitment. It is simply to say that forming, joining, splitting, and leaving associations are as personally significant as communitarian "belonging"; indeed, they are a prelude to it. Liberty and discontent produce associations, after all, including "traditionalist" ones. The objective is to create conditions for the independence and proliferation of groups, indirectly increasing the likelihood that individuals will find their way into associations where there is a "fit" with their moral needs.

Equally important as a condition for effective moral uses of pluralism is a strong background of public institutions and democratic political culture that impresses on us our identity as members of a larger political society. Public policy encourages *both* shifting involvements and appreciation for political community when it ensures that our rights, welfare, and public standing are unaffected by our associations or by changes in affiliation. It can do this by disconnecting health care benefits and pensions from specific places of employment, for example, or by insisting that even self-contained religious communities such as the cultish Alamo Foundation or the Amish pay members minimum wages for their work and contribute to Social Security taxes, so that economic dependency does not make leaving inconceivable.[27] Homeowners in residential associations resist what they call "double taxation," but municipalities should require them to pay property taxes in full as well as internal assessments, dispelling any thought that they are separate enclaves and that membership substitutes for local citizenship.

I have outlined an indirect role for government: supporting the moral uses of pluralism by individuals. In its policies toward groups, government does not aim directly at creating civic associations with a view to character formation.

Indirection does not address the "root causes" of bad attitudes and vicious associations. Ultimately, the moral uses of pluralism are linked to these deeper structural concerns. If families instill basic trust in children, one "root cause" argument has it, they are more likely to go on to cooperate in beneficial associations as adults. True, but surely that is not the principal reason for public concern about families and the well-being of children. And it ignores the fact that many experiences intervene to reinforce or undermine early learning; civic renewal cannot begin and end with children. Similarly, because the workplace is a principal arena for recruitment into groups of all kinds, mandatory or guaranteed employment is almost certainly relevant to a flourishing civil society. But the link between employment and voluntary association is not the best criterion for policy on welfare and work. In the same vein, groups delivering social services, from Catholic Charities to the Boys Clubs, are publicly subsidized, often on the order of 70 percent or more of their funding, in what Lester Salamon calls "third party government."[28] Government support for these projects is justified in terms of social needs and efficiency. But here, too, the significance these groups have for personal moral development is an indirect consequence of participation in their activities, not a reason to subsidize these programs in the first place.

I do not mean to reject entirely direct public encouragement and support for associations judged particularly beneficial to civic renewal. Government has a role as tutor and promoter of civic renewal, and we can expect public officials to single out exemplary groups for recognition and support. I doubt that this is more effective than indirect support for pluralism and shifting involvements, though.

Moreover, a direct public policy of civic renewal through associations carries the danger of creating expectations—peculiarly sensitive and ambitious expectations—that we cannot afford to have disappointed. We should recognize that the civic-minded groups most likely to benefit from a public imprimatur are unable to reach everyone, least of all the worst off. They are even less likely to operate on a scale capable of turning around the perception of civic decline. In any case, we cannot reasonably expect that if public incentives channeled people into "the right sort" of group, be it benign religious associations or civic ones, membership would have the desired moral effects, for all the reasons I have discussed.

The *existence* of a dense array of associations—congruent and incongruent—does little to ensure civic renewal. I have argued that shifting involvements are necessary if individuals are to exploit, willfully or inadvertently, the moral possibilities of associational life. Not civil society, simply, but the *experience of pluralism*, by men and women personally and individually, is what counts. Efforts to create or support exemplary associations have their place. But they should not eclipse sustained commitment to ensuring overall conditions that encourage pluralism and shifting involvements.

NOTES

1. For an extended discussion, see my *Membership and Morals: The Personal Uses of Pluralism in America* (Princeton, N.J.: Princeton University Press, 1998).

2. Samuel L. Popkin, *The Reasoning Voter* (Chicago: University of Chicago Press, 1991).

3. Robert Lane, "The Joyless Polity," in *Citizen Competence and Democratic Institutions*, ed. Stephen L. Elkin and Karol Edward Soltan (University Park, Penn.: Pennsylvania State University Press, 1998).

4. William A. Galston, "Won't You Be My Neighbor," *American Prospect*, no. 26 (May–June 1996): 16–18.

5. Michael Walzer, "The Idea of Civil Society," *Dissent* (Spring 1991): 304. The thought is echoed by liberals who once disparaged civil society as reactionary and by the left who had characterized it as "bourgeois" or "bad privacy."

6. Christopher Beem, "Civil Society in America: A Public Debate about Political Theory," unpublished paper, 29.

7. Walzer, "The Idea of Civil Society," 293, 298.

8. In *Making Democracy Work*, Robert Putnam correlates "intense horizontal interactions" to civic engagement, and vertical patron-client relations to democratic dysfunction. For an extended discussion, see my "Democratic Character and Community: The Logic of Congruence," *Journal of Political Philosophy* 2 (1994): 67–97, and "Civil Societies: Liberalism and the Moral Uses of Pluralism," *Social Research* 61, no. 3 (Fall 1994): 539–62.

9. Joan Didion, *Slouching towards Bethlehem* (New York: Farrar, Straus, & Giroux, 1968), 84.

10. Beem, "Civil Society in America," 26.

11. We think of ethnic or racial identity groups. But the real "multiculturalism" of the United States is not necessarily linked to ethnicity or race; there are innumerable other sources of self-identity and affiliation, from traumatic experience to professional status.

12. Joan Didion, *Miami* (New York: Simon & Schuster, 1987), 13.

13. I specify these areas with regard to particular types of association—

religious associations, homeowners' associations, quasi-civic associations, political parties, secret societies and hate groups, militias, and others—in *Membership and Morals.*

14. Robert Wuthnow, *Sharing the Journey: Support Groups and America's New Quest for Community* (Princeton, N.J.: Princeton University Press, 1994).

15. Nancy L. Rosenblum, "Navigating Pluralism: The Democracy of Everyday Life," in *Citizen Competence and Democratic Institutions*, ed. Elkin and Soltan.

16. Evan McKenzie, *Privatopia: Homeowner Associations and the Rise of Residential Private Government* (New Haven, Conn.: Yale University Press, 1994), 143 (italics added).

17. Uriel Reichman, "Residential Private Governments: An Introductory Survey," *University of Chicago Law Review* 43 (1976): 263.

18. For data, see Robert Jay Dilger, *Neighborhood Politics: Residential Community Associations in American Governance* (New York: New York University Press, 1992), 140; and Stephen E. Barton and Carol J. Silverman, "The Political Life of Mandatory Homeowners' Associations," in *Residential Community Associations: Private Governments in the Intergovernmental System?* (Washington, D.C.: Advisory Commission on Intergovernmental Relations, May 1989), A-112.

19. David Popenoe, "The Roots of Declining Social Virtue: Family, Community, and the Need for a 'Natural Communities Policy,' " in *Seedbeds of Virtue: Sources of Competence, Character, and Citizenship in American Society*, ed. Mary Ann Glendon and David Blankenhorn (Lanham, Md.: Madison Books, 1995), 97, 94.

20. Raphael S. Ezekiel, *The Racist Mind* (New York: Viking, 1995), 24, 288.

21. Cited in Ezekiel, *The Racist Mind*, 154, 32, 150.

22. John Rawls, *A Theory of Justice* (Cambridge, Mass.: Harvard University Press, 1971), 298–300, 441.

23. It is worth noting that this is an implicit brief for expansive freedom of association, which conforms to popular commitment to this civil liberty.

24. Arthur M. Schlesinger, "Biography of a Nation of Joiners," *American Historical Review* 1, no. 1 (October, 1944): 1–25, 15.

25. Rawls, *A Theory of Justice*, 441, 544, 545.

26. Sally Jacobs, "Male Order Distress Grows," *Boston Globe*, 31 May 1993, 1.

27. See my "The Moral Uses of Pluralism: Freedom of Association and Liberal Virtue Illustrated with Cases on Religious Exemption and Accommodation," Working Paper no. 3, the University Center for Human Values, Princeton University.

28. "Gingrich's Welfare Vision: Charities Find It in the Clouds," *New York Times*, 4 June 1995, 30; Lester M. Salamon, *Partners in Public Service: Government-Nonprofit Relations in the Modern Welfare State* (Baltimore: Johns Hopkins University Press, 1995), 34. Salamon finds little evidence that public subsidies have led to association dependency, co-optation, dilution of advocacy, or loss of autonomy.

11

Civil Enough

Toward a Liberal Theory of Vice (and Virtue)

Loren E. Lomasky

I

The contemporary debate about "civil society" is, in one measure, a debate about virtue and vice. It is a debate about character—the kinds of character needed by citizens to sustain liberal democracy—and the institutions that form and cultivate character, for good or ill. As Nancy Rosenblum notes in the preceding chapter, "official 'seedbeds of virtue' such as public schools and local government cannot do the work of character formation . . . alone."[1] Indeed, in our liberal polity, we may be wary of any "official" character formation at all. Hence the contemporary interest in the formative effects of the families and face-to-face associations within which we spend most of our lives.

It is not clear, though, how we can rekindle a language of virtue and vice in a culture that is fundamentally liberal or even whether doing so would be desirable. Modern moral philosophy is uncomfortable with the concept of vice. It is not entirely at ease with the virtues either, but to remark on someone's virtues is to initiate a friendly act of praise or commendation. To characterize a person's dispositions as vices is not friendly. Rather, it is to throw down the gauntlet in a manner likely to be a prelude to hostilities. And since modern moral philosophy directs itself above all else toward deriving rationally well-grounded articles of peace that might substitute for the Hobbesian war of all against all, a nose for sniffing out vice is a nose for trouble.

Old-fashioned reprobation speaks in the language of vice, but modern moral criticism prefers to talk of rights and their violation. By a *right* is meant a maximally weighty claim entailing duties with which others *must* comply. (The "must" is normative rather than causal or epistemological.) Robert Nozick characterizes rights as *side-constraints*,[2] Ronald Dworkin as *trumps*.[3] The two notions differ in subtle ways—a side-constraint is such only insofar as it constrains, while a trump remains a trump even when overtrumped—but are fundamentally similar. The doctrine of rights establishes for each individual a property in the life that is her own. Holders of rights homestead an expanse of moral space within which they are free to attach themselves to those ends they find personally compelling and to pursue them wholeheartedly. Wholeheartedly but not without limit: if persons in the service of their diverse projects follow wheresoever the main chance leads, they will regularly encroach on the moral space of others. Therefore, if a semblance of peace, let alone cooperation, is to be preserved, there is need for markers that indicate precisely what does and does not constitute trespass. Rights are those markers. Just so long as one does not infringe the rights of others, no liability has been incurred. This account of rights advances a conception of individuals as beings both free and equal: equal insofar as they are one and all endowed with a patch of moral space within which they are entitled to develop their own conceptions of the good, and free to act as they see fit in the pursuit of this good just so long as they do not abridge the similar prerogative of others.

Within this fundamentally liberal framework, it is tempting to see vice and virtue as either otiose or dysfunctional. If a vicious act is one that violates the rights of someone else, then it ought to be condemned forthrightly as such; we do not need a separate vocabulary of vices so as to be able to express our disapproval. If, however, the allegedly vicious action takes place within the ambit of what the individual rightfully may do, then it would seem that criticism is off-limits. At best, unsolicited clucks of disapproval are a failure to mind one's own business; at worst, they pose the threat of border crossings. In either case, it seems that references to vice are eminently dispensable. So too, but less ominously, are ascriptions of virtue. For a liberal morality the preeminent desideratum is tolerance, and immoderately to prize certain dispositional traits above others that are equally rights-respecting may be seen as putting tolerance at risk.

Although no summary account of three centuries of philosophical ethics can be definitive, it is instructive to observe the awkwardness with which the two dominant frameworks of the modern era, utilitarianism and Kantianism, attempt to address considerations of virtue and vice. For the utilitarian, an individual acts rightly on a particular occasion if and only if from among all the alternative actions open to him he chooses the one that will produce the greatest amount of happiness (or pleasure or preference satisfaction: I abstract from the innumerable variations on variations within the family of utilitarianisms) for all parties concerned. To choose in any other manner is to act wrongly. Ethical behavior so conceived is an exercise in unconstrained maximization, and all willful failures to maximize are culpable.[4] No special significance attaches to those suboptimal behaviors traditionally thought of as manifesting vice. To be sure, as utilitarians have noted, virtues (vices) can be given a derivative sense as those traits of character that are conducive (detrimental) to skill in utility maximization coupled with a persistent propensity to exercise that skill, but they are not estimable (discreditable) in any respect other than with regard to the consequences they engender. A utilitarian ethic is binary: one either does one's duty or one fails to do so. There simply is no room between these on-off states for the numerous distinct forms of estimability and culpability that underpin the commonsense morality from which references to vices and virtues have not yet been completely expunged.

Within the academic taxonomy of moral philosophies, Kantian ethics is standardly presented as the polar opposite of utilitarianism: while for the utilitarian it is the *consequences* of people's actions that carry all moral weight, for the Kantian consequences do not matter. Rather, moral value is solely a function of the *motives* brought to action. The only thing good without qualification, insists Kant, is the will that directs itself by the signal of duty. Duty, in turn, is understood as that which pure reason commands, and the voice of reason in practice is the Categorical Imperative, bidding us to act only in accord with precepts that are universalizable. Kantianism thus entirely rejects the utilitarian criterion of consequentialist maximization. To phrase the contrast spatially, utilitarianism peers outward in businesslike fashion at the effects in the world that one's actions can engender, while the Kantian gazes inward at the maxims that guide choice.

Despite the considerable gulf separating the two theories, Kantianism marches in step with utilitarianism to a binary beat. Although common morality readily distinguishes between merely doing what is required and acting conspicuously above and beyond the call of duty, with Kantianism as with utilitarianism there is no room for distinctions of quality among morally positive modes of action. That follows directly from Kant's dictum that there is nothing higher than doing one's duty for the sake of that duty. No zeal for righteousness, compassion for the downtrodden, or commitment to projects that shape the moral contours of a life is acknowledged as elevating even by a hair's breadth the standing of conscientious attention to duty. Quite the contrary: Kant characterizes these as submoral "pathologies" of practical reason. Similarly, although this is less clear from the texts, there does not seem to be any consistent way in which Kantians can recognize degrees of substandardness in people's performances. The theory requires that there at least be a distinction between conduct that lacks all moral value, either positive or negative (as is the case, for example, with the behavior of infants and imbeciles who lack a capacity for deliberative moral agency), and that which is disvaluable in the extended sense of being evil. Kantianism is, however, embarrassingly short of resources for establishing that contrast, let alone for discriminating among evils of differing types and magnitudes. As with utilitarianism, the richness of common morality is wedged into a Procrustean bed into which it fits only with the assistance of a nip here, a tuck there, amputations all around.[5]

The past several centuries have, in summary, been hard on vice and virtue. (I restrict that comment to matters of theory, though one might suspect that they have fared no better in practice.) Liberal political philosophy is inclined to regard them as indelicate affronts to sensibilities of toleration, and the two dominant forms of contemporary ethics squeeze categories of moral salience into a conceptual conduit too narrow for them to fit. So whither vices and virtues?

My goal in this chapter is to rehabilitate a robust conception of vice and virtue within a framework that is demonstrably liberal. I duly avail myself of the standard caveat that the attempt offered here is preliminary and far from synoptic. I do hope, though, to indicate with some clarity and conviction what the elements of that to-be-awaited synoptic account will comprise. By way of anticipation, the theory will accord distinctly less prominence to considerations of justice and injustice than liberal theorizing usually incorporates. And it will accord considerably more prominence than is customary to manners and other informal conventions of social order. In keeping with good building practices, I commence with the foundations and work upward.

II

A moral philosophy that assigns a prominent place to vice and virtue without thereby declaring war on the deliverances of the modern moral consciousness will have the following features.[6] First, it will recognize a baseline of minimally acceptable conduct. These are the prescriptions correlative on the rights of others. One may (and, of course, should) do more than avoid trespass against the rights of others, but one *must not* do less. And because the demands consequent on rights are maximally weighty, they are also sharply restricted in scope so as to leave a wide territory within which individuals are at liberty to act in accord with their own lights. Thus, second, the theory assigns great latitude and moral significance to personal discretion. Because there are innumerable varieties of rights-respecting conduct, all of which are in the broadest sense permissible, choices matter. They are not merely a selection among near-indiscernibles, like occasions of picking out wallpaper patterns or car options, but instead range over the portentous concerns that shape a life. This realm of choice is not expressible in the apodictic *musts* and *must nots* of the language of rights and duties but is instead a nuanced and multifaceted discourse of suggestion and persuasion. It offers and entreats but does not command.

Third, it follows that most matters of moral salience occur within the realm of discretion. This discretionary spectrum extends from the baseline upward to the furthest reaches of heroism and sainthood. It is at these strata rather than at the level of minimal acceptability that vice and virtue have most of their purchase. To be sure, we can correctly speak of vices that drag individuals down below the baseline of moral acceptability and virtues that buoy them up above it. But these are limiting cases; it is no more satisfactory to equate virtue and vice with the maintenance of minimal standards than it is to identify the art of gastronomy with techniques for averting starvation. Leaving aside mere respect for rights, there are innumerable ways in which individuals can craft lives that ascend beyond the mediocre, and there are innumerable pitfalls that can give them a tumble. Virtues are those habits of body, intellect, and temperament that conduce to the former and inoculate against the latter. Some virtues are general-purpose tools for successful living, deployable across a wide range of projects and conceptions of the good: resourcefulness, diligence, prudence, for example. Others are of more specialized application, such as the particular excellences of a mountain climber or monk. No complete catalog of virtues (or vices) is possible because modes of living well are in large part a matter of creation, not discovery. Their range is the product of human imagination, ingenuity, and intelligence applied to nature's endowments and therefore does not stay fixed over time or place.

Although such a mapping of morality may not altogether satisfy contemporary fashions, it is nonetheless thoroughly liberal. As with other liberal strains, it accords maximally urgent status to the requirements consequent on rights. But unlike a rights-intoxicated liberalism, it does not stop there. It not only acknowledges but emphasizes the moral significance of people's character and convictions. Because most of what is morally significant about our lives is lived above the baseline, questions about whether conduct is rights-respecting do not monopolize practices of moral appraisal and choice. No less central to the moral life are evaluations concerning the particular forms that conduct takes. The two types of inquiry are, however, distinguishable with respect to *on whom* that centrality devolves. Whether an individual is constrained in her conduct by the rights of others is a matter of urgency not only to her but also to all those with whom she (actually or potentially) interacts. That the baseline be observed is everybody's business. But how one comports oneself beyond that point is—if not exclusively, then predominantly—the agent's own business. This is to announce a division of moral labor within which the vast majority of questions about the selection of appropriate modes of life are definitively answered at the individual level by and for the person whose life it is. Systematic *decentralization of judgments of value* underpins liberal toleration. And although liberalism is sometimes faulted for being atomistic (I return to this criticism in Part IV), that indictment does not apply here. Tolerance is not equivalent to isolation. Others may advise, cajole, remonstrate; even more tellingly, they can emulate or avoid. What they may not do is foist their valuational wares on unwilling customers.

The conception is, additionally, *pluralistic,* not simply in the negative sense of countenancing different modes of life—that would merely reprise toleration—but as a positive affirmation of multiple varieties of value. There is an indefinite number of worthwhile modes of life, and although no one person can partake of more than a minute sample of that richness, one benefits vicariously from goods and virtues that are not one's own possession. Pluralism celebrates sociality, not in the insular manner of communitarian theories ancient and modern that define the relevant society in terms of a narrow range of shared allegiances, but as an arena in which the limitations of the individual self can be transcended. (And liberal friendship stands in sharp contrast to the Aristotelian conception in which the true friend is a "second self" in whom one's own virtues are to be observed.) To be sure, not all perceived differences will be agreeable, but pluralism is the standing wager that externalities are, on balance, more positive than negative.

Finally, the account is *individualistic.* It holds that values are individuated by reference to the persons whose goods and evils they are. Entities more comprehensive than the individual such as classes, races, nations, or species are not recognized as having claims or responsibilities of their own; rather, whatever moral standing they may possess is reducible without remainder to that which attaches to distinct persons. Moreover, in labeling the account individualistic we are also placing a constraint on ethical justification, specifically that it be responsive to individuals' particular interests. That some action or policy is alleged to advance evolutionary fitness or the happiness of the greatest number or the Tide of History is not an adequate response to someone's complaint that it involves the sacrifice of her deep concerns. "What's in it for me?" is not a question that dishonors the inquirer; rather, it captures the essence of moral interchange. To put it another way, the conception of morality under development here is not Olympian: it rejects impersonal appraisals *sub specie ae-*

ternitatis. What permissibly may be asked of people and imposed on them is, it insists, ineliminably perspectival.

III

Virtues are dispositions of body and mind, acquired through practice, conducive to the identification and securement of that which is worth believing, having, making, or doing.[7] Vices, correspondingly, are habitual traits that direct one away from these goods. Not all virtues and vices display a distinctively moral nature; we readily identify virtues and corresponding vices of sound reasoning, artistic design, athletic achievement, and the like. (By adding the adverbial qualifier that these are not *distinctively* moral, I mean to affirm in passing that moral significance is not confined to some arcane, specialized corner of human activity but rather extends across all the contours that make up a life.) Some (e.g., prudence) are mostly self-regarding, while others (e.g., gregariousness or envy) are defined by the characteristic relations in which they put us to others.

Liberal theory's attentiveness to the virtues has been directed disproportionately to justice. To call it disproportionate is not to deny that justice is a crucial virtue, arguably the one that is most indispensable to social life and therefore that on which all others rest.[8] Rather, the problem with justice-centered renderings of morality is that precisely because justice is so special a case, attempts to extrapolate from the theory of justice to a comprehensive geography of the moral landscape will almost invariably be distorted. (Utilitarianism and Kantian ethics are essentially theories of justice writ large; I have already commented on their inability to offer a secure place to other virtues.) Justice is the most universal of the virtues insofar as it involves a disposition to give to all persons their due. It is in this way quite unlike charity or loyalty or kindliness, the objects of which are a select—and selected—subset of those with whom one interacts. Justice abstracts from relations of particular regard or affection— hence the familiar image of justice as blindfolded and impartially weighing measure against measure. The virtue most sharply contrasting with justice is friendship, the disposition to identify and respond to particular others on the basis of special affective ties. It is, therefore, entirely understandable why justice-centered conceptions of morality have no place for friendship as a moral virtue, instead treating it either with suspicion as a potential source of illicit partiality or as what one does "on one's own time" once the constraints of morality have been fully satisfied.

So deep-seated by now are justice-centered theories that universalizability is often presumed to be a defining feature of morality—of *all* stances insofar as they evince moral significance. I shall not attempt here to spell out in detail the manifold unfortunate ramifications of this conception because I wish instead to turn to two correlative features of universality. First, because justice is to be extended to all, it is a least common denominator. Inability to distinguish between the claims of saints and scoundrels is a grievous species of moral idiocy, but in this respect saints and scoundrels are to be treated alike: to each is owed what is justly hers. One may elect not to socialize with boors and braggarts, but one must not shortchange them. And that formulation points us to a second feature, one especially relevant to the current discussion: justice alone among the virtues operates via a language of imperative. Precisely because it sets out standards of minimally acceptable conduct, compliance is not optional. Justice is what one *must do*—period.

Confusions surrounding justice's minimal demandingness and maximal weight are legion. One could write a nearly comprehensive history of recent moral philosophy simply by detailing their course. One chapter would be given over to charting the astonishing proliferation of rights claims that punctuate every variety of policy agitation: not for contemporary philosophers merely the Rights of Man, but to these are superadded animal rights, children's rights, gay and lesbian rights, smokers' rights, ecosystem rights, rights ad infinitum, rights ad nauseam. Another chapter would address confusions sired in the name of so-called *social justice*, that branch of advocacy that gives itself over to translating expressions of programmatic wishes and utopian ideals into the jarringly inappropriate language of duties of justice. Yet another chapter would treat the arcane topic of *imperfect duties* (of justice), those things we are somehow obliged to do despite enjoying discretion whether to do them or not. But so as to avoid transforming this discussion into a preface to that volume, I offer no more chapter summaries. The preceding remarks will suffice to suggest why justice is indeed sui generis, not a proper template for the study of the virtues in general; now it is time to turn specifically to these other virtues and their corresponding vices.

Even with justice duly singled out for its unique status and sequestered in its own private room, it would be another venture in nonergonomic theory design to attempt to present the virtues, or even the moral virtues, as a homogeneous family. Some are of global import, whereas others are restricted with regard to time and place; some could hardly be altogether lacking in a life we would deem well lived, whereas others are the possession of a small set of initiates and of no concern to the vast generality of human beings. Still, the following five observations more or less adequately apply to most of the traits we would identify as virtues/vices.

First, virtues and vices go a long way toward defining the shape of a person's life. In this regard they resemble personal projects and commitments. When we know of someone that he is amiable or a tightwad or a coward, we have thereby learned a good deal about his life, both how it appears from the outside and how it feels from the inside. It is in no small measure through our virtues and vices that our identities are constituted.

But second, and in apparent tension with the preceding observation, virtues are exemplary. In wishing to lead a life of a certain sort, I identify in its masterly practitioners the dispositions that make for doing well, and I apprentice myself as their understudy. One who aspires to a life of piety learns from imitating the practices of the devout spiritual masters how that is done; if it's cricket that is one's game, one takes the batting excellences of Bradman or Botham as models for emulation. This is not to maintain, of course, that any and all recognition of the traits that someone possesses as virtues will motivate one to make those traits one's own. Cricket, after all, may *not* be one's game. The relationship is more accurately expressed as a subjunctive conditional: I identify a disposition that someone possesses as a virtue if it is the case that were I to do what she does, I would wish to do it as she does it. Because not all worthwhile modes of life are compassable, one will frequently have reason to acknowledge value in that which one rejects as an object of pursuit for oneself. So a proper schooling in virtue will include lessons not only in what to do but also what to admire in doings that are distant from one's own modes of activity.

Third, by way of synthesizing the preceding thesis and antithesis, making a virtue one's own manifests individuating self-determination. Even more so does ongoing attachment to the integrated set of virtues that, along with one's projects and ideals, lends distinctive form to the life that is one's own. Because not all good things neatly fit together in one comprehensive package, whether one is going to embrace a particular virtue at all and, if so, then in what manner and to what extent, does not admit of a one-size-fits-all resolution. The distinctive virtues of the cricket player or the pious man of faith may have no place at all in a life that is nonetheless lived well. And even if any satisfactory life demands some amount of kindness to others, to whom one will be kind and the means via which that kindness will be bestowed are matters that different people will, legitimately, resolve differently. I do not mean by this to say that one can spell out in precise measures of tablespoons and teaspoons the recipe of virtues that constitute one's life, if for no other reason than that biographies are not static. Nor do I wish to suggest that the mix is entirely or even for the most part under one's immediate voluntary control. As Aristotle pointed out, the habituation that goes to form character begins early in childhood and is more a matter for ongoing ratification and fine-tuning than for once-and-for-all decision. But it bears emphasizing that assumption of responsibility on a continuing basis for the conceptions of the good and dispositions of character that guide one's activity is itself a virtue: the virtue of integrity.

Fourth, virtues are excellences. They merit esteem. We praise the generous man for his generosity, the meek individual for his humility. And to the extent that we are disinclined to believe that such praise is merited, we thereby express doubt concerning whether these dispositions genuinely are excellences. To possess a virtue is to possess access to an aspect of the good that would not be accessible without that virtue. Whatever uncertainties and epistemological hurdles attach to our knowledge of the good thus attach to our theory of the virtues. What's so great, we might ask, about meekness—or even about the ability sharply to strike a cricket ball? It isn't news to anyone that during the final years of the twentieth century, these uncertainties are profound. Is it possible to construct a postmodern theory of the virtues? I am inclined to think not. At any rate, that is a task I willingly leave to others.

Fifth, and in partial response to the preceding remark, though one may wash down one's moral theorizing with copious draughts of skeptical brew, individuals in their capacity as agents necessarily place their bets concerning that which is worthy of pursuit and that which ought to be shunned. And that is to take a stand, if not with explicit full conscious awareness then at least implicitly, concerning which virtues are to be acknowledged as central to one's makeup. Each of us is stuck with some conception or other of the virtues, if only as a consequence of inadvertence and omission. In this respect, virtues are not a shabby cousin to rights and duties within personal morality. Rather, they define who we are and what we're about in a manner for which there is no substitute.

Certainly attention to the demands of justice, although necessary and admirable, is altogether disqualified from functioning as such a substitute. Justice abstracts from particular conceptions of the good. Because it aspires to universality, justice cannot limn the fine grain of people's lives. And fidelity to justice, except in rare cases, merits no special esteem. "You've gone a whole day without stealing from me—thanks!" is either an insult or a joke. But generosity, compassion, wit, or bravery do elicit a regard that goes beyond mere absence of reproach. Excellences that individuate and that inspire admiration and emulation operate at a level above and beyond the call of duty.

IV

Many of the characteristics of vices can simply be extrapolated from an account of the virtues, with necessary inversions performed along the way. As with virtues, knowing a man's vices is to possess information concerning the shape of his life. Once we understand him to be, say, a miser, we can estimate with a fair degree of accuracy which ends will move him and which will leave him cold, what trade-offs he is prepared or not prepared to make, where we do well not to rely on him. What is true for vices taken singly holds all the more for swarms of vices that define a character.

Moreover, like virtues, vices are exemplary. The indolent, intemperate person is a model for us of what we do not wish to be, a cautionary example for our children of how they are not to grow up. This observation is not restricted to the moral vices. It applies equally well to the athlete who trains diffidently or the journalist who customarily allows pretentiousness to substitute for precision in her prose: if we aspire to success in their vocations we do well to shun their example. Vices, then, have their uses, but it is the sort of utility that instances of disease provide to the healthy. And like diseases, vices are deficiencies, though with this difference: the primary victim may not be the one who suffers from the deficiency but rather those with whom she interacts. A yet more critical difference between them is that disease calls forth sympathy and compassion, whereas vice is reprehensible. We hold people responsible for their vices. The ultimate justification of these judgments runs into a multitude of paradoxes surrounding the compatibility of freedom and causation, but all that needs to be said here is that yet more fundamental than recriminations we bring to the failings of others is our capacity to identify in ourselves our own vices and to hold ourselves accountable for them. With regard to other people, to know all may—I have my doubts—be to forgive all, but that is not the case with first-person judgments. To perceive oneself to have acted without sufficient courage or alacrity or prudence elicits feelings of shame or self-reproach. This capacity for self-monitoring and consequent navigational alterations is requisite for agency. Lacking it, we would be mere spectators of people's lives, our own included. This is another aspect of what was meant by saying that while one's vices and virtues are legitimately subject to appraisal by others, the moral division of labor affords primary responsibility to the individual whose vices and virtues they are.

Among the vices, injustice is unique. An unjust person is one who does what she must not do, who falls below the moral baseline constituted by the legitimate claims of those with whom she interacts. Therefore, injustice, more than any other vice, calls forth reprobation from others. That is not to say that the unjust individual is relieved from responsibility for tending her own character. But injustice is specifically the disposition to trespass across the moral space that belongs to others, and being trespassed against affords one status as primary complainant. It is no accident of social evolution that we have courts of justice but not, say, courts of gluttony or sloth. Socrates may be right—though again I have my doubts—when he maintains that it is worse for a person to do injustice than to be the object of another's injustice, but the allegedly lesser seriousness of the latter does not detract from its capacity to stand as a basis for indictments. It is as serious an error in ethical theorizing to take injustice as emblematic of vices in general as it is to take justice as one's paradigm of the virtues. Perhaps it is even more serious, for this is the characteristic error of perfectionists, paternalists, puritans, busybodies, inquisitors, and totalitarians of all stripes.

So much for the symmetries between virtues and vices. I close this brief disquisition on vice with two important asymmetries. First, the relation between virtues and corresponding vices tends to be not one-to-one but one-to-many. That is because, to use Aristotelian language, there is one way of hitting the Golden Mean dead on, but there are innumerable modes and degrees of misfiring. Perhaps it is this dazzling multiplicity of vices that accounts for the much greater number of engaging scamps and sinners in literature than heroes or saints. It is not because Milton is deficient in piety that the Devil gets all the best lines. Second, we voluntarily make our virtues truly our own, if not by selecting them de novo then by nurturing and ratifying them through our ongoing choices. There is, however, a sense in which we do not choose our vices but, rather, they choose us. It is probably something like this that Socrates has in mind when he issues the outrageous but hard-to-refute conjecture that no person does wrong voluntarily. No one, I think, aspires to cowardice or boorishness as such, but these traits are, as it were, the undesirable accompaniments to persistently myopic or misestimated evaluations of which goods it is worth surrendering to achieve which others. And in this regard familiarity breeds not contempt but, what is worse, complacency and acceptance, such that what were once unwelcome visitors become over time cherished family retainers.

V

The flourishing life, according to Aristotle, is one that manifests complete virtue over an extended period of time. It also requires a tolerable stock of external goods such as money, physical vigor, and a decent social environment. For few of us, alas, is this ideal fully realizable. Not only may fortune shortchange us with regard to the external accoutrements of happiness, but, more ominously, we are creatures notoriously susceptible to vice's manifold charms and seductions. It is one thing to say that we ought to steel ourselves sedulously to despise or at least to resist these enticements, quite another to expect most people to approximate this blessed state. In society as in school, not everyone will score highest marks. Fortunately, there are more diplomas to go around than there are valedictorians. Avoiding failure is not the equivalent of graduating magna cum laude, but neither is it nothing. For this reason, censoriousness is itself a vice. It is to suppose that nothing but the best will do despite the clear fact that often the best we can do is to make do. The moral to be drawn from these reflections is that in morality as in economics, we need alongside a theory of perfectly functioning interactions a theory of the second best.

Toleration eschews perfectionistic credos so as to acknowledge the (minimal) acceptability of all activity conducted above the moral baseline. It thereby establishes itself as the liberal virtue par excellence. In large measure, this explains the contempt for liberal morality maintained by ideologues and utopians of both the left and right. I do not mean to claim that responsiveness to human frailty is the only underpinning of toleration; it also can be justified in terms of respect for individual autonomy, adherence to the dictum "Judge not that ye be not judged," even avoidance of the horrors of the Hobbesian war of all against all. Like a Swiss army knife, toleration has numerous uses. Not least among them is that for individuals who are driven to acknowledge that sainthood is in short supply among their associates, and (casting a rueful inward glance) even in themselves, toleration is a splendid lubricant for countering social frictions. Toleration, then, is a necessary ingredient of the moral theory of the second best.

Once again, justice presents itself as a special case. To be sure, we ought to tolerate many failings and transgressions, but we may not tolerate injustices. People's rights *must* be upheld. A limited exception can be made for discretionary authority on the part of those who have suffered encroachments to pardon those who have wronged them, but the point worth emphasizing is that such discretion is indeed limited: we hold criminal invasions to be not only injuries to the individual who suffers trespass but also offenses against the state, in which lodges ultimate prosecutorial authority. It is precisely this intolerance toward injustice that secures for individuals the moral space within which they may enjoy opportunities to construct for themselves lives of greater or lesser excellence. Toleration is a virtue, but tolerating the intolerable is not.

Justice and injustice aside, primary responsibility for virtues and vices lodges in the individual. Preceding remarks should suffice to explain why it is a gross confusion to infer from this allocation of responsibility the proposition that liberal society is indifferent to distinctions between better and worse, higher and lower. The error is analogous to the supposition that economic markets must be irrational and disorderly because they lack a central planner charged with superintending all transactions. Similarly fallacious is the oft-voiced criticism that liberal toleration amounts to a doctrine of "atomistic" individuals. The criticism rests on erroneous moral chemistry. The odd noble gas aside, our lives are thoroughly molecular. Some of the bonds are stable and others evanescent. Taken together, they constitute richly plural and individuated patterns of association that belie the charge of atomism. To espouse toleration is not to endorse solipsistic isolation but rather to insist that the valences that draw people together (and pull them apart) be their own rather than imposed from without.[9]

Further, ascriptions of primary responsibility are not grants of monopoly. As John Stuart Mill observed,[10] not for the first time but perhaps most eloquently, toleration leaves ample scope for morally significant responses to perceived quality distinctions in people's characters. First, each of us enjoys a prerogative to extend admiration and disapproval as we see fit; it is an atomism of the rankest sort to suppose that these must be impotent unless underscored by the fist in the glove. Second, we can emulate that which we find admirable and shun that which we find base. Third, we possess a wide liberty to undertake initiatives in persuasion. We may cajole, plead, suggest, remonstrate, proselytize, petition, endorse, warn, implore; we can also set an example. (The supposition that tolerant individuals refrain from subjecting others to "value judgments" is yet another gross misunderstanding of the implications of liberal morality.) Fourth, we may offer or withhold association. In all these ways and variations thereon, fully consonant with the strictures of tolerance, one can amply respond to differences between virtue and vice.

Targets of remonstration can respond in a variety of ways to would-be reformers. One, of course, is gratitude followed by conversion. Its contrary is the response "That's *my business*; back off!" Both are legitimate. The second of these can, alternately, be phrased "That's *none of your business*," but there is a subtle difference in meaning between these formulations. Whereas the former affirms one's own controlling stake in the matter under question, the latter goes beyond that to deny to anyone else even a subsidiary legitimate interest. But is that really a theorem of liberal morality? Or is it rather the case that liberal toleration countenances a rationale for regarding another's rights-respecting conduct as falling to a limited extent within one's own purview?

The answer, I think, is that we do have something of a direct interest in how others comport themselves within their own allotment of moral space, and that for much the same reason that nations have a significant interest in how other nations conduct their internal affairs. Put most simply, borders now respected can later be crossed; that which is not now injurious may nonetheless constitute a threat of subsequent injury. This is not to withdraw the earlier claim that a propensity to police the vices of others is itself a vice—nor, for that matter, should the present analogy be interpreted as denying that many so-called preemptive defensive strikes by one nation against another are in fact acts of naked aggression. Nonetheless, and with full acknowledgment of the dangers of self-serving biases and slippery slopes down which one might careen, it is implausible to maintain that a liberal morality allows severe reprisals after infringements of rights have occurred but entirely rules out advance measures to thwart such breaches.

It is not possible here even to gesture toward formulation of the conditions necessary and sufficient to legitimize preemption. So blithely assuming that task away, let us look instead at the problem as it presents itself to someone who understands that others may have reason from their perspective to launch preemptive incursions and who wishes to avoid supplying provocations that render likely such an onset of hostilities. One effective way of addressing the problem is to broadcast convincing evidence of one's inoffensiveness. Consider again the conduct of internal affairs by potentially hostile nations. One country builds a reactor that it maintains is for the peaceful generation of nuclear power, but the other isn't so sure. If the intent of the first country is indeed pacific, it might do well to become a party to international protocols governing the use of nuclear materials, throw its nuclear installation open to inspection by neutral parties, employ a reactor design that all authorities acknowledge cannot easily be turned to bellicose purposes, and so on. Similarly, when in private arenas suspicions run high, individuals may be well advised to take special pains to render their intentions transparent to those who fear an imminent launching of incursions.

What is the relevance of this to a liberal theory of vices and virtues? It is that the perils of vice are wider-reaching than may be immediately apparent. Even "self-regarding" ones may place others at risk insofar as they are liable to expand into the realm of the other-regarding. Vices, at least some of them, are peaceful reactors that are all too susceptible to transformation into producers of the moral equivalent of weapons-grade plutonium. Those with whom one interacts have an interest in being given an assurance that the sloppy overflow of one's own vices will not engulf them.

To say this is not to allow the hectoring intrusiveness that was barred at the front door to sneak in through the back. Much vice is simply negligible from the perspective of others. If you are inclined toward sloth and forgetfulness, I might do well not to make any early morning appointments with you, but otherwise I can be benignly indifferent to your habitual lack of punctuality. Moreover, in a world brimming with risks of one sort or another, only the fanatic (vainly) demands total assurance from all quarters. To repeat: with vices as with virtues, primary responsibility devolves on the individual in question. Qualifications duly noted, it is nonetheless reasonable to be wary of individuals in rough proportion to the extent that they are in the grip of their vices. One of the most important symptoms of the moral vices, often ascending to a defining feature, is that they promote self-absorption and thereby lead one to be insufficiently responsive to the interests of others.

Our vocabulary of virtues and vices has atrophied during this century, no doubt reflecting in large measure the discomfort modern moral theory has with these concepts. We tend to restrict our moral appraisals to conduct that infringes people's rights. It is, therefore, revealing that among the features held in common by the diminished list of dispositions onto which we still tend to pin the not-quite-obsolescent rubric "vice" is a pronounced tendency to generate impermissible crossings of the borders that secure the moral space of others.

Some examples: habitual drunkenness is inimical to powers of cogitation and is bad for the liver. These are self-regarding deficiencies. But it is also notoriously the case that drunkards' inordinate love of the grog leads them to neglect obligations owed to others. They perform poorly as husbands or mothers or friends; their work at the factory or office is sloppy; they commit mayhem on the highways. When the need for the next drink and the seven after that takes highest priority in one's life, other concerns, including attentiveness to the interests of others, inevitably move down on the queue. And what is true of alcohol holds true, mutatis mutandis, for other addictions. Whether it is the heroin addict who steals to get money to pay for his next fix or the cigarette smoker for whom the urgency of lighting up outweighs regard for the breathing preferences of those in her immediate vicinity, the habitual consumption of drugs puts civility at risk.

Gamblers are moved by the lure of the big payoff, but they also relish the action for its own sake. When from an occasional invigorating pastime the urge to place a bet—and another, and another—grows into a central preoccupation of one's life, the track, slot machines, and point spread crowd out other objects of concern. One will imprudently put at risk one's own well-being, that of one's children, or anyone from whom a line of credit can be solicited. All to double down on black or draw to the next straight.

Drink and gambling dispose one toward self-absorption. Sexual passion deviates from this pattern insofar as it heightens fixation both on self and on the object of one's desire. Sexuality, unlike addiction, is not solipsistic; it naturally finds its home in intimate two-person worlds of its own construction. However, the correlative of capturing within one's orbit and being captured by the one who is desired is exclusion of all other persons from the duality's gravitational field. Sexual activity and its various anticipations, postludes, auras, and penumbras weave around the partners a phenomenological curtain that blocks awareness of the outside world or makes its affairs seem small, commonplace, too humdrum to merit full attention. Lust, therefore, as with cravings for drink or gambling, is a jealous passion that does not easily brook competition. Much of the world's great literature—and an even greater percentage of its potboilers and Hollywood schlock—presents lovers consumed by their passion. Frequently they are star-crossed; frequently their story ends in tragedy. These denouements may be considered self-regarding, at least if we reconceptualize the "self" to be the double-backed beast of the Greek poets, but this literature is also replete with other-regarding side effects. For the sake of the beloved—and the beloved's beloved—one will cheat, lie, dissemble, kill, forsake vows, give oneself over to treachery and disloyalty without limit. The horrifically intense single-mindedness of lust is what makes it so lovely a medium for a wallow, either firsthand or vicarious.

VI

A world without intoxicating drugs, gambling parlors, and passion-driven romance would be a much safer world. It would also be unbearably tedious. No doubt we should all pursue these pleasures only in moderation, always squarely hitting the virtuous mean. But this is a pipe dream. In all our activities, and most especially those in which intense pleasures are engaged, we overshoot, undershoot, shoot ourselves in the foot. We pose risks to ourselves and, by extension, to others. A theory of the vices, if it is to be practical, cannot confine itself to the injunction: Avoid! It must, as was urged previously, incorporate in addition a theory of the second best.

Systems of manners and decorum are practically responsive to that theoretical demand.[11] Good manners are, no doubt, adornments that add luster to all departments of one's life. But they are especially critical as accompaniments to one's vices. In at least two respects, rules of etiquette render the practice of vice less risky. First, a decorously practiced vice is intrinsically less dangerous. By confining the practice of vice in accordance with rules of time, place, quantity, and quality, manners check tendencies toward excesses that might inflict harms on oneself or others. But second and less obviously, attentiveness to etiquette has a crucial epistemological function. Through punctilious observance of conventional forms, one indicates one's continued allegiance to norms of interpersonal civility, including the most fundamental precepts of the social contract. Manners demand attentiveness to boundaries between self and others. They afford visible indicators that one retains control of one's vices rather than being controlled by them. Conversely, erosion of manners presents an early-warning signal of disorders liable to engulf others in their wake.

For these and other reasons, contemporary infatuations with the quasi-Rousseauian cult of "authenticity" and "acting naturally" are to be deplored as loosening the constraints that temper our vices and hold them in check. Rules of etiquette are disparaged as artificialities, invidiously contrasted with our natural impulses. But the natural human condition is laced with ignorance, enmity, aggression, and premature death. These are meliorated by the virtues. An invaluable second line of defense, though, is the mannerly pursuit of vice. Whatever may be the case with regard to our command of the virtues, we are demonstrably less well endowed with tools to domesticate vice than were our nineteenth- and eighteenth-century forebears. They possessed elaborate codes and ceremonies that manifested wariness concerning and simultaneously guarded against the attractive and centrifugal forces of familiar vices. We have, for better or worse, mostly consigned these to oblivion. I say "for better or worse" in open acknowledgment of the fact that codes of etiquette may be tiresome, invidiously discriminatory, stultifying. Caveats duly noted, it nonetheless is worth considering whether in tossing out the bathwater of class-ridden, Victorian arcana we may have inadvertently overlooked a baby or two hidden amidst the suds.

Why don a particular item of apparel reserved for the occasion and exile the gentlemen from the ladies before one is permitted to indulge one's taste in tobacco? By contemporary standards, this ritual must surely be seen as unacceptably formalistic and sexist. However, the custom aspired to and in large measure succeeded in preventing smoke damage to the fabric of the social contract. It implicitly acknowledged that while some individuals take great pleasure in the consumption of tobacco, others find it offensive to be a recipient of secondhand smoke. Admittedly, the supposition that the boundary between tobacco partisans and disdainers runs neatly along the sexual divide was too facile, and after the application of persistent pressure from feminists who demanded equal access to the cigarette box as well as the ballot box, it gave way. But imperfect as the etiquette of smoking may have been, it was nonetheless of considerable utility in preventing damage to social relations. Cloaking the practice of smoking in a mantle of manners afforded explicit recognition of the moral salience of its other-regarding aspects. By voluntarily separating themselves prior to the time for ignition, smokers conveyed to nonsmokers their intention not to give offense. Nonsmokers reciprocated with an implied message that although they themselves found effusions of tobacco clouds unwelcome, they were not inclined to impose their tastes on reluctant others. Also significant is that the separation was for a fixed duration that was preceded and succeeded by periods of conviviality between members of the two groups. Confining indulgence of the vice in accord with accepted albeit imperfect principles of time, place, and gender signaled its domestication.

Today, the smoking jacket, the garment designed to capture and sequester residual smoke aromas, has ascended to fashion heaven where it joins the codpiece and bustle. Are we happier for its demise? Not obviously. After years of suffering obnoxious smoke blown in their faces, nonsmokers have snatched power from the smokers and firmly taken the offensive. Smokers are thrust into tobacco apartheid and may be glimpsed outside of office buildings huddling together for warmth and spiritual solidarity in subfreezing temperatures as they snatch a few coveted puffs before shuffling back to their desks. Evangelists against tobacco censor commercial speech, paste citations from prohibitionist scriptures where smokers will be forced to view them, and with unflagging zeal deliver antinicotine sermons to reluctant auditors. Meanwhile, dispirited by the dramatic slide in their fortunes, consumers of tobacco mutter imprecations and appeal for redress in the name of a heretofore unobserved curiosity called "smokers' rights." Every so often a nonsmoker shoots an offending smoker, or vice versa, although admittedly this usually happens in places such as California where even modest impositions inspire fusillades. Legislation fills the vacuum created by the withdrawal of an acknowledged informal order of manners, and whatever else one might say about the result, it bespeaks a diminished level of civility.

Similar reflections attach to other familiar vices. In bygone days, much ceremony attended the quaffing of wine and spirits. For each beverage a specified time and manner of presentation was observed during the evening's festivities. Proprieties governed selection of stemware, placement of the candle while decanting the port, and subsequent distribution of the various liquid treasures. The ritual was far from empty. Alcohol, it was well known, could master a man, and so the etiquette of drinking served, among other functions, to supply visible indication of mastery over it. To be sure, it was not unknown for some imbibers to get a head start on intoxication or to pursue it long after others had set down their glasses, but ladies and gentlemen took the extra drams with as much surreptitiousness as they could muster, so as to give lip (and palate) service to conventional forms. To dismiss such dissembling as the hypocritical tribute that vice pays to virtue is to fail to attend with sufficient seriousness to the fact that payments of tribute do indeed matter. They convey a message that one's breaches of conventions, even if periodic and frequent, are accompanied by continued acknowledgment of the conventions' legitimacy. Transgression was thereby distinguished from rebellion. (Compare with the practice of civil disobedience.) *Victorian* has become a byword for a culture of sexual repressions and subterranean sublimations. Yet despite their straitlaced facades, the Victorians were not altogether unfamiliar with the manifold entertainments of adulteries and fornications. Indeed, the strictness of their codes of sexual conduct bespoke an awareness that carnal pleasure is a remarkably potent solvent, and that the disorder it engenders within the primal society of the domestic union tends ineluctably to ripple outward so as to fray other social ligatures. Thus, to the extent that sexual indulgences not sanctified by bonds of matrimony resist eradication through reminders of the spiritual joys of chastity, they must be confined so as to minimize damages that will otherwise ensue. Those who were parties, either directly or indirectly, to illicit sexual congresses had a keen interest in keeping them private, and when they broke into public view via messy suits for divorce or the sort of prosecution that landed Oscar Wilde in Reading Gaol, all sides were losers. Although statistics of an accuracy that would satisfy social scientists are unavailable, it does seem to be the case that the Victorians achieved a considerable degree of success in regulating by a regimen of manners even this most unruly of human passions.

That is not to deny that our predecessors paid a considerable price reckoned in repressions, gender and class discriminations, dissimulations, and neuroses to maintain the effectiveness of their informal orders. We may speculate concerning whether the gains thereby accrued outweighed these costs and whether the Victorians might have availed themselves of more efficient and less oppressive instruments for securing the desired ends. At any rate, nostalgia for anachronistic codes of etiquette is pointless, and attempts to restore those practices are worse than pointless: insofar as they tend to bring all concern for manners into disrepute, they are counterproductive. We do not need and could not live with conventions that reflect the modes of life of a thoroughly defunct epoch. We do, though, remain very much in need of a theory and concomitant practice of the morally second best. Without it, we will experience continued raveling of the social fabric and find ourselves increasingly driven to stretching patterns of justice and injustice, rights and duties, where they do not fit. Liberal morality will either overcome its discomfort with vice and virtue or else become increasingly incapable of sustaining an ethical environment in which ordinary men and women might flourish.

NOTES

1. Nancy L. Rosenblum, "The Moral Uses of Pluralism" (chap. 10 in this volume).

2. Robert Nozick, *Anarchy, State, and Utopia* (New York: Basic Books, 1974), 28–35.

3. Ronald Dworkin, *Taking Rights Seriously* (Cambridge, Mass.: Harvard University Press, 1987), xi.

4. Let me add, however, that whether in a particular case it is appropriate to blame or punish is a practical determination that must itself pass through the utilitarian filter.

5. I note for the record that numerous sophisticated utilitarians and Kantians have attempted to fill in these lacunae. It is not possible here to lend even a cursory glance at those inventions; I judge even the best of these to be more ingenious than satisfying. But even if one believes that utilitarianism or Kantianism can with some effort in fact make some place for virtues and vices, the difficulty of that project is itself revealing.

6. The sketch that follows is derived from my book *Persons, Rights and the Moral Community* (New York: Oxford University Press, 1987).

7. The following characterization basically follows, with occasional embellishments, that of Aristotle in *Nicomachean Ethics*. As will be apparent, however, I do not accept the Aristotelian thesis of the unity of the (moral) virtues.

8. So, for example, John Rawls, "Justice is the first virtue of social institutions," in *A Theory of Justice* (Cambridge, Mass.: Harvard University Press, 1971), 3.

9. What is to be made of calls for civic renewal predicated on the proposition that practices of voluntary association have dangerously atrophied in recent years? I am reluctant to address the question, both because I possess no special expertise on the topic and because so many other contributors to this volume do. Nonetheless, it would be unsporting not to dip an oar into the water, so I offer the following impressionistic observation. Because the liberal conception of human nature is not atomistic, liberals generally assume, in the absence of strong evidence to the contrary, that people left to their own devices will form social ties sufficient unto their needs. Alexis de Tocqueville's theorization of associational dynamics within liberal democracies remains uncontravened. It does, however, require two addenda. First, it is likely that a kind of Gresham's law is operative such that bad association tends to drive out good. Specifically, instrumentalities of a state possessing the power to tax and the power to regulate can, in virtue of those advantages and not because of any inherent superiority of political structures, displace the functions of voluntary associations. Affection for the latter ought to engender a presumption against the former. That presumption is, of course, defeasible, but it is not negligible. Second, nothing serves better as a pretext for rolling out the big guns of the policy-making arsenal than do crises, whether these be real or mirages. I do not profess knowledge concerning whether people are in fact bowling alone more frequently these days, nor do I have any serviceable intuitions concerning whether, if true, that is a bad thing. I am, though, willing to wager that scores of pundits and politicians will find in this alleged fact grounds for copious legislation and fiscal appropriations to meet the emergency. These siren songs can most safely be listened to while firmly lashed to the liberal mast.

10. See John Stuart Mill, *On Liberty*, especially chap. 3, "Of Individuality, as One of the Elements of Well-being."

11. The normative significance of etiquette receives further discussion in my review of Judith Martin's *Miss Manners Rescues Civilization* in *Reason* 28 (April 1997): 61–65.

PART FOUR

RELIGION AND RACE

12

Religion, Philanthropy, and Political Culture

Kathleen D. McCarthy

Jeremiads are a time-honored American tradition. Initiated by the Puritans, honed and perfected in the colonial era, and amplified over the course of the nineteenth century, they reached new levels of statistical authority in the twentieth century. One of the most provocative contemporary jeremiads holds that community and political participation have precipitously declined at the threshold of the twenty-first century. Observers lament that Americans are abandoning long-standing bonds of communal cohesion. To quote the noted political scientist Robert Putnam, we are increasingly "bowling alone."

Several contemporary indices seem to bear this out. Perhaps the most striking figures indicate a waning faith in the efficacy of government. Three and a half decades ago, during the heyday of American liberalism, 76 percent of Americans expressed their "trust of the government in Washington," a figure that dipped to 25 percent in 1995. Voter participation plummeted to less than 50 percent in the presidential election of 1996, the smallest turnout since the 1920s. Overall, voter turnout has steadily declined since 1966, with only a reported 45 percent of Americans voting for public office or on political issues at any governmental level.

Public opinion polls further underscore the depth of the country's malaise: 67 percent of the respondents in one poll complained of a "long-term moral decline," while 78 percent reported that they were "dissatisfied with moral values." Who or what is responsible for the country's fin-de-siècle crisis of confidence? Is Americans' faith in the country's social institutions dissolving in a sea of "civic non-participation" and "widespread cynicism"?[1]

The answer to these questions is vitally important to the nation's future. But the cause of this much-heralded decline is extremely difficult to pinpoint, particularly when focusing on such nebulous and highly alluring concepts as "civil society." Civil society has been variously defined as the interstices between the family and the state (Hegel); the "public sphere" that fosters citizen interchange (Habermas); and the voluntaristic arena in which "trust" is generated and social capital accumulated (Putnam). Some definitions include the market; others do not. But the common denominator that runs through almost every definition of civil society is the nonprofit sector: those social, educational, and charitable services and volunteer groups that facilitate citizen participation outside the formal contexts of elected office and "for-profit" commercialism. And philanthropy—the giving of time, money, and/or valuables for public benefit—is a major force in the development and survival of this "voluntary sector."[2]

Is America unraveling, as the statistical jeremiads suggest? Or do some institutions within this vast universe of civil society actors remain stronger than others, providing clues to ways in which national participation as a whole might be strengthened? In this chapter I explore one type of voluntary organization—religious institutions—tracing the contemporary and historical roles of these groups in fostering civic and political participation.

RELIGION AND CIVIC PARTICIPATION: CONTEMPORARY TRENDS

Viewed from the perspective of the altar rather than the polling booth, citizen participation seems far healthier than current jeremiads would suggest. Although faith in government may be waning, philanthropic participation remains widespread. According to statistics compiled by Virginia Hodgkinson and Murray Weitzman for Independent Sector, an estimated ninety-three million Americans volunteered in 1995, contributing approximately $201 billion in donated time. Almost 70 percent of the households polled reported charitable gifts. Moreover, religion played a strikingly important role in marshaling this participation:

- In 1996, 55 percent of the church members polled reported participating in volunteer activities, as opposed to 34 percent of nonchurch members. Between 1987 and 1996, levels of voluntarism among church members fluctuated between 50 and 59 percent.
- Seventy-six to 80 percent of the respondents who were church mem-

bers reported making household contributions for philanthropic purposes, as opposed to 50 to 64 percent among nonchurch members.
Frequency of church attendance was also a factor, with giving levels
highest among those who attended religious services on a weekly
basis: 3.4 percent of household income was donated by weekly atten-
dants, 1.4 percent by those who attended sporadically, and 1.1 percent by those who did not attend religious services.
- Sixty-four percent of those who *regularly* attended religious services
volunteered, and 83 percent reported household contributions.

Contrary to views that cast the United States as a relatively secularized
nation, religious participation is on the upswing. According to Hodgkinson and Weitzman, membership in religious organizations grew between
1987 and 1993, and "held steady in 1995." The number of religious institutions is also growing: 20 percent of the approximately 260,000 religious
congregations for which data were available in 1991 were founded after
1971.[3]

These activities have political as well as civic implications. Giving, voluntarism, and the support they provide to voluntary associations lie at
the heart of civil society. Religion plays a critical part in these activities. It
has often been noted that America is one of the most generous, if not the
most generous, country in the world, and a major portion of that generosity flows through religious coffers. Statistics compiled by the American
Association of Fund-Raising Counsel over the past three decades indicate
that approximately 45 to 50 percent of all dollars given by any source—
individuals, foundations, and corporations—are given to religious organizations. Much of this money comes from small donations dropped in
the weekly collection plate. Far from an elite monopoly, these are practices that resonate through every level of society.[4]

Nor is this beneficence limited to sectarian purposes. As noted in Independent Sector's study of religious giving and voluntarism, *From Belief to
Commitment*:

- In 1991, religious congregations spent $53.3 billion, including $34.2
billion in cash donations and $19.2 billion in volunteer time.
- Of this, approximately 60 percent went for religious activities, with
the remaining 40 percent allocated for health, education, and welfare
services in the following ratios:
   education: 14 percent
   human services: 8 percent
   health and hospitals: 8 percent
   arts and culture: 2 percent
   human justice and social benefit: 1 percent

environment: 1 percent
international: 1 percent
other: 4 percent

In effect, religious participation not only encourages people to give and volunteer, and to do so more generously than the majority of unchurched Americans, but it does so in ways that are deeply woven into the fabric of civil society at the community, national, and international levels, both within and beyond the context of individual congregations.[5]

Moreover, churches are often heavily involved in nonprofit service delivery, with approximately 92 percent of all 236,000 religious congregations for which data were available in 1992 reporting "one or more programs in human service and welfare, including 73 percent with . . . youth programs." In addition, 62 percent were involved in foreign relief, 53 percent in education, and 90 percent in health-related efforts. Many served as community centers as well: six out of ten congregations reported sharing their facilities with other groups in their communities.[6]

Clearly, religious institutions have assumed an important and growing role in conscripting volunteers, encouraging giving, and increasing the resources available to other types of voluntary associations. They provide charitable, educational, and social welfare services, and constitute a "public sphere" for community interchange and social action. They also enhance political participation. As political scientists such as Sidney Verba have pointed out, "it is incomplete and misleading to understand citizen participation solely through the vote." Instead, Verba defines any organization that "takes stands on public issues either nationally or locally" as political, emphasizing the centrality of religious congregations in drawing people of all classes into volunteer work and providing them with opportunities to hone their political skills through community service.[7]

HISTORICAL TRENDS: VOLUNTARISM AND POLITICAL CULTURE

Verba's findings stress that American democracy and political participation extend well beyond the ballot box, a theme reiterated with growing forcefulness by historians—especially women's historians—since the 1980s. Instead of looking solely at voting patterns as the measure of political participation, these scholars argue, it is necessary to examine the entire *political culture*, including "any action, formal or informal, taken to affect the course or behavior of government or the community." Cast in these terms, even once-disfranchised groups, such as women and African Americans, suddenly emerge as political actors.[8]

For women, the links between religion, voluntarism, and political activism have historically been strong, alliances that date from the country's infancy. Although the earliest women's voluntary associations were not always specifically denominational in intent, churches were a significant force in mobilizing female volunteers. Two kinds of charitable organizations were founded by middle- and upper-class white women in the decades immediately following the Revolution: charities for women and children, and asylums. And these earliest organizations provide a lens for examining the relation between female voluntarism and political culture in the country's formative decades.

Although no women's voluntary associations have been traced to the colonial era, they began to proliferate in the 1790s. Philadelphia's first citywide women's charity, the Female Society for Assisting the Distressed, was founded in 1795. By 1798, the founders were providing outdoor relief for females of all races, religions, and ethnic groups, and had established a house of industry where impoverished women received food and day care services while they spun linen for wages. By 1800 a Female Association for Poor Women with Children and a Magdalen Society had also been created to help the city's female poor, while the Society for the Relief of Poor Widows with Small Children ("Widows' Society") performed similar services in New York.

The timing of the creation of the Widows' Society was fortuitous. Shortly after it was founded by two Scotch emigrées, Isabella Graham and her daughter, Joanna Bethune, in 1797, New York was racked by yellow fever, leaving legions of "respectable, industrious women" with neither work nor food. Within months, over 190 subscribers and approximately a thousand donors of one-time gifts had come forward with contributions. Graham captured the sense of emergency, noting that "the poor increase fast; emigrants from all quarters flock to us, and when they come they must not be allowed to die for want."[9]

Many of their clients apparently did die over the following disease-laden summers, and in the 1810s Joanna Bethune and a group of younger women took the lead in founding the city's first orphanage. Inspired by Benjamin Franklin's description of a European orphan asylum, it was one of several female orphanages created by elite white women after the turn of the century. In addition to the "home" in New York, similar institutions appeared in Boston in 1800; Savannah in 1801; Norfolk, Virginia, in 1804; and Petersburg, Virginia, Fayetteville, North Carolina, Natchez, Mississippi, Philadelphia, and Baltimore over the ensuing decade. The women who pioneered in the creation of these institutions aided the poor, but they also helped themselves by creating expanded public roles outside the domestic sphere. The trickle of charities that began in the 1790s, and the flood of religiously oriented societies that followed, provided new levels of public, political, and economic authority for their female sponsors in ways that had not previously existed.

Participation in charitable organizations also gave married women a political identity that they lacked as individuals. Membership in a chartered nonprofit organization enabled wives to collectively own and alienate property, a right denied them under the common-law doctrine of *femme couverte*. Indeed, married women's inability to control property was one of the primary rationales for excluding them from direct political participation, in the belief that "only men secure in their property could be virtuous."[10]

A charter enabled an organization to "make binding rules for self-government, to function in law as a single person with the right to hold property and to sue and be sued—and so protect its assets—and to persist after the lifetimes of its founding members." In effect, corporations were considered "agencies of government . . . for the furtherance of community purposes." Attaining a charter was a political act, with each petition considered on a case-by-case basis by state legislatures. To win their charters, women used the same right of petition that was guaranteed under the First Amendment. Although "the most primitive of political mechanisms," petitioning opened the way to public roles in the alternative provision of services.[11]

Women's groups were able to gain charters, despite their members' lack of political authority, because they provided needed services for cash-starved and overburdened governments. As a result, these practices were not only tolerated but encouraged, often through the addition of public funds, which were mingled with donations from a variety of sources: subscriptions pledged over the long term, one-time donations from both women and men, investments, and income-generating projects ranging from fund-raising fairs to quasi-commercial ventures. Sometimes women's charities received municipal contracts for their products. On other occasions, they netted outright donations. Municipal grants to private charities acknowledged the role of these institutions in lessening the burdens on the public till and in reducing almshouse populations. Women's charities received public allocations in several cities during the early national period, including Philadelphia, Baltimore, New Orleans, New York, and even rural North Carolina. New York City and state were particularly generous, providing women's, immigrant, and African-American groups and a variety of religious denominations with public land, housing, and funds for their charitable and educational work in the early nineteenth century. All of these constituencies thus assumed a direct role in the allocation of municipal resources and services.[12]

The point here is twofold. First, voluntarism enabled even disfranchised groups to participate politically when, in terms of voting behavior, they were essentially invisible. Second, the notion that there was once a "golden age" in which public and private responsibilities were totally separate is a serious misreading of the historical record. Charities and the educational institutions created by white male elites regularly received public donations of cash and land during the colonial era, practices which expanded after the Revolution to include women and (in a few instances) African Americans. Nor were these purely local practices. Missionary Societies received public funding for their educational work in Indian territories, and the federal government relied heavily on organizations such as the American Philosophical Society for advice and aid. America's nonprofit sector was often intertwined with different levels of government in the provision of public services, processes that began with legislative deliberations in granting charters to individual charities. Thus, voluntarism and nonprofit organizations provide an important perspective for reassessing the meaning of American democracy, even among disfranchised groups.

HISTORICAL TRENDS: RELIGION AND CIVIL SOCIETY

Women's philanthropy was born of the Revolution, but it matured in the church. By the 1810s, women's institutional networks began to expand exponentially, weaving grids of female organizational activity across the breadth of the new republic. Religion was a major catalyst in these developments. The activities that Isabella Graham and Elizabeth Seton, the founder and the first treasurer of the Widows' Society, pursued after the turn of the century exemplified the impact of different religious currents on the development of female voluntarism. Protestantism and Roman Catholicism each left a distinctive imprint on civil society, as well as on women's political roles.

Protestantism

Protestantism—especially evangelical Protestantism—was the single most important factor in the growth and elaboration of American nonprofit activities during the early national period, not only because of its numerical strength, but because of the extent to which doctrinal and organizational structures influenced parishioners' public lives. Far from discouraging the growth of religious institutions, the disestablishment of state churches that Thomas Jefferson and James Madison set in motion in the 1780s (culminating with the disestablishment of Congregationalism in Massachusetts in 1833) spawned a kaleidoscope of sects. It "built the churches into the structure of civil society," reshaping American Protestantism into a "mass enterprise" in the decades following the Revolution.[13]

The driving engine behind much of this expansion was the Second Great Awakening, the rush of religious enthusiasm that began in the 1790s and crested in the Jacksonian era. In the process, churches became increasingly "feminized." Estimates place the proportion of female converts in northeastern revivals as high as 70 percent between 1795 and 1815, giving women a commanding presence within a growing variety of Protestant institutions.[14]

As women increasingly filled the pews, they also assumed much of the responsibility for raising funds, which in turn bolstered their authority. Both black and white women assumed substantial responsibility for supporting capital improvements and church-related social services, including charitable relief. Fund-raising was particularly important. In addition to serving the needs of their immediate congregations, Protestant women developed a host of cent, mite, missionary, tract, and Bible societies during the first quarter of the nineteenth century. By the 1810s, the movement to create fund-raising auxiliaries gathered an astonishing momentum, accounting for more than a thousand organizations in New England alone. Nor was this solely a sectional phenomenon. Nashville had a Female Bible and Charitable Society by 1817, and Charleston's Female Domestic Missionary Society was launched the following year. Virginia, too, had a number of women's Bible, tract, and missionary societies by 1820. These groups raised substantial sums, initially for local goals, but increasingly for national causes and institutions. By 1816, they began to consolidate into centralized, national organizations designed to promote a variety of religiously oriented endeavors under the guidance of prominent male trustees, from the American Bible Society to the Presbyterians' powerful American Board of Commissioners of Foreign Missions, which mingled women's donations with federal funds.[15]

Women provided critical support for these infrastructures, and they assumed a particularly prominent managerial role in the development of the nation's Sunday Schools. Isabella Graham founded one of the country's first Sunday Schools in 1792. By 1829, more than 40 percent of all the children in New York were enrolled in these institutions, more than double the number that attended the city's schools. Nationally, estimates placed the number of students in the American Sunday School Union's seven hundred auxiliary networks at fifty thousand in 1825; five years later that number had increased tenfold, with operations in every state.[16]

Middle-class laywomen organized many of these classes, volunteering to teach reading, writing, and Bible studies. Their efforts fostered a stunning upsurge in national literacy rates. In 1780, only about 50 percent of the women in New England could sign their names; by 1840 almost all could. In an era when comprehensive, compulsory public education was still in the future for most states, Sunday Schools fueled the democratization of basic education in tandem with the other national religious groups that comprised the Benevolent Empire.[17]

At one level, these activities represented the growing financial and social power of religiously oriented associations. But the statistics hold a deeper, more profound meaning, not just for women's activities but for the growth of civil society. Religious disestablishment and the Second Great Awakening brought a new kind of religious experience to the fore. While Anglicans clung to their liturgy and rituals, and orthodox Congregationalism retained a stern emphasis on predestination, disestablishment cleared the way for more vigorous proselytizing by evangelical sects: Baptists, Methodists, Presbyterians, and non-Calvinistic Congregationalists. Unlike many of their predecessors, these sects emphasized the power of individual conversion, grace, and human perfectibility. For them, the ability to read the Bible for oneself was the basis of religious faith. Eschewing ritual and learned texts, they promoted a more accessible version of religious belief. And the key to that religious experience was literacy.

Evangelicalism was the primary impetus for the rapid spread of Bible and tract societies. It was the driving force behind Sunday Schools. Its popularity also provides the key to understanding the impact of Protestantism in promoting the development of civil society in the United States after 1800. The ability to read brought with it the ability to transmit ideas; to correspond with like-minded groups; to argue one's case in print as well as in person. And that ability sparked an avalanche of organizational activity that both fed and was nurtured by evangelical Christianity. Women provided the bulk of the converts and funds for its expansion, and as they were schooled in the Bible, they taught others to read as part of their religious duties.

Evangelical injunctions to go out and save the world provided an additional stimulus to organizational elaboration and reform. The doctrines of immediate grace and human perfectibility were deeply empowering, giving female converts as much of a stake in defining and acting on social ills as men. Christianity became "a liberating force; people were given the right to think and act for themselves rather than depending on the mediation of an educated elite," trends which increasingly led Protestant laywomen into advocacy and social reform by the 1830s. From antebellum female moral reform societies and abolitionist campaigns, to the massive Gilded Age networks of ladies' missionary societies and the Women's Christian Temperance Union, Protestantism was a major force in drawing American women into social advocacy and reform.[18]

This, then, was the Protestant legacy after disestablishment turned the nation's churches into voluntary associations in the wake of the Revolution: (1) women's increasing visibility, numbers, and power within a rapidly expanding array of congregations; (2) their increasingly central economic roles, which accorded them authority within the church, as well as ministerial backing for their charitable work; and (3) the growing predominance of a cluster of doctrines that stressed literacy, charity, and advocacy—all of which encouraged evangelical laywomen to assume a prominent part in building civil society. In the process, American Protestantism opened expanding opportunities for women's participation in political culture through service provision and social advocacy, charity and social reform—and a relentlessly proliferating universe of voluntary associations.

Catholicism

Like her colleague Isabella Graham, Elizabeth Seton played a pioneering role in the creation of new types of women's voluntary and nonprofit organizations. Each was reared with a post-Revolutionary veneration for learning, and each devised ways of translating that reverence into distinctively religious terms. Yet there were telling differences as well. In particular, while Graham marshaled support for her ventures independently among the laity, Seton's work increasingly developed within the context of an emerging religious hierarchy.

One of the unintended legacies of Seton's success in building the Sisters of Charity of St. Joseph, America's first indigenous order of nuns, was that it helped edge Catholic laywomen to the voluntaristic sidelines, where they were tapped as parish-based fund-raisers and supporters, but little more. Both during the early republican phase of American Catholicism, which was marked by a high degree of lay autonomy, and in the ensuing phase of episcopal consolidation, laywomen were accorded markedly narrower volunteer roles than their Protestant counterparts.

Unlike Protestantism, the Catholic Church commanded only modest numbers of adherents prior to the massive influx of Irish immigrants during the 1840s and 1850s. Estimates place the number of Catholic churches at slightly more than fifty in 1780, a figure that doubled three decades later. At the time of Washington's election in 1789, there were fewer than thirty thousand Catholics in the United States, most of whom resided in the Middle Atlantic region. Within this milieu, churches were scattered, episcopal authority was limited, and parishes were often highly independent.[19]

One of the earmarks of the early national period was a deeply ingrained suspicion of centralized authority, a suspicion that played out among Catholics in a drive for local congregational autonomy that replicated the decentralization of many Protestant denominations. As in other sects, the laymen who supported these churches initially had a decisive hand in controlling their affairs. Within Catholic congregations, this translated into a dual emphasis on trusteeism: the right of lay trustees to own and control church properties, and to select and dismiss their parish priests. In effect, Protestant precedents influenced the laity's vision of the appropriate contours of an American Catholic church. Yet despite the fact that women often constituted the majority of Catholic parishioners, they were excluded from positions of trusteeship and control over church properties such as the orphanages and schools managed by nuns. Nor were they encouraged to participate in most antebellum social reform movements. Catholic revivalism, where it occurred, tended to promote devotional practices rather than a messianic faith in human perfectibility.[20]

American religious orders began to appear after the turn of the century. When John Carroll, the country's first bishop, assumed the Baltimore episcopacy in 1789, the American church was still bereft of educational or charitable institutions. Seton was an unusual candidate to fulfill Carroll's vision of an activist order of nuns. Reared in a prominent Episcopal family in New York, she had married well and was a member of the upper echelons of the city's gentry when a string of personal disasters destroyed what had seemed a secure and comfortable destiny. Her husband went bankrupt, and they lost their house in 1800. Her father died the following year, and her spouse contracted tuberculosis. He died in Italy in 1803, where they had journeyed in a vain attempt to restore his health. Widowed at the age of 28, Seton was left with five young children to care for on her own. This in turn precipitated the crisis of faith that resulted in her conversion to Catholicism in 1805. It also headed her down the road to self-support. After opening a school in Baltimore, she was befriended by Carroll, who encouraged her in her spiritual development and vocational aspirations.

Perhaps as a result of the severity of her recent history, as well as her growing spirituality, Seton began to gravitate toward a religious vocation, an extremely complicated proposition given her desire to keep her family intact. With Carroll's encouragement, she opted to start an order of her own, backed by his pledge that she would have a great deal of autonomy in developing the new venture. She established her fledgling convent in Emmitsburg, Maryland, in 1809, adding a day school in a nearby log cabin a year later. Moreover, she created these institutions with very little monetary support from the Church, relying instead on private donations and income generated by the school and through the sale of cloth and clothes manufactured by the nuns. These revenues in turn supported not only the convent, but also its educational programs for children of the poor.

By 1817, the order had grown to encompass two more convents, one in Philadelphia, where the nuns ran an orphan asylum for Trinity Church, and one in New York, where they directed a similar venture supported by a blend of public and private funds. The division of labor in the New York asylum exemplified the lingering decentralization of parish life. Parish trustees owned the land and controlled the asylum's financial affairs, while the nuns exercised control over the institution's management. Additional funding was provided by a Ladies Charitable Association of parish laywomen, while state and private allocations supported the physical plant. The congregation donated $40 per annum for the nuns' personal use, including their clothing. Clearly, this was a system that depended not only on the sisters' managerial abilities, but also on their vows of charity and service. Voluntarism by nuns sustained the country's first Catholic charities, coupling service with their ability to generate revenues through fees for services and the sale of goods. The order continued to grow after Seton's death, giving rise to a network of orphanages and schools that stretched from Baltimore to Indiana by 1835. The nuns also ventured into hospital work, managing the infirmary at the University of Maryland at the state's request.[21]

Their ability to maintain themselves at minimal cost endowed these early orders with a substantial amount of leeway in developing their programs. In contrast to Protestant fund-raising efforts, support for early Catholic charities was spotty at best. Some parishes developed fraternal organizations to raise funds, and parish laywomen sometimes banded together to collect the modest sums needed for the nuns' personal maintenance. Special collections at Easter and Christmas also provided limited amounts of cash, which were occasionally augmented by individual bequests and donations. But unlike their Protestant counterparts, Catholic laywomen never developed the highly organized fund-raising activities necessary to subsidize a concerted, national program of institutional development and elaboration. Instead, they focused their energies on parish-based sewing and altar societies and short-term local fund-raising campaigns.

Like Graham, Seton was an experienced fund-raiser from her days as treasurer of the Widows' Society in New York. As part of her responsibilities there, she had successfully lobbied the state legislature for permission to conduct a state-sponsored lottery to raise $15,000 for the Society's work. Catholic charities and schools were also granted municipal allocations in New York in this era, policies that benefited Seton's order when it took over the management of the city's Catholic orphanage. Although public allocations for parochial education ended in the mid-1820s, when educational funding was consolidated under the Protestant-dominated Free School Society, support for asylums continued on a limited but regular basis. Catholic charities also netted modest but ongoing municipal allocations in other cities, such as New Orleans and San Francisco.

Other Catholic sisterhoods managed to forge public-private partnerships, too, especially during the cholera-ridden 1830s, when they were frequently contracted to manage public almshouses and hospital wards. The governments of major cities such as Philadelphia, Baltimore, and smaller towns such as Augusta, Georgia, all enlisted the services of Catholic sisterhoods during these pestilent years.

Seton and her contemporaries developed their convents and charities in a unique milieu. By the 1820s, the episcopal hierarchy began to consolidate its control over the Church's growing network of parishes and charities as part of a larger plan of centralization emanating from Rome. Voluntarism was also made to conform to ecclesiastical standards. To quote one historian, "bishops did not look favorably on even limited autonomy in female activities, whether lay or religious, and the women's benevolent societies did not have even the modest legal protections enjoyed by the sisterhoods." In the process, Catholic clerics discouraged lay overtures to undertake national benevolent programs, advising their flocks to "focus their energies" on "their own dioceses" instead.[22]

Prior to the 1820s, individual Catholic churches and religious orders enjoyed a significant amount of autonomy, but because Catholics were limited in number and their ranks dispersed, the system that emerged was highly fragmented, often focusing on parish institutions. Subsequent episcopal policies discouraged both lay autonomy and the development of national organizations. Nor did Catholic theology motivate individuals to participate in social reform movements to the same degree that evangelicalism kindled Protestant benevolence.

The end result was a system in which Protestant laywomen pursued political roles through the acquisition of nonprofit charters, public-private funding arrangements, and social reform. Catholic laywomen, on the other hand, raised funds for charities and churches run by the religious sisterhoods, male lay trustees, and priests. The greatest difference was in the area of reform, where Catholic initiatives lagged behind those of Protestants—especially evangelical Protestants—for both organizational and doctrinal reasons. But whether as donors, reformers, or organizational entrepreneurs, the philanthropic endeavors in which these women engaged increasingly drew them into webs of interdependence between their churches, their communities, and the state.

CONTEMPORARY RELEVANCE

Are these patterns still relevant today? Work by scholars such as Sidney Verba suggests that they are. According to his research, Protestant congregations have continued to play a particularly significant role in political mobilization, especially among disadvantaged groups. Verba attributes this to the smaller size of Protestant congregations, the fact that they tend to be more decentralized and less hierarchically structured than their Catholic counterparts, and the fact that "most Protestant denominations allow for greater lay participation," such as "serving on a committee to hire a new minister or oversee the church budget." As a result, Verba and his coauthors were able to document

> a dramatic difference between Catholic and Protestant respondents in terms of both opportunities to exercise politically-relevant skills in church, and time devoted to church-related educational, social and charitable activity. . . . Protestants are much more active, and more likely to practice civic skills, than are Catholics.

This has continuing gender implications as well: "the more restricted role of women in the Catholic church might diminish skill acquisition" among different groups of female parishioners, such as Latinas. In effect, the skills learned in church-related charities and management often provide a bridge to political mobilization.[23]

If Verba is correct in assuming that religious institutions have continued to "play a special role" in "providing opportunities for the development of civic skills to those . . . who otherwise would not be in a position to acquire them," and if we know that, statistically, religious participation has remained strong, how does this relate to larger patterns of civic engagement that seem to be on the wane? Religiously motivated charitable endeavors and social advocacy campaigns often provide the primary point of access for politically disadvantaged groups to public policy-making roles. Moreover, the pattern of public-private alliances that emerged in the colonial era and was expanded in the wake of the Revolution continues to undergird the nonprofit sector today. In effect, the "barn-raising myth"—the idea that philanthropy and government are separate and separable—has little historical *or* contemporary validity.[24]

American nonprofits traditionally survived, and continue to survive, on a mix of private donations, fees for service, governmental outlays, and volunteer time. This type of diversified portfolio provides a major source of longevity and strength, since organizations with multiple sources of support are less likely to falter on the fortunes or whims of a single donor. Recent statistics indicate that fees for service currently constitute the largest source of nonprofit support across the board, followed by government grants and contracts and private donations. In 1989, the breakdown was as follows:

- For all nonprofits: fees, 51 percent; government, 31 percent; private giving, 18 percent
- Health: fees, 55 percent; government, 36 percent; private giving, 9 percent
- Education: fees, 63 percent; government, 17 percent; private giving, 19 percent
- Social and legal: fees, 23 percent; government, 42 percent; private giving, 35 percent
- Civic: fees, 23 percent; government, 41 percent; private giving, 35 percent
- Arts and culture: fees, 26 percent; government, 11 percent; private giving, 63 percent

As these statistics reveal, arts organizations were the only nonprofits to receive a majority of their revenues from private donors, and even in this politically embattled field, philanthropic support was far from exclusive.[25]

Public-private partnerships have historically constituted an important, albeit unheralded, social compact among governments, nonprofits, citizens, and communities, providing a key element of the infrastructure through which citizen participation is marshaled for public benefit. Since 1980, these alliances have increasingly been called into question. Although not as severe as initially anticipated, government cutbacks have both exacerbated demands on nonprofit services in some fields and reduced their organizational resources for addressing those demands. Moreover, projected cuts under the congressional budget resolution of 1996 included an 18 percent drop in federal social welfare outlays by the year 2002. Research has clearly demonstrated that private giving cannot make up these shortfalls. Over the past two decades, nonprofits have relied most heavily on increased fees-for-service to compensate for funding shortfalls—a practice that has often placed them in direct competition with small businesses and endangered their ability to provide pro-bono or low-cost services for the poor. And although American giving remains high, private donations actually fell as a proportion of nonprofit revenues between 1982 and 1992, from 15 percent to 11 percent.[26]

At the same time, politicians have increasingly endorsed measures that threaten to undermine nonprofits and Americans' incentives to give and volunteer. For example, charitable deductions for nonitemizers were tested, then scrapped during the 1980s, despite the obvious benefits to nonprofits. Several of the recent "flat tax" proposals would have reduced or eliminated charitable deductions for individuals and/or businesses. Contrary to "trickle down" notions that tax cuts will encourage generosity, donations by taxpayers with adjusted gross incomes of $1 million or more declined by 55 percent between 1983 and 1992. Giving by bequest also diminished. Although the real value of estates increased by nearly 75 percent between 1977 and 1992, the proportion of estates containing charitable bequests dropped from 22.1 percent to 18.6 percent.[27]

Meanwhile, nonprofits themselves have come under fire. Policy makers in Pennsylvania and Colorado recently debated whether the tax-exempt status of certain types of nonprofits might be rescinded, measures designed to bring additional revenues into public coffers. Perhaps the most volatile initiative was the narrowly defeated (but far from defunct) Istook Amendment, which would have regulated the amount of *private* revenues that nonprofits receiving federal funding could devote to advocacy, broadly defined to include public education efforts before any level of government from school boards to federal agencies.

So, to return to the original question: if church membership and religiously inspired giving and voluntarism remain strong, and if much of this generosity is parlayed into participation within the broader community, what has declined? Is it civic participation per se, or is the malaise more specifically focused on government, as the statistics suggest? And if there is a split between citizen participation in the public and nonprofit spheres, why has it occurred?

The public opinion polls and voter turnout records clearly suggest that Americans' faith in the government's ability to respond to their needs has plummeted, and that this decline began at the high tide of liberalism and has continued its downward slide ever since. Vietnam, Watergate, and the recent scandals concerning political contributions and the selling of the White House have doubtless contributed to Americans' growing skepticism about federal politicians and political morality. But based on the statistics, it is also possible to argue that almost two decades of government attacks on publicly supported social welfare programs have played a role as well.

Religious institutions have historically served as key nodes for social and political mobilization. They are also wellsprings for giving and voluntarism. Church members tend to be more involved than unchurched citizens in charitable, educational, and cultural activities both within and beyond their congregations. These services have been the direct targets of the political initiatives of the past two decades, as donors, volunteers, nonprofit personnel, and the constituencies they serve have increasingly been asked to do more with less. The end result is that Americans who have been directly involved with these institutions through their investments of time and money have had firsthand experience in dealing with the impact of government policies within their own communities. From volunteers in programs for the homeless, to residents who value the ways in which cultural institutions improve the quality of life in their cities and towns, Americans have had ample opportunities to question the government's responsiveness to the issues and institutions that have an immediate impact on their daily lives.

If this is the source of the discontent so vividly tracked by pollsters over the past three decades, if growing numbers of Americans no longer believe in the ability of elected officials to address their priorities, then we need to fundamentally rethink the jeremiads for the lost soul of civil society. We need to recast our understanding of the scope and nature of the dilemma, and focus instead on the implications of sundering the social contracts that have traditionally bound citizens, nonprofits, and government together in common cause. In effect, we need to shift our line of vision from politics to political culture, recasting our concerns in more incisive terms.

NOTES

1. National Commission on Civic Renewal, Press Release (13 November 1996), 2, 1. These statistics are drawn from a Chilton Research Services poll for ABC, a 1996 *Los Angeles Times* poll, a General Social Survey, and U.S. Census Bureau data, respectively.

2. Georg Hegel, *Philosophy of Right*, trans. T. N. Knox (Oxford: Clarendon, 1942; originally published 1821); Jürgen Habermas, *The Structural Transformation of the Public Sphere*, trans. T. Burger and F. Lawrence (New York: Cambridge University Press, 1989); Robert Putnam, *Making Democracy Work: Civic Traditions in Modern Italy* (Princeton, N.J.: Princeton University Press, 1993). The fullest account of the various theories of civil society is Jean L. Cohen and Andrew Arato, *Civil Society and Political Theory* (Cambridge, Mass.: MIT Press, 1992). See also Craig Calhoun, ed., *Habermas and the Public Sphere* (Cambridge, Mass.: MIT Press, 1992), and Adam B. Seligman, *The Idea of Civil Society* (Princeton, N.J.: Princeton University Press, 1992).

3. Virginia A. Hodgkinson and Murray S. Weitzman, *Giving and Volunteering in the United States: Findings from a National Survey* (Washington, D.C.: Independent Sector, 1996), 3, 5, 6; Virginia A. Hodgkinson, Murray S. Weitzman, Arthur D. Kirsch, Stephen M. Noga, and Heather Gorski, *From Belief to Commitment: The Community Service Activities and Finances of Religious Congregations in the United States* (Washington, D.C.: Independent Sector, 1993), 3. The methodology used in *Giving and Volunteering*, as described by the authors, included survey information on in-home personal interviews conducted by the Gallup Organization and "based on a representative national sample of 2,719 adult Americans 18 years of age or older. The sample included oversamples of blacks, Hispanics and affluent Americans with household incomes over $60,000," but not the very wealthy (those

with incomes above $200,000) because they constitute such a small percentage of the population. "The error rate for the total sample is plus or minus 3 per cent" (xiv). The value of volunteer time was estimated at the average hourly wage for nonagricultural workers ($12.84 in 1995), plus 12 percent for fringe benefits (I-30).

4. AAFRC Trust for Philanthropy, *Giving USA* (New York: AAFRC Trust for Philanthropy, issued annually). In 1995, the figure was 45.3 percent.

5. Hodgkinson et al., *From Belief to Commitment*, 1.

6. Hodgkinson et al., *From Belief to Commitment*, 2–3.

7. Sidney Verba, Kay Lehman Schlozman, and Henry E. Brady, *Voice and Equality: Civic Voluntarism in American Politics* (Cambridge, Mass.: Harvard University Press, 1995), 23, 59.

8. Paula Baker, "The Domestication of Politics: Women and American Political Society, 1780–1920," *American Historical Review* 89, no. 3 (June 1984): 622. For a more recent elaboration on the theme of women's political culture, see Kathryn Kish Sklar, *Florence Kelley and the Nation's Work* (New Haven, Conn.: Yale University Press, 1995).

9. Society for the Relief of Poor Widows with Small Children, *Annual Report* (New York, 1800), 12; Isabella Graham, letter to Mrs. Walker, 1798, in Joanna Bethune, *The Power of Faith: Exemplified in the Life and Writing of Mrs. Isabella Graham of New York* (New York: J. Seymour, 1816), 234.

10. Joyce Appleby, "Republicanism and Ideology," *American Quarterly* 37 (Fall 1985): 265. For an excellent discussion of these themes, see Linda Kerber, *Women of the Republic: Intellect and Ideology in Revolutionary America* (Chapel Hill: University of North Carolina Press, 1980).

11. Appleby, "Republicanism and Ideology," 255; Pauline Maier, "The Revolutionary Origins of the American Corporation," *William and Mary Quarterly*, 3rd Series, 50, no. 1 (January 1993): 55; Kerber, *Women of the Republic*, 287.

12. One of the best explications of the public role of charitable corporations remains Oscar Handlin and Mary Flug Handlin, *Commonwealth: A Study of the Role of Government in the American Economy, Massachusetts, 1774–1861* (Cambridge, Mass.: Harvard University Press, 1947). Much of this interpretation is drawn from a book I am currently writing on "Democracy, Philanthropy, and Civil Society in the United States, 1776–1865."

13. Patricia Bonomi, *Under the Cope of Heaven: Religion, Society and Politics in Colonial America* (New York: Oxford University Press, 1986), 217. See also Nathan O. Hatch, *The Democratization of American Christianity* (New Haven, Conn.: Yale University Press, 1989). Some of the other political roles played by evangelical sects in the antebellum era are discussed in Richard J. Carwardine, *Evangelicals and Politics in Antebellum America* (New Haven, Conn.: Yale University Press, 1993).

14. Mary P. Ryan, *Cradle of the Middle Class: The Family in Oneida County, New York: 1790–1865* (New York: Cambridge University Press, 1981), 77.

15. Trends in New England are described in Conrad Edick Wright, *The Transformation of Charity in Postrevolutionary New England* (Boston: Northeastern University Press, 1992).

16. Paul Boyer, *Urban Masses and Moral Order in America, 1820–1920* (Cambridge, Mass.: Harvard University Press, 1978), 34. For a detailed discussion of the

Sunday School movement, see Anne M. Boylan, *Sunday School: The Formation of an American Institution, 1790–1880* (New Haven, Conn.: Yale University Press, 1988).

17. Nancy F. Cott, *The Bonds of Womanhood: "Woman's Sphere" in New England, 1780–1835* (New Haven, Conn.: Yale University Press, 1977), 15.

18. Hatch, *The Democratization of American Christianity*, 11.

19. Patrick M. Carey, *People, Priests and Prelates: Ecclesiastical Democracy and the Tensions of Trusteeism* (Notre Dame, Ind.: University of Notre Dame, 1987), 107. See also Jay P. Dolan, *The American Catholic Experience* (Garden City, N.Y.: Doubleday, 1985).

20. Dolan notes that "church attendance was largely female" throughout the nineteenth century, citing a survey of church attendance in Manhattan that documented that "73 percent of all Catholic churchgoers were women" in one of the nation's most heavily Catholic areas as of 1902 (*The American Catholic Experience*, 233).

21. For a fuller discussion of the role of women's voluntary associations in subsidizing the development of public social welfare services, see Kathleen D. McCarthy and John Patrick Diggins, eds., *The Liberal Persuasion: Arthur Schlesinger, Jr., and the Challenge of the American Past* (Princeton, N.J.: Princeton University Press, 1997), 142–50.

22. Mary J. Oates, *The Catholic Philanthropic Tradition in America* (Indianapolis: Indiana University Press, 1995), 28, 27.

23. Verba et al., *Voice and Equality*, 321–22, 324.

24. Verba et al., *Voice and Equality*, 328.

25. Virginia A. Hodgkinson, Murray S. Weitzman, Christopher M. Toppe, and Stephen M. Noga, *The Nonprofit Almanac: Dimensions of the Nonprofit Sector* (San Francisco: Jossey-Bass, 1992), 147.

26. Lester M. Salamon, *Holding the Center: America's Nonprofit Sector at a Crossroads* (New York: Nathan Cummings Foundation, 1997), xiv.

27. Salamon, *Holding the Center*, 22, 24–26.

13

Will the Circle Be Unbroken?

The Erosion and Transformation of African-American Civic Life

Fredrick C. Harris

Scholarly and popular debates about rekindling America's civic health are fraught with contradictions. Although social, political, and economic changes over the past decades have undoubtedly altered the meaning and nature of civil society in contemporary America, just how and to what degree these changes have affected the nation's civic life remains largely unsolved. Misconceptions and contradictions abound, particularly when we consider the nature and meaning of civic life in African-American politics and society. If we are convinced by the indicators of civic decay—declines in voter participation, group membership, political participation, trust in government, morality, and the traditional family structure—then the civic health of black America is in serious crisis.

Social theorist Cornel West, in a widely received and controversial essay titled "Nihilism in Black America," assesses the crisis in black civic life by citing moral decay as the basis for the "shattering of black civil society."[1] This decay is manifested in what West describes as the "nihilistic threat" in black America, a mood typified by "the lived experience of coping with a life of horrifying meaninglessness, hopelessness, and (most important) lovelessness." This threat to black society is, for West, not totally the result of economic devastation in black poor and working-class communities, nor is it derived from a declining sense of political empowerment. Rather, erosion in the civic fabric of black life is linked primarily to "the profound sense of psychological depression, personal worthlessness, and social despair."

West pinpoints two factors that contribute to the nihilistic threat. One cause is the corrosive effects corporate market institutions have generally on American society and specifically on African-American society. West argues that these market institutions foster a "seductive way of life, a culture of consumption that capitalizes on every opportunity to make money." They undermine "traditional morality" in order to gain profit. The second cause West gives for civic erosion is the inefficacy of black leadership. West attributes this leadership crisis to the lack of accountability between leaders and black publics, the leadership's preoccupation with racial issues, and black elected officials' inability to deal with an "electoral system with decreasing revenues, loss of public confidence, self-perpetuating mediocrity, and pervasive corruption."

West's two explanations only scratch the surface of why civic life is declining in black America. And like other scholars who have offered interpretations of American civic life, West's emphasis on traditional morality understates the importance of black social institutions and how these institutions have structured black civic life over time. To argue that moral decay would undermine the "traditional morality" of blacks any more than it would for most Americans is an interesting proposition, especially given that allegations of low moral character have historically legitimized black exclusion from the nation's social and civic spheres and justified the state's neglect in addressing racial and economic inequalities.[2] Moreover, by couching decay in black society and politics as a "disease of the soul" or as a problem of "collective clinical depression," West inadvertently romanticizes the very period and society that supposedly kept the nihilistic threat at bay.

Indeed, West sees segregated black communities of yesteryear as spaces that created "powerful buffers to ward off the nihilistic threat," equipping segregated blacks "with cultural armor to beat back the demons of hopelessness, meaninglessness, and lovelessness." But at least some of these "demons" existed during the era of Jim Crow. West's characterization of contemporary black life resembles sociologist E. Franklin Frazier's take on the black middle class just before the civil rights movement. To Frazier, the black middle class was hardly a model of civic virtue. He alleged that as a privileged class in a segregated society, middle-class blacks (like today's "underclass") suffered from pathologies; they exploited poor and working-class blacks, led meaningless lives, indulged in conspicuous consumption, were sexually promiscuous, and suffered from racial self-hatred—some of the same ills that West and others attribute to loss of community in contemporary black life.[3]

Contradictions and misinterpretations of black civic life also prevail when we pay close attention to explanations given for the general decline in the nation's civic health. For instance, scholars and politicians point to mounting cynicism toward government as a sign of civic decay. If we took this claim at face value, we would conclude that government distrust among blacks is like that of whites: cynicism among both would stand as an example of declining civility. We would mistakenly conclude that the recent controversy over alleged CIA links to the crack cocaine epidemic in inner-city neighborhoods represents yet another example of how paranoia has crept into the nation's consciousness. To see black distrust of the CIA merely as one more instance of sagging confidence in the nation's institutions, however, would ignore how race has historically shaped the contours of American politics and society.

This chapter contributes to our understanding of African-American civic life—and indeed American civic life more broadly—in two ways. First, it challenges some of the assumptions and highlights omissions in the civic renewal debate, and it explores how these misconceptions distort interpretations of black civic life. I argue that (1) mistrust in government institutions combined with a belief in the legitimacy of government is not necessarily a sign of civic decay, (2) social movements are a vital though largely overlooked component of American civic life, and (3) African-American political behavior is characterized by a participatory norm that is similar to yet distinct from the participatory norm of mainstream civic life.

A second aim of this chapter is to assess the current state of civic life in black America by examining survey data on black social and political activity. Using the 1960s as a benchmark, I examine both the nature and intensity of black participation during the thick of the civil rights movement—a peak period of black activism in the post–World War II epoch—and compare patterns of participation then with patterns in the contemporary period. In addition to examining changes in a variety of formal modes of political participation, such as campaigning for political candidates or contributing to a political campaign, this chapter also estimates changes in group membership and participation in community-oriented activities. An assessment of group membership and community-oriented activities is important because it will allow us to detect the extent to which the availability of "social capital" may have changed over time. By social capital I mean what Robert Putnam defines as the "features of social organization, such as trust, norms, and networks," that enable participants to act together more effectively to pursue shared objectives.[4]

Assessing the vitality of group membership and community-oriented activities is important for another reason. By examining patterns in organizational life across social class, we will be able to speculate on how poverty in inner-city communities may have disrupted the ties that kept black civic life intact for generations. Current findings by political scientists Michael Dawson and Cathy Cohen suggest that living in a community with high concentrations of poverty greatly reduces the formation of social capital. As their findings suggest and as we will later see in detail, group membership and participation in community-based activities among poor blacks has dropped precipitously since the 1960s.

But before we present evidence on participatory patterns in black politics and society, we first need to tackle some assumptions and misconceptions about the nature of civic life in America.

GOVERNMENT DISTRUST AND BLACK CIVIC LIFE

Scholars who study black political life have consistently discovered that blacks have higher levels of cynicism toward government institutions than the mainstream population.[5] In theory, confidence in governmental institutions makes for a strong democracy and should therefore encourage citizens to participate in the workings of the polity. But for blacks, distrust in government and lack of belief in the efficacy of government institutions has a paradoxical link to civic engagement. Political scientist Richard Shingles and others have shown that what motivates black political activism is feelings of black solidarity, which in turn are stimulated by a combination of confidence that one can make a difference in the political process (internal political efficacy) and cynicism toward government.[6] The combination of efficacy and mistrust is particularly important in motivating blacks to participate in modes of political action that require a great deal of personal initiative. As Shingles explains, cynicism and feelings of competence create a "mentally healthier and politically more active black citizenry."[7]

Intuitively, African-American cynicism about government makes sense when we consider that government policies and practices have historically legitimized and constructed systems of racial exclusion in American politics and society. If southern blacks during the age of segregation had had absolute confidence in government's will to abolish racial segregation, the civil rights movement would not have taken place. So suspicion about the efficacy of government is not necessarily a barrier to a healthy civic life. Indeed, revelations in recent years regarding the government's covert syphilis study of black men in Tuskegee, Alabama, and efforts by the FBI's counterintelligence program (COINTELPRO) to disrupt the civil rights and black power movements only *reinforce* already existing levels of cynicism within the black population.

For example, a year after the assassination of civil rights leader Martin Luther King, Jr., three-quarters of blacks in a 1969 Gallup poll believed that King's death was "a result of a conspiracy," whereas only 6 percent believed that one man acted alone. In that same survey a considerable portion of respondents indicated a lack of confidence in the police—40 percent reported that police brutality occurred in their neighborhood, 45 percent believed that their local police were more harmful than helpful in protecting "Negro rights," and nearly half reported that the police did not do a good job of preventing crime in their neighborhood.[8] That suspicions of police and an interest in reinvestigating King's death have resurfaced in our public discourse thirty years later points to the *endurance* of blacks' distrust in some of the nation's civic institutions.

WHITHER SOCIAL MOVEMENTS?

An important omission in the civic renewal debate is the role social movements play in the nation's civic life. This omission is curious, because social movements—and the activities that are associated with them—are a vital facet of American political life. One place where the discussion of movements has surfaced is in Robert Putnam's speculation about whether the civil rights movement contributed to the erosion of organizational membership through "white flight." Putnam finds that "avowedly racist or segregationist whites have been no quicker to drop out of community organizations . . . than more tolerant whites."[9] But what is interesting about the civil rights movement's influence on American civic life has less to do with white flight (especially since residential segregation has changed little over the years) than with how the civil rights movement inspired other movements for social change and helped legitimize protest as a political resource in American politics.

While some analysts lament the erosion of commitments to traditional civic associations, there might be more cause for optimism about the nation's civic health if civic renewal crusaders turned their attention toward social movements. Assessing whether movements have decreased or multiplied in American society is somewhat difficult, because activities associated with movements are rarely included in standard surveys of American political behavior. Moreover, nonviolent tactics that were associated with the civil rights movement and movements that followed—the free speech, anti-war, and feminist movements—were considered by many to be disruptive, "unpatriotic" modes of political expression that threatened the civic order's stability. But these movements have had a lasting effect on American civic life, serving as models for subsequent movements for social change—particularly the gay and lesbian movement, the environmental movement, the disability movement, and the antiabortion movement. Indeed, nonviolent movements are no longer viewed as fringe elements that threaten the fabric of the nation's civic life. One rarely hears of antiabortion protesters being labeled "un-American."

The spread of social movements in American life since the 1960s and 1970s suggests that there has been a "strange endurance" of protest (or at least its acceptance) in contemporary American politics.

Recent surveys confirm this endurance. Sidney Verba, Kay Schlozman, and Henry Brady report in their book on civic voluntarism that about 6 percent of Americans engage in protest activities. Although this level of political activity may seem insignificant when compared with the number of Americans who vote or contact public officials, engagement in protest activities is only slightly less than participation in campaign work (8 percent).[10] Furthermore, Verba and his colleagues found that an overwhelming majority of protesters (89 percent) said that their participation reflected a "desire to do their duty as a member of the community, to make the community or nation a better place to live, or to do their share." This suggests that protesters viewed their activism in terms of civic virtue. Moreover, social movements engender the very type of values and norms that crusaders of civic renewal find wanting. Movements thrive on social networks, cultivate social trust between actors, operate on norms of reciprocity, nurture bonds of solidarity, and generate opportunities for the learning and practicing of democratic skills. They are rich in social capital.

Given that social movements do so well at generating social capital, why is it that advocates of civil renewal privilege system-oriented activities and overlook participation in protest activities? Is challenging the Catholic Church's stand on homosexuality by disrupting a religious mass less civically engaging than attending a school board meeting? Is organizing protesters to block abortion clinics any less virtuous than rounding up neighbors for a block party? And could it be that, as a counterpart to Putnam's virtuous "civic generation" that came of age during the 1940s, the "movement generation" of the 1960s and 1970s has taken on alternative forms of civic engagement that involve participation in groups such as feminist collectives rather than the Junior League, or the Promise Keepers rather than the Lions Club?

Now that I have raised questions about the legitimacy of social movements in American civic life, I would now like to turn to a related subject: the unique participatory norms that make up the civic life of African Americans.

PARTICIPATORY NORMS IN AFRICAN-AMERICAN CIVIC LIFE

Before we can assess whether there have been changes in the civic life of African Americans, we must first consider the distinct participatory norms that exist in African-American politics and society. Research during the 1950s and 1960s showed that, when controlling for education and other indicators of social class, levels of social and political participation were higher for blacks than for whites. Two main explanations were put forward. Either blacks "overparticipated" because they needed to compensate for their exclusion from mainstream society by joining numerous groups, or they participated more than whites because they were part of an "ethnic community" that nurtured norms of community involvement.[11] The compensation theorists marked greater-than-white participation as "pathological," "excessive," "exaggerated," and "a mark of oppression," while the ethnic community theorists did (at least indirectly) acknowledge that greater levels of black participation engendered social capital and should not be viewed as aberrant behavior.

By the 1980s, however, blacks no longer outparticipated whites in social and political activities.[12] In fact, Sidney Verba and his colleagues show that the average numbers of political acts for blacks and whites are today nearly identical. While whites are involved more in some activities (voting, contributing money to campaigns, contacting elected officials, affiliating with a political organization), blacks participate more than whites in others (campaigning for political candidates, protesting, and engaging in informal community activities).

These divergent patterns in participation suggest that participatory norms operate differently in African-American politics and society. These norms embrace what Aldon D. Morris, Shirley J. Hatchett, and Ronald E. Brown describe as the "orderly and disorderly" sides of the political process.[13] By "orderly and disorderly" they mean that blacks have been socialized into employing political tactics that lie both within and outside of normal political processes. In other words, boycotting, picketing, and joining protest marches are just as legitimate as a tool of political expression as voting, campaigning for candidates, or contacting an elected official about a problem.

This characteristic mixture of protest and system-oriented participation has been sustained historically by what I describe in detail elsewhere as an oppositional civic culture.[14] Black mainstream institutions—churches, social clubs, masonic orders, community organizations, schools—have traditionally nurtured norms that both legitimized the civic order and, subtly and at times overtly, served as sources of opposition to white supremacist practice and discourse. Gabriel Almond and Sidney Verba have shown how social institutions and system-supporting attitudes contribute to a society's civic culture and hence to its stability. A sense of obligation to the polity, for example, is transmitted through a complex process that involves the "family, peer group, school, work place, as well as the political system itself."[15] But while the culture and institutions of marginal citizens perform this civic role, they also transmit values that counter the dominant society's ideology of subordination, and they employ these values to justify and legitimize oppositional movements. As sociologist Aldon Morris explains, "the groundwork for social protest has been laid by the insurgent ideas rooted within churches, labor unions, voluntary associations, music, informal conversations, humor, and collective memories of those elders who participated in earlier struggles."[16]

This oppositional civic culture has deep roots in African-American communities. It operated during the "racial uplift" and antilynching crusade of the National Association of Colored Women at the turn of the century;[17] it sparked the boycott of segregated streetcars in southern cities after the 1896 *Plessy* decision;[18] it stirred the demand for black citizenship rights through the Niagara Movement and the founding of the National Association for the Advancement of Colored People (NAACP); it stimulated the black nationalist movement of Marcus Garvey's Universal Negro Improvement Association (UNIA) after World War I; and it fostered A. Philip Randolph's push for unionizing Pullman Porters as well as the 1941 March on Washington movement, which he organized but later canceled after Franklin Roosevelt abolished racial discrimination in government jobs and contracting during World War II.

These moments of political activism could not have taken place without a vibrant associational life in black communities. For instance, it was the women's convention of the all-black National Baptist Convention that provided the early leadership and the networks for the secular-based black women's club movement.[19] Middle-class organizations such as the black college sorority Delta Sigma Theta mobilized on behalf of women's suffrage.[20] Alpha Phi Alpha fraternity, whose founding was inspired by W.E.B. Du Bois's call for "race leadership," developed citizenship schools in the urban South and with its slogan "A Voteless People Is a Hopeless People" registered hundreds of blacks during the 1930s, decades before the Southern Christian Leadership Conference (SCLC) and the Student Non-Violent Coordinating Committee (SNCC) launched their citizenship schools in the 1960s.[21] Working-class masonic organizations provided the infrastructure for local chapters of Garvey's UNIA and served as a mechanism for recruiting men for the Pullman Porters' Union.[22]

These participatory norms were not restricted to activities outside "normal" politics. When opportunities for participation in electoral politics expanded with the migration of blacks north, black civil society accommodated both normal politics and protest politics in its tactical repertoire. Chicago provides perhaps the best example of an equilibrium between the two. Blacks in Chicago became an important and significant component of the Democratic party machine during and after the New Deal; they were also an important part of the city's Republican machine before the New Deal. In both cases, blacks were elected to Congress, the state legislature, and city council.

But black electoral success and political representation did not preclude the employment of "disorderly" tactics. In their landmark study of black Chicago, St. Clair Drake and Horace R. Cayton recorded the various forms that the "organization of discontent" assumed in Chicago's black belt during the 1920s and 1930s.[23] These included picketing and boycotting department stores and trade unions that refused to hire blacks, filing lawsuits against realtors who practiced discrimination through racially restrictive covenants, organizing tenant strikes against high rents, and initiating consumer boycotts against companies that refused to hire blacks.

How a civic culture of opposition has changed in black civic life since the 1960s should be the focus of discussion about black America's civic health. Such a focus would raise important questions, some of which are beyond the scope of this investigation: Have patterns in black associational life declined or been transformed since the civil rights era? Has the concentration of poverty eroded the transmission of an oppositional civic culture in black inner-city communities? Have some segments of black society become more oppositional than civic while others have become more civic than oppositional? And how do trends in the nation's body politic encourage or dampen a civic culture of opposition? Before we ponder some of these questions, we should first take a look at the nature of black political participation during the 1960s and assess what changes have taken place.

CHANGES AND CONTINUITIES IN BLACK CIVIC LIFE

The unique participatory norm that combines civically directed participation with protest strategies is evident when we consider patterns in black participation during the 1960s. Although this era is an atypical period in black political history, it nonetheless provides a guidepost for exploring changes in black participation since the passage of the Voting Rights Act and other measures that promoted black inclusion in American politics and society.

Figure 13.1, taken from the 1966 Harris-*Newsweek* Survey on Race Relations, shows the frequency of participation in eleven modes of political action. These modes include civically directed activities such as asking others to register and vote, working for a political candidate, contributing money to a political candidate, or contacting a public official. They also include protest-oriented activities such as boycotting a store, marching in a demonstration, picketing an establishment or taking part in a sit-in.[24] Political scientists who study participation usually consider system-ori-

Figure 13.1   Frequency of Black Political Activism During the Civil Rights Movement

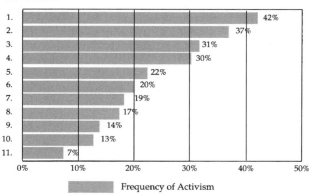

Source: 1966 Harris-*Newsweek* Race Relations Poll

ented and protest activities as separate participatory spheres. But to explain the relative frequency of activities in this sample of blacks in the mid-1960s, we must attend not to the distinction between protest and system-oriented activities but rather to the difference between those activities that require high levels of individual initiative and resources, and those that do not.

System-oriented activities such as asking people to register to vote (42 percent) or asking others to vote for one candidate over another (30 percent) took just as much energy as participation in consumer boycotts (31 percent)—and, in this historical context, less personal risk as well. Similarly, activities that required more energy (and in some cases more risk) included both system-oriented and protest activities; about an equal number of blacks reported marching in demonstrations (22 percent), writing or speaking to their congressional representative (20 percent), working in a political campaign (19 percent), and contributing money to a political candidate or party (17 percent).

Other activities represent more aggressive modes of action and are exclusively protest-oriented. They entailed even greater personal costs to actors, as indicated by the small proportion who engaged in sit-ins (14 percent) or pickets (13 percent), or who had gone to jail as part of their activism (7 percent). Again, these patterns of black political activity during the mid-1960s demonstrate a participatory norm that embraces both protest tactics and system-oriented activities. Just as they did in the pre–civil rights period, black Americans employed both strategies during the movement, a movement that led to the inclusion of black Americans into mainstream politics. This inclusion was brought about by the passage of the 1964 Civil Rights Act and, especially, the 1965 Voting Rights Act. In some ways, the Voting Rights Act, along with civil rights organizations, steered the participatory norm of protest *and* institutionalized activities toward dominance of system-oriented activities linked to black electoral success.

However, some evidence suggests that this participatory norm has recently been employed to mobilize behind quality-of-life issues. The 1984 National Black Election Study (NBES) and the 1993 National Black Politics Survey (NBPS) show changes and continuities in blacks' involvement in protest and system-oriented activities. The 1984 survey asked two questions that measured protest:

1. In the last five years have you ever attended a protest meeting or demonstration?
2. In the last five years have you ever picketed, taken part in a sit-in, or boycotted a business or governmental agency?

Although these questions combine four protest activities into two questions, they do allow us to make some comparisons to the 1960s. About 15 percent of respondents in the NBES reported participation in protest meetings and demonstrations. If we compare this figure with the percentage from the 1966 sample who marched, participation in protest demonstrations has declined by seven percentage points. Only 8 percent of respondents in the 1984 sample had picketed, taken part in a sit-in, or boycotted a business or governmental agency, representing about a 5 to 6 percent drop-off in either picketing or joining sit-ins, or possibly a 23 percent decline in boycotting.

But these findings only tell part of the story. Figure 13.2 shows patterns in black political participation from the 1993 National Black Politics Survey. The NBPS asked questions on participation in system-oriented activities,[25] but it also probed black respondents on protest activities in a uniquely different way:

> I'm going to read you a list of things people have done to *protest* such things as neighborhood crime, drug trafficking or school reform. Please tell me if you have done any of these things in the last five years.

The survey asked whether they had contacted a public official or agency, attended a protest meeting or demonstration, taken part in a neighborhood march, or signed a petition in support of or against an issue. When these modes of participation are probed in the context of issues (crime, drugs, or school reform) and "protest," participatory patterns over time reveal interesting results. For instance, about a third of the

Figure 13.2   Frequency of Black Political Activism in the Post-Civil Rights Era

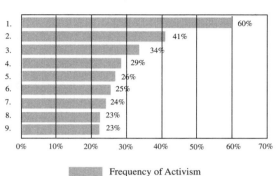

Modes of Political Action

1. Signed a petition in support/against something
2. Signed a petition in support of a candidate
3. Protested an issue by contacting a public
official or agency
4. Attended protest meeting of demonstration
5. Attended fund-raiser for a candidate
6. Gave people ride to the polls on election day
7. Gave money to political candidates
8. Took part in neighborhood march
9. Handed out campaign material

Frequency of Activism

Source: 1993 National Black Politics Survey

1993 sample reported attending a protest meeting or demonstration (29 percent), a 14 percent *increase* in protest from 1984 and a 7 to 15 percent *increase* from 1966. If we compare the 1966 Harris-*Newsweek* question on marching for "Negro rights" with the 1993 NBPS question on participation in neighborhood marches, the frequencies are nearly identical. It appears that the participatory energies that were once devoted to smashing Jim Crow during the 1960s have now been deployed to address quality-of-life issues in black communities.

Admittedly, protest activism in the 1990s does not involve the sort of high-risk, nationally coordinated campaigns that were mounted in the 1960s. What these patterns do confirm, nonetheless, is the endurance of participatory norms that have characterized black civic life for over a century. In the National Black Politics Survey, respondents were just as likely to attend a fund-raiser for a candidate (26 percent), give rides on election day (25 percent), or donate money to candidates (24 percent) as they were to attend a protest demonstration (29 percent) or join a neighborhood march (23 percent).

The current trend in the deployment of participatory norms in contemporary African-American politics and society is best symbolized by the 1995 Million Man March on Washington. As the largest political gathering of African Americans in the twentieth century, the march focused on the same values that civic renewal crusaders want to strengthen—personal responsibility, self-help efforts, social trust (specifically among blacks themselves), and participation in civic groups. As Minister Louis Farrakhan declared in his speech to participants, civic life in black America needs renewal:

> Go back, join the NAACP if you want to, join the Urban League, join the All
> African People's Revolutionary Party, join us, join the Nation of Islam, join

PUSH, join the Congress of Racial Equality, join SCLC—the Southern Christian Leadership Conference, but we must become a totally organized people and the only way we can do that is to become part of some organization that is working for the uplift of our people.[26]

But Minister Farrakhan may have been preaching to the converted. Many march participants were already firmly engaged in civic life. The gathering on the Mall represented a solid core of black civil society: (male) family members, fraternity brothers, masonic orders, church groups, black nationalist organizations, Boy Scout troops, black student unions, neighborhood groups, and even black gay organizations, among many other groups. A poll of march participants by the Howard University department of political science shows that marchers were on average considerably more active in political life than both the black and white populations at large. The poll asked more than a thousand participants about their views on the march and their involvement in political activities.[27] Nearly all (87 percent) reported that they had signed a petition for some cause; half had contacted a public official by phone or by writing (55 percent); slightly less than half had contributed money to a political campaign (46 percent), volunteered or served in a political campaign (45 percent), or attended a public policy hearing (44 percent); and a significant number reported visiting a public official (38 percent) or attending a state or national convention (22 percent).

But if the march attracted a considerable number of male political activists from the nation's diverse black communities, it also indicated the widening class divisions in African-American civic life. Most participants at the Million Man March were not from the poor or even from the marginal working-class segments of black society. As the Howard University research team reported, most marchers came "primarily from the middle and upper social and economic strata of the Black community." Nearly half had grown up in two-parent homes, about 40 percent made over $50,000 a year, and nearly 60 percent had some college or had graduated from college. The march in some ways can be viewed as the "rage of a privileged class."[28] This finding reveals that class may be structuring participation in black society and politics more than it did a generation ago. We now consider class by examining changes in participation in group membership and community-oriented participation.

THE POOR AND THE DISAPPEARANCE OF FREE SPACES

Two surveys are analyzed to compare group membership and community-oriented activity by social class and over time. They are Sidney Verba and Norman Nie's 1967 survey for the _Participation in America_ study and the 1987 General Social Survey (GSS). The 1987 GSS replicated questions on social and political participation from the 1967 Verba-Nie study. This twenty-year span allows us to estimate changes in black participation. The 1987 survey, like the 1967 survey, has an oversample of black respondents. Using educational attainment as a rough measure of social class, I estimate mean rates of participation in social groups and community-based activity by educational categories. Rates for participation in community-based activities are computed by the sum of the standardized response to questions measuring those activities (see Table 13.1); the scale has a population mean of zero and a standard deviation of one. Positive estimates indicate that educational groups score above average, while negative scores indicate that an educational category on average participates less, not negatively. These scores should be viewed as "participation units."[29]

Figure 13.3 shows the mean number of organizational memberships for blacks in four educational categories: grammar school, some high school, high school, and more than high school. With the exception of blacks in the high school category, participation in organizations declined in the two-decade period. Unexpectedly, the greatest decline occurred among blacks in the highest educational category, from an average of about 2.5 memberships to about 1.6 memberships. This drop suggests that, on average, blacks on the highest end belonged to one fewer organization than they did in 1967. Participating substantially less than the black population

Table 13.1   Participation in Community-Based Activities, 1967 and 1987

	All		_Whites_		_Blacks_	
	_1967_	_1987_	_1967_	_1987_	_1967_	_1987_
Worked with Others on Local Problems	30%	34%	30%	34%	33%	32%
Contacted Local Official about a Problem	14%	24%	15%	26%	7%	17%
Helped Form Group to Solve Local Problem	14%	17%	14%	18%	17%	16%
Sample Size	3095	1819	2660	1222	406	544

Source: Norman H. Nie, Sidney Verba, Kay L. Schlozman, Henry E. Brady, and Jane June, _Participation in America: Continuity and Change,_ transcript, January 1990. The estimates for 1967 are from a survey conducted by Verba and Nie for their book _Participation in America: Political Democracy and Social Equality_ (New York: Harper & Row, 1972). The estimates for 1987 are from the General Social Survey, which repeated questions asked in the earlier survey.

Figure 13.3   Mean Membership Rate by Education among African Americans: 1967 and 1987

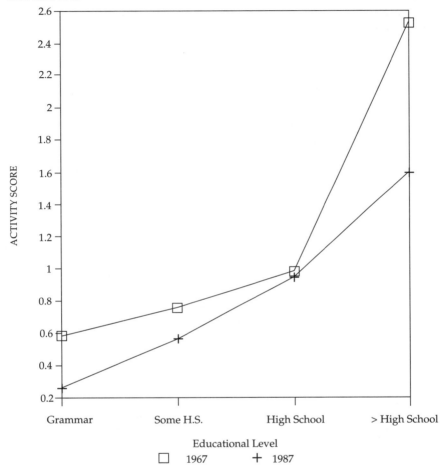

Source: 1967 *Participation in America* Study and 1987 General Social Survey

at large, blacks in the lowest educational categories (grammar school education or less and some high school) were also less engaged than before. For whites, the overall pattern shows only slight erosions for all four educational categories (figure not shown).[30]

With the exception of active participation in church organizations, patterns in group membership within each educational category were more or less consistent across group types. For the highest educational category, there was a sharp decline in membership in expressive organizations (sports clubs, social clubs, fraternal groups, and veteran groups), while the rate remained unchanged in the other educational categories. Similar patterns emerge when we look at "instrumental" group membership (membership in political groups, work-related/professional groups, unions, school groups, nationality groups, and service organizations). Again, it is in the highest educational category that we see the greatest decline (from two and a half standard deviations above the mean to near one standard deviation above the mean); each of the three other educational categories shows marginal declines. The only group membership that shows stability and, in some categories, increases is activity in church-related groups. Activities in church-related groups grew substantially in the lowest and two highest educational categories.

Patterns in participation across social class are complicated even more when we examine community-oriented activities. Table 13.1 shows changes in community-oriented activities from 1967 to 1987 for the general population, whites, and blacks. Participation in community-oriented activities is measured by whether respondents worked with others on local problems, contacted a local official about a problem, or helped form a group to solve a local problem. These participatory acts entail neighborly activities, the type of participation that promotes and sustains social connectedness, trust, and networks. The findings suggest that little has changed for blacks or whites in the two-decade period. In fact, in the general population there has been an increase in community-oriented activities.

More Americans report working with others on local problems (4 percent increase), contacting a local official about a problem (10 percent increase), and helping form groups to solve a local problem (3 percent increase) than at the time of the 1967 survey. For blacks, the patterns show increases or only insignificant declines. Just as many blacks worked on local problems and helped form groups to solve local problems in 1967 as they did in 1987, while contacting a local official increased by 10 percent. These findings are counterintuitive to arguments that there has been a decline in the civic activities of black Americans, especially those activities that enhance community.

But a look at community-oriented participation by social class tells a different story. Figure 13.4 shows the summed standardized responses to the community-oriented activity questions by education. Changes over the two-decade period are startling. Although group membership among blacks in the highest educational category has declined, the rate of participation among this group in community-oriented activities has remained the same. But for each category below the highest educational group, there has been significant erosion. The two lowest educational categories witnessed the greatest declines. Their scores hovered near half a standard

Figure 13.4   Mean Participation Rate in Community-Oriented Activities among African Americans: 1967 & 1987

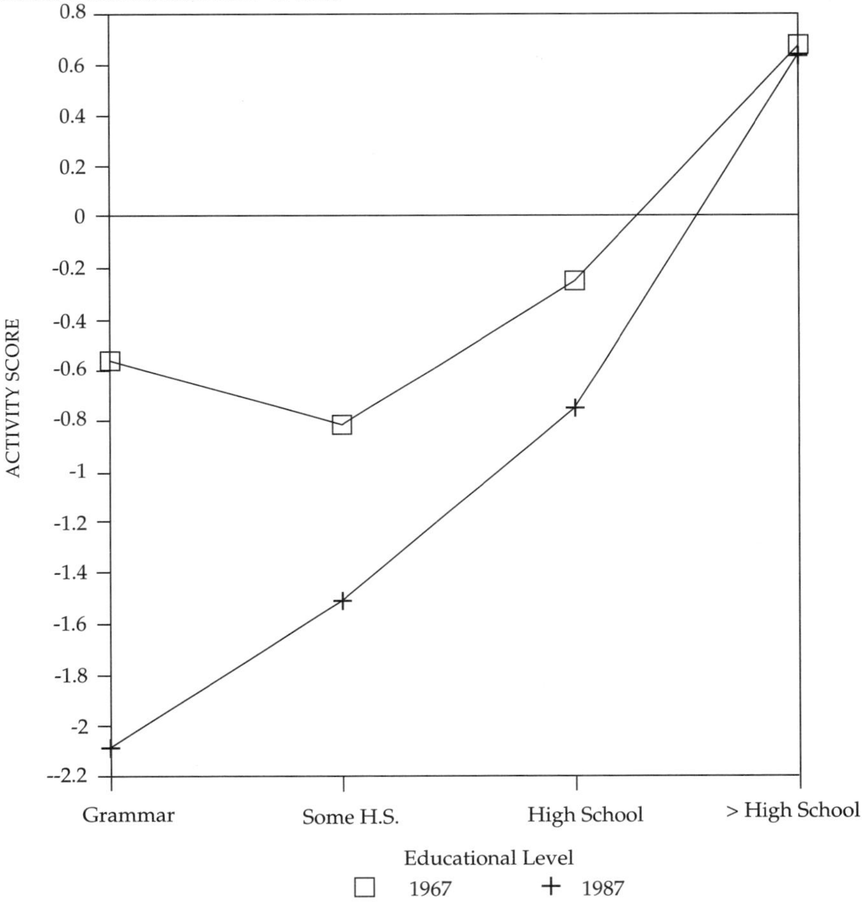

Source: 1967 *Participation in America* Study and 1987 General Social Survey

deviation below the average for all blacks in 1967; by 1987 their score plummeted toward two standard deviations below the population mean. These findings suggest that the increasing economic inequalities within the black population are also reflected in civic life. They partly confirm sociologist William Julius Wilson's claim about the increasing social isolation of poor blacks, and they raise serious questions about the transmission of participatory norms that have characterized black civic life for generations.

As I mentioned at the beginning of this chapter, recent work by political scientists Cathy Cohen and Michael Dawson shows the devastating effects of poverty on black civic life.[31] Their analysis of the effects of neighborhood poverty on black political and social life in Detroit demonstrates that civic life has virtually disappeared in poor black communities. Survey respondents who lived in census tracts that had more than 30 percent of residents living in poverty were less likely to engage in civic and social activities than blacks who lived in communities with less poverty. Residents in severely poor neighborhoods were less likely to belong to a church or social group, talk about problems with family and friends, attend a meeting about a community problem or issue, or (not surprisingly) contribute money to a political candidate. The effects of living in "deadly neighborhoods" hold up even after taking into account individual levels of poverty and personal attributes like education and income.

Cohen and Dawson's findings, along with the evidence I have presented on educational variations in group membership and community-oriented activities, point to the disappearance in many inner-city communities of those institutions that Sara Evans and Harry C. Boyte have called "free spaces"—"environments in which people are able to learn a new self-respect, a deeper and more assertive group identity, public skills, and values of cooperation and civic virtue."[32] They also suggest that the institutions of civil society among the poor can no longer sustain an oppositional civic culture, leaving open the possibility that the "organization of discontent" might lead to "uncivil," disruptive alternatives. Without the institutions to instill the twin virtues of civic engagement and *organized* opposition against forces that perpetuate racial-economic inequalities, prospects for civic renewal for those at the margins of American society seem dim.

WILL THE CIRCLE BE UNBROKEN?

Rebuilding and strengthening civic life in inner-city communities will take an enormous commitment and effort. Voluntarism and role modeling can only touch the surface of the vast problems facing inner-city communities. I doubt that the "remnants of the talented tenth" can overcome the barriers to engagement that citizens who live in those communities face every day. Moreover, institutions that have historically transmitted a civic culture of opposition are crumbling or no longer exist, and feelings of group solidarity may be weakening throughout the black population as other identities and interests begin to take shape. There is no longer *a* "black community" whose political interests are defined strictly by the experiences of racism alone.

Recent trends in black political attitudes are telling. Although nearly three-quarters of blacks in the 1993 National Black Politics Survey agreed that "American society is unfair to black people," nearly 40 percent also agreed that "economic divisions in the black community have grown so much that black people as a group no longer share common interests." Class, gender, religion, nationality, and increasingly sexuality are also influencing the character of black society and politics—a phenomenon that is occurring in American society at large. On the other hand, race still remains the great social divide in American society and politics. Greater racial polarization in American society may actually reinforce feelings of black solidarity even though greater differentiation within the black population is taking place.[33]

So what is to be done? Just as a combination of participatory norms has historically characterized black civic life, multiple strategies must be deployed to rebuild and transform civic life in poor and working-class inner-city communities. This means helping citizens transform their own communities by nurturing leadership *within* those communities. It means reviving and sustaining the "organizing tradition"[34] in which residents themselves—rather than charismatic figures or well-meaning volunteers with little knowledge of inner-city communities—teach and recruit other residents to organize. It means fostering associations and institutions—rather than personalities—that can nurture and sustain social capital.

The late civil rights organizer Ella Baker warned us about the dangers of charismatic leadership in her assessment of the civil rights movement, and her words are just as instructive today as we ponder how to foster social capital in poor neighborhoods:

> I have always felt it was a handicap for oppressed people to depend so largely on a leader, because unfortunately in our culture, the charismatic leader usually becomes a leader because he has found a spot in the public light. It usually means that the media made him, and the media may undo him. There is also the danger in our culture that, because a person is called upon to give public statements and is acclaimed by the establishment, such a person gets to the point of believing that he is the movement. Such people get so involved with playing the game of being important that they exhaust themselves and their time and they don't do the work of actually organizing people.[35]

The organizing tradition of group-centered leadership and the participatory norms that characterize black civic life will have to be deployed to attack the problems affecting poor neighborhoods. Those efforts, for instance, should encourage residents to demand that police and elected officials deliver equitable services and keep streets safe. They should challenge financial institutions that redline poor communities as well as corporations that refuse to reinvest in those communities. They should foster entrepreneurship, make *all* elected officials accountable for their (in)actions, and establish free spaces (YMCAs, Boys Clubs, after-school programs in schools and churches) where residents can participate in community-enhancing activities. Finally, they should offer incentives for multiclass, highly structured institutions such as masonic groups that can coordinate youth and community programs and thus become even more engaged. Only with the cultivation of indigenous leadership and free spaces can civic life in poor communities begin to take root.

NOTES

1. Cornel West, "Nihilism in Black America," *Dissent* (Spring 1991): 221–26.

2. For a discussion on the historical uses of moral decline in American politics and society and its link to the politics of race, see William Morone, "The Corrosive Politics of Virtue," *American Prospect*, no. 26 (May–June 1996): 30–39.

3. E. Franklin Frazier, *Black Bourgeoisie* (New York: Free Press, 1965; first edition, 1957).

4. Robert D. Putnam, *Making Democracy Work: Civic Traditions in Modern Italy* (Princeton, N.J.: Princeton University Press, 1993), 167.

5. High confidence in government by blacks is also determined by the degree to which blacks are represented in public office. Recent research suggests that blacks show higher levels of political engagement and confidence in government than whites in cities where a black is elected mayor. See Lawrence Bobo and Franklin Gilliam, Jr., "Race, Socio-Political Participation, and Black Empowerment," *American Political Science Review* 84 (1990): 377–93.

6. Richard D. Shingles, "Black Consciousness and Political Participation: The Missing Link," *American Political Science Review* 75 (1981): 76–91.

7. Shingles, "Black Consciousness and Political Participation," 89.

8. Percentages are from a 1969 Gallup Survey on Black Americans ($N = 977$); the study number is GO6955. The survey was made available through the Roper Center at the University of Connecticut, Storrs.

9. Robert D. Putnam, "Tuning In, Tuning Out: The Strange Disappearance of Social Capital in America" (The Ithiel de Sola Pool Lecture, American Political Science Association, 1995), *P.S.: Political Science and Politics* 27 (1995): 672–73.

10. Sidney Verba, Kay Lehman Schlozman, and Henry Brady, *Voice and Equality: Civic Voluntarism in American Politics* (Cambridge, Mass.: Harvard University Press, 1996), 51. The question asked, "In the past two years . . . have you taken part in a protest, march, or demonstration on some national or local issue (other than a strike against your employer)?"

11. See, for example, Marvin Olsen, "Social and Political Participation of Blacks," *American Sociological Review* 35 (1970): 682–97; Shingles, "Black Consciousness and Political Participation"; Thomas M. Gutterbock and Bruce London, "Race, Political Orientation, and Participation: An Empirical Test of Four

Competing Theories," *American Sociological Review* 48 (1983): 439–53; Bobo and Gilliam, "Race, Socio-Political Participation, and Black Empowerment."

12. Bobo and Gilliam, "Race, Socio-Political Participation, and Black Empowerment."

13. Aldon D. Morris, Shirley J. Hatchett, and Ronald E. Brown, "The Civil Rights Movement and Black Political Socialization," in *Political Learning in Adulthood*, ed. Roberta S. Sigel (Chicago: University of Chicago Press, 1989).

14. Fredrick C. Harris, *Something Within: Religion in African American Political Activism* (New York: Oxford University Press, forthcoming).

15. Gabriel Almond and Sidney Verba, *The Civic Culture: Political Attitudes and Democracy in Five Nations* (Princeton, N.J.: Princeton University Press, 1963), 367.

16. Aldon D. Morris and Carol McClurg Mueller, eds., *Frontiers in Social Movement Theory* (New Haven, Conn.: Yale University Press, 1992), 370.

17. Paula Giddings, *When and Where I Enter: The Impact of Black Women on Race and Sex in America* (New York: Bantam, 1984).

18. August Meier and Elliott Rudwick, "The Boycott Movement against Jim Crow Street Cars in the South, 1900–1906," *Journal of American History* 55 (1969): 756–75.

19. Evelyn Brooks Higginbotham, *Righteous Discontent: The Women's Movement in the Black Baptist Church, 1880–1920* (Cambridge, Mass.: Harvard University Press, 1993).

20. Paula Giddings, *In Search of Sisterhood: Delta Sigma Theta and the Challenge of the Black Sorority Movement* (New York: Morrow, 1988).

21. Charles Harris Wesley, *The History of Alpha Phi Alpha: A Development in College Life* (Washington, D.C.: Foundation Publishers, 1953).

22. William H. Harris, *Keeping the Faith: A. Philip Randolph, Milton P. Webster, and the Brotherhood of Sleeping Car Porters, 1925–37* (Urbana: University of Illinois Press, 1991).

23. St. Clair Drake and Horace R. Cayton, *Black Metropolis: A Study of Negro Life in a Northern City* (Chicago: University of Chicago Press, 1993), 730–44.

24. The sample size for the 1966 Harris Poll is 1,037 black respondents. Questions on participation in protest asked, "In the cause of Negro rights, have you personally or has any member of your family taken part in a sit-in, marched in a demonstration, picketed a store, or gone to jail?" Questions on system-oriented participation simply asked, "Have you ever . . . belonged to a political club or group, worked for a political candidate for office, asked people to register and vote, asked people to vote for one candidate over another, gone to a political meeting, written or spoken to your congressman, or given money to a candidate or political party?"

25. The survey asked seven questions that gauged participation in system-oriented activities. It asked whether in the past two years respondents had helped with a voter registration drive, given rides to the polls on election day, given money to political candidates, attended a fund-raiser for a candidate, handed out campaign material, or signed a petition supporting a candidate running for office.

26. Transcript from Minister Louis Farrakhan's Remarks at the Million Man

March, 17 October 1995 (http://www.cldc.howard.edu/~bah/text/Farrakhan_ Speech.html).

27. "Million Man March: Preliminary Report on the Survey," Howard University Political Science Faculty and Researchers: Lorenzo Morris, Joseph McCormick, II, Maurice Carney, and Clarence Lusane, 1 November 1995. Survey organized by the Wellington Group/OMAR and the Howard University Political Science Department.

28. See Ellis Cose, *The Rage of a Privileged Class* (New York: HarperCollins, 1993).

29. Sidney Verba and Norman H. Nie, *Participation in America: Political Democracy and Social Equality* (New York: Harper & Row, 1972), 128.

30. Organizational membership declined for whites as well during the same period, though the decrease is more uniform among the four educational groups. Among the highest educational groups, black participation declined dramatically compared with that of whites in the same group. In 1967 blacks in the highest educational group outparticipated their white counterparts. By 1987 the highly educated white group outparticipated their black counterparts while mean participation among the black group dropped below two (mean memberships).

31. Cathy Cohen and Michael C. Dawson, "Neighborhood Poverty and African American Politics," *American Political Science Review* 87, no. 2 (June 1993): 286–302.

32. See Sara Evans and Harry C. Boyte, *Free Spaces: The Sources of Democratic Change in America* (New York: Harper & Row, 1986), 17.

33. For further discussions on the transformation of black solidarities, see Michael Dawson's *Behind the Mule: Race and Class in African-American Politics* (Princeton, N.J.: Princeton University Press, 1994).

34. See Charles Payne's excellent book on the civil rights movement in Mississippi for a fuller discussion of group-centered leadership: *I've Got the Light of Freedom: The Organizing Tradition and the Mississippi Freedom Struggle* (Berkeley: University of California Press, 1995).

35. Quoted in Payne, *I've Got the Light of Freedom*, 93.

PART FIVE

PUBLIC DELIBERATION

14

Beyond the Public Journalism Controversy

Judith Lichtenberg

Public journalism—the term *civic journalism* is also becoming common—is a movement that has taken hold over the past few years at several newspapers across the country and among some theorists of the trade. Its development has been anything but predictable; as my colleague Peter Levine has written, "diverse ideals and projects" are often advanced in its name.[1] For this reason, trying to figure out what exactly public journalism is, and how it differs from the kind of journalism with which it is contrasted (for lack of a better term, I shall call it traditional journalism), can be frustrating.

It can also be contentious. Sometimes, proponents seem to regard public journalism simply as a synonym for good or in-depth or serious journalism—probing the issues that voters really care about, say, rather than providing horse-race election coverage—leading a bystander to wonder why anyone would oppose it. But those who revile public journalism—and among traditional journalists there seem to be many—naturally describe it in different terms.

Two features of public journalism stand out. One is its proponents' ready acknowledgment that their values shape what they do. In contrast to the "just the facts, ma'am" stance of the traditional journalist intent on maintaining objectivity, neutrality, and detachment, public journalists believe their values not only do, but ought to, shape their reporting. More specifically, they see themselves not as adopting the iconoclastic stance of much contemporary journalism—where the point is not simply to state the facts but to expose them—but as playing a role in creating what Jay Rosen, the leading academic theorist of public journalism, calls "a healthy public climate."[2] Journalists, Rosen insists, shouldn't just report the news; there is "also the job of improving the community's capacity to act on the news, of caring for the quality of public dialogue, of helping people engage in a search for solutions, of showing the community how to grapple with—and not only read about—its problems."[3]

The other noteworthy feature of public journalism is its asserted reliance on "the people"—the readers of a newspaper or the viewing audience—as a source of decisions about what stories and issues to cover. "In a democracy," writes Arthur Charity, "the public arena ought to be arranged on the public's own terms. So public journalists have invented ways to let Americans set the terms of the 'national debate' themselves."[4]

Examples of public journalism include the *Charlotte Observer*'s decision to tap its readers for ideas about how to cover the 1992 presidential campaign; the same paper's "Taking Back Our Neighborhoods" project, aimed at identifying the sources of crime in Charlotte and encouraging the community to find solutions; a project in Madison, Wisconsin, to increase public deliberation through town-hall meetings, debates among candidates, and interactive civic exercises; and the efforts of the *Huntington Herald-Dispatch* in West Virginia to galvanize its community to deal with vanishing jobs and a crumbling economy.[5]

However admirable these projects appear to some, many hard-nosed journalists recoil from them. "When journalists begin acting like waiters and taking orders from the public and pollsters, the results are not pretty," David Remnick writes in the *New Yorker*. Reacting to the *Norfolk Virginian-Pilot*'s mission statement, which exhorts its journalists to revitalize a sick democracy and to "lead the community to discover itself and act on what it has learned," Remnick responds, "Excuse me while I run screaming from the room."[6] Leonard Downie, executive editor of the *Washington Post*, is slightly more restrained but no less critical: "Too much of what's called public journalism appears to be what our promotion department does." The sole responsibility of journalists, he says, is to give people "as much as possible of the information they need to conduct their lives."[7]

My aim in this chapter is to sort out the issues that divide public journalists from their critics—or seem to—and to see how far we can go in resolving the controversy between them.

PUBLIC JOURNALISM AS "NICE" JOURNALISM?

Begin with public journalism's assertion that journalists should help foster a healthy public climate, that they should participate in the public's search for solutions to social and political problems. This might seem a rather innocuous claim. Who, after all, could be against a healthy public climate; who could oppose solving our society's pressing problems? The only question, we might think, is how best to achieve these goals.

Traditional journalists who object to this commitment to health and solutions seem to have two things in mind. One is a fear that journalists will become lapdogs rather than watchdogs—that public journalism is "nice" journalism, exhorting reporters to *accent*uate the positive, *elim*inate the negative. And nice journalism, it can be inferred, is not good journalism. Without necessarily going so far as to claim that good news is no news, the critics believe that much news is bad news, and that public journalists aim to bury the bad news.[8] (Or that even if they do not *aim* to bury the bad news, that will be the upshot of their rose-colored view.)

The good news/bad news controversy is harder to evaluate than might at first appear. For one thing, it's not always easy to tell the good news from the bad news. Consider this example. A recent *New York Times* story headlined "New Test Finds 2 in 3 Know Basics of Science" began this way: "In what education officials hailed as progress toward meeting national goals in science, a test of fourth, eighth and 12th graders from across the country showed that 2 in 3 have a basic understanding of the subject."[9] The same day, the headline on the front page of the *Washington Post* read, "U.S. Students Do Poorly in Science Test." The lead: "A rigorous new test of what American students know in science has revealed that many of them are not demonstrating even basic competence in the subject in certain grades."[10]

Is the difference between public journalism and traditional journalism that one sees the glass as half-full, the other as half-empty? How do we decide whether two in three students demonstrating competence is a lot or a little, something to be celebrated or deplored? We may be able to find no answer better than "Compared to what?" Whether we should be optimistic or pessimistic depends in large part on which way the trend is going. But even that may be difficult to determine.[11]

More often, perhaps, the dispute is not so much about how to spin a particular set of facts but which facts to spin at all. The question is sometimes put in terms of reporting on solutions versus reporting on problems. For example, as part of its two-year "Taking Back Our Neighborhoods" project, the *Charlotte Observer* devoted considerable energy and resources to "talking and writing about solutions" to neighborhood crime, according to assistant managing editor Jim Walser. The paper tried to draw "a picture of what had worked in other neighborhoods that had faced similar problems," and it emphasized "local revitalization efforts."[12]

Do traditional journalists mean to say that stories of this kind, that focus on "solutions," aren't newsworthy? It is hard to believe that they do. Solutions are solutions *to* problems, and without understanding the problems to be solved you could hardly report workable solutions. The *Observer*'s project began by analyzing crime statistics for every neighborhood in Charlotte. The paper identified the ten most violent neighborhoods and conducted polls asking residents, among other things, what *they* saw as the problem and what their lives were like. This is not just feel-good journalism.

On the other hand, it would be equally absurd to maintain that stories about "problems" that do not also emphasize solutions are not newsworthy. Again, it is hard to believe that public journalists would disagree. So what's the dispute? Is it simply a matter of emphasis? Isn't there room for both—for many—kinds of stories?

NEUTRALITY VERSUS ENGAGEMENT

What really worries the critics of public journalism is perhaps something else—something that goes to the heart of the traditional conception of the journalist's role. They fear that the seemingly laudable commitment to contribute to a healthy public climate and to help the public solve its problems pushes journalists over the line from their proper stance of detachment to an improperly engaged posture, thus hampering their ability to report the news fairly and without bias.

Now, one response to this objection would be explicitly to challenge the traditional journalistic commitment to detachment, to embrace wholeheartedly a conception of the journalist as an advocate, a passionate political animal who seeks to bring about social change. And certainly we can think of journalists (I. F. Stone comes to mind) whose commitment to a cause in no way undermined their fidelity to truth. How that balance between the desire for a particular social goal and the unwavering commitment to truth can be maintained is an interesting and important question, but answering it is not necessary to counter the current charge against public journalism.

The reason is that this objection to public journalism rests on two related confusions. One is a confusion about different levels on which one might or ought to be value-neutral. It makes sense to say that journalists should not allow their political beliefs to distort their coverage.[13] In attempting to provide the public with useful information, journalists must be careful not to cast those whose beliefs they share in too favorable a light or to give those with whom they disagree short shrift. But from these platitudes it does not follow that a journalist must be value-neutral about whether her society solves its problems. Why would someone become a journalist in the first place if she didn't care whether the country survived or thrived? (Well, there might be lots of reasons—excitement, the desire for celebrity, a love of words—but surely public-spiritedness might be among them.)

Indeed (and this brings us to the other point), it is impossible to make sense of the special privileges allocated to the press in our society— privileges of which journalists constantly remind us, trotting out the First Amendment at every opportunity—except on the assumption that the press is supposed to serve some important public good. Why is the press exempt from restraints and restrictions that fall on others? Because we believe that the information journalists provide contributes to the search for truth, to democratic citizenship, and to the solution of social problems. If journalism doesn't serve these goals, then it is nothing more than a business (some would agree immediately) and deserves no special protections. Press freedom rests on foundations that are not value-neutral.

Opponents of public journalism might reply that even if such "values" are the bedrock on which press privilege rests, it does not follow that flesh-and-blood journalists need to embrace them. As long as their work contributes to the public good, we might say, press privileges are justified; journalists themselves may be indifferent to the uses to which their work is put. But although this is abstractly true (we cannot know what motivates journalists, after all, and some may work simply for fun or profit), it can hardly be said that journalists have failed or fallen short if they do care about the public good.

So the criticism that public journalists' commitment to a healthy public life represents a departure from standard and defensible journalistic norms of detachment is misguided. Journalists must remain detached in the sense that their particular political views must not distort what they say, but they need not be indifferent to the welfare of their communities, and their concern about such matters is a legitimate motivation in choosing what issues to cover and in what manner.

Can a journalist perform competently and be committed to more specific "values" than simply the well-being of her community? Can she cover abortion fairly if she opposes abortion? Can a journalist who is the white mother of an adopted black child cover transracial adoption? No doubt some journalists are incapable of reporting on issues about which they hold strong opinions. But if all journalists suffer from this failing, we are in trouble, for the opinionless journalist is an ideal both impossible and undesirable.

SETTING THE AGENDA

Perhaps the thorniest question in the controversy about public journalism concerns decisions about what is news and where these decisions come from. Proponents often suggest that the terms of public discussion, and the standards for what is newsworthy, ought to be set *by* the public: the people are supposed to let it be known what they are interested in or find important, and journalists are to follow their lead in deciding what stories and issues to cover.

Critics of public journalism find this approach problematic, and it is easy to see why they might be worried. What sort of commitment to the public's interests do public journalists make? Are they indeed, in Remnick's phrase, "acting like waiters and taking orders from the public and pollsters"?

A look at what newspapers have actually done in the name of public journalism suggests that the answer is no. Consider, again, the *Charlotte Observer*'s series "Taking Back Our Neighborhoods." The impetus for the project, as Walser describes it, came from editors and reporters who felt that the standard police blotter approach to reporting urban violence didn't fully capture the problem or the experience of people in the affected communities. As the series developed, *Observer* staff continually had to make judgments about how to report events at the neighborhood level. Who were the local activists whose stories ought to be told? How could the success of revitalization efforts be judged, and which ones might serve as models for other communities? At every stage, essential decisions had to be made by the journalists themselves, not at the behest of pollsters.

More worrisome, to many critics, is the approach the Charlotte paper took in covering the 1996 Senate race between Jesse Helms and Harvey Gantt. The *Observer* convened citizen panels that identified issues they wanted to see the candidates address, with the understanding that reporters would emphasize those issues in their stories. (Reporters were free, however, to cover other issues as well.) The paper didn't merely send pollsters door to door, tabulate the surveys, and then allow people's unreflective judgments to guide its coverage—although you might get that idea from listening to some of public journalism's critics. Instead, it offered citizens through a process of deliberation an opportunity to develop their sense of what issues were important.

Contrary to Remnick's view, then, these public journalists didn't simply take orders from the public. They responded to beliefs that had been submitted to deliberation and dialogue—procedures meant to transform mere public opinion into the informed and reflective judgments of citizens.

But some critics take public journalism to task for reasons just the opposite of Remnick's. According to Michael Kelly, the citizen panels convened by the *Observer* identified eight important issues, but the *Observer* decided to concentrate on only four. Moreover, Kelly notes that although the panels ranked "Taxes and Spending" equal in importance with "Families and Values," the *Observer* chose to ignore the latter, which was clearly a more contentious, divisive issue. (The "nice" journalism complaint rears its head again.) Kelly argues on this basis that the paper's stated commitment to having citizens set the agenda was not entirely sincere—and that under cover of the citizen panels, the paper actually imposed its own agenda, limiting its coverage to those issues that *it* felt were most important and had less potential for turning ugly.[14]

THE EXISTENTIAL JOURNALIST

It now becomes clearer why the controversy about public journalism is hard to grasp: although traditional journalists protest public journalism's deference to the public as a source of decisions about what to cover, they may also object upon learning that public journalism is not as deferential as it appears. The first objection is that when journalists allow the public to set the news agenda, they cede their independence and an essential part of their role, becoming followers where they should be leaders and allowing others to usurp their autonomy. The second objection is that, in practice, public journalists take *too active* a role: what they should do—what journalists have traditionally done—is let others set the news agenda and not assume this task for themselves. To do otherwise is to abandon the journalist's tradition of detachment and objectivity.

These contradictory objections reflect an unresolved tension in traditional journalists' understanding of how they should go about their business. Journalists want to be independent of external pressures, whether from elites or from the public at large—but not so independent that they can be accused of setting the political agenda. They want to be responsive to external events, but not so responsive as to be manipulated—whether by politicians and spin doctors or by the unwashed public with its vulgar demands. And so public journalists get it from both sides: accused by some of arrogance and agenda-setting, by others of subservience and passivity.

For many journalists, it is almost an article of faith that their job is simply to "report the facts." But this supposition is naive. The problem is not that there are no facts (no postmodernist am I) but that there are way too many. The standard formulas say little or nothing about the journalist's act of *deciding* what to cover. And so they fail to address the fundamental, it is tempting to say existential, significance of that act. The question of selection—which facts and which stories, out of the vast if not infinite number available, a newspaper or news program should report—is the single most important question confronting journalists and news organizations, and constitutes the true heart of the problem of objectivity.[15] News organizations have managed to convey to their audiences the illusion of inevitability, from Walter Cronkite's famous sign-off, "And that's the way it is, Tuesday, January 13 . . .," to that authoritative look about the front page of the daily paper. But there is nothing inevitable about what ends up as news; many reasonable choices are possible.

Now, the public journalist might assert that this is precisely his point—that the news could be, and should be, different than it is, that there should be less coverage of certain sorts of events and issues and more coverage of other sorts of events and issues. Nevertheless, the rhetoric of public journalism, like that of traditional journalism, oversimplifies the process by which news *becomes* news.

It is not enough to say, as Arthur Charity does, that "the public arena ought to be arranged on the public's own terms." For even public journalists, as we have seen, must *decide* what's news; they can never pass this responsibility along to anyone else, whether the public or the politicians. Leonard Downie's assertion that journalists should simply give people "as much as possible of the information they need to conduct their lives" also implicitly acknowledges that choices must be made to determine what, of the vast quantities of information out there, people "need." Journalists can never abdicate autonomy of judgment. In this, their predicament parallels the one in which we all find ourselves. That someone (no matter who) says something is never sufficient reason for believing it; that someone (no matter who) commands something is never sufficient reason for doing it. Always required is the individual judgment on the part of the listener or the commanded that this person ought to be believed or obeyed. For the journalist, the judgment takes the form "This is worth reporting."

There is a danger that journalists will take this view in the wrong way. It is not a license to do just as you please. It does not render reporters immune to criticism, on the grounds that "it's up to us to decide" or that "we journalists are the experts here; we know better than anyone else." The autonomy principle does not mean there are no criteria for good journalism, although it says nothing about what these criteria are. The autonomy principle tells you only that you have to make up your own mind; it doesn't tell you how to go about doing so.

What, then, are the criteria for good journalism? Public journalists have rendered a valuable service in reminding us of the special roles that journalism is supposed to play in a democratic society. Let us see whether, taking into account what has already been said, we can be more explicit.

JOURNALISM AND DEMOCRATIC THEORY

Defenders of a free press, and of the First Amendment privileges our political system affords journalists, are quick to remind us of journalism's importance in a democratic society. They tell us that people in a democratic society need information to be good citizens—so that they can make up their minds about important public issues. To the question "What should journalists cover?" one answer, then, is "What people need to know to be sufficiently informed to perform their functions as citizens."

Several things are worth noting about this criterion for journalistic selection, the need to know. First, there is an obvious difference between what you want to know and what you need to know. You may want to know all sorts of things you do not need to know—certainly not for the purposes of good citizenship generally cited in connection with the journalist's role, possibly not under any reasonable analysis of need.[16] This point is relevant also to the much-discussed "right to know." People—*the* people, *some* people—have a right to know some things, but there is no general right to know; so it must always be demonstrated that a given set of people have a right—a moral or legal entitlement—to a particular piece or kind of information. (Because the claim of a *right* to know tends to beg the question unless a case has been made for such a right, I shall speak instead in terms of the somewhat less contentious *need* to know.) Furthermore, those who need to know some set of facts, arguments, or the like, may not know *that*, or *what*, they need to know. Indeed, this situation is common. As Socrates explained, to know that you don't know (and, by extension, to know what you don't know) is halfway to wisdom. Many people do not make it that far.[17]

These points can help us sort out the dilemmas public journalism brings to light—dilemmas implicit in all journalism that justifies itself in terms of its democratic functions—about the role of public opinion generally and its influence in decisions about the content of news. That what you need to know and what you want to know are different might seem too obvious to be worth mentioning, except that an enormous amount of journalism rests on the significance of markets and polls, which (at best) measure preferences, not needs. Football games and celebrity funerals regularly preempt media coverage of substantive political events. Local television news programs are increasingly dominated by crime stories, despite the sharp decline in the crime rate over the last few years. Stations that try to buck the trend, by covering stories more significant than the 400-pound man accused of sitting on a toddler, risk losing market share; most viewers watch the big crime channels instead.[18] What we need to know concerns the public interest; what we want to know, the public's interests.

Some critics believe that public journalism endorses the use of markets and polls. After all, don't these reflect what the public wants? If, as Arthur Charity claims, "the public arena ought to be arranged on the public's own terms," don't these tell us best what the public's terms are? It may be that some journalists who call themselves public journalists have appealed to polls as a way of gauging the public's interest. It is clear, however, that this is not what the best public journalism does.

Why not? Polls, as well as markets, are flawed for a variety of reasons. People's responses are indelibly shaped by which questions are asked or by which products are offered to them. That questions have to be framed, and framed in one way rather than another, is just one further proof that "the people" never speak in a vacuum and that their responses are always shaped by the formulations of journalists, or pollsters, or *someone*. The question whether it would be desirable to know people's brute preferences doesn't in fact arise. Their preferences are not brute. The implicit belief of many news organizations that polls tell us something especially real or legitimate is an illusion.

At least as important, the views revealed by ordinary polling are often rooted in ignorance. How seriously should we take people's opinions about complex subjects such as health care or national security if these opinions develop without the knowledge that is relevant to making sound judgments about such issues? This question is related to one of the most enduring debates in democratic theory: whether democratically elected representatives ought to be bound by the opinions of those who elect them, or whether instead, as Edmund Burke believed, they must be free to decide what is "in the best interests of their constituents" after they have "had the opportunity to hear and discuss the arguments together."[19]

Informed by the latter view, contemporary democratic theory has focused on the importance of public deliberation and judgment, as opposed to (mere) public opinion. The idea is that democracy is not simply about citizens registering their preexisting preferences and opinions; it requires citizens to deliberate about policy, so that the interests they express are informed by dialogue and debate rather than simply being data for, or endorsements of, the decisions of political leaders.

Although the connections are not always explicit, public journalism—or at least public journalism at its best—can be seen as an element in the theory of deliberative democracy. It rejects the ordinary poll as a device for finding out people's opinions; more precisely, it rejects the idea that we should be interested in people's mere opinions. More in keeping with the values of public journalism is the deliberative poll, a device developed and employed over the last decade by James Fishkin:

> The idea is simple. Take a national random sample of the electorate and transport those people from all over the country to a single place. Immerse the sample in the issues, with carefully balanced briefing materials, with intensive discussions in small groups, and with the chance to question competing experts and politicians. At the end of several days of working through

the issues face to face, poll the participants in detail. The resulting survey offers a representation of the considered judgments of the public—the views the entire country would come to if it had the same experience of behaving more like ideal citizens immersed in the issues for an extended period.[20]

Deliberative polling is one way of generating public deliberation. Other approaches include focus groups and town meetings, less ambitious and perhaps better suited to the constraints of most news organizations.

Public journalism can play several different roles in the enhanced conception of democracy implicit in the requirement of public deliberation. First, journalism can *serve* public deliberation, by providing the kind of information citizens need to make informed decisions. This role is uncontroversial; indeed, it is part of the standard view of the press's role in a democratic society. Second, journalism can *cover* public deliberation. As we have seen, the dispute between public and traditional journalism seems to center partly on the extent to which journalists cover sites of public deliberation—town meetings, the school board, and the like—rather than crimes and scandals, occasions when something has gone awry.

Finally, journalists can *organize* or "cause" public deliberation, by bringing people together into groups designed for that very purpose. Fishkin's deliberative poll is one example; focus groups and town meetings of the kind organized by the *Charlotte Observer* and other newspapers are another. This function is the most controversial of the three, because it calls into question the journalist's role as detached observer: the journalist is making something happen that probably would not happen otherwise.

No doubt there are dangers in these kinds of journalistic initiatives. But dangers lurk in any version of the journalist's role, a point we cannot fail to notice once we disabuse ourselves of the picture of the journalist as passive transmitter of "the news." As we have seen, traditional polls also shape public responses. And Downie's what-the-public-needs-to-know standard contains an unlovely paternalism if, in setting the news agenda, it neglects public deliberation and forswears active exchange with groups of deliberating citizens. Of course, any view that treats polls and markets with skepticism will also be subject to the charge of paternalism. Journalists inevitably steer an uneasy course between two accusations of manipulation: that they are manipulators, and that they are manipulated.

PUBLIC JOURNALISM AND CIVIC RENEWAL

Public journalism has emerged in the last few years alongside the revival of interest in civil society and civic participation. There are at least three connections. First, public journalism is supposed to improve the quality of public discussion of politics—for example, by replacing horse-race election coverage with coverage of substantive issues. The point, however, is not simply to improve the quality of news coverage but also to change the nature of public discussion. Thus, second, public journalism is supposed to bring the public in, giving it an enhanced role as an actor in the public sphere rather than as just a spectator of debates among elites. In so doing public journalism reinterprets the cliché about a free press giving citizens in a democratic society the information they need to make decisions; it can also give them *opportunities* to make decisions (by organizing or acting as catalyst to public meetings and discussions) as well as new ways to *conceive* the choices before them.

The third connection between public journalism and civic renewal concerns journalists themselves. Public journalism rejects the model of the journalist as outsider, the neutral observer who tells us how things are but plays no further role in public life. I have been calling into question the coherence of this model, arguing that it makes no sense to think of the role of informant as being as passive as the model suggests. We might then see public journalism as making a virtue of necessity, or rendering explicit what has been implicit: reporters do shape public discourse and guide public life, and therefore they might as well do these things self-consciously. The journalist is also a citizen—perhaps a citizen first and then a journalist; at the very least a citizen and a journalist at the same time.

In thinking about the purposes of public journalism, we may find ourselves wondering how exactly it differs from more traditional approaches. Don't these ideas sound familiar? Haven't we heard them a million times in connection with the justification of the First Amendment and the role of the press in a democratic society? Haven't theorists of the media been talking for years about the agenda-setting function of the press? I have met reporters who are angered by what they take to be the meaning of public journalism but who (in the spirit of Molière's *bourgeois gentilhomme*) seem to have been public journalists all their working lives, covering underreported communities and telling stories from the point of view of those communities' members.

We may suspect that much of the disagreement between public journalists and their critics is terminological. Such tiresome disputes persist when people speak in vague generalities. Although they may sometimes disagree when they get down to cases, my guess is that, more often than not, journalists will reach consensus about what constitutes *good* journalism. Or at least they should.

NOTES

1. Peter Levine, "Public Journalism and Deliberation," *Report from the Institute for Philosophy and Public Policy* 16, no. 1 (Winter 1996): 1–5.

2. Jay Rosen, "Public Journalism as a Democratic Art," 4. Rosen, an assistant professor of journalism at New York University and director of the Project on Public Life and the Press at New York University, is the leading academic proponent of public journalism. His essay is adapted from a presentation to the Project's fall seminar on public journalism at the American Press Institute, Reston, Virginia, 11 November 1994.

3. Rosen, "Public Journalism as a Democratic Art," 3.

4. Arthur Charity, "Public Journalism for People," *National Civic Review* 85 (1996): 9–10.

5. See *Civic Lessons: Report on a 1996 Evaluation of Four Civic Journalism Projects Funded by the Pew Center for Civic Journalism* (Philadelphia: Pew Charitable Trusts, 1997); and Arthur Charity, "What Is Public Journalism? Five Communities, Five Examples," *National Civic Review* 85 (1996): 14. The Madison project involved the *Wisconsin State Journal*, Wisconsin Public Television, Wisconsin Public Radio, a CBS television affiliate, and a public relations firm.

6. David Remnick, "Scoop," *New Yorker*, 29 January 1996, 42.

7. Quoted in Tony Case, "Public Journalism Denounced," *Editor and Publisher*, 12 November 1994, 14–15.

8. For further discussion of this issue, see Judith Lichtenberg and Douglas MacLean, "Is Good News No News?" *Report from the Institute for Philosophy and Public Policy* 8, no. 4 (Fall 1988): 5–8.

9. *New York Times*, 22 October 1997, A28.

10. *Washington Post*, 22 October 1997, A1.

11. Both optimistic and pessimistic claims often rely on dubious comparisons. When the SAT was "recentered" a few years ago to render the median score 500, as it had been when the SAT was designed in the 1940s, some people bemoaned the decline in intelligence of our high school students, whose median scores had sunk in 1995 to 428 (verbal) and 482 (math). They neglected to note that the original SAT had been administered in 1941 to ten thousand students from private high schools, whereas today some two million students of diverse cultural and socioeconomic backgrounds take it every year. Statistics come from Michele A. Hernandez, *A Is for Admission: The Insider's Guide to Getting into the Ivy League and Other Top Colleges* (New York: Warner, 1997), 40–41.

12. "*Charlotte Observer*: 'Taking Back Our Neighborhoods,' " *Newsletter of the National Commission on Civic Renewal* 1, no. 2 (Autumn 1997): 10–11.

13. This does not mean, of course, that journalists shouldn't *have* beliefs about the issues they cover or that they shouldn't express them in other fora—contrary to the view of the *Washington Post* executive editor Leonard Downie, who refuses to vote on the grounds that to express a political preference through casting a ballot is incompatible with his professional role. Journalists can, and generally do, manage to keep their particular political beliefs out of their coverage, but that

does not mean that news reporting is free of bias. But the biases are more likely to result from other factors (e.g., the economic interests of media corporations or the pressures and constraints on news gathering) than from the particular politics of the reporter.

14. Michael Kelly, "Media Culpa," *New Yorker*, 4 November 1996, 45–49.

15. For an extended discussion of the idea of objectivity in journalism, see my chapter "In Defense of Objectivity Revisited," in *Mass Media and Society*, 2d ed., ed. James Curran and Michael Gurevitch (London: Arnold, 1996), 225–42.

16. People are not merely citizens, of course, and thus they may "need to know" other things for their other roles—for example, in their capacities as consumers, parents, and so forth. But the standard theories of freedom of the press emphasize the civic functions of the people, and I shall concentrate on those here.

17. See James H. Kuklinski, Paul J. Quirk, David W. Schwieder, and Robert F. Rich, " 'Just the Facts, Ma'am': Political Facts and Public Opinion," *Annals of the American Academy of Political and Social Science* 560 (1998): 143–54, which argues that people are not simply uninformed about facts relevant to public policy but misinformed—that is, they get the facts wrong but believe they have them right.

18. See Michael Winerip, "Looking for an 11 O'Clock Fix," *New York Times Magazine*, 11 January 1998, 31. The difference in profits—based on the price a station can charge for its advertising spots, which is in turn based on audience share—between first and third place in a market such as Orlando, Florida (the twenty-second largest in the country), which Winerip examines, is $3 million. In New York City, the difference between first and third place is $100 million.

19. James S. Fishkin, *The Voice of the People: Public Opinion and Democracy*, with a new afterword and appendices (New Haven, Conn.: Yale University Press, 1997), 31.

20. Fishkin, *The Voice of the People*, 162.

15

The Changing Role of Expertise in Public Deliberation

Robert Wachbroit

The relationship between experts and the public lies at the center of a number of concerns regarding the state of civil society and civic engagement. It is an important element in assessing the character of public deliberation, particularly when a scientific or medical issue must be addressed. What should the role of experts and expertise be in the public's deliberations? Moreover, when a scientific discovery becomes a public issue, what role should the public itself play in its resolution?

In this century, a great many voluntary associations have been formed in large part to mediate between experts and the public. These associations range from professional organizations, such as the American Association for the Advancement of Science, to health charities, such as the American Lung Association or the March of Dimes, to various grassroots activist groups and disease support groups. Insofar as these associations form part of the fabric of civil society, it is important to examine their social function and their attitudes toward expertise.

Understanding the relationship between experts and the public is also an important element in analyzing the nature and extent of trust in society. Most of the public's ordinary dealings with experts demand trust, because most individuals are not able to assess the validity of expert claims for themselves. Indeed, even the identification of experts turns on a trust in various institutions, since such identifications are usually based on institutional credentials and pedigrees rather than on an examination of the expert's knowledge itself. For example, most people place an extraordinary amount of trust in their doctor as medical expert. Beyond noting some certificates on a wall and gaining an overall impression of the physician's manner, people rarely know anything about their physician's command of the subject or his track record or even what other doctors think of his abilities. They will rarely question his views by seeking a second opinion. Although trust of this sort is not identical to the trust one might place in government or in one's neighbor—kinds of trust that have been taken as measures of the health of civil society—they are nevertheless intricately linked.

There is reason to believe that the relationship between experts and the public has changed in the past few decades, with consequences regarding the role of expertise in public deliberation, the character of various voluntary associations that stand between experts and the public, and the nature of the trust we place in experts. I want to present this case by focusing on medicine. Not only are people's dealings with health professionals one of the most common interactions between the public and experts, but they also provide one of the most vivid illustrations of the changes I have in mind. Even with this focus, however, the topic is large, and so my remarks, though touching on many of the themes noted, will be sketchy but suggestive. A good deal of research by philosophers, historians, and sociologists is needed in this area. Let me begin by first addressing more generally how the contribution of experts to public deliberation has typically been understood.

OUTSIDERS AND INSIDERS

In the literature on expertise and deliberation, two conceptions of the experts' role are dominant. The first conception describes experts acting in what we might call a "technocratic" or "outsider" mode. Here, science (expertise) sets the limits of the possible for reasonable public deliberation. Expertise is not part of the public sphere—the space within which public deliberation can take place—but rather helps determine its boundaries. For example, whether tuberculosis is a hereditary disease is not a question for public deliberation. The experts pronounce on the matter, and thus place it outside the public sphere. A failure to accept the authority of expertise presumably reflects ignorance, confusion, or irrationality. Insofar as some people are persistently guilty of such failures, they should not be involved in reasonable public deliberation.

In making this point, I should emphasize that "public deliberation" is being understood normatively and not just descriptively. To be sure, if enough people are talking about a certain issue, it is thereby an issue in the public sphere. My concern, however, is with a more restricted notion of public deliberation in which the conclusions of such deliberation have a normative force and not merely the force of numbers.

The technocratic mode easily allies itself with the supposedly sharp and simple contrast between "hard" facts and "soft" values. Public deliberation over values—including how and when to bring them into play—is entirely appropriate; public deliberation over facts is not only absurd but invites disaster. To be sure, disagreements can arise over whether the core issue in a policy debate is factual or normative. But there is no disagreement, according to the technocratic mode, over the scope of the experts' authority. It is up to them to determine the facts; the public deliberation and any resulting decisions should be framed entirely within that determination.

The second conception of the experts' role describes what could be called the "adversarial" or "insider" mode. On this view, the function of expertise is not to set the limits of what is possible for public deliberation but rather to serve as an element in the justification of any conclusion of public deliberation. In this conception, different groups acknowledge the cachet of scientific expertise and seek to appropriate it, or at least to counter any advantage their opponents might gain by appealing to expertise in defense of *their* positions. Whereas the experts are located outside the realm of public deliberation in the technocratic mode, in the adversarial mode they are the "hired guns." Is there a greenhouse effect, and are we threatened by global warming? Is AIDS caused by HIV, or is it the result of drug overload? Participating in the public deliberation on such issues demands having some experts on one's side.

This conception is plainly reminiscent of the role of expert witnesses in our adversarial legal system, in which each side presents its own experts to counter the other side's experts. Indeed, it might even be considered bad lawyering to let any unfriendly expert go uncountered or unchallenged. In the formal procedure of a trial, however, there is, in the end, a judge or jury who is charged with making a determination regarding which experts are credible. In the less structured arena of public deliberation, no such clear determination is made. Credibility can turn on the number of experts on a particular side, their prominence, or their alleged motives.

The adversarial conception need not reject the sharp contrast of facts and values, nor need it rest on a mistrust of science. It simply begins with the recognition that science is not a strictly cumulative enterprise. Scientific claims, laws, and theories have always been open to revision in the light of new observations, new experiments, and new theories, and we have every reason to expect this process to continue. Furthermore, the practice of science often requires making judgment calls. Is a particular hypothesis worth testing, or has it been sufficiently tested already? Are the data points that don't quite fit the curve a matter of insignificant random errors (noise) in the experimental setup, or do they indicate serious shortcomings in the underlying theory? Finally, the adversarial conception recognizes that science is an institution within society. Its members are subject to many of the same pressures and temptations as other people occupying other roles, and as a result their judgments may be biased or otherwise distorted. The presence of opposing experts goes some way toward diminishing the effects of bias.

I should emphasize that in identifying these two conceptions, I am describing only the role of expertise in public deliberation and not the character of the deliberation itself. There may well be an adversarial flavor to a deliberation—a sharp to-and-fro—even if the adversarial mode (of expertise) does not govern it. In the technocratic mode, however, the public debate and controversy will not be over the scientific findings themselves.

Each of these conceptions has its place. The technocratic mode presupposes a consensus among the experts on the relevant scientific issues. When there is none, the adversarial mode may be more appropriate. One ought not to use the adversarial mode regarding the claim that the Earth goes around the sun, nor the technocratic mode regarding the claim that the planet is suffering from a greenhouse effect. Because the character of scientific consensus can change as new discoveries or developments in theory arise, there is a dynamic between the technocratic and adversarial modes, so that over time, one mode might give way to the other as the appropriate one to govern deliberation.

We should note, finally, that the presence of a scientific consensus does not render an adversarial mode impossible. Consensus rarely entails unanimity. Dissenting experts, even in the face of consensus, are not uncommon.

The two modes both require education of the public, but there will be some differences. When the technocratic mode is accepted, associations will typically be deferential; their educational aim will be to help the public understand what is known, to inform the public of the facts (according to the consensus of experts). When the adversarial mode is in play, the task is still to educate the public but with obvious modifications: education may involve argumentation to show that one group of experts is more credible than another on a particular issue.

To these two conceptions of the experts' role one might formally add a zero option (i.e., the "zero mode," discussed later) in which expertise is deemed to play no role in public deliberation. Nevertheless, as far as the positive role of expertise in public deliberation goes, these two modes appear to be the dominant ones that have governed public deliberation.

There is, however, a third positive conception, setting forth what could be called the "participatory" mode. In one sense, of course, science is uncontroversially a participatory enterprise. Go to any scientific conference or read typical research reports, and you will notice that claims and proposals are put forward by various scientists, whose findings are meant to be discussed, analyzed, and argued over by their colleagues. Disagreements are sometimes quickly settled, but other times they become topics of extended debate and controversy, only to be clarified by further research. Such participation and deliberation are crucial to the practice of science. They characterize the process by which scientific consensus arises, disappears, or is revised. They are, however, participation and deliberation by the experts—not public deliberation.

In any account of the participatory mode, it must also be remembered that the term *expert*, as I have already suggested, is a rough social classification, reflecting more a pedigree than the possession of any particular body of knowledge. Someone is not a scientist by virtue of what she knows or believes but because she possesses certain public credentials. This is perhaps as it should be: expertise cannot require expertise for its identification; otherwise the public would be unable to tell who is an expert. This understanding therefore leaves open the possibility that some people will know at least as much about a topic as the experts do, even though these people are not "experts" themselves. Such people would not be part of the deliberation that routinely goes on in the practice of science; they would not be accorded any voice. (Sometimes the knowledgeable nonexpert is called the "community-based expert," leaving the expert to be called the "establishment expert." These labels are perhaps too loaded to be useful here.)

When experts as experts disagree with each other on a scientific finding that has become a public issue, we have the adversarial mode. If the disagreement is resolved, typically the agreement results from a deliberation among experts. But when experts and knowledgeable nonexperts disagree, a new possibility opens up in which experts and knowledgeable nonexperts engage each other in deliberation. When this occurs, the resolution of a scientific issue may no longer be determined by the experts alone; the experts may have something to learn from the nonexperts. Indeed, such deliberation may transform (the practice of) expertise, and thus the understanding of what constitutes good science.

These different conceptions can be linked to different kinds of voluntary associations. Commentators have noted that recent developments in some associations suggest movement toward the participatory mode. Let me therefore shift from my initial level of abstraction to some actual examples.

The two types of examples I want to examine are voluntary health agencies and support groups. Because of the wide variety in each case, substantive generalizations about these associations are difficult to come by. Nevertheless, interesting differences can be noted by examining a leading representative of each type: first, the American Lung Association, and then the loose coalition of activists and AIDS support groups that is sometimes called the "AIDS movement." I have chosen these particular organizations for discussion for several reasons. Both were among the first examples of their type, and both have been regarded as models for subsequent associations. The social character of the diseases at issue— tuberculosis and AIDS—is strikingly similar. And the importance of educating the public has been recognized as crucial to any effective control of the spread of either disease. These similarities make their differences regarding deliberation and expertise and the relationship between experts and the public all the more striking.

FIGHTING TUBERCULOSIS

Although the American Lung Association is concerned with all manner of respiratory disease, it was originally an association devoted entirely to the problem of tuberculosis. Founded in 1904 as the National Association for the Study and Prevention of Tuberculosis, the organization revised its mission as the public health threat posed by tuberculosis receded, adopting its current name in 1972. (Similarly, with the advent of the Salk and Sabine vaccines against polio, the National Foundation for Infantile Paralysis revised its mission to address problems of birth defects and renamed itself the March of Dimes.) The American Lung Association is therefore the oldest as well as one of the largest national voluntary health agencies or "health charities," as commonly understood.

At the turn of the century, tuberculosis was a leading cause of death in the United States. As many as 10 to 15 percent of all deaths were attributable to tuberculosis, far exceeding deaths attributable to heart disease or cancer. Only pneumonia may have claimed more lives, but the evidence is uncertain: misdiagnoses were not uncommon, and there is a rough similarity in some of the signs and symptoms, so that many reported cases of pneumonia or bronchitis could well have been cases of tuberculosis instead. Indeed, these confusions were sometimes deliberate, since there was a social stigma attached to the disease. Victims were frequently poor, urban dwellers—often immigrants—living in grim circumstances.

Tuberculosis was, of course, not confined to the poor, but there was little understanding at the time of how the disease spread. During the late nineteenth century, the dominant scientific debate was over whether consumption was contagious or hereditary, and this uncertainty in turn affected the meaning of the social stigma. Did someone develop the disease because of where he had been, or because of his family's constitution or "stock"? (Interestingly, even though Koch's famous experiments were reported in the 1880s, American physicians seemed particularly reluctant to accept the finding that tuberculosis was not hereditary.)

Despite the prevalence of tuberculosis—the "white plague," as it was so often called—it was not feared as much as many other epidemics, such as cholera or smallpox. There seemed to be a sort of passive (or fatalistic) acceptance of tuberculosis among the public. No one seemed to know how it arose or how to treat it, though a variety of opinions was put forward. Some insisted that tuberculosis was not a specific disease but rather a generalized morbid wasting process—hence the term *consumption*—that arose from a previous disease. Public health actions, such as the sanitation movement, which were so effective against infectious diseases such as cholera, had no apparent impact on tuberculosis. Special "lung hospitals" were established, but these served more to isolate victims than to offer any effective treatment. Sanatoriums arose, catering mostly to the afflicted in the middle and upper classes, but these were based on a cumulative lore regarding the general benefits of marine or mountain air, exercise, and rest—nothing specific to tuberculosis.

As scientists came to learn how to prevent and treat tuberculosis, they were faced with the challenge of translating that information into action. The National Association for the Study and Prevention of Tuberculosis was the creation of some of the leading physicians of the time. Its mission was to educate the public and advise the government and other institutions on how to respond to the disease. No such voluntary effort against a specific disease had ever been undertaken before. The organizers quickly realized that membership would have to be expanded to make the Association effective, and so its rolls were soon opened to "laypeople." To be sure, "laypeople" did not mean everyone; rather, it referred to professionals who were not physicians (i.e., health officers and social workers). Still, the recruitment of nonscientists had an immense influence on the anti-tuberculosis movement. As one historian has noted:

> Social reforms, led entirely by laymen, had acquired an evangelical quality during the 1800's; while in contrast those led by scientists, such as the sanitary campaign, had usually remained coldly objective. The tuberculosis movement combined these two qualities to mutual advantage. Because of medical direction, the tuberculosis societies rarely viewed their objective as a moral issue or indulged in the emotional enthusiasm which this might have involved. At the same time, thousands of laymen came to support the movement with increasing fervor. They provided aid which scientists could not have given, yet such aid was tempered at all times by scientific guidance. This blend of qualities was something new under the social sun.[1]

The Association's efforts at public education—developing traveling exhibits for display at town halls and county fairs, issuing press releases, and organizing lectures by prominent physicians—had two aspects. First, they tried to inform people about ways to avoid exposure to tuberculosis. This was crucial, because control of the disease required the public's active cooperation. Outbreaks of diseases such as cholera or typhoid could be controlled through supervision of the community's water and milk. Yellow fever, malaria, and plague could be controlled through the extermination of insect and rodent vectors and reservoirs. Tuberculosis control, however, required changes in the attitudes and behavior of the public. "If the crusade against tuberculosis was to succeed, the public had to learn not to spit, to open windows, to seek diagnosis before the disease became hopelessly advanced, and to submit to strict medical control rather than relying on patent medicine or flight to a favorable climate for treatment."[2]

But the Association had a larger public health goal as well: to inspire the formation of voluntary societies which would campaign for necessary laws and institutions. Charles Winslow's remarks on this feature of the antituberculosis campaign are often quoted: "the discovery of the possibilities of widespread social organization as a means of controlling disease was one which may almost be placed alongside the discovery of the germ theory of disease itself as a factor in the evolution of the modern public health campaign."[3] Another historian adds:

> Under these circumstances, governmental action might be delayed; but it was at least assured of popular support before it came. This was not only in keeping with a democratic tradition but was especially helpful in a disease like tuberculosis, in which popular cooperation was so essential to any control program.[4]

Eventually, the boundaries of the public deliberation regarding tuberculosis would be set by the experts as organized by the Association. Deliberation would be confined to questions regarding priorities and trade-offs in the control of tuberculosis (e.g., the allocation of resources, the use of tuberculosis screening in the military, etc.).

It should be clear from its structure and membership that the Association was deferential to the expertise of the medical establishment. Informing the public about controversies regarding the etiology or treatment of tuberculosis was not deemed part of its educational mission. George Palmer, president of the Illinois State Association for the Prevention of Tuberculosis, stated in 1915:

> We will have to adopt [sic] our creed and doctrines and present them to the laity as though they were unanimously adopted and almost spontaneously created. Our controversies of orthodoxy and faith should be reserved for the inner chambers of our scientific and professional conferences.[5]

These sorts of misrepresentations are unlikely to be endorsed now. Nevertheless, for the most part this deference to medical expertise continues in the Association's modern incarnation as well as in other major health charities. This should not be at all surprising. Many health professionals serve as volunteers and sit on the boards of these associations, which consider themselves partners with clinicians and researchers. Challenging medical expertise or voicing skepticism about its findings would be seen as irresponsible.

THE AIDS MOVEMENT

One of the striking developments of the past few decades in the area of voluntary associations has been the growth of support groups for people with a particular disease, behavioral problem, or emotional condition. Hundreds if not thousands of these groups have been formed, varying in size from small groups that meet occasionally in someone's kitchen, to large organizations that have a national presence. Their structures and meeting agendas can be formal and specific, or they can proceed much more haphazardly. Despite this variety, however, we can divide support groups into roughly two broad types. In the first type, the primary purpose is therapeutic. People join such a group in the hope that by participating in its activities, they can resolve their problem (or cope more effectively with its consequences). Examples of such support groups would be twelve-step programs such as Alcoholics Anonymous (AA), Overeaters Anonymous, or Co-Dependents Anonymous, as well as groups with different internal structures, such as the various bereavement groups.

In the second type of support group, the primary purpose is to mediate between patients and the community, the government, and the health professions by serving as a clearinghouse for information and a coordinator of action. No one joins this type of group thinking that her disease or problem can be treated by participation in the group's activities. Examples of such support groups would be the AIDS Coalition to Unleash Power (ACT UP), Gay Men's Health Crisis (GMHC), and the National Breast Cancer Coalition. In this discussion, I refer to the first type as therapeutic support groups, and to the second type as mediating support groups.

To be sure, many actual groups (including, arguably, some of the examples already mentioned) fall in between, combining both missions. For example, many mediating support groups, by their very existence, provide their members with needed emotional support. Nevertheless, there is a clear difference between a group such as AA, which is primarily noted for meetings in which members are helped to overcome their alcohol addiction, and a group such as GMHC, which is primarily noted for its education and advocacy, enabling its members to understand and pursue various treatment options. It may be best to think of the two kinds of groups as marking off the ends of a spectrum.

Mediating support groups have been especially prominent with regard to the AIDS epidemic. Almost from the time the disease was first noticed—when it was still being characterized as a "gay disease" or more formally as "Gay-Related Immune Deficiency" (GRID)—support groups were formed to provide information and to alert certain populations of risk. These groups did not simply pass on the latest expert findings, such as special reports from the Centers for Disease Control and Prevention (CDC). In the mid-1980s, the established experts were quite divided over the nature of the disease and so over what the identifiable risk factors were. Some thought that the disease was caused by a virus. Others suspected that certain recreational drugs, apparently popular in some gay communities, caused a general deterioration of the immune system. While some support group or community publications merely followed the controversy, others took sides. By no means did the support groups simply defer to the experts.

As the etiology of AIDS became better understood and a rough consensus regarding the causal importance of HIV was formed, attention turned to treatment and the testing of various drugs. While developments were duly reported in the various medical journals as well as the CDC's *Morbidity and Mortality Weekly Report*, alternative support group and community publications, such as GMHC's *Treatment Issues* and *AIDS Treatment News*, had also begun to appear. These newsletters drew on a broad range of treatment reports, anecdotes, and unofficial testings. According to some commentators, many clinicians and researchers consulted these newsletters to obtain information they could not find in the standard medical journals.

Several of the various activities that have come to constitute what is called "AIDS activism" have a familiar ring. Treatment and research in AIDS is affected by U.S. health policy and science policy. Accordingly, some groups were formed to lobby the government to budget money for research and treatment and to shape research priorities at the appropriate government-funded research centers. There is little that is special or unexpected in this. In their general aim (and in some of their tactics), AIDS lobbyists are not so different from earlier advocates concerned about other diseases. During the late 1960s and early 1970s, people with ESRD (end-stage renal disease) were brought, sometimes with medical devices attached, before members of Congress in a successful effort to secure full funding for dialysis treatment.

The new, perhaps trendsetting, feature of several AIDS support groups was their decision to engage in public deliberation with scientists over the conduct and interpretation of research. The relationship between the experts and the public seems to fall into what I earlier called the participatory mode. Let me illustrate this point by describing the public issue of clinical trials.[6]

A clinical trial is a blunt way, conceptually speaking, of determining the effect of a drug. Its chief advantage is that it does not require a great deal of knowledge about the pathophysiology of the disease, how the drug works, or why. In the many situations where science remains in a state of considerable ignorance, clinical trials are often the only means of clearly determining a drug's effect. In essence, a clinical trial consists of comparing, in a way reminiscent of John Stuart Mill's simple methods of induction, people who have taken the drug in question with those who have not.

Several controversies have arisen concerning clinical trials of various AIDS therapies, including questions about confidentiality and privacy, the use of placebos, and when a Phase II trial should be terminated. Of particular interest, for our purposes, has been the debate over the researchers' demand for "clean data."

Given the ignorance that usually attends clinical trials, no one knows what kind of interaction or interference, if any, occurs if the subject is taking other medication along with the investigational drug. To eliminate this complication, researchers will typically demand that their research subjects be "clean"—that they not take other medications—unless it is known that these medications will have no effect on the research results.

The problem with this demand regarding AIDS clinical trials was that many HIV-infected people could not meet it. The lack of passivity, to say the least, that characterized many HIV-infected people manifested itself by a willingness to seek out and try all sorts of drugs in an effort to combat the disease. Under the circumstances, they believed that they had nothing to lose. Because many also wanted to participate in clinical trials—the typical motive being to have access to the latest experimental drugs—some potential research subjects would lie about their medication history, while others would forgo even taking aspirin to qualify as research subjects.

The issue of clean data is not only a matter of research ethics or policy; it also has to do with what constitutes a scientifically meaningful clinical trial. Researchers could well concede that questions of ethics or policy do not fall within their expertise. But the proper way to design a clinical trial so that it will yield an interpretable result is a different matter: it would seem that questions about experimental design ought to be debated among experts themselves. In this case, however, experimental design became a public issue in which certain support groups of nonexperts engaged the experts. As a result, what had constituted expert practice was revised.

Several AIDS activists challenged the demand for clean data. By imposing this requirement on research subjects, they argued, scientists ran the risk of having the results of a clinical trial not clearly apply to "real-world conditions." So-called "clean data" were of doubtful clinical use. On the other hand, experts pointed out the uncertainty in applicability when the data are *not* clean. Because the data would be unclean in different ways, reflecting different possible drug interactions, how could any generalizable results be obtained?

Interestingly, the controversy over clinical trials proceeded in accordance with the participatory mode. The debate took place on newspaper op-ed pages, in letters to the editor in professional journals, in comments at professional meetings, and in discussions by institutional review boards. Eventually, the experts conceded the point, including one who wrote an article in the *New England Journal of Medicine* entitled, "You *Can* Teach an Old Dog New Tricks: How AIDS Trials Are Pioneering New Strategies."[7] The scientific consensus (the "biomedical norms governing the acquisition of knowledge through AIDS clinical trials") shifted as a result of public deliberation.

FAILED DELIBERATION AND THE ZERO MODE

In other recent scientific disputes, however, the participatory mode has not come into play as it did in the debate over clinical trials. Consider the public controversy over the cause of AIDS. During the early 1980s, the scientific merits of various hypotheses regarding the cause of AIDS quickly became a public issue. Whereas a growing number of experts favored some sort of viral cause, several AIDS groups, at least initially, refused to accept this hypothesis, presumably because of its implications regarding what populations were at risk and what sort of behaviors (i.e., "safe sex") would reduce risk. As a consensus formed among experts in favor of the view that the HIV family of retroviruses caused AIDS, many AIDS groups also came around. Nevertheless, some did not. Rather than continue with deliberation, these groups fell into the adversarial mode: they identified experts who did not share in the expert consensus (this is often possible, as we noted earlier, because a consensus does not require unanimity) to justify their rejection of the HIV hypothesis. In this case, a general scientific issue was indeed at stake: how relevant were Koch's postulates, since HIV does not clearly satisfy the standard criterion for an agent's being the cause of a disease? As the expert consensus solidified, the dissenters appeared to dig in their heels with dramatic but irresponsible offers to be injected with HIV to "prove" their position.

A different example of this phenomenon, in which different voluntary groups are pitted against each other, can be found in the case of cancer therapies. Several associations, including the International Association of Cancer Victims and Friends, which publishes the *Cancer News Journal*, and the Cancer Control Society, which publishes *Cancer Control Journal*, believe, contrary to the expert consensus, that cancer is not a tumor disease but rather a metabolic disease in which the tumor is merely an obvious symptom. Cancer treatment should not consist in destroying tumors so much as changing diet and administering various enzymes, most notably the apricot-pit extract known as laetrile. Other associations, such as the American Cancer Society and the AMA, have denounced these groups as promoting quackery.

Nevertheless, despite the expert consensus against laetrile, various experts who were part of the consensus tried to initiate deliberation with the proponents of laetrile by performing animal experiments, clinical trials, and retrospective case reviews, even though the initial negative data on laetrile would not normally have led to further investigation. For the most part, these efforts had little impact on the dissident groups. In some cases, instead of seeking deliberation about the expert consensus, these groups adopted the adversarial mode, identifying experts who were sympathetic to their cause. In other cases, however, what we might call the "zero mode" prevailed.

In the zero mode, experts are deemed to have no status whatsoever, on the grounds that the issue is not one about which there can be expertise. In the case of cancer therapies, some of the associations promoting laetrile seem animated chiefly by the principle that people should have the freedom to choose their therapy, regardless of expert opinion, and not by scientific questions, such as whether the standard tests are adequate in assessing laetrile's efficacy. For some, interest in laetrile is part of a broader interest in holistic medicine, natural therapies, and alternative medicine that is often based more on New Age and other forms of modern spiritualism than on specific scientific issues. Invoking any of the other conceptions of the experts' role—technocratic, adversarial, or participatory—in debating therapies misses the point.

The zero mode was also invoked in the controversy over the etiology of AIDS. Several associations (some apparently religious) reject the HIV hypothesis, but, unlike some of the AIDS groups mentioned earlier, they do not base their rejection on a scientific issue such as the satisfaction of Koch's postulates. These associations maintain that AIDS is caused by the "sin" of homosexuality, and so is the manifestation of God's anger. In effect, the causal issue is deemed not to be a matter of expertise.

I do not wish to suggest that the zero mode is necessarily antiscience or is invoked only by small minorities or groups considerably out of the mainstream. Especially if we look at expertise in areas other than biology and medicine, there are several public controversies in which analysis by experts might seem useful or appropriate but in which the zero mode reflects the prevailing sentiment. Although some people claim expertise on such issues as drug legalization, crime prevention and punishment, and race relations, for the most part experts play little if any role in these debates. The prevailing judgment is that the (important) issues in these debates are not a matter of expertise.

A TREND?

In assessing the role of contemporary voluntary associations in mediating between experts and the public, it would be rash to generalize solely from the contrasts between the tuberculosis movement at the turn of the century and the AIDS movement of the past two decades. To make a strong claim—that changes in the character of voluntary associations formed around specific diseases have altered the relationship between experts and nonexperts—we would plainly need first to establish some generalities about the variety of associations that identify themselves as voluntary health agencies or support groups. The problem is that we face a "messy dynamism" in these groups. As I noted earlier, the line between voluntary health agencies (health charities) and mediating support groups is both fuzzy and evolving. Many consist of both national and local entities, their records are not always centralized, and some are more fastidious than others in keeping records. Under the circumstances, suggestive cases are the best we have.

It might be objected that, even as a case, AIDS is too exceptional—and so are many AIDS organizations—to be representative of possible trends in health-related associations. First, AIDS support groups are often tied in various ways to the broader political concerns of many gays and lesbians, whose early activities and consciousness-raising efforts predate the AIDS epidemic. Members of these groups have long been skeptical of the government's responsiveness to their protests regarding stigma and discrimination. Consequently, as AIDS was at least initially perceived to be a disease that affected only gays, many AIDS support groups were not inclined to trust the medical establishment's findings or efforts. The women's health movement, which also predates the AIDS epidemic, had already set the stage for questioning medical authority. Furthermore, the gay community affected by AIDS has been, to a considerable extent, an affluent, well-educated part of the population. This combination of features helps explain why many AIDS groups would not wait on expert findings but instead were inclined and able to deliberate with the experts on the subject matter of their expertise.

Nevertheless, these special features do not mean that other groups cannot replicate some of the strategies of the AIDS movement. Indeed, to some extent the AIDS movement has come to be seen as a model for other disease organizations. For example, several commentators have noted the rise of breast cancer support groups whose success in getting research and treatment issues on the public agenda owes a good deal to techniques borrowed from the AIDS movement. Although most of the media attention has been focused on their successful efforts at fund-raising and lobbying, the breast cancer groups have also deliberated with the experts. Let me illustrate with a recent example.

At the beginning of 1997, a public controversy arose over the use of mammograms for women in their forties. There is a consensus among experts that periodic mammograms for women 50 or older should be performed: the risk of contracting breast cancer substantially increases at that age, and early detection from a mammogram would usually indicate an optimistic prognosis. Experts were divided, however, over whether to recommend breast cancer screening also to women in their forties.

The National Institutes of Health (NIH) periodically hold what they felicitously call "Consensus Development Conferences" in which the leading experts are gathered to deliberate among themselves on medical issues that seem ripe for forging a consensus. A Consensus Conference was called regarding the advisability of recommending mammograms for women in their forties, and the expert panel concluded that such tests should not in general be recommended for these women.

When the panel's findings were announced in January 1997, several experts disagreed with its conclusion. But the controversy was not seen as a debate among experts that should be settled by experts. Whether to recommend testing of women in their forties became a public issue, with Congress holding hearings on the matter even though it was not clear what legislation was in question.

Given the lack of expert consensus (though there was an "official consensus"), one might have thought the adversarial mode would come into play. In that scenario, people who supported the panel's conclusion would appeal to the expertise of those assembled by the NIH as well as the American College of Physicians, while people who opposed it would appeal to the expertise of those from the National Cancer Institute and the American College of Radiology, who favored mammograms for women in their forties.

Although some groups indeed behaved according to this mode, others acted more in accordance with the participatory mode. Various groups weighed in to debate the interpretation of findings, focusing on several studies on the reduction of mortality attributable to breast cancer screening in various age groups. They also debated the sort of expertise called for in making recommendations about breast cancer screening to women and their doctors. The Senate, hardly a body of medical experts, also weighed in. Hearings were held, and at least one senator, Kay Bailey Hutchison of Texas, claimed that the expert panel's report contained factual errors.[8] The result was that a nonbinding resolution in favor of recommending screening was passed 98 to 0. Although the public has not reached any such consensus, it seems likely that any resolution of the matter will not be determined solely by the experts.

It is perhaps worth noting that the issue was whether there was evidence supporting a universal recommendation for mammography for all women in their forties. No one denied that some women, based on their medical histories and concerns about risk, would be well advised to discuss the matter with their physician and perhaps seek mammography. And certainly no one claimed that mammography should never be offered to women in their forties. Unfortunately, some of the heat in the public controversy—such as public accusations that the panel's report condemned American women to death—seemed to come from distortions of what was at issue. A clearer understanding of the issue might have caused a different mode to govern the public debate, or it might have kept the matter from becoming a public issue in the first place.

Assuming that a current trend favors the participatory mode in addressing scientific and medical controversies that become public issues, is this a change for the better? In some sense, it surely is. The public's choices are not limited to the technocratic, the adversarial, or the zero mode; nonexperts are not required to be deferential, skeptical, or dismissive with regard to expertise. Even when faced with an expert consensus, members of the public need not believe they must always either defer to the experts or question the legitimacy of expertise in the matter altogether. Adoption of the participatory mode can lead to alteration of an existing consensus or help clarify to a broader audience the compelling reasons for that consensus.

Sometimes, however, the participatory mode is not an option. If there are no knowledgeable nonexperts, there can be no participatory mode governing public deliberation; if there is no expert consensus for the knowledgeable nonexperts to challenge, then the participatory mode, as I have described it, cannot be invoked. Moreover, although the knowledgeable nonexpert's challenge may begin by alleging that the experts' entrenched perspective blinds them to certain considerations, it cannot rest there. The challenge must ultimately rest on arguments that the experts can acknowledge and assess and then reply to or accept. If the nonexpert has no such arguments, or if the experts' replies are not seriously offered or seriously considered, there can be no deliberation. Although the participatory mode has its place, it doesn't belong everywhere. Indeed, one might argue that if the experts deserve their name, only in rare cases will the expert consensus need to be challenged or corrected.

Still, I wish to conclude by pointing to one likely and tangible benefit that may follow from the availability of the participatory mode: its effect on levels of trust, both on the part of the public toward experts and on experts toward the public. In the technocratic mode, the public's trust in the experts is mainly *assumed*. In the participatory mode, appropriately applied, trust is *built* in both directions. Voluntary groups in our own day are presumably less likely to obey Palmer's call to present the experts' claims as "almost spontaneously created." His suggestion that the public should be led to believe that there is no deliberation in science, that the facts somehow speak for themselves, and that subsequent deliberation with nonexperts is irrational, is no longer tenable. That is quite likely a good thing for the public and the experts alike.

NOTES

1. Richard Shyrock, *National Tuberculosis Association 1904–1954: A Study of the Voluntary Health Movement in the United States* (New York: National Tuberculosis Association, 1957), 57.

2. Michael Teller, *The Tuberculosis Movement: A Public Health Campaign in the Progressive Era* (New York: Greenwood Press, 1988), 55.

3. Charles Winslow, *The Life of Hermann M. Biggs* (Philadelphia: Lea & Febiger, 1929), 200.

4. Shyrock, *National Tuberculosis Association*, 56.

5. George Palmer, "The Need for Uniformity in Anti-Tuberculosis Education," *Journal of the Outdoor Life* 12 (1915): 38.

6. See Steven Epstein, *Impure Science: AIDS, Activism, and the Politics of Knowledge* (Berkeley: University of California Press, 1996).

7. T. Merigan, "You *Can* Teach an Old Dog New Tricks—How AIDS Trials Are Pioneering New Strategies," *New England Journal of Medicine* 323 (1990): 1341.

8. Jessica Mathews, "Bad Science in the Senate," *Washington Post*, 10 February 1997, A19.

PART SIX

INTERNATIONAL CIVIL SOCIETY

16

Civil Society and Transitional Justice

David A. Crocker

"There is no more important new subject on the international agenda," remarks *Washington Post* columnist Jim Hoagland, "than the necessity of balancing the human need for justice and retribution with the state's interest in stability and reconciliation."[1] This claim is especially true when the state in question is a new democracy making a transition from a deadly internal conflict or a prior authoritarian government. The term *transitional justice* is increasingly used to address the question of how emerging democracies should deal with past human rights abuses perpetrated by opponents in a civil conflict or by the nation's prior regime.

This chapter has two main sections. In the first section I discuss the challenge of transitional justice and develop a normative framework for meeting this challenge. I identify a variety of tools—from trials, through truth commissions, to amnesty—that fledgling democracies have employed in reckoning with past human rights atrocities. I then examine the fundamental objectives that transitional democracies should strive to accomplish. In the second section I discuss the idea of civil society and then bring together the usually separate discussions of transitional justice and civil society. A nation's civil society is often well suited to contribute to the selection and implementation of transitional tools. Moreover, *international* civil society can play a helpful and even indispensable role in helping a newly forged democracy achieve justice. As we will see, the most promising approaches to both transitional justice and civil society—whether domestic or international—involve the ideals of the public sphere, discursive democracy, and public deliberation.[2]

MEANS, RISKS, AND ENDS

The question of reckoning with past evil has been framed in several ways. The most general query concerns "what nations should do about a difficult past," in the words of Timothy Garton Ash.[3] Another commentator, Carlos Nino, formulates the challenge in two questions: "How shall we live with evil?" and "How shall we respond to massive human rights violations committed either by state actors or by others with the consent and tolerance of their governments?"[4] Although these questions are important in certain contexts, they fail to put the specific question of this chapter. For our purposes, Ash's question and Nino's first question are too broad: they fail to emphasize, as I shall usually do, how an *emerging democracy* should cope with its past. Nino's second question is too narrow: it neglects atrocities committed by nonstate actors against a prior authoritarian regime or in a prior internal conflict. Hence, the question of "transitional justice," as I shall be employing the term, is "How should a fledgling democracy reckon with severe human rights abuses (i.e., extrajudicial killing, disappearance, rape, torture, or severe ill treatment) that earlier authoritarian regimes, their opponents, or combatants in an internal armed conflict have committed?"[5] What national and international institutions should implement transitional justice, however conceived, and how and when should they do so? What ethical and practical considerations should guide reasonable answers to these questions, and who should try to answer them?

Societies have employed a variety of means or tools in responding to human rights violations committed by a prior regime or its opponents. These measures embrace but are not limited to the following: international war crimes tribunals and punishment; domestic and foreign criminal trials and punishment; domestic and foreign civil suits; truth commissions and other investigatory bodies; public access to police or military records (e.g., the Stasi files in the former East Germany); public or individual acknowledgment of and apology to victims for harm done; purging or banning perpetrators from public office (lustration); public commemoration such as monuments, museums, or days of mourning; reparation to or compensation of victims or their families; social shunning or stigmatization of perpetrators; individual or blanket amnesty (prohibition on prosecution of alleged rights violators); pardon or reduced sentences for past crimes; repeal of exculpatory laws (amnesties or pardons); impunity (ignoring or accepting past rights violations).

To decide among these tools, as well as to fashion, combine, and sequence them, a society ideally would consider what it is trying to accomplish. One contribution of ethical analysis is to consider which goals have the greatest moral urgency. In assessing candidates for morally justifiable ends, however, we must guard against a rigid and overly specific universalism. The particularities of each situation are enormously important in determining what ought to be done in that context. Even if there are—as I believe—transcultural ethical principles, each society has more or less idiosyncratic features to be taken into account as it decides how to respond to prior human rights violations.

For instance, what transitional justice requires will depend to some extent on what the transition is *from*. Is the prior situation one of a government's military defeat in a war between nations (World War II); a government's collaboration with an occupying military (Vichy France, the Ustashe regime in Croatia); a civil war in which one side is victorious (Rwanda, Democratic Republic of the Congo); a stalemated civil war (El Salvador, Guatemala); a military dictatorship (Argentina, Uruguay, Chile); two distinct nations (West and East Germany); a unified nation (Yugoslavia or Czechoslovakia); or apartheid (South Africa)? Does the country have a prior history of democratic institutions (Chile, Uruguay), colonialism (Rwanda), ethnic conflict (Rwanda, South Africa), or military repression of and systematic terror against its own citizens (Guatemala)? How long did the human rights violations last? What percentage and sectors of the population were directly or indirectly responsible for human rights violations? What percentage and sectors of the population were victims?

Equally important is what the transition is *to*. Is the nation the result of unification of prior states (Germany), only one of which violated basic rights, or is the nation the result of a disintegration of a prior state (Czechoslovakia) that committed administrative atrocity? Does the successor and democratic society to some extent perpetuate, perhaps in a new guise, the ruling party, judicial system, and military of the old regime? Or have one or more of these been replaced with (more) democratic institutions? What is the strength and progressive potential of the government, democratic institutions, market, and civil society? How poor or prosperous is the society, and what internal or external resources might be made available for reckoning with past human rights abuses? To what extent has civil strife been eliminated and relative stability established, and to what extent are these conditions dependent on occupying forces or other international institutions? What are the operative values in the new society? What domestic political alignments and conflicts exist in the new order?

Finally, *how* has the transition to a new democracy been made? By force, imposed from without (Nuremberg) or within? By negotiation and agreement, including agreement among former enemies? By democratic vote? Some mixture of these three modes?[6]

In most cases, the challenge of transitional justice will be integrally linked to the challenge of protecting, legitimating, and strengthening the society's new or embryonic democratic institutions. There are certain things that a fragile democracy should not do and other things that it must do if it is to reckon with an evil past, distinguish itself from a prior repressive regime, and not imperil its own existence.

MORALLY JUSTIFIED GOALS

Given these challenges and the array of available tools described earlier, what should be an emerging democracy's basic purposes as it pursues transitional justice? I have argued elsewhere that revenge—whether private or in the public form of "victor's justice"—is not a legitimate purpose; at the other extreme, the resolve simply to "forget and move on" is equally unacceptable.[7] But, assuming that these two ends—revenge and oblivion—should not be the goals of societies seeking transitional justice, what are some morally defensible goals that might guide these transitions? I would argue that a society's choice of measures to achieve transitional justice, and of the most appropriate version of any particular measure, should be made in the light of at least the following objectives:[8]

1. *Truth.* There should be investigation and disclosure of the truth about whose moral and legal rights were violated, by whom, when, where, and why. This information should include at least a general picture of the institutional ethos and chain of command that resulted in rights violations. Truth about the past is important in itself; one way to make this point is to say that victims and their descendants have a moral right to know the truth about past abuses. Moreover, without reasonably complete truth, none of the other goals of transitional justice are likely to be realized.

2. *A public platform for victims.* There should be the provision to victims or their families of a platform—in a trial, investigatory hearing, historical account, or public commemoration—to tell their stories and have their testimony publicly acknowledged. Secrecy about and threats pursuant to the disclosure of human rights abuses are among the conditions that made possible extensive campaigns of terror. Enabling victims to give their accounts expresses respect for the victims, is a means to getting at the truth, and nurtures trust in peacemaking and democratic institutions.

3. *Accountability and sanctions.* There should be fair ascriptions to individuals and groups on all sides of responsibility for past abuses and the meting out of appropriate sanctions to these perpetrators. Sanctions may range from legal imprisonments, fines, and the payment of compensation to public shaming and prohibitions on holding public office. Past violators should get what they deserve and be educated about societal norms.

Potential future violators should be deterred from committing similar crimes.

4. *Rule of law.* The transitional society should comply with the rule of law, which, as David Luban argues, is one of the abiding legacies of Nuremberg.[9] Rule of law is especially important in a new and fragile democracy bent on distinguishing itself from prior authoritarianism or lethal conflict.

5. *Compensation to victims.* Compensation, in the form of income or opportunities, should be paid to individuals and groups whose rights have been violated.

6. *Institutional reform.* There should be identification and attacks on the likely causes of the past abuses as well as reform in the law and basic institutions to reduce the possibility that such violations will be repeated. Basic institutions include the judiciary, police, military, land tenure system, tax structure, and systems providing economic opportunities.

7. *Reconciliation.* A transitional society should aim to reconcile former enemies and reintegrate them into society. Reconciliation should mean at least that, though they may continue to disagree and even be adversaries, former enemies live together nonviolently and as fellow citizens ("liberal social solidarity").[10] A more robust interpretation of reconciliation—for example, as healing or mutual forgiveness—is both less practically feasible and less normatively compelling.

8. *Democratization and economic development.* A transitional society should protect and deepen its democracy and promote just economic development, including the opportunities for all to live minimally decent lives.[11]

9. *Public deliberation.* A transitional society should engage in and promote a public discussion of and deliberation about its goals and strategies for transitional justice. It is unlikely that in any given society full agreement will exist about the aims and means for dealing with past abuses. What can be aspired to is that disagreements about ends and means will be reduced through public deliberation that permits a fair hearing for all and promotes morally respectable compromises. Such public deliberation, embodied and promoted in various institutions, increases the chances that whatever policies are adopted can be justified to all and practically forges links between transitional justice and democracy building.

For our purposes here, a few comments about these objectives are called for. First, each of the proposed ends may also be a means contributing to the attainment of one or more of the others. Determining accountability and sanctions sometimes contributes to truth about the past. Truth about the past is necessary for allocating responsibility, sanctions, and compensation as well as for making recommendations about removing the causes of the human rights abuses.[12] Holding individuals morally and legally accountable helps diminish stereotyping and enmity between groups and thereby contributes to their reconciliation.[13] Public deliberation about transitional justice both contributes to and is benefited by reconciliation and democratic development. Moreover, the various tools mentioned earlier often serve more than one objective at once. For instance, a truth commission's determination of individual accountability may be indispensable to other institutions that sanction perpetrators and compensate victims.

At the same time, it must be admitted that in some situations, the achievement of one end will be *at the expense of* (full) achievement of another. Legal sanctions against former human rights violators can imperil a fragile democracy in which the military responsible for the earlier abuses still wields social and political power. Compliance with the rule of law in fact can protect human rights abusers if prior authoritarian governments pass blanket laws that prohibit investigations or prosecution. The principle of nonretroactivity—the rule which says that someone may be charged and punished only under statutes in force when he committed the act—may clash with the goals of penal sanctions and the deterrence of future rights violations.[14] A trial determining the past guilt or innocence of an individual accused of human rights violations is not a very good means of achieving *general* truth about past atrocities.[15] To protect witnesses or secure testimony from alleged perpetrators, a truth commission's interrogation of witnesses or alleged perpetrators sometimes may have to take place behind closed doors.

Each of the goals, I would argue, must be considered with respect to its relevance for a particular transition. If possible, however, none of them should be completely sacrificed—at least in the long run—to obtain one or more of the others.

Finally, although all nine objectives are important, the final objective—the public deliberation objective—has a certain priority. This goal requires that a society in transition engage in a society-wide discursive process in which the merits of various proposals for the ends and means of transitional justice are publicly debated and judged. This process should go on in public rather than behind closed doors, and it should be accessible—linguistically and in other ways—to every citizen. For example, South Africa's Truth and Reconciliation Commission (TRC) met in various locations throughout the nation, and its proceedings were accessible in a variety of South Africa's languages. Likewise, democratic bodies, accountable to the public, should decide how and why the society should reckon with past evil. Moreover, the results of these choices—such as legal decisions or investigatory reports—should be publicly available.

A society's response to prior human rights violations need not issue from or yield a consensus about the specific meanings of or foundations for the nine objectives. In a society aspiring to be liberal and democratic, public deliberation expresses the commitment to respect one's fellow citizens, to engage in give-and-take, and to forge compromises with which all can live nonviolently.[16]

Now that we have considered the challenges, tools, and goals of transitional justice, we can ask what roles civil society can (and should) play in this process. In what follows, I pursue this question while exploring the *idea* of civil society, both domestic and international.

THREE MODELS OF CIVIL SOCIETY

A nation's civil society is often well suited to specify and prioritize the ends of transitional justice as well as choose and implement the means. To defend this claim, and to argue for a role for *international* civil society, requires some clarification of the term *civil society*. Civil society is a fashionable and contested concept.[17] Its multiple meanings permit people of almost every political stripe to employ it, usually in a celebratory way, as a beneficial institution to be protected or an ideal to be aimed for. The various civil society debates, however, have a special hue in the context of societies undergoing democratization and reckoning with prior human rights abuses.

Michael Ignatieff, writing about the aspirations of East European intellectuals in the 1970s and 1980s, tries to capture their ideal of civil society: "the kind of place where you do not change the street signs every time you change the regime."[18] This one-liner nicely captures the antigovernmental approach to civil society, made popular after the fall of the Berlin Wall. "Civil society," on this interpretation, is a rallying cry for individuals and groups, such as churches and capitalist enterprises, to get governmental spies, police, economic planners, and bureaucrats out of their affairs. The recent enthusiasm for privatization, advanced in different ways by the 1994 Republican "revolution" in the United States and by the International Monetary Fund and the World Bank around the world, echoes this approach. Civil society exists if and only if people and their groups are free to pursue their own conception of the good, especially their economic self-interest, without government interference.

This model usefully provides a basis to undermine state authoritarianism and corporatism, for it envisions a zone of life free of government control. When a government has violated human rights or permitted such violation, the antigovernment approach to civil society opens space to criticize and undermine state oppression and to build a different kind of government and society. Nongovernmental groups, often working underground, help people survive repression or civil war and then begin the

onerous process of democratization. The antigovernmental model is illuminating to the extent that this civil ferment is composed of a variety of
groups—sometimes in alliance with each other—such as churches, self-
help and mutual support groups, and human rights organizations in addition to the mass media and other business and professional associations.

However, this model of civil society in a transitional justice context is
also misleading. Whatever legitimate role nongovernmental groups may
play, when a society in the process of democratization grapples with prior
human rights violations, that society's national *government* has important
and often unique democratic responsibilities. These duties embrace protecting its citizens' present democratic rights and promoting their future
economic opportunity. Government obligation also extends to reckoning
with the rights violations perpetrated by the prior nondemocratic regime.
One or another branch of government is often best situated to employ
certain tools—such as prosecution, investigation, compensation, or commemoration—designed to achieve transitional justice.

Furthermore, what democratization and transitional justice often require is not a rejection of government but a reform of some branch of government—for example, bringing the military and police under ("civilian") control by elected officials or ensuring that the judiciary becomes
more independent of executive or private pressures. An antigovernmental approach to civil society in a context of transitional justice also neglects
the myriad ways in which the government and nongovernmental groups
can work together and supplement each other's efforts. Honduras's
human rights commissioner, Leo Valladares, uses the resources of his office to help strengthen that part of civil society playing a positive role in
transitional justice. Government and civil society need not be at odds, and
each can contribute something important to democratization and transitional justice. The antigovernmental model of civil society provides no
basis to grasp and approve of such collaboration.

A narrower approach to civil society, which in the U.S. debate has been
termed the *associational* model, excludes for-profit groups and commercial
organizations and emphasizes private voluntary associations such as
churches, self-help groups, amateur sports leagues, and groups pursuing
common hobbies. On this view, civil society is a "third sector," differing
from both state and market. The state coercively protects or promotes the
public good. In the market, private producers and consumers freely exchange goods and services. In civil society, private individuals freely join
together to pursue some noneconomic common passion or project.[19] Inspired by the nineteenth-century social critic Alexis de Tocqueville, Robert Putnam has recently argued that voluntary associations of this kind

promote trust of others, social cooperation, and civic engagement.[20] To what extent is this model of civil society relevant to societies confronting the challenge of transitional justice?

One problem with this model is that it includes such a heterogeneous list of groups. Some, such as certain church groups or the Argentine Madres de la Plaza del Mayo, have played an important role in ending government repression, promoting democratization, and advancing transitional justice.[21] These beneficial groups may themselves be quite diverse. Some may be primarily inwardly oriented or self-help groups, such as the Madres, whereas others, such as human rights groups, may see their basic mission as that of promoting transitional justice. The associational model, however, also covers other voluntary groups that are indifferent to, or have limited consequences for (at least in the short term),[22] transitional justice (e.g., amateur soccer teams) or that oppose and are detrimental to transitional justice (e.g., paramilitary associations, the right-wing Catholic organization Opus Dei). Enemies of democratization, these latter groups may be bent on either private revenge or public forgetting.

While the first model emphasizes civil society's freedom from state invasion and the second emphasizes the capacity of associations within civil society to generate social trust and other valuable products, a third model emphasizes a different aspect of civil society. It focuses on the communicative activity generated by civil society's groups and on its potential to strengthen democracy. The continual public conversation generated by civic improvement associations, religious groups, political and social movements, advocacy groups, and the like, filtered through media organs such as newspapers and television, constitutes a "public sphere" that supports the formation of public opinion, a necessary ingredient in democratic politics. This third model has been worked out most fully by Jürgen Habermas, Jean Cohen, and James Bohman. Cohen contends that "the concept of the public sphere . . . [is] the normative core of the idea of civil society and the heart of any conception of democracy."[23] Explicitly indicating her indebtedness to Habermas, Cohen defines the "civil public sphere" as

> a juridically private (nonstate) "space" in which individuals without official status can communicate and attempt to persuade one another through argumentation and criticism about matters of general concern. Ideally, participation in discussion is universally accessible, inclusive, and freed from deformations due to wealth, power, or social status. Argumentation and critique involve the principles of individual autonomy, parity of discussants, and the free and open problematization of any issue that is of common concern, including the procedural principles guiding discussion.[24]

Given this idealization of the public sphere, the third model is especially interested in civil society associations whose internal structure mirrors the structure of the public sphere itself: they are egalitarian, democratic, and inclusive. The public sphere model highlights those inwardly democratic, outwardly oriented, nonstate, nonmarket groups that deliberate about and try to protect and extend democratic forms. Included would be democratically organized unions, human rights and other advocacy groups, think tanks, and so forth. Cohen remarks that "the political role of civil society [in the sense of the civil public sphere] is not directly related to the conquest of power, but to the generation of influence, through the life of democratic associations and unconstrained discussion in a variety of cultural and informal public spheres."[25] One effect of this public deliberation in the context of transitional justice has been—*pace* Ignatieff and sometimes with state help—*to* change the names of streets and buildings to commemorate the victims of human rights abuses.

Yet, although this third model in effect highlights groups that are internally democratic and egalitarian, its main point seems to be that civil society is constituted by groups, often dissimilar in internal structures and missions, which accept each other as partners in a public conversation about societal concerns. Civil society breaks down when public debate ceases and violence begins (again).

THE CONTRIBUTIONS OF CIVIL SOCIETY TO TRANSITIONAL JUSTICE

Our discussion of the three models highlights different aspects of civil society relevant to our inquiry about transitional justice. We have seen that civil society can be a bulwark of freedom against the state; that private associations can generate both civically valuable by-products (social trust, civic capacities) and civically noxious attitudes (clannishness, private revenge, resistance to democratic change); and that civil society groups, especially those that are internally democratic and egalitarian, nourish the kind of informed public opinion that makes viable democratic government possible. The models alert us to the positive and negative roles civil society organizations can play in transitional justice and to the challenge that social pluralism poses to a just and democratic transition. Let us consider some of civil society's contributions, limitations, and dangers. There are at least five kinds of contributions: public deliberation, victim assistance, investigation, adversarial public action, and mass media and the public sphere.

Public Deliberation

With respect to the challenge of transitional justice, civil society can play an important role in deliberating about, formulating, scheduling, and prioritizing goals and in forging measures to realize them. A particularly important occasion for such public deliberation is during peace negotiations between the two opposing sides in a military conflict.

A crucial element in negotiating the end of a conflict is an accord between former enemies about how past human rights violations will be treated once peace is obtained. In the difficult and drawn-out peace negotiations between the Guatemalan government and the twenty-year-old guerrilla movement, the Guatemalan National Revolutionary Union (URNG), civil society played a strong and increasingly institutionalized role. The UN-brokered Framework Agreement signed in January 1994 "recognized the role played [in earlier negotiations] . . . by the various sectors of organized civil society and gave them a legitimate place within the negotiating process in an Assembly of Civil Society (ASC)."[26] Chaired by the highly respected cleric Monsignor Quezada, the ASC comes closest to the first model of civil society discussed earlier, for it was composed of representatives not only of grassroots nongovernmental organizations but also of political parties, universities, and small and medium business associations. It should be noted, however, that the assembly, though representing many business groups, did not include the most powerful one, the Comity Coordinador de Asociaciones Agrícolas, Comerciales, Industriales, y Financieras (Chamber of Agricultural, Commercial, Industrial, and Financial Associations).

The Guatemalan ASC formulated consensus positions on the various topics being negotiated, including the formation of a truth commission, an agreement on indigenous rights, and an agreement on socioeconomic goals, and transmitted these positions to the negotiating parties and the UN mediator. According to Teresa Whitfield, the ASC helped broaden the peace negotiations to address the original sources of a conflict that had cost over 150,000 lives since 1960.[27] Moreover, the opposing parties also presented each negotiated accord to the ASC for its consideration and endorsement. Although many human rights activists were and remain very dissatisfied with the accord on the Guatemalan truth commission, Whitfield remarks that the consultative process both "fueled public discussion and enhanced the validity of the peace process within Guatemalan society at large."[28]

Here we see civil society engaged in public deliberation, achieving consensus on some basic policies and disagreement on others, stimulating further public discussion, and lending democratic legitimation to the peace process and transitional justice. James Bohman articulates the ideal:

[P]olitical decision making is legitimate insofar as its policies are produced in a process of public discussion and debate in which citizens and their representatives, going beyond mere self-interest and limited points of view, reflect on the general interest or on their common good.[29]

It is not that the ASC was the only embodiment of civil society, let alone of public deliberation about transitional justice. After all, the peace negotiations, initially brokered by the Catholic prelate, were themselves a form of public deliberation, and such deliberation also occurred—albeit unevenly and with much narrower representativeness—within the Guatemalan parliament. Nor does the mere existence of an Assembly of Civil Society guarantee that diverse citizens will do more than rubber-stamp the decisions of the political or military leadership. Sometimes, especially following years of brutal repression, civil society is too weak to advance and widen public deliberation. In the Guatemalan case, however, the ASC arguably played a helpful role in getting the peace negotiators to tackle the root causes of the conflict and to create the outlines, at least, of some remedies. It is less clear that Guatemalan civil society in general or the ASC made a significant impact on the issue of *accountability* for past rights abuses.

Victim Assistance

In societies making a democratic transition, civil society can offer support in assisting and unofficially compensating the victims of human rights violations. In Chile and other countries, various civil society groups—especially families, religious groups, human rights groups, legal and medical clinics, and neighborhood support groups—provide often crucial assistance in rehabilitating victims—especially exiled or displaced persons—and helping them reintegrate into the larger society. In Chile, this activity often continues the work of clandestine neighborhood and professional groups that emerged during the Pinochet dictatorship to aid victims of official oppression and their families.[30] One worry is that aid-giving nongovernmental organizations (NGOs) flourish only under repressive conditions, and that they will decline if not altogether disappear during democratization. But it now appears that different types of NGOs have emerged to perform the same beneficial function. Still, a new democratic government sometimes can and should take over the task of rehabilitating and compensating victims, especially when it recognizes that it has a responsibility to restore certain basic opportunities as redress for past governmental abuses.

Investigation

Civil society groups can be enormously helpful and even indispensable in obtaining the truth about the past. During the seventeen-year Pinochet dictatorship, two religious organizations—the Roman Catholic Church's Vicaría de la Solidaridad and its ecumenical predecessor, the Comité de Cooperación para la Paz en Chile—collected thousands of judicial transcripts concerning disappearances. Such records were invaluable for the investigations of the presidentially appointed National Commission for Truth and Reconciliation, which had to complete its work in only eighteen months. In Uruguay, a nongovernmental report on governmental abuses committed between 1972 and 1985 was, according to Priscilla B. Hayner, more comprehensive, accurate, and widely distributed than the little-known government report.[31]

In Guatemala, dissatisfaction with the limited mandate, resources, and initially slow progress of the official Historical Clarification Commission has resulted in a parallel effort by an influential group within Guatemalan civil society. The Guatemala City archdiocese's human rights office sponsored the Project for the Recovery of Historical Memory (REMHI). Margaret Popkin has called REMHI's work "the most comprehensive civil society effort to investigate a country's past atrocities."[32] Local citizens, whom REMHI trained as "ambassadors of reconciliation," recorded more than six thousand testimonies, which communal leaders, elected by their villages, gave in their native (Indian) language. The resulting report, published on 24 April 1998 as "Guatemala: Nunca Mas," alleged that the army and so-called civilian self-defense patrols were responsible for about 80 percent of the 150,000 deaths and 50,000 disappearances in the war, while the leftist rebels were cited for about 9 percent of the deaths. Because Guatemalan illiteracy is so high, diffusion of the report will employ theater, radio, videos, public workshops, and ceremonies. REMHI has directly contributed to truth about the past, manifested respect for victims by providing them a platform in their own language, and spurred on the government's Historical Clarification Commission.

The importance of, but also dangers involved in, uncovering truth about past evil were tragically underscored two days after the REMHI report's release: Auxiliary Bishop Juan Gerardi Conedera, the director of the archdiocese's human rights office and coordinator of the report, was brutally bludgeoned to death in his home in Guatemala City. In a public ceremony releasing the report two days earlier, Gerardi Conedera situated the report in relation to both the past and future:

> We want to contribute to the building of a country different than the one we have now. For that reason we are recovering the memory of our people. This

path has been and continues to be full of risks, but the construction of the Reign of God has risks and can only be built by those that have the strength to confront those risks.[33]

Although usually appointed by a government's executive or legislature, truth commissions can be viewed either as parts of civil society or as hybrid entities that mediate between the state and civil society. Truth commissions are normally composed of prestigious and respected citizens not holding public office, and often these citizens represent important NGOs, a spectrum of political outlooks, and commercial groups. Desmond Tutu, for example, who heads South Africa's TRC, is an Anglican archbishop.

Unlike judicial proceedings, truth commissions usually lack subpoena power (South Africa's is an exception). Moreover, adversarial defense and cross-examination of witnesses do not take place. Still, public deliberation occurs if and when truth commissions publicly deliberate about the focus of their investigation and make their proceedings accessible to a live audience or through the mass media. Public acknowledgment occurs when perpetrators of human rights abuses admit their involvement if not their guilt and when victims or their families accept disclosures if not confessions and repentance. In South Africa, a mixture of amnesty and social stigmatization occurs when perpetrators exchange disclosure, acknowledgment, and sometimes confessions of guilt for legal protection from future prosecution. Investigatory commissions also engage the wider public sphere when they defend their aims, procedures, and costs in public debate and in response to public criticism.

Adversarial Public Action

Some organizations in a nation's civil society adopt as one of their main goals the monitoring and evaluation of the government's (and wider society's) actual steps toward achieving peace, democratization, and ways of handling past human rights violations. One role of civil society is to constitute an independent site to assess whether promises are kept and rhetoric becomes reality. Such monitoring and assessment is part of what Amartya Sen calls public action—action of NGOs designed to advance the public good.[34] Possible actions include public petitions, protests and marches, strikes, press conferences, and complaints addressed to public officials.

Each of these activities helps undermine what Leo Valladares, the human rights commissioner of Honduras, calls the "culture of impunity." In such a culture, government officials, the police and military, and ordinary citizens break the law without fear of punishment, for there is a shared understanding that each person will be silent about the other's abuses as long as the favor is returned. Many NGOs in transitional societies are seeking to replace such a culture of impunity with a "culture of responsibility" or a "culture of rights" in which citizens are responsible for respecting human and legal rights and publicly protest their violation. As the 1996 report of Honduras's National Commission of Human Rights puts it:

> Civil Society ought to join forces so that judicial reform is a reality, and this requires the strengthening of a democratic and human rights culture in order to halt the epidemic of corruption and be able to save our democratic institutions. As the Commissioner has expressed it: "Democracy is shown not only at the ballot box but also by accusations, by opposition to official abuse and corruption, and by the system of justice. Hence, democracy ought to fight so that injustice is the exception and justice the rule."[35]

Not only do such advocacy groups fight impunity and advance citizenship in the wider culture, but groups within civil society, especially those that are internally democratic, become schools for democratic citizenship.

Three such organizations struggling to promote transitional justice in Guatemala are REMHI, discussed earlier, the Myrna Mack Foundation, and the Center for Human Rights Legal Action. The Mack Foundation has been described as "generating public debate and legislative change on key issues such as judicial, police and intelligence reform."[36] The group is named for an internationally renowned anthropologist who investigated the forced displacement of indigenous peoples in Guatemala and who was savagely killed in the streets of Guatemala City in 1990; one of the foundation's goals is to bring to justice the military intelligence officers accused of her murder. The Center for Human Rights Legal Action aims to end impunity for Guatemala's human rights abusers, implement human rights in the Guatemalan peace process, and promote "the involvement of a broad cross section of civil society representatives in the process."[37] These three Guatemalan NGOs have joined many other groups[38] in domestic civil society to pressure the official Guatemalan truth commission to name specific perpetrators and not merely profile the general pattern of human rights abuses.

Mass Media and the Public Sphere

The civil public sphere clearly functions in countries undergoing transitional justice insofar as the mass media foster a society-wide debate that evaluates and seeks to improve the ends and means of transitional justice. For instance, South African newspapers and television reported daily on the TRC's work. They also provided fora for a spectrum of critics and defenders of the Commission. Likewise, since the mid-1980s, many Guatemalan newspapers have enlarged and invigorated the public sphere by reporting and commenting on the peace process and by opening their pages to a variety of opinions.

LIMITATIONS AND DANGERS OF CIVIL SOCIETY WITH REGARD TO TRANSITIONAL JUSTICE

The foregoing examples illustrate what a country's civil society, however conceived, and its civil public sphere in particular may do to advance the aims of transitional justice. Civil society, however, is not without some limitations, and there are some dangers in putting undue (and the wrong kind of) emphasis on it. Groups in civil society, especially following prolonged authoritarianism, may be very weak and disunited, which limits their potential impact on transitional justice. Just as civil society groups can differ considerably within a given national society, so too the civil societies of particular nations or regions exhibit much variety. Civic groups and a nation's civil society as a whole differ with respect to longevity, vitality, formality, resources and sustainability, orientation (inward or outward), internal structure (democratic vs. hierarchical), and external relations (grassroots, regionally/nationally federated, or internationally linked). Depending on their type and social context, many groups and networks are limited in what they can contribute to transitional justice, for they often have scant resources, outreach, and staying power. They may rise and fall before they are able to make much of a difference in the lives of their members or the larger society. Their knowledge of similar groups or networks also may be limited, so that they are unable to learn from each other. Their scope may be entirely at the grass roots, preventing them from influencing national institutions. National governments may be indifferent or hostile to their activities. Because of these deficiencies, national governments or international institutions may have important roles in helping create, strengthen, and form alliances among various civic groups.

Societies undergoing transitional justice should beware of certain dangers in thinking about the potential roles of civil society in meeting the challenges of transitional justice and democratic development. First, civil society must not be absolutized as the new source of salvation, permanently assuming roles that other actors, including national and local governments, should play. As innovator, facilitator, critic, educator, and (temporary) substitute, civil society can contribute to transitional justice. Yet, here as in other areas, the state must be "brought back in."[39] For government has an indispensable role with respect to some forms of prosecution, punishment, investigation, compensation, and commemoration. And just as civil society can supplement and correct the state, a democratizing state may fortify and help unify a weak, timid, and fragmented civil society.

A second peril is the opposite of the first—namely, that civil society will narrow its scope, functioning as exclusively inward-oriented voluntary associations, and thereby fail to assess, debate with, and influence other institutions that affect transitional justice. Although Putnam is concerned with the decline of civic culture, Cohen correctly sees that his conceptual framework prevents him from sufficiently emphasizing the activist and deliberative potential of civil society. An inward-looking self-help group of human rights victims or perpetrators, though important in a free and pluralistic society, is not all that civil society can be in relation to the challenge of transitional justice.

Inflexibility is a third danger for civil society and its advocates. Depending on historical developments and what the state and market in a society currently are doing or failing to do, civil societies in diverse social formations have *diverse* roles to play. The role of civil society in Chile, where—prior to Pinochet—there was a long and rich democratic history, is quite different from the role of civil society in Guatemala, where repression lasted longer and democracy had shallower roots. The challenges to civil society and the public sphere vary with the circumstances.

INTERNATIONAL CIVIL SOCIETY

It is in relation to the strengths, limitations, and weaknesses of domestic civil societies and national governments that we can best understand the ways in which international civil society may contribute to a nation's approximating the goals of transitional justice. International civil society (ICS), I argue, can fortify, supplement, and correct domestic civil society, strengthen the hand of local democrats, and reinforce or (temporarily) substitute for a society's own institutions, including its government and civil society.

A domestic civil society (DCS) consists of groups whose members are (predominantly) citizens of that nation and whose concerns, if they go beyond the group itself, (predominantly) are contained within the borders of the nation-state. The weasel word *predominantly* is used to acknowledge that the concepts of domestic and international civil society are fuzzy. A paradigm case of ICS, as I shall use the term, would be a group whose membership consists of citizens from many countries and whose activities or concerns extend to many countries and to international structures and issues. The Roman Catholic Church, Physicians without Borders, the International Campaign to Ban Land Mines, the International Red Cross, and the International Soccer Federation would be clear examples of ICS. However, a group whose members were all citizens in one country, such as Costa Ricans for World Peace, could also be part of ICS if its members had global concerns or activities.

In relation to transitional justice, it is useful to distinguish two types of ICSs and a closely related type of international institution: civil society groups from one country that aid the efforts of civil society groups in a country undergoing transitional justice; international not-for-profit organizations and movements; and transnational institutions such as the Organization of American States and institutions within the United Nations system. The first type, an internationally oriented DCS, is illustrated by the Washington Office on Latin America (WORL), a group that emphasizes police, judicial, and economic reform as well as transitional justice in the narrower sense. Composed largely of U.S. citizens, this advocacy group supplies moral and financial support and U.S. speaking opportunities to such groups as the three Guatemalan NGOs discussed earlier. Moreover, WORL may transmit lessons that DCSs learn about transitional justice in one country to DCSs confronting the challenge of transitional justice in their own country.

The second type of ICS is illustrated by a profusion of heterogeneous international NGOs and movements.[40] The term *globalization* is often used to denote global capital flows and transnational economic institutions. There is, however, another kind of globalization—movements and NGOs that investigate, debate, and help implement policies of many kinds in particular nations and regions. This network is constantly changing and often lacks formal institutional definition; sometimes an ICS is little more than a "virtual community" committed to a common cause and linked by E-mail, fax, and list servers. Still, the contributions to transitional justice by groups of this second type should not be underestimated. For example, international investigatory/advocacy groups conduct inquiries into human rights violations, monitor human rights compliance, and make recommendations as to how past abuses should be treated and future violations prevented. By providing international attention and support, these international groups can also lend legitimacy to and strengthen the hand of domestic civil groups and democratically elected governments in pursuing the goals of transitional justice.[41] Funded by a variety of private and national sources, these ICSs include Amnesty International, Human Rights Watch, the NGO Coalition for an International Criminal Court, and the Joint Evaluation of Emergency Assistance to Rwanda, the latter being an international team that investigated the international response to the Rwandan massacres.[42] Through their published documents and press conferences, these sorts of groups can inform domestic and world opinion and contribute to public deliberation about what should be done.

Closely related to international civil society, but a product of intergovernmental cooperation, are those organizations of the United Nations system that play a variety of roles in national transitional justice. Just as the increasing power of transnational corporations and decreasing power of national governments require a reconceptualization of international relations, law, and political economy, so the roles of the UN system require a rethinking of civil society and its relation to states, markets, and international forces and institutions. Not a superstate with coercive power, the UN seems at present to be best understood as an international body interacting with international civil society. Although the UN has been beset with financial problems (largely because the United States has not paid its membership dues), waste, and inefficiencies, it has contributed to transitional justice in several significant ways, ranging from peacemaking and accords on transitional justice, through investigatory bodies, to international war crimes tribunals.

In Guatemala, the United Nations Human Rights Observer Mission in Guatemala (MINUGUA), especially its representative Jean Arnault, facilitated the peace negotiations, including agreements between the contending parties with respect to truth commissions and other measures of transitional justice.[43] MINUGUA's mission was later expanded to verify that both sides complied with the peace accords. In 1991, responding to a request by the Salvadoran government and the political opposition, the UN established, funded, and provided personnel to the Salvadoran truth commission.

The UN also established and funds two ad hoc international criminal courts, the International Criminal Tribunal for the Former Yugoslavia (ICTY) and the International Criminal Tribunal for Rwanda (ICTR). The ICTY was established in May 1993 to "prosecute persons responsible for serious violations of international humanitarian law committed in the territory of the former Yugoslavia since 1991."[44] It has the authority to prosecute individuals with respect to four clusters of offenses: (1) grave breaches of the 1949 Geneva Conventions; (2) violations of the laws or customs of war (e.g., the mistreatment of noncombatants and prisoners in time of war); (3) genocide (i.e., acts committed to destroy a national, ethnic, racial or religious group); and (4) crimes against humanity.

The consensus seems to be that the ICTY, after a shaky and unimpressive start, is making surprising and steady progress: several suspects have been arrested and brought into custody; other suspects have turned themselves in; verdicts are being rendered and sentences meted out, appealed, and reduced; even among some Serbs, the court is gaining the reputation of being fair and impartial.[45]

Building on the ICTY, the UN in late 1994 belatedly set up an International Criminal Tribunal for Rwanda (ICTR) as an international response to genocidal massacres there.[46] Two and one-half years after its creation, the ICTR had achieved little: it had indicted just thirty-five people, held only twenty-five in custody (although some were Hutus accused of playing major roles in planning or ordering the massacres), had one trial in progress, but had convicted no one.[47] In May 1998, however, in the ICTR court in Arusha, Tanzania, Jean Kambanda, the Rwandan prime minister in 1994, both admitted guilt to and was pronounced guilty of four charges of genocide and two charges of crimes against humanity. This plea and verdict are momentous in several ways.[48] This was the first time that a guilty plea had been entered before any international tribunal, including Nuremberg. It was also the first time that any Rwandan suspect had admitted that his or her actions were genocidal in intent and not merely part of a civil war. Finally, the plea and verdict represented an important step toward the transitional justice goal of holding *individuals*—especially leaders who planned and gave orders—accountable for human rights violations.

Further work on this topic would assess the strengths and weaknesses of the three types of international civil society and the measures they might employ in transitional justice. Let us conclude, however, by suggesting some distinctive merits, effects, and limitations of ICS when assessed in relation to the roles of national governments and civil societies.

We have seen that international civil societies (and international regimes) can promote transitional justice by providing to domestic civic groups and democratically elected governments such things as material resources, relevant tools, international legitimacy, and moral support. Such assistance may be indispensable as domestic civil groups and fledgling democracies confront the forces seeking revenge or hoping to "forget and move on." ICS can also adopt an adversarial role and criticize or substitute for domestic civic groups and national governments when there is good reason to believe that these have succumbed to unjust or antidemocratic forces.

In these various activities ICS often appeals to or applies international (human rights) law and promotes a transnational culture of universal human rights. Naomi Roht-Arriaza describes the situation:

> Over the last ten years or so, the insistence by human rights lawyers and institutions on the legal limits to government choices in this area [of transitional justice] has had an impact, albeit an indirect one. That impact has come through norm creation and diffusion, the creation of an authoritative vision of what is right.[49]

This "authoritative vision" is one impetus for what Nelson Mandela calls "the creation of an international community predicated on human dignity and justice."[50] International civil society is deepened and widened by appeal to a fundamental normative perspective. The vision takes two forms. First, it is embodied in international human rights conventions, treaties, and interpretations. These norms, among other things, send a global message about individual criminal accountability (thereby avoiding the problem of retroactivity), proscribe a nation's ignoring past violations, and insist that states have a duty to investigate and punish human rights violations, especially torture and genocide. Second, the normative vision is an ethical outlook, the result of attempts to clarify and defend a global or world ethic, whose principles are used to develop and assess international law and offer guidance as to which package of legal and nonlegal tools is ethically most appropriate for particular situations. Decisions about optimal international law and institutions, such as international criminal courts, and how they might best be combined and sequenced with other tools cannot be made without reference to those ethical principles that emerge through cross-cultural dialogue as well as the capabilities of and constraints on particular societies.

Of course, in a world of putatively sovereign nation-states and powerful global economic forces, many national governments and some international bodies routinely ignore these norms. Moreover, international norms can be used as smokescreens under the cover of which powerful countries dominate weaker countries or ethnic groups contend with each other.

But newly democratic governments often ratify human rights treaties and international conventions, and human rights proponents in domestic civil society advance transitional justice in their own countries by insisting on compliance with these international norms:

> Before the 1980s, it was widely believed that decisions about prosecution, investigations, amnesties, and the like were entirely within the sphere of each country's domestic jurisdiction. That has now changed; both governments and nongovernmental organizations now compile information, issue protests, rate government performance, and condition aid and trade on the treatment of past human rights violations as well as on the prevention of current abuses.[51]

Yet we must be wary here, not just out of political realism but also on moral grounds. For, as Carlos Nino rightly insists, too great an international response or the wrong kind of response to a country's past rights violations can do more harm than good for democratization and transitional justice.[52] International involvement and appeals to universal human rights can give some factions in a nation—for instance, the military—the pretext to reject, as an "outside job," international recommendations or pressure. In El Salvador, the fact that three non-Salvadorans composed the Salvadoran Truth Commission was used by the government as a pretext to declare (the week after the commission's report was released) a general amnesty for all those individuals charged with violating rights during the civil war.

CONCLUDING REMARKS

Michael Walzer observes, "There is today an international civil society, the very existence of which raises questions about the usefulness of the state."[53] He is correct in recognizing that ICS exists and raises issues about the state's role. He is incorrect, at least in relation to the challenge of transitional justice, if he assumes or implies that the state has no role. Rather than seeing civil society at odds with or replacing the nation-state, I have argued that national and international civil societies can and often should act in ways that enable emerging democratic governments to reckon with prior human rights violations. National governments are not obsolete if and when their sovereignty is limited, corrected, and supplemented by global norms generated, diffused, and implemented by domestic and international civil societies.

NOTES

I am grateful to Trudy Govier, Margaret Popkin, Peter Quint, Wilhelm Verwoerd, and my colleagues at the Institute for Philosophy and Public Policy and the School of Public Affairs—especially Sue Dwyer, Arthur Evenchik, Robert K. Fullinwider, and William A. Galston—for helpful comments on earlier versions of this chapter. I also owe thanks to the following conferences, in which I was invited to give the paper on which it is based: North American Society for Social Philosophy, Fourteenth International Social Philosophy Conference, Queens University, Kingston, Ontario, 18–21 July 1997; Conference on War Crimes: Moral and Legal Issues, Global & International Studies Program, University of California, Santa Barbara, 14–16 November 1997; Beas Foundation Seminar, "Human Rights and Asian Values/Transitional Justice and Civil Society," Bryn Mawr College, 21 November 1997; New Jersey Regional Philosophical Association Meeting, Montclair State University, 25 April 1998.

I dedicate this chapter to Ken Aman, whose untimely death prevented him from publishing on this topic but whose pioneering work continues to stimulate my own research.

1. Jim Hoagland, "Justice for All," *Washington Post*, 19 April 1998, C7.

2. Although philosophers and other ethicists have not entirely ignored the topics of transitional justice and civil society, it is legal scholars, social scientists, policy analysts, and activists who have made the most helpful contributions. The best multidisciplinary collections on transitional justice are Neil J. Kritz, ed., *Transitional Justice: How Emerging Democracies Reckon with Former Regimes*, I, *General Considerations*; II, *Country Studies*; III, *Laws, Rulings, and Reports* (Washington, D.C.: United States Institute of Peace Press, 1995). Kritz is preparing a fourth volume on transitional justice in Guatemala, South Africa, and Bosnia. In the 1980s, moral and legal philosophers Ronald Dworkin, Owen Fiss, Thomas Nagel, and Thomas Scanlon attended hearings in Argentina and conferences in the United States on transitional justice. Two prominent Argentine philosophers, Gregorio Klimovsky and Eduardo Rabossi, were members of the Argentine investigatory commission, the National Commission on Disappeared Persons (CONADEP), and contributed to the drafting of CONADEP's report, *Nunca Mas* (Buenos Aires: Editorial Universitaria de Buenos Aires, 1985). In December 1996, the International Development Ethics Association and the Committee on International Cooperation of the American Philosophical Association sponsored a panel entitled "Justice, Amnesty, and Truth-telling: Options for Societies in Transition."

3. Timothy Garton Ash, "The Truth about Dictatorship," *New York Review of Books* 45, no. 3 (19 February 1998): 35–40.

4. Carlos Nino, *Radical Evil on Trial* (New Haven, Conn.: Yale University Press, 1996), vii.

5. This is not to say that it is not also important to consider other forms of evil such as what Ash calls "millions of tiny Lilliputian threads of everyday mendacity, conformity, and compromise" (Ash, "The Truth about Dictatorship," 36).

6. See Nino, *Radical Evil on Trial*, 108.

7. See David Crocker, "Transitional Justice and International Civil Society: Toward a Normative Framework," *Constellations* 5, no. 4 (December 1998): 495–96.

8. For the first four of these objectives, see Margaret Popkin and Naomi Roht-Arriaza, "Truth as Justice: Investigatory Commissions in Latin America," *Law and Social Inquiry* 20 (Winter 1995): 79–116.

9. David Luban, "The Legacies of Nuremberg," in *Legal Modernism* (Ann Arbor: University of Michigan Press, 1994), 344–46. In describing what constitutes the rule of law, Luban draws on Lon Fuller's analysis. To order society, law must guide human action, and it does this insofar as the law contains rules that (1) are public; (2) are not retroactive or ex post facto; (3) show some congruence between the law as announced and law as administered, which implies that like cases are treated alike and that private revenge and other means of "noncongruence" are prohibited. In addition, adjudication in a society ruled by law (4) respects due process, in the sense of procedural fairness, publicity, and impartiality. See Lon Fuller, *The Morality of Law*, rev. ed. (New Haven, Conn.: Yale University Press, 1963), 33–39.

10. Mark Osiel argues that what he calls "liberal" or "discursive social solidarity" can be promoted "through public deliberation over continuing *dis*agreement, a process by which rules constrain conflict within nonlethal bounds and often inspire increasing mutual respect among adversaries." Mark Osiel, *Mass Atrocity*,

Collective Memory, and the Law (New Brunswick, N.J.: Transaction, 1997), 17, n. 22; see also 47–51; 204, n. 136; 263–65.

11. Martha C. Nussbaum and Jonathan Glover, eds., *Women, Culture and Development* (Oxford: Clarendon, 1995).

12. Osiel, *Mass Atrocity*, 54–55.

13. See Robert C. Johansen, "A Turning Point in International Relations? Establishing a Permanent International Criminal Court," *Report: The Joan B. Kroc Institute for International Peace Studies* 13 (Fall 1997): 3.

14. For an extremely subtle discussion of the variety of attempts in Germany to confront the problem of retroactivity in relation to deeds committed by border guards and leaders in the former East Germany, see Peter Quint, *Imperfect Union* (Princeton, N.J.: Princeton University Press, 1997), 196–205. Some Germans, according to Quint, appeal to the German legal theorist Gustav Radbruch, arguing that the nonretroactivity principle can be set aside: in exceptional cases "there are some extreme situations in which another value . . . may be even more important" (203). In the case of Nuremberg that value was "the importance of imposing sanctions on acts of extraordinary evil" (203). Quint, however, questions whether acts by German border guards and leaders are sufficiently evil to justify setting aside the principle of nonretroactivity (see 204–5).

15. During the trial of Maurice Papon, one reporter noted, the French nation debated "more than one man's wartime role":

> What kind of responsibility do the French bear for the extermination of 75,000 French Jews? How representative of occupied France's collective spirit was Vichy, the Nazis' French Puppet government? How representative was Papon, the loyal civil servant who claimed he was, while a Vichy official in Bordeaux, also an active undercover member of the anti-Nazi Resistance?

But French prime minister Lionel Jospin argued that the trial of one man cannot yield truth about an era: "Justice does not establish history. History is not made in the dock." Charles Trueheart, "France's Papon Case Puts an Era on Trial," *Washington Post*, 22 October 1997, A23; see also Trueheart, "Letter from France," *Washington Post Book World*, 2 November 1997, 15.

16. For a thorough clarification of this concept of public deliberation, in contrast to rational consensus, political bargaining, and aggregation of given preferences, see James Bohman, *Public Deliberation: Pluralism, Complexity, and Democracy* (Cambridge, Mass.: MIT Press, 1996).

17. The locus classicus for the historical and analytic treatment of civil society is Jean L. Cohen and Andrew Arato, *Civil Society and Political Theory* (Cambridge, Mass.: MIT Press, 1992). Discussions of international issues appear in Adam B. Seligman, *The Idea of Civil Society* (New York: Free Press, 1992), and Michael Walzer, ed., *Toward a Global Civil Society* (Providence, R.I.: Berghahn, 1995). For an accessible sample of the American debate, see *Brookings Review* 15 (Fall 1997).

18. Michael Ignatieff, "On Civil Society: Why Eastern Europe's Revolutions Could Succeed," *Foreign Affairs* 74 (March/April 1995): 128.

19. See Benjamin R. Barber, "Clansmen, Consumers, and Citizens: Three Takes on Civil Society" (chap. 1 in this volume).

20. See Robert D. Putnam, "Bowling Alone: America's Declining Social Capi-

tal," *Journal of Democracy* 6 (January 1995): 65–78; "Bowling Alone Revisited," *Responsive Community* 5 (1995): 18–33; "The Strange Disappearance of Civic America," *American Prospect*, no. 24 (Winter 1996): 34–48; "Robert Putnam Responds," *American Prospect*, no. 25 (March–April 1996): 26–28.

21. See, for example, Jean Bethke Elshtain, "The Mothers of the Disappeared: Passion and Protest in Maternal Action," in *Real Politics: At the Center of Everyday Life* (Baltimore: Johns Hopkins University Press, 1997), 284–302.

22. I readily accept the point, which Trudy Govier has urged, that "apparently neutral or irrelevant groups may be positive in their impact" on transitional justice. It is indeed true that associations with no intent to further transitional justice, such as amateur soccer leagues, in the long run may nurture communal and deliberative virtues on which transitional justice depends (Trudy Govier, Comments on David A. Crocker, "Transitional Justice and International Civil Society," New Jersey Regional Philosophy Association, 25 April 1998, 2). For example, by expanding women's opportunities to play and watch soccer, both amateur and professional soccer organizations in Iran are having a secularizing and egalitarian if not democratizing effect, a phenomenon widely recognized as Iran's national soccer team prepared for its participation in the 1998 World Cup. See Jere Longman, "A Renewed Secular Passion is Gripping Iranians: Soccer," *New York Times*, 22 April 1998.

23. Jean L. Cohen, "American Civil Society Talk" (chap. 3 in this volume).

24. Cohen, "American Civil Society Talk."

25. Jean L. Cohen, "Interpreting Civil Society," in *Toward a Global Civil Society*, ed. Walzer, 38.

26. Teresa Whitfield, "The Role of the United Nations in El Salvador and Guatemala: A Preliminary Comparison," paper presented at the conference "Comparative Peace Processes in Latin America," Woodrow Wilson International Center for Scholars, Washington, D.C., 13–14 March 1997, 16–17.

27. Whitfield, "The Role of the United Nations in El Salvador and Guatemala," 17.

28. Whitfield, "The Role of the United Nations in El Salvador and Guatemala," 17.

29. Bohman, *Public Deliberation*, 4–5 (footnote omitted).

30. See Ken Aman and Christián Parker, eds., *Popular Culture in Chile: Resistance and Survival* (Boulder, Colo.: Westview, 1991).

31. Priscilla B. Hayner, "Fifteen Truth Commissions—1974–1993: A Comparative Study," in *Transitional Justice*, ed. Kritz, I: 232–33.

32. Margaret Popkin, personal communication, 22 April 1998.

33. Press release, "Guatemala's Bishop Gerardi Assassinated," Guatemalan Archdiocesan Human Rights Office, 29 April 1998, World Wide Web site of the Guatemala Human Rights Commission/USA (http://members.aol.com/PeaceGuate/INDEX.HTM).

34. Amartya Sen and Jean Drèze, *Hunger and Public Action* (Oxford: Oxford University Press), 275–79.

35. *El Difícil tránsito hacia la democracia: Informe sobre derechos humanos, 1996* ([Tegucigalpa]: Comisionado Nacional de los Derechos Humanos, 1996), 20–21. The translation is my own.

36. Announcement of briefing, "Guatemala after the Peace Accords," Washington Office on Latin America and Center for Human Rights Legal Action, Washington, D.C., 6 March 1997.

37. Announcement, "Guatemala after the Peace Accords."

38. The names of some of these groups reveal their concerns: the Alliance against Impunity, the Association of Families of the Detained-Disappeared of Guatemala, the Mutual Support Group of Relatives of the Disappeared, the Group of Mutual Aid.

39. See Theda Skocpol, ed., *Bringing the State Back In* (New York: Cambridge University Press, 1985), and Michael Schudson, "The 'Public Sphere' and Its Problems: Bringing the State (Back) In," *Notre Dame Journal of Law, Ethics and Public Policy* 8 (1994): 529–46.

40. See, for example, Elise Boulding, *Building a Global Civic Culture* (Syracuse, N.Y.: Syracuse University Press, 1990), and Trudy Govier, *Social Trust and Human Communities* (Kingston, Canada: McGill-Queen's University Press, 1997), 228–29.

41. Naomi Roht-Arriaza, "Conclusion: Combating Impunity," in *Impunity and Human Rights in International Law and Practice*, ed. Naomi Roht-Arriaza (New York: Oxford University Press, 1995), 302. See also Osiel, *Mass Atrocity*, 235–36.

42. See *The International Response to Conflict and Genocide: Lessons from the Rwanda Experience* (Odense, Denmark: Steering Committee of the Joint Evaluation of Emergency Assistance to Rwanda, 1996). In this five-volume study, see John Erickson, ed., *Synthesis Report*, chap. 4, especially 37–39, and *Study 4: Rebuilding Post-War Rwanda*, chap. 9.

43. Whitfield, "The Role of the United Nations in El Salvador and Guatemala," 16–23. It should be mentioned, however, that substantial criticisms of the UN have been made in the contexts of peacemaking or international justice, alleging that it has failed to take adequate account of the requirements of international law with respect to both individual accountability and limitations on amnesty. I owe this point to Margaret Popkin.

44. http://www.un.org/icty/facts2.htm.

45. See Gary Jonathan Bass, "Due Processes," *New Republic*, 20 March 1998, 16–19, and Tina Rosenberg, "Defending the Indefensible," *New York Times Magazine*, 19 April 1998, 46–56, 69–70. Rosenberg notes, however, that many Serbs have rejected the ICTY because they believe it is rigged against them. The process would gain more legitimacy in Serb eyes, she writes, if at least one Serb were found innocent of human rights violations.

46. The Rwandan case is not (yet) one of transitional justice in our sense, since the predominantly Tutsi government in Rwanda is far from democratic.

47. See Bass, "Due Processes," 18. Perhaps because of this meager international judicial response to past evil, Tutsi-dominated Rwandan authorities are holding as many as 130,000 Hutus in custody, have tried 350 people, and found all but twenty-six guilty. Of those found guilty, about a third have been sentenced to death, the supreme punishment in Rwanda. On 24 April 1998, twenty-two Hutus were executed by firing squads in four sites throughout the country. While thousands of Tutsis cheered and talked about both retribution and the deterrence of Hutu guerrillas in the countryside, international observers had grave worries. Not

only were there clear signs of victor's justice—for instance, many of those executed had neither legal counsel nor sufficient time to prepare their cases—but the perceived lack of justice could result in Hutu reprisals rather than reconciliation. See James C. McKinley, Jr., "Massacre Trials in Rwanda Have Courts on Overload," *New York Times*, national edition, 2 November 1997, 3; and "As Crowds Vent Rage, Rwanda Executes 22 for '94 Massacres," *New York Times*, 25 April 1998, 1, 6.

48. Stephen Buckley, "Ex-Leader in Rwanda Admits to Genocide," *Washington Post*, 2 May 1998, 1, 16; James C. McKinley, Jr., "Ex-Premier Admits He Led Massacres in Rwanda in 1994," *New York Times*, 2 May 1998, 1, 7.

49. Roht-Arriaza, "Conclusion: Combating Impunity," 294.

50. Nelson Mandela, "Foreword," in *Transitional Justice*, ed. Kritz, I: xi.

51. Roht-Arriaza, "Conclusion: Combating Impunity," 294.

52. Carlos Nino, "Response: The Duty to Punish Past Abuses of Human Rights Put into Context: The Case of Argentina," in *Transitional Justice*, ed. Kritz, I: 417–36. See also Diane F. Orentlicher, "A Reply to Professor Nino," also in *Transitional Justice* I: 437–38.

53. Michael Walzer, "Introduction," in *Toward a Global Civil Society*, ed. Walzer, 3.

17

Democracy and Uncivil Societies

A Critique of Civil Society Determinism

Xiaorong Li

Civil society has often been prescribed as the irreversible path to democracy and a panacea for political repression in authoritarian countries. Those who subscribe to this *civil society determinism* tend to use the term *civil society* to refer to any private or associational life (including productive, commercial, or consumerist activities) existing apart from the state.[1] Civil society, its proponents suggest, exists anywhere and anytime there is a "market-regulated, privately controlled or voluntarily organized realm."[2] This tendency is found in recent scholarship on democratization in authoritarian-communist countries and in policy arguments for "engaging" authoritarian governments through diplomacy and trade.

The tendency to oversell the *nonstate model of civil society*—to exaggerate its potential to foster stable democratic regimes—has been undermined by the recent proliferation of collapsed, dysfunctional, and strife-torn states, and by the example of assertive authoritarian regimes in the "economic miracle" countries of Asia, Bosnia, Algeria, Sri Lanka, Somalia, and Rwanda are instances of the first type of problem. In these countries, elements of nonstate forces were present or even vibrant before their descent into ethnic, tribal, religious, or political violence. These forces included anarchist, intolerant, or hatred-motivated social currents whose existence has been understated by some proponents of nonstate civil society. Countries such as China, Singapore, Malaysia, and Indonesia illustrate the second type of problem. In these countries, market forces have not brought democratic changes in a timely, meaningful fashion. Where democratization has indeed begun, as in South Korea and Taiwan, market forces certainly helped, but other factors were also at work. Asia's older democracies in India and Japan were not produced or nurtured primarily by a free market. In the history of Western Europe, capitalist forces were not especially conducive to social-liberal democracy and were bedfellows at different times and places with absolute monarchies, juntas, and fascist regimes. A nonstate civil society can be flourishing even as democracy is not.

In this chapter I will consider what roles nonstate forces, economic or societal, might play in strengthening or undermining democracy or the prospect of it, and what else is required for these forces' pro-democratic components or potentials to grow and overpower the uncivil or antidemocratic ones.

WHAT SORT OF DEMOCRACY?

A first reaction to the deterministic claim that civil society leads to democracy is to ask, "What sort of democracy?" To tackle this question, let me first consider the argument that a free-market economy inevitably leads to democracy. There is no denying that a genuine market economy can go a long way toward cleaning up government and politics and ushering in the rule of law. If the results generated by the "invisible hand" and by a minimal state that merely protects negative freedoms are what a people want from democracy (as John Locke argued in the eighteenth century that they had reason to), then the nonstate civil society may indeed be the best hope for transition to such a libertarian democracy. In such a democracy, the government has little to do with, so there will be no need for, a free public space for deliberating about any "public good" independently of the "goods" generated by the market economy itself. Nor will there be a need to protect a broad range of liberties and rights—including the right to deliberate about the public good—from infringement by market forces.

However, liberal democratic states are more than mere traffic cops for market activity and are bound to protect a great many rights of the people—rights to assemble, deliberate, and agitate for a conception of the public good. Not only do profit-driven market forces sometimes threaten these rights and liberties, but other societal forces—particularly the sorts that have been operating in the failed states mentioned earlier—threaten the rule of law which even the minimal, libertarian state requires.

The argument for a causal connection between a nonstate civil society and democracy faces a tougher challenge where liberal democracy is concerned. Liberal rights can be infringed not only by the state but also by communal violence, anarchy, social disintegration, and the tyranny of "invisible hands" driven by profit. One alternative to the nonstate model is thus a model that allows a sanctuary for rights and deliberation about the public good. The *middle-space model* has emerged as such an alternative. On this model, civil society is conceived as a realm situated between, and sheltered from, both state coercion *and* the realms of private, profit-driven, parochial, and anarchist impulses. This space is conditioned on a vibrant nonstate realm/marketplace, on the one hand, and on a state that acts to safeguard liberal rights and democratic deliberation about the public good, on the other.

The sociopolitical history in which the two models of civil society have evolved can shed some light on their definition. The nonstate concept of civil society was a child of the cold war era. The current enthusiasm with civil society stemmed from the perception that the civil society movement led by Eastern European intellectuals hastened the demise of communism and ended the cold war. Communist states typically outlawed voluntary nongovernmental associations. Their Marxist ideology derided civil society as a bourgeois fraud. It regarded the idea of voluntary, autonomous associations serving to counterbalance the state as a fig leaf for class domination. In any case, a classless communist society, in which the state is abolished, would have no need for civil society. The Eastern European dissidents identified liberal rights as the missing piece in their societies and the attainment of those rights as their highest political priority. Understandably, the need to secure liberal rights against state infringement overshadowed the importance of insulating the space of civil liberties from other sources of constraint, such as parochial communal or ethnocentric interests and other divisive and intolerant forces, which would break into the open soon after communism collapsed in Eastern Europe.

During the cold war, the Reagan administration's policy for promoting democracy and human rights abroad took the market-libertarian approach (i.e., undermine authoritarian states by promoting a market economy). The policy advocated support for the nonstate economic sector in authoritarian countries that were considered allies of the United States. The idea was that if market practices were established, more poor people would become involved in making their own economic decisions, and wealth would trickle down and extend to larger masses of people. Increased economic mobility would create a critical mass of propertied individuals with demands for sharing political power. This trickle-down policy may have worked in bringing down a few dictators. But it did not work as desired in poor countries, where capitalism accelerated the concentration of wealth within a small elite and widened the gap between the privileged few and the destitute masses, making the prospect of majority power more remote.

Toward the end of the cold war, a different philosophy was introduced in U.S. foreign aid and pro-democracy policy. The export of capitalism was qualified by efforts to achieve a fit between market efficiency and social fairness. The objective was to meet basic needs of the poor masses in these countries so as to enable and expand political participation.[3] In the 1990s, however, the Clinton administration has seemed to return to the market trickle-down legacy in its policy toward such powerful authoritarian countries as China and Indonesia. The administration's "engagement" policy toward these nations has sometimes been backed by the sort of arguments characteristic of market–civil society determinism. Toward dictators in less significant world players such as Cuba, Iraq, and Burma, the administration seems to have a different philosophy: it insists on global economic sanctions and isolation to undermine state economic power and to encourage opposition forces (civil society) to emerge from among the angry masses. A preliminary assessment of these two approaches will emerge later when I discuss the conceptual issues they raise.

CIVIL SOCIETY AND THE DEMOCRATIC STATE

The recent American debate about our own civil society—in contrast to the transition-to-democracy debate—dwells on the question of how best to reinvigorate U.S. democratic institutions or, more precisely, what roles social-associational, corporate, and governmental entities can or should play in such a task. The debate has something in common with a debate within international development circles and democratization studies about how best to facilitate transitions from authoritarianism to democracy in developing countries. These two debates are related in the following sense. Where a liberal democracy is already in place, civil society is invoked as one of the causes of its consolidation (or deterioration); where democracy does not yet exist, civil society is invoked in assessing the prospects for democratization.

In each area of interest, *civil society* is used both as a normative concept and as an empirical description. As a normative concept, it prescribes the ideal conditions for effective self-governance. As a descriptive concept, it identifies certain existing and viable social activities, civic dispositions, and nonstate institutions that seem to be linked to democracy.

So far, I have tried to sort out the different usages of *civil society* by differentiating first between nonstate and middle-space conceptions, and then between normative and descriptive conceptions. This exercise yields four conceptions of civil society: normative nonstate, descriptive nonstate, normative middle-space, and descriptive middle-space. A comparison of these various concepts is important for a critique of civil society determinism.

According to the normative middle-space conception advanced by Benjamin Barber, civil society should consist in a select set of voluntary associations and activities that foster such civic virtues as trust and public-mindedness (being conscious of or attentive to the public good). Barber characterizes the "golden age" of eighteenth- and nineteenth-century American civil society in terms of its orientation toward the public good:

> Although in eclipse today, civil society was the key to America's early democratic energy and civic activism. Its great virtue was that it shared government's regard for the commonweal, yet unlike government made no claim to exercise a monopoly on legitimate coercion. Rather, it was a voluntary, "private" realm devoted to "public" goods.[4]

Barber goes on to define *civil society* as "a space that unites the virtue of the private sector—liberty—with the virtue of the public sector—concern for the general good." It is through citizens who have cultivated these virtues and are conscious of their rights and responsibilities in self-governance that this space can be fortified against both bureaucracy and consumerism.[5] For Barber, only certain associations would qualify as members of civil society—namely, those that orient people toward the public good, including those that support democratic institutions. Associations that are hostile to liberal democratic values (such as intolerant religious or racist organizations) should not be considered members of civil society. Indeed, the normative middle-space definition cautions against the destructive role played by such groups in a democracy.

Barber also blames the ailing civil society in the United States on corporations, which encroach on the public space and thwart governmental efforts to protect such a space. Though the state is sometimes said to be guilty of diminishing and crowding out civil society, Barber places the lion's share of blame on "market arrogance." He recounts how private, for-profit corporations have taken over schools, churches, and foundations. As a result, he writes, these associations no longer aspire to enhance the public good; instead, they aspire to represent the private ends of their members.[6]

It is important to remember that this normative middle-space definition makes specific suppositions about the political institutions that support civil society: they have to be liberal-democratic. On the one hand, the power of the state should be limited by citizens' civil-political rights, and on the other hand, the state is to interact actively with civil society to facilitate citizens' enjoyment of freedom and their ability/disposition to deliberate about the public good. By empowering citizens on the basis of equality, the state maintains broad political participation in—and thus the health of—democratic institutions. These suppositions about the dependence of civil society on the state have not often been made explicit.

Those who use the term *civil society* descriptively have referred either to the nonstate sector in general or to a middle space between the state and the private-economic realms. The descriptive middle-space model, unlike the nonstate models, does not count economic, for-profit, and other private pursuits as part of civil society; but unlike the normative middle-space model, it includes noneconomic associations of every kind. On this definition, certain associations such as neighborhood crime watches, sports teams, baby-sitting co-ops, self-help groups, book clubs, and the like may not have a pronounced pro-democracy political agenda, but they belong to a middle-space civil society nonetheless, because they can serve as a training ground for such qualities as self-governance, responsibility, equal respect, and a sense of fair play. Certain voluntary associations, such as some whites-only country clubs, might be run on the basis of equal respect for all members. Such associations can be said to have mixed functions in a democracy. Voluntary associations that advocate racist or other intolerant ideas, as long as they operate peacefully, are also included in the descriptive middle-space model. This, of course, raises the question of how these groups can be conducive to democracy.

The descriptive definitions, which are based on empirical observations, tend not to make explicit or to recognize the extent to which the character of civil society depends on the character of the government and of the larger society in which the civil society is located. But some participants in the American debate have called attention to this point. According to Jean Cohen, for example, the particular qualities of American (and European) civil society—the "third sector" associations in Cohen's descriptive middle-space definition—have been fostered by the norms of the political institutions in which they are embedded—namely, constitutional protection of the rights to free speech, association, and assembly; public accountability of government officials; and transparency of legislative, judicial, and executive procedures.[7]

This dependence of civil society on democratic governance identifies, in Cohen's view, the empirical link between civil society and democracy in American and European history. A relatively consolidated civil society is the protegé of democratic institutions and normative procedures. Associations that are pro-democratic have tended to flourish under a democratic regime. Even groups with nondemocratic structures or antidemocratic mandates, which do not disappear under democracy, tend to operate within the restraints of democratic norms and procedures.

This dependence explains why we cannot automatically expect civil society formed under far different conditions to deliver democracy. In contemporary Russia, for example, the totalitarian state has dissolved and individuals have an unprecedented degree of personal, social, and economic freedom. However, the organizations that have formed or re-emerged in this newly opened space reflect not a history of democracy and limited government but a thousand years of autocratic rule and established religion. Private economic organizations often look more like criminal syndicates, and the Orthodox Church is once more reaching for state power to quash other forms of religious expression.

Civil society determinism is a normative claim to the effect that market and societal developments under a nondemocratic/authoritarian regime are desirable because they guarantee the outcome of democracy. This claim rests on an implicit assumption about the independence of civil society from the political and social environment in which it develops. To address the normative claim, I will argue later that civil society determinism equivocates between a descriptive nonstate concept of civil society and a normative middle-space conception. But in this section, I have drawn attention to arguments that counter the underlying assumption regarding civil society's independence.

THE NONSTATE MODEL IN DEMOCRACY STUDIES

On the nonstate models, a "civil society," as Ernest Gellner remarked, "may, indeed, be pluralistic and centralization-resistant," but its members may belong to a "segmentary community which avoids central tyranny by firmly turning the individual into an integral part of the social sub-unit," a subunit that may undermine or hinder the development of democracy.[8] The moral resources within a civil society for supporting democracy must, on these models, coexist with potentially extensive anti-democratic or intolerant social and market forces, and often they must so coexist without state protection. Thus, the nonstate models would seem to offer no assurance that an extensive civil society will lead to democracy.

Nevertheless, the nonstate conception continues to underlie many studies of civil society and democratization. On the nonstate model, the structural relation between civil society and the state is binary: civil society is in fact society itself, confronting the state as its only threat. For example, India's failure to forestall outbreaks of religious and political violence has been blamed mostly on the state, on the grounds that with its penetrating power and its emergence as a hegemonic actor in the public realm, it has devoured Indian civil society. Meanwhile, insufficient attention has been paid to the ways that ethnic and religious conflicts affect the civic space for deliberating about the public good and for consolidating democracy in India.[9]

Some historians of the late Qing period in China also seem to use civil society in this binary way. In their accounts of a rapidly declining dynastic regime that proved incapable of effective rule in the face of growing threats from Western imperialist powers, these historians find the binary conception a handy tool for analyzing the efforts by largely local societal elites to assert power in areas of concern to both society and the weakened state authorities. A new generation of historians of the late Qing Dynasty and early Republican China (late nineteenth to early twentieth centuries), in particular, has tried to demonstrate the existence of what seem to be nascent elements of a civil society existing in a binary relation to the state. These studies tend to cite economic or other associational life outside state control as evidence of a civil society. As one such study finds:

> A distinct pre-modern civil society existed in the form of corporate groups and voluntary associations: guilds, native place associations, clans and lineages, surnames associations, neighborhood associations, and religious groupings such as temple societies, deity cults, monasteries, and secret societies. Perhaps the most important shared principle of these organizations was that they were formed outside of, or independent of, the state.[10]

Such scholars as William Rowe, Mary Rankin, and David Strand also see evidence of a civil society in spheres that were not completely controlled by the state in premodern China.[11]

The excitement of these historians and others over their discoveries seems to indicate that the signs of nonstate civil society in the late Qing Dynasty have been interpreted, implicitly perhaps, as precursors to an emerging Chinese democracy. This may explain why scholars of contemporary Chinese political changes and prospects for democratization have by and large used *civil society* in the binary sense. Several, for instance, have tried to identify a nascent or fragile Chinese civil society in the networks or independent organizations of urban elite intellectuals and students.[12] Such a civil society is characterized by its relative autonomy, a result of the recent decentralization of the economy. A number of studies of civil society in contemporary Taiwan and other so-called Confucian countries in East Asia have also clearly subscribed to the binary conception of civil society as a sphere of social life in opposition to the state.[13]

EQUIVOCATION AND CONFUSION

The differences between the nonstate and middle-space conceptions should not themselves generate inconsistencies, as long as those who use them stay within their proper explanatory limits. For example, because the nonstate conception treats market institutions and for-profit associational activities as integral parts of civil society, it is consistent for those who adopt this definition to view the vitality and expansion of the decentralized economy as evidence of a viable and growing civil society. Likewise, it is consistent for those who adopt the middle-space definitions to insist that expanding for-profit (market) forces may constitute a threat to civil society.

One problem with civil society determinism, however, has been its equivocation of these two concepts. To arrive at its optimism over the role of the market economy in transforming authoritarianism to democracy, civil society determinism has used the two concepts interchangeably. For example, in an essay on "the search for civil society in China," Heath Chamberlain writes that the loosening of state control over economic and social life that was associated with the collapse of communist regimes in Eastern Europe is "currently appearing in somewhat similar guise in China, bringing in its train 'democracy' (albeit 'with Chinese characteristics')."[14] The argument seems to be that, because the market is an integral part of civil society, market development means civil society development; and, because civil society is in opposition to the state, a growing civil society is thus a growing counterforce to the authority of the state, checking and balancing its power—an essential function of democratic rule. But this move from nonstate expansion to democracy seems to conflate elements of the nonstate and middle-space notions without acknowledging their differences. This equivocation enables one to conclude that liberal democracy is the inevitable outcome of expanding nongovernmental and market engagement.

This inference contains a two-segment argument: (1) flourishing markets and societal forces means a growing nonstate civil society, and (2) a growing civil society in turn indicates political liberalization and a transition to democracy. The deductive relation between decentralized economic/societal development and a nonstate civil society in the first segment is by definition valid. The inference from a civil society to (liberal) democracy that appears in the second segment can only be valid if *civil society* is used in the normative middle-space sense. This is because liberal democracy can only have meaningful prospects in a civil society where the virtues and skills necessary for effective self-government (and the social fabric that nurtures these virtues) are cultivated. And such a civil society is a normative middle-space civil society. But there is little connection between the first and the second segment. Deductive certainty does not transmit from one to the other. It breaks down where the meaning of *civil society* is switched from the one conception to the other.

Behind this equivocation lies another confusion. Civil society, by all four definitions, possesses a certain *autonomy* from the state. The state does not control its activities. However, civil society's autonomy from the state does not imply its *independence*. The latter is a thesis about the causal relations between state and society. If civil society were independent, then its character would not depend on the character of the state, including the legal protections that envelop civil societies in liberal democracies. It would be "detachable" from a particular state context and "implantable" within a different context yet produce similar effects. This is what civil society determinism supposes. But the supposition rests more on the elision of the difference between autonomy and independence than on any empirical demonstration.[15]

ASSESSING PROSPECTS FOR DEMOCRACY

Civil society determinism has an optimistic, forward-looking, dynamic, and evolutionary outlook on global political changes; it confidently predicts the arrival of a global convergence toward democracy in the era of global capitalism. In comparison, the middle-space conception, particularly as it is used in the context of American politics, has a relatively conservative, retrospective, and sometimes pessimistic outlook. David Brooks has commented on this general mood:

> Civil society theory begins with the notion that America, though based on liberty, is being undone by excessive liberty. Unchecked individualism saps institutions, like the family, that build character. Unfettered choice weakens the bonds that keep us together. . . . The adherents of "civil society" want individual choice to be exercised inside a thick web of local bonds. . . . Civil society theorists tend to emphasize community more than the heroic individual, organic structures more than dynamic change, local serenity more than national greatness, authority more than freedom, stability more than change.[16]

The optimism of civil society determinism, however, is hardly justifiable. As my analysis has shown, an ensemble of just any decentralized, nongovernmental, local groups does not have the necessary dynamics, or sufficient resources, to evolve into the kind of civil society that prepares the social conditions for liberal democratic self-governance. Civil society determinism underestimates the complicated and unpredictable effects of such an ensemble on the preconditions of liberal democracy. For-profit market institutions and intolerant groups or racist communities, for instance, have a mixed impact on the strength and quality of the civic space required for liberal democratic governance.

As previously mentioned, pro-democracy and public-minded civic forces can be overpowered or devoured by for-profit, self-interested, or parochial communal forces that coexist with these forces within a non-state civil society. In this sense, a flourishing nonstate civil society has little meaning for liberal democracy. Since the Berlin Wall came down, oppositional (or nonstate) civil society has been granted the long-sought-after freedom to flourish in Eastern Europe and Russia. But the oppositional agents that were expected to support the new democratic state and to engage in deliberation about the public good are being silenced or shouted down, crowded out, or overwhelmed by forces hostile to democracy or the public good. The same Eastern European public intellectuals who risked their lives to foster an oppositional civil society are now complaining about social incohesion, lack of national debate on the public good, and the collapse of social institutions.

The concept of a nonstate civil society is an ineffective tool for a realistic appraisal of the prospects for democracy. If it is to be used, its proper limits in making predictions about democracy should be clearly drawn. The nonstate conception is also not very useful in studying how to consolidate dysfunctional democracies. By "dysfunctional democracies," I refer to countries where elections might be regularly held but political power is still concentrated in the hands of elites, and where state institutions are corrupt or incompetent, such that individuals' basic liberties are effectively unprotected from endemic social or political violence. Some have also called such a democracy "illiberal democracy."[17] Violent gangs, secret societies, and racist or other intolerant groups as part of a nonstate civil society all directly threaten any kind of democratic self-governance. Recent events in Algeria, Sri Lanka, and the Balkan region offer some concrete examples of democracies becoming dysfunctional in the presence of a strong nonstate civil society.

In any case, an open-ended prediction (e.g., "Marketization and proliferation of NGOs will eventually bring about democratic change") is rather barren, because it does not say anything about when the changes will take place and what else needs to be done to hasten them. Alternatively, one may try to set a relatively specific timetable such that, say, within a couple of generations, democratization on the basis of a nonstate civil society should be well under way in a specific country. As soon as a timetable is set, any predictions of democratization can then be actually tested. If democracy has not emerged in due course, then the time-specific predictions about democracy should be considered falsified. An open-ended prediction, however, is unfalsifiable.

The nonstate model has very limited explanatory power in a theory about why democracy did not develop in places with a vibrant nonstate civil society. Nonstate civil society has existed in almost every type of human society, and in various stages of their history. Antagonism against state authority—be it oligarchy, monarchy, autocracy, or democracy—has been perpetual and universal. Such a civil society is by no means the unique new creation of modernization and capitalist globalization. In fact, one could find evidence of such a civil society (or at least its components) in almost any developing or underdeveloped country today— Egypt, Algeria, Somalia, Cuba, Sri Lanka—or, in terms of decentralized economic activities, in Russia and China. If democracy were to follow inevitably from such a civil society, some of these societies would have long been among the world's oldest democracies or have a secure future of democratization. But neither is the case.

CAPITALIST AUTHORITARIANISM

The expression *capitalist authoritarianism* has often been dismissed as a contradiction in terms. This response suggests that market/nonstate civil society determinism is deeply entrenched among students of democracy. But this alleged contradiction must now be faced up to as a reality.

In assessing the prospects for democratization in developing countries, civil society determinism has understated a growing obstacle to democracy in authoritarian countries with rapidly growing economies—the economic empowerment of the authoritarian state. The nonstate model is right to emphasize the antiauthoritarian nature of nonstate agencies, including the marketplace. But this model does not adequately recognize the mutually beneficial relationship between the authoritarian state and the business sector. Civil society determinism pays little attention to the fact that a top-down market reform initiated and directed by an authoritarian government, often for the purpose of boosting its own political legitimacy and consolidating power, enables the state to be selective about the extent and scope of social-economic liberalization so as not to undermine its own power.

The European experiences before the world wars—with booming capitalist economies side by side with oligarchic or authoritarian regimes— seem now to be repeated in Singapore, Malaysia, Indonesia, and China. In these countries, the antidemocratic power of ruling elites has in some sense been strengthened by economic development. The possibility for democratization seems remote, because the regimes (which control legislatures, courts, police, and the military as well as many of the key industries and banks) continue to exercise their monopoly and selectively use their coercive power to eliminate what they consider to be threatening groups in intellectual, religious, or cultural communities. For example, the Chinese government continues to oppress any nongovernmental associations or peaceful expressions that challenge its policies concerning important public issues, from the environmental consequences of development projects such as the Three Gorges Dam, to labor protection, unfair farm levies, and lack of government accountability. The government has not hesitated to use its new revenues and modern technology to tighten its grip over activities it deems to be "endangering national security." China adopted elaborate new laws in 1997 to restrict the use of the Internet, citing the need to "safeguard national security and social stability."[18] The government used its monopoly over the telecommunications system to promote trade communication but also to block access to more than one hundred Web sites, including those of the *New York Times*, Amnesty International, and Human Rights Watch, as well as those of dissident groups abroad.

These instances say much about the reality of operational capitalist authoritarianism. The consolidation of government in tandem with economic growth in authoritarian countries deserves more attention from students of civil society and democracy. No assessment of the conditions of civil society in such societies should be isolated from a study of the possible roles that authoritarian states can play in either shaping or suppressing pro-democratic forces within society and in strengthening their own monopoly on power.

DEMOCRACY AND THE MIDDLE CLASS

A seemingly corroborating thesis to civil society determinism is what we might call a "middle-class" determinism. This view states that marketization is almost always (or most of the time) a liberating and progressive process, in that it spreads wealth and thereby creates or expands the "middle class." This class will demand mobility, autonomy, political participation, and rights in general. And democracy as majority rule requires such a middle class, which provides the critical mass needed to counterbalance the traditional power elites in politics. The link between a strong middle class and a democratic polity is valid as long as the "middle class" in question lives up to the expectation; that is, it forms that critical mass which is powerful enough to sway political decisions and force the elites to make concessions.

That democracy requires such a middle class was long realized in Western political theories. Aristotle, for example, pointed out the important role of a "middle class" in good governance.

> In all states therefore there exist three divisions of the state, the very rich, the very poor, and thirdly those who are between the two. . . . [T]hose who have an excess of fortune's goods, strength, wealth, friends and the like, are not

willing to be governed and do not know how to be . . . while those who are excessively in need of these things are too humble. . . . And also this [middle] class of citizens have the greatest security in the state; for they do not themselves covet other men's goods as do the poor, nor do the other classes covet their substance as the poor covet that of the rich. . . . It is clear therefore also that the political community administered by the middle class is the best, and that it is possible for those states to be well governed that are of the kind in which the middle class is numerous, and preferably stronger than both the other two classes.[19]

Aristotle's observation about viable popular governance in a class society has influenced theories about the democratic transition from feudal hierarchical societies. Thus, on the eve of those transitions in Europe, the political philosopher Machiavelli remarked that "corruption and incapacity to maintain free institutions result from . . . great inequality" and that a middle class was necessary to equalize political participation.[20]

The great importance of economic and social equality—of which a strong majority middle class is a structural indicator—for effective popular power sharing was further articulated by Jean-Jacques Rousseau:

[B]y equality, we should understand, not that the degrees of power and riches are to be absolutely identical for everybody; but that power shall never be great enough for violence . . . and that, in respect of riches, no citizen shall ever be wealthy enough to buy another, and none poor enough to be forced to sell himself.[21]

Along similar lines, Alexis de Tocqueville attributed the vitality of nineteenth-century American democracy to its empowerment of the majority members of society who constituted the middle class:

[E]xperience has shown that it is no less dangerous to place the fate of these classes exclusively in the hands of any one of them than it is to make one people the arbiter of the destiny of another. When the rich alone govern, the interest of the poor is always endangered; and when the poor make the laws, that of the rich incurs very serious risks. The advantage of democracy does not consist, therefore, as has sometimes been asserted, in favoring the prosperity of all, but simply in contributing to the well-being of the greatest number.[22]

Capitalist market economies created the majority middle class by breaking down kinship- or royalty-based, rigid class hierarchies. The middle class's well-being, in turn, motivates its political activism to force out the oligarchy. Economically and socially, the middle classes are capable of overpowering the small minority constituted by the wealthy ruling elite.

This class analysis supports the claims that democracy is predicated on a strong middle class, and that free trade and the global capitalist economy create such a middle class. Capitalist development, it seems, then, goes together with democracy. However, this class analysis is misleading when applied out of context. The so-called "middle class" created by capitalist economic development in authoritarian societies such as Indonesia and China, populated by vast poor masses, is often a minority class. This will continue to be the case given the prevalence of poverty, which takes years and even generations to ease. To transform most of the poor into middle-class citizens will at best be a slow and precarious process.

There is one more disconcerting factor. While the authoritarian elites in these countries continue to rule, the upper class will continue to amass wealth and consolidate power by taking advantage of its ability to engage in political cronyism. Those who manage to rise above the poor masses, but lack the political connections to advance into this upper class, will constitute a vulnerable middle class, at least as long as the authoritarian elites hold on to power and privileges. A capitalist global economy will first and mostly enrich and strengthen this upper ruling class. Some wealth trickles down to the middle class. But large profits will also provide incentives for the politically unaccountable ruling elites to neglect or exploit the poor masses and, in so doing, perpetuate poverty—by failing to regulate labor practices at foreign joint-venture enterprises, for example, or otherwise preserving a national competitive advantage that comes of employing cheap and unprotected labor.

Lastly, the middle class in such societies has an economic or business interest in building alliances with the ruling elites and perpetuating mass poverty. For example, it may seek to ensure its own competitive advantage by maintaining the pool of cheap laborers and low-cost labor conditions. Though the bourgeoisie emerging from this process has its own political demands for power sharing, its members also have an antidemocratic political interest. They will not accept majority rule by the poor, who will be the majority in these societies for the near future. Democracy, it may seem to them, allows the poor masses to sway politics and policy decisions, which may threaten the interest of the middle class.[23]

The links between a capitalist economy, a middle class, and democracy in authoritarian developing countries are thus much more precarious and less predictable than the "(middle) class analysis" makes them out to be.

CONCLUSION

Having rejected civil society determinism, we are in no way prevented from saying that the emergence of nonstate civil society forces in nondemocratic and/or anarchist societies is a source of hope, if not a guarantee, for future democratization. Economic decentralization can weaken authoritarian state control over society. This would certainly be a step in the direction of political liberalization. Some China observers, for example, have pointed out, rightly in my view, that the penetration of market forces in formerly state-controlled sectors, increased economic freedom, and the greater share of wealth among certain social groups tend to liberate social life and nurture demands for political freedom and democracy.[24] But these effects, though clearly possible, are by no means certain.

In fact, one can only make limited predictions about the prospects for democracy on the basis of a nonstate civil society. Flourishing nonstate sectors *may* benefit pro-democracy forces but not necessarily ensure democratization. Although eroding the pervasive control of the authoritarian state is an essential condition for democratization, market-regulated economic activities and localized or regional strife can also dash its prospects. For example, as the Chinese state has dismantled central planning and introduced a market economy, nonstate forces have grown in various directions. Income disparity has generated discontent, envy, and adversity among the population. Rich coastal provinces have resisted providing their share of poverty assistance to less developed inland rural regions and threatened to break away. Illegal smuggling rings and bandits run rampant despite the government's harsh and swift punishment, threatening public safety. These developments in state-society relations render the prospects for a middle-space civil society and a liberal democracy anything but certain.

It might be more productive for students of democracy to avoid referring to nonstate civil society overall as the precondition of democratization in authoritarian developing countries. Instead, one should sort out the forces or elements that are either conducive or hostile to democracy in such a civil society. One should study the specific and often opposing roles played by various nongovernmental associations and their networks. The potential of a nonstate civil society to deter democracy should not be underestimated. Additionally, any international efforts to promote democracy in such countries should seek to identify and nurture pro-democracy forces, or forces that are not harmful to democracy, within a nonstate civil society, instead of putting all their eggs in one basket—the nonstate civil society as a whole.

NOTES

1. David L. Blaney and Mustapha Kamal Pasha, "Civil Society and Democracy in the Third World: Ambiguities and Historical Possibilities," *Studies in Comparative International Development* 28 (Spring 1993): 11.

2. John Keane, "Introduction," in *Civil Society and the State: New European Perspectives*, ed. John Keane (London: Verso, 1988), 1.

3. I thank Jerome Segal for drawing my attention to this historical background.

4. Benjamin R. Barber, "The Search for Civil Society: Can We Restore the Middle Ground between Government and Markets?" *New Democrat* 7 (March/April 1995): 13.

5. Barber, "The Search for Civil Society," 13, 17.

6. Barber, "The Search for Civil Society," 15.

7. Jean L. Cohen and Andrew Arato, *Civil Society and Political Theory* (Cambridge, Mass.: MIT Press, 1995), 425–26, 429, 440–42.

8. Ernest Gellner, *Conditions of Liberty: Civil Society and Its Rivals* (New York: Allen Lane, Penguin, 1994), 8.

9. See the review of recent Indian studies in Blaney and Pasha, "Civil Society and Democracy in the Third World," 13–16.

10. Mayfair Mei-hui Yang, "Between State and Society: The Construction of Corporateness in a Chinese Socialist Factory," *Australian Journal of Chinese Affairs* 22 (July 1989): 35–36.

11. See William T. Rowe, *Hankow: Commerce and Society in a Chinese City, 1796–1889* (Stanford, Calif.: Stanford University Press, 1984); William T. Rowe, "The Public Sphere in Modern China," *Modern China* 16 (July 1990): 309–29; Mary Backus Rankin, *Elite Activism and Political Transformation in China: Zhejiang Province, 1865–1911* (Stanford, Calif.: Stanford University Press, 1986); and David Strand, *Rickshaw Beijing* (Berkeley: University of California Press, 1989).

12. Michel Bonnin and Yves Chevier, "The Intellectual and the State: Social Dynamics of Intellectual Autonomy During the Post-Mao Era," *China Quarterly* 127 (1991): 569–93; Andrew Nathan, *China's Crisis: Dilemmas of Reform and Prospects for Democracy* (New York: Columbia University Press, 1990); Merle Goldman, *Sowing the Seeds of Democracy in China* (Cambridge, Mass.: Harvard University Press, 1994), 358–59.

13. See Edward Shils, "The Virtue of Civil Society," *Government and Opposition* 26 (Winter 1991): 3–20; and Thomas Gold, "Civil Society in Taiwan," in *Confucian Society in East Asian Modernity*, ed. Tu Wei-ming (Cambridge, Mass.: Harvard University Press, 1996).

14. Heath B. Chamberlain, "On the Search for Civil Society in China," *Modern China* 19 (1993): 199–200.

15. I have benefited from a comment by Robert Fullinwider on the difference between autonomy and independence of a civil society from the state.

16. David Brooks, " 'Civil Society' and Its Discontents," *Weekly Standard*, 5 February 1996, 18–19.

17. Fareed Zakaria used this phrase in noting that "democracy is flourishing; constitutional liberalism is not" in today's world. See his op-ed article, "Democracies That Take Liberties," in *New York Times*, 2 November 1997, 15.

18. Erik Eckholm, "China Cracks Down on Dissent in Cyberspace," *New York Times*, 31 December 1997, 3.

19. Aristotle, *Politics*, trans. H. Rackham (Cambridge, Mass.: Loeb, 1967), IV: xi (1295a25*ff.*)

20. Niccolo Machiavelli, *The Discourses*, trans. Christian E. Detmold (New York: Modern Library, 1950), 167.

21. Jean-Jacques Rousseau, *The Social Contract*, trans. G.D.H. Cole (London: J.M. Dent, 1993), 225.

22. Alexis de Tocqueville, *Democracy in America*, trans. Henry Reeve and Phillips Bradley (New York: Vintage, 1954), 248–49.

23. Peter Levine has been particularly helpful in my thinking through these points. He generously provided references to the earlier quotations from the classic philosophers.

24. See Chamberlain, "On the Search for Civil Society in China," for an analysis of this trend.

Index

About the Editor and Contributors

Benjamin R. Barber is Walt Whitman Professor of Political Science and director of the Walt Whitman Center for the Culture and Politics of Democracy, Rutgers University. Among his books are *An Aristocracy of Everyone: The Politics of Education and the Future of America* (Oxford University Press, 1994) and *Jihad vs. McWorld: How the Planet is Both Falling Apart and Coming Together* (Ballantine, 1996).

Jean L. Cohen, associate professor of political science at Columbia University, is the coauthor of *Civil Society and Political Theory* (MIT Press, 1992).

David A. Crocker is senior research scholar at the Institute for Philosophy and Public Policy. Among his recent writings are "Toward Development Ethics," *World Development* (1991), "Functioning and Capability: The Foundation of Sen's and Nussbaum's Development Ethic," *Political Theory* (1992), and "La metacritica de Cerutti a la filosofia de la liberacion," *Cuadernos de Filosofia* (1993).

Robert K. Fullinwider, senior research scholar at the Institute for Philosophy and Public Policy, writes in several areas where educational and social policy intersect with political theory. He is the author of *The Reverse Discrimination Controversy: A Moral and Legal Analysis* (Rowman & Littlefield, 1980).

Fredrick C. Harris is assistant professor of political science at the University of Rochester. Among his publications are "Something Within: Religion as a Mobilizer of African-American Political Activism," *Journal of Politics* (1994) and "Religious Institutions and African-American Political Mobilizing," in *Classifying By Race*, ed. Paul Peterson (Princeton University Press, 1995).

431

Xiaorong Li is research scholar at the Institute for Philosophy and Public Policy. Among her publications are "Cultural Relativism and Gender Inequality in China," in *Women, Culture and Development*, ed. Jonathan Glover and Martha C. Nussbaum (Oxford University Press, 1995), and "License to Coerce: Violence against Women, State Responsibility and Legal Failure in China's Family Planning," *Yale Journal of Law and Feminism* (1996).

Judith Lichtenberg, research scholar at the Institute for Philosophy and Public Policy, is editor of *Democracy and the Mass Media* (Cambridge University Press, 1990) and numbers among her writings "Within the Pale: Aliens, Illegal Aliens, and Equal Protection," *University of Pittsburgh Law Review* (1983) and "Nationalism: For and (Mainly) Against," in *The Morality of Nationalism*, ed. R. McKim and J. McMahan (Oxford University Press, 1997).

Loren E. Lomasky is professor of philosophy at Bowling Green State University. He is the author of *Persons, Rights, and the Moral Community* (Oxford University Press, 1987) and coauthor of *Democracy and Decision: The Pure Theory of Electoral Preference* (Cambridge University Press, 1993).

Kathleen D. McCarthy is professor of history and director of the Center for the Study of Philanthropy, City University of New York Graduate Center. She is the author of *Noblesse Oblige: Charity and Cultural Philanthropy in Chicago, 1849–1929* (University of Chicago Press, 1982), and *Women's Culture: American Philanthropy and Art, 1830–1930* (University of Chicago Press, 1993), among other works.

Nancy L. Rosenblum is professor of political science at Brown University. She has written *Another Liberalism: Romanticism and the Reconstruction of Liberal Thought* (Harvard University Press, 1987) and, most recently, *Membership and Morals: The Personal Uses of Pluralism in America* (Princeton University Press, 1998).

Mark Sagoff, senior research scholar at the Institute for Philosophy and Public Policy, is the author of *The Economy of the Earth: Philosophy, Law and the Environment* (Cambridge University Press, 1990).

William A. Schambra is director of general programs at the Lynde and Harry Bradley Foundation and the author of several essays on civil society and government. Earlier, while at the American Enterprise Institute, he edited a series of volumes on the Constitution.

Kathryn Kish Sklar, Distinguished Professor of History at SUNY-Binghamton, is the author of *Catherine Beecher: A Study of American Domesticity* (Norton, 1976) and *Florence Kelley and the Nation's Work: The Rise of Women's Political Culture, 1830–1900* (Yale University Press, 1995).

Steven Rathgeb Smith is the coauthor of *Nonprofits for Hire: The Welfare State in the Age of Contracting* (Harvard University Press, 1993). An assistant professor in the Graduate School of Public Affairs at the University of Washington, he runs the School's Nonprofit Management Program and edits the journal *The Nonprofit and Volunteer Sector Quarterly*.

William M. Sullivan is professor of philosophy at La Salle University. His books include *Reconstructing Public Philosophy* (University of California Press, 1986) and *Work and Integrity: The Crisis and Promise of Professionalism in America* (HarperCollins, 1995).

Robert Wachbroit, research scholar at the Institute for Philosophy and Public Policy, has written, among other works, "Rethinking Confidentiality: The Impact of Genetics," *Suffolk Law Review* (1993), "Il Cancro come malattia genetica: Problemi sociali ed etici," *L'Arco di Giano: Revista di Medical Humanities* (1995), and "Concepts of Health and Disease," *Encyclopedia of Applied Ethics* (Academic Press, 1998).

David Wasserman is research scholar at the Institute for Philosophy and Public Policy. His writings include "DNA Fingerprinting," in *Encyclopedia of Bioethics* (Macmillan, 1993), "Let Them Eat Chances: Probability and Distributive Justice," *Economics & Philosophy* (1996), and *A Sword for the Convicted* (Greenwood, 1990). He is the coauthor of *Disability, Difference, Discrimination* (Rowman & Littlefield, 1998).

Robert Wuthnow, Gerhard R. Andlinger '52 Professor of Social Science at Princeton University, is the author of many books, among them *Acts of Compassion: Caring for Others and Helping Ourselves* (Oxford University Press, 1993), *Producing the Sacred: An Essay on Public Religion* (University of Illinois Press, 1994), and *Learning to Care: Elementary Kindness in an Age of Indifference* (Oxford University Press, 1995).